LEADERSHIP AND RESPONSIBILITY
IN THE SECOND WORLD WAR

Robert Vogel, 1981

Leadership and Responsibility in the Second World War

Essays in Honour of Robert Vogel

EDITED BY
BRIAN P. FARRELL

McGill-Queen's University Press
Montreal & Kingston · London · Ithaca

© McGill-Queen's University Press 2004
ISBN 0-7735-2643-9 (cloth)
ISBN 0-7735-2731-1 (paper)

Legal deposit second quarter 2004
Bibliothèque nationale du Québec

Printed in Canada on acid-free paper.

This book has been published with the help of a grant from the Canadian Federation for the Humanities and Social Sciences, through the Aid to Scholarly Publications Programme, using funds provided by the Social Science and Humanities Research Council of Canada.

McGill-Queen's University Press acknowledges the support of the Canada Council for the Arts for its publishing program. It also acknowledges the financial support of the Government of Canada through the Book Publishing Industry Development Program (BPIDP) for its publishing activities.

National Library of Canada Cataloguing in Publication

Leadership and responsibility in the Second World War : essays in honour of Robert Vogel / edited by Brian P. Farrell.
Includes bibliographical references and index.
ISBN 0-7735-2643-9 (bnd)
ISBN 0-7735-2731-1 (pbk)
1. World War, 1939–1945 – Political aspects – Great Britain. 2. Political leadership – Great Britain – History – 20th century. 3. Command of troops – History – 20th century. I. Vogel, Robert. II. Farrell, Brian P. (Brian Padair), 1960–
D743.L42 2004   940.53'41   C2003-906962-1

Typeset in Palatino 10.5/13
by Caractéra inc., Quebec City

Contents

Contributors

SIDNEY ASTER teaches British and international history at the University of Toronto.

TREVOR BURRIDGE, after many years of teaching history at the Université de Montréal, is retired and living in Oxford.

NEIL CAMERON teaches history at John Abbott College in Montreal.

PAUL D. DICKSON teaches military history at Queen's University's International Study Centre in Herstmonceux Castle, England.

BRIAN P. FARRELL teaches military history at the National University of Singapore.

PETER HOFFMANN teaches German and European history at McGill University.

AARON KRISHTALKA teaches history at Dawson College in Montreal.

ROBERT VOGEL taught history at McGill University from 1959 until his death in 1994. See xix–xxvii.

Preface

Mrs Shirley Vogel, Robert Vogel's widow, endorsed and supported this volume from the start, and the editor and contributors hope that she will be satisfied with the final outcome. Terry Copp gave valuable early assistance, as did Carman Miller and Georgii Mikula. People who played a role in this project but were ultimately unable to contribute a paper included Chandar Sundaram, Allen Hertz, and especially Sid Parkinson, for whose counsel and assistance over several years the editor is most appreciative. Aaron Krishtalka and Neil Cameron gave the editor more help than just their excellent contributions to this volume. Francesca Hills provided valuable assistance in proofreading and copyediting.

It took a very long time to bring this manuscript to the stage where all obstacles to publication were at last cleared away, and Aurele Parisien at McGill-Queen's University Press offered indispensable advice and support from start to finish. Two anonymous colleagues who wrote reviews that made this book stronger deserve our thanks. Official records and private papers, whether we authors consulted them in an archive or obtained them, we use with permission, for which we are grateful.

Above all, of course, we dedicate this volume to the memory of Robert "Bob" Vogel, in the hope that his many friends and former students will accept this tribute that we all had hoped to present to him in person.

Brian P. Farrell
Singapore

Introduction:
Leadership and Responsibility

BRIAN P. FARRELL

The president of the United States at the end of the Second World War, Harry S Truman, had a sign on his desk that said, "The buck stops here." This terse definition of leadership is more stirring than that found in the *Concise Oxford Dictionary* (COD): "a person that leads, a person followed by others."[1] The word, and Truman's encapsulation, resonate with the concepts of power, authority, and command. Leadership was an exalted status, a position of power and prestige. But Truman's aphorism focused not on power but on responsibility. The power and the authority to give orders and commands, to make decisions that others must live by, come with a catch. Responsibility is defined as "the state or fact of being responsible, the holding of authority to make decisions." Responsible means further "liable to be called to account" (COD). Put those concepts all together, and this is what you get: a leader is a person (or persons) with the power and authority to make decisions who is liable to be called to account for the outcomes of those decisions. Leadership is a duty, not just an opportunity.

Simple to define, so difficult to really grasp, let alone perform. What authority does the leader have? Whence does it derive, and how secure is it? Does the power to see decisions implemented reflect this authority, or does it fall short? If the latter, how can the leader fairly be called to account by anyone for anything? As for being called to account, the questions multiply. By what or whom? On what grounds? With what sanction? The notions of leadership and responsibility always have been and always will be intertwined, at least in principle. Studying them systematically could well involve studying the history of the human race in a truly comprehensive analysis.

This is not the forum to pursue such a broad trail. But even a sensible and coherent narrowing of focus can leave a great deal to be considered. Such a focus can emerge by examining those recognized by their society as having the right and the duty to make decisions, to give orders, to lead. Political office, be it elected, appointed, or acquired, is one familiar field of leadership. Military command is another. Diplomatic and civil-service appointment can be a third. All three can encompass the right and duty to advise as well as to command and the liability to be held accountable for that advice as well.

Leaders from these three different realms shared common ground as officers of the state. This is the general focus of the studies in this volume: the experience of leadership and responsibility during the Second World War, particularly in the British Empire, as exemplified by political decision-makers, military commanders, and diplomats or other senior officials. The historical essays collected here do not pretend to study even British leadership at this time in all its forms. But they do examine a range of examples of wartime leaders facing – or shirking – responsibilities, and they pose many interesting and valuable questions. How important was individual character in leaders' exercising leadership and facing responsibility? Was there any relationship between facing responsibility and success or failure? How did leaders understand responsibility and accountability? Why have the failures of some to stand accountable been so controversial? Did they share any common causes? If the task of leaders is to lead, the task of historians is to understand and explain.

Power without responsibility was aptly described as the prerogative of the harlot throughout the ages. Leadership in every field is all too often irresponsible, in both senses of the word. Foolish and ill-considered decisions litter the pages of history, as do leaders who wanted to exercise the power and authority their position bestowed but had no desire to stand accountable in any way, to anyone or anything, for whatever happened. Often enough, just such leaders made the foolish decisions. But not always. Fools and knaves sometimes died venerated as great men. And sometimes leaders more than willing to take the consequences made foolish or ill-considered decisions that led to disaster. This very unpredictability is what surely makes the study of history so fascinating. Humanity is a paradox, capable of greatness and fecklessness in the same breath. The study of leadership can bring out that very human quality, or dilemma, very sharply. This volume does not aim to provide any systematic theory or explanation of leadership, even in its chosen time period and its three chosen areas. Rather, it seeks to provoke some reflection, and suggest some insights, on the nature of leadership and responsibility as it was seen and practised in the real world, before and during the Second World War, especially by statesmen, soldiers, diplomats, and officials in the British Empire.

The first part of this book examines leadership as exercised by holders of public office. An example of failure is analysed in the first essay (chapter 1) – an almost-completed draft left by Robert Vogel himself, the last thing on which he worked.[1] With minimal editorial alterations, it is his considered study of Neville Chamberlain and British foreign policy in the 1930s, especially from 1937 to 1940. Drawing on years of studying why British political leaders failed to prevent the outbreak of another world war, Vogel argues that the passionate controversy over the policy of appeasement can surely now be assessed calmly – and then proceeds to argue passionately (!!), but carefully, that Chamberlain was the driving force in British foreign and defence policy from 1931 on, that as prime minister from 1937 on he pursued his policy with confidence and resolve, but that for several reasons it failed disastrously, and that he is accountable to history for the greater part of that failure. While there is little here that is truly new to the specialist, Vogel's essay not only gives us a synthesis of this important issue and a taste of his own ability and sympathy as a historian, but also sets the tone for the volume. Vogel examines the responsibility of a powerful head of government to both his nation and to history for failing to prevent the war that became perhaps the central event of the century.

Aaron Krishtalka continues (chapter 2) this examination of the role played by British political leaders in the coming of the Second World War by going one step down the ladder of responsibility. He focuses on a group of politicians not commonly identified as leaders – backbench members of Parliament in Chamberlain's Conservative government, or "old Tories," and how they saw their role as supporters of a prime minister trying first to prevent war, then to win it. Krishtalka argues that while the group supported Chamberlain's foreign policy because they sympathized with it, when war broke out they determined not to support the government uncritically but rather to watch over it, press it if necessary, to make sure that it directed a vigorous fight. This showed a sense of responsibility to the nation, not just to the party, which swayed them to turn against Chamberlain when crisis exposed his leadership as inadequate.

Trevor Burridge rounds off this part (chapter 3) by examining the leader of the other major force in British politics – the Labour Party – in the tumultuous period before, during, and after the war. This biographer of Clement Attlee reconsiders his subject's political career, in terms of the general theme of leadership and responsibility. Burridge argues that by any measurement Attlee was a great success in both areas, and he rejects the notion that he benefited from circumstances to rise at the expense of better men. Instead, Attlee's very strength of character and personality made him a sensitive, conscientious, but also strong and sensible party leader, minister, and prime minister. Attlee – an "ideological pragmatist" – exercised quiet leadership and shouldered great burdens to help steer both party and country through two decades of war and turmoil and leave both in better shape than he found them.

The second part of the volume examines the experience of appointed government officials responsible for advising statesmen and thus sharing the burden of exercising state leadership and responsibility. Both contributors continue with the British experience before and during the Second World War. Neil Cameron (chapter 4) examines the experience of British scientists turned officials, working with statesmen. This is a study of Nobel Laureate A.V. Hill and the role of scientists in advising on British defence policy before and during the war. Cameron challenges C.P. Snow's famous critique of "war science," arguing that Snow, by pursuing his own agenda, missed the deeper problem. The fate of Hill, a truly central figure, illustrates how total war refuted two generally held assumptions – that throwing enough money at a problem can solve it and that only the accident of personalities prevents the right people from assuming the right positions to give the right advice. During the war, there was no easy or obvious way to fit the disparate community of scientists into a decision-making chain of command that had to be improvised on the job and made to work with an eccentric but indispensable leader. Hill found that out the hard way, and his fate illustrates the whole problem.

Sidney Aster (chapter 5) turns to the world of diplomacy, in a study that sheds further light on Chamberlain's ultimately doomed effort to prevent another world war. Aster analyses the mission of Chamberlain's man in Moscow, Sir William Seeds, British ambassador to the Soviet Union in 1939, and his role in the controversial negotiations that failed to produce an alliance to deter Germany from war. Aster asks what can be expected of an ambassador working in a hostile environment and given little to offer, whether the talks failed despite Seeds or whether he must share the blame, and whether he was made a scapegoat following their collapse. Bolstered by unique access to Seeds's own private papers, cited here for the first time, Aster argues that the diplomat did more than one might have expected in a job made all but impossible by his own government's inability to be decisive and was later sacrificed for it. The conclusion is that no diplomat can succeed when the home government cannot decide once and for all what it wants and on what terms.

The book's final part reflects Robert Vogel's main interest in his last years of research and writing – military commanders and their leadership in the Second World War. The first essay provides a useful counterpoint to the volume's emphasis on the British experience. It studies a classic episode involving leadership and responsibility in that other potent military organization in which Bob was so interested and on which he wrote so much: the German army. Peter Hoffmann, the leading historian of German resistance to the Nazis and biographer of the Stauffenberg brothers, re-examines (chapter 6) the question of why Claus von Stauffenberg took it on himself not only to oppose but also to assassinate Hitler. Hoffmann argues that Stauffenberg made a moral decision to commit tyrannicide when he heard reliable evidence that a war of racial extermination was being waged in the east. Stauffenberg believed that as a German officer and patriot, a Catholic, and a man of principle, he was obliged by his conscience to act against a policy so evil that it overrode the obligation to defend the country at war. This assumption of moral leadership contradicts the accusation that Stauffenberg, like others who turned against Hitler, did so only to save their own lives when Germany started to lose the war.

Brian P. Farrell combines the focus on British military leadership and the empire's experience by analysing (chapter 7) the role of Field Marshal Wavell in the defence and fall of Singapore in 1942, in his capacity as Allied supreme commander in Southeast Asia. Farrell argues that while there was nothing Wavell could have done to prevent the fall of Singapore, it is nevertheless worthwhile to examine how he performed at this highest level of command in very adverse circumstances.

For five weeks Wavell had command authority over the defence of Singapore; did he help or harm that effort, did he do the best possible job at the time? How did he assign blame for its fall, and did he accept any himself? Finally, what difference does all that make? Farrell argues that Wavell made some avoidable errors which accelerated the loss of Singapore but took almost no responsibility for them. He also drew reasonable conclusions about why it fell but then lent his name to finger pointing and scapegoating that had enduring consequences. All this reveals Wavell's mediocrity, underlines the importance of supreme command in all circumstances, and sheds new light on the running controversy over this great British military disaster.

Robert Vogel used to say only half-jokingly that "history ended in 1945"; accounts of anything later were still journalism. Certainly the latter years of the war were the subject of his own most important publications, concentrating on the Canadian army and its role in the campaign in northwest Europe. So it is fitting that the final contribution to this volume deals with a Canadian problem of command responsibility in that campaign. Paul Dickson (chapter 8) focuses on the leadership efforts of General Harry Crerar, the General-Officer-Commanding-in-Chief (GOC-in-C) of the First Canadian Army, between the breakout from Normandy and the operations to clear the approaches to Antwerp. Crerar found himself caught in an ambiguous situation between being responsible to his government, army, and nation for the lives of his men and being responsible to his superiors in a coalition for military operations aimed at winning the war as fast as possible. Crerar tried to manage both tasks while feuding with his superior, Field Marshal Montgomery, but in the end he leaned more towards preserving his army when circumstances jeopardized its staying power. Crerar found that he could not ignore the responsibility of leadership and acted accordingly.

Robert Vogel will never see this volume, dedicated to his life, work, and memory. But its theme, its topics, and its arguments all bear an imprint of his that will be visible to all who knew him. The authors are of course responsible for whatever shortcomings its essays may have, but they all offer the scholarship within as their effort to thank him for all the support and inspiration he gave them as teacher, historian, friend, and colleague. Robert Vogel never shirked any responsibilities in his own life and was never impressed by any leaders who did so or who would not stand accountable for their power. The authors feel he would have found food for thought in these historical studies of problems of leadership and responsibility faced by statesmen, soldiers, diplomats, and officials, and we hope they will find readers who share his interest in such important problems of history.

NOTE

1 With thanks to Terry Copp and Aaron Krishtalka for making the draft available and helping with its preparation.

Robert Vogel:
A Life in History

BRIAN P. FARRELL

The essays in this volume reflect the interests of the man to whose memory it is a tribute – Robert "Bob" Vogel. Bob spent his life studying, writing, and above all teaching history. It was his passion, and he taught it in big bold colours, round the clock, all year round. The only things Bob loved more than history were his family and perhaps McGill University, the institution where he earned his PhD in 1959 and at which he taught history for the next 36 years. Bob Vogel was born in Vienna in 1929.[1] His father died when Bob was very young, but his mother soon remarried, and the young boy developed a good relationship with both mother and stepfather. This must have stood the family in good stead in the tumultuous years of Bob's childhood and youth. The Anschluss left the Jewish family in a perilous situation, even though Bob's father had served in the imperial air force in the First World War and been wounded. Bob rarely talked about what happened to his life after the Nazi takeover, but longtime friends gathered that he had encountered persecution, including expulsion from his school. The family was able to emigrate to England by early 1939, just in time for the Battle of Britain, in which the young boy saw fighter duels sketched out by contrails in the sky and the Blitz. But when his stepfather was again wounded, while serving as a civil-defence volunteer, the family moved to Wales. Bob spent several happy years there, developing a love for the country, its people, and its music. In later years he occasionally called himself Welsh. He once declared to me that he did not consider himself involved in the latest storm of Quebec politics, despite having lived in the province for over 40 years – after all, he was Welsh!!

That sense of humour must have helped him shortly after the war ended. In 1948, on leaving high school, Bob won a scholarship for a place in Oxford University from Glamorgan County. But by this time his parents had decided that the opportunities in the postwar United Kingdom were too limited for Austrian refugees and decided to emigrate to Canada. After much soul-searching, Bob decided to forgo Oxford and to emigrate with his parents, to help them settle on a new continent. Montreal was Bob's main residence for the rest of his life. Oxford gave ways to Sir George Williams College, now part of Concordia University, where Bob studied history from 1949 to 1952. He took on a variety of part-time jobs, such as driving a taxi, to help his family, on his way to winning the Lieutenant-Governor's Silver Medal for History on earning his BA in 1952.

That success launched Bob Vogel on his career – that of an academic historian. Bob went across town to McGill that same year and never really left that university. An MA followed in 1954, leading to work on a doctorate under Noel Fieldhouse. Between stints teaching part-time for the Army Apprentice Training Corps, and at Sir George, Bob completed and submitted his dissertation on British foreign policy between the two world wars. He earned his PhD in 1959 and published his thesis as *A Breviate of British Diplomatic Blue Books 1919–1939* (Montreal: McGill University Press, 1963). Meanwhile Bob stepped right into what became his permanent home, McGill's Department of History.

From 1959 until his death in April 1994, Bob Vogel was a fixture at the department and at McGill. He was promoted professor in 1969, chaired the department from 1966 to 1971, served as dean of the Faculty of Arts from 1971 to 1981, and sat on innumerable bodies and committees in and around the university, including the Senate, the Board of Governors, and the Editorial Board of McGill-Queen's University Press. All who knew him will agree that Bob never walked away from a good fight and threw himself with vigour into the perennial task of trying to improve McGill for everyone. Not everybody agreed with him, but no one could ignore him. But history always remained Bob's passion, and while his research and publishing really picked up only after his long stint as dean, his dedication to teaching was constant and truly remarkable. There was very little in history that did not interest Bob, but his particular passion was for the history of Western civilization, particularly its politics, international relations, and wars. Bob was famous at McGill for teaching the survey of Western civilization – the "Plato to NATO" course – by himself, for many years. His initial interest in British diplomatic history shifted somewhat in later years to a greater interest in more military matters – echoes, perhaps, of those 1940 contrails in the sky? The Second World War in particular always fascinated Bob. He came to regard it as the central event of the twentieth century, devoted most of his later research to it, and developed an undergraduate lecture course and graduate seminar course devoted to it, both remembered fondly by all lucky enough to attend them.

Despite his broad interests, Bob spent most of his time on British and British Empire military, diplomatic, and political history, especially the interwar period and the Second World War. Over the years he supervised 22 MA theses (including those of three contributors to this volume) and nine PhDs (three contributors, including me). When he died, four PhD and six MA students lost a supervisor. Of those 40-odd theses, nearly all reflected Bob's interests largely or completely, and many have since been published. The last time I saw Bob Vogel was as I left McGill in 1993, having just spent a year as a colleague rather than as a student. I told him he was synonymous with military history at McGill, the best mentor any student could hope to have, and an example to any teacher. I know that a great many people, including all the writers in this volume, will agree with all of that.

Bob Vogel showed me by example what it meant to be an academic historian and a university teacher. He exulted in his students' successes, never forgot any of them, and indeed probably let his work as a teacher get too much in the way of his own research and publishing. None the less, his published work is impressive in both quality and quantity. In addition to his dissertation and a goodly number of articles, papers, and review essays, Bob's largest work was the five-volume study on the campaigns of the Canadian army in northwestern Europe in 1944–45 – *Maple Leaf Route* – that he co-wrote with Terry Copp and that appeared from 1983 to 1988. Bob's broad and deep knowledge of military history, the Second World War, and the German armed forces and their language did much to make the series the great success it deservedly became. One of the best days of my life was when, representing the Canadian Committee for the History of the Second World War, I was able in 1992 to present Bob and Terry with the C.P. Stacey Award for excellence in the study of Canadian military history for *Maple Leaf Route*. Yet I feel sure that if we could ask Bob today what pleased him most regarding those publications, he would cite the help he gave his former student and good friend Terry Copp to build a second career as a highly regarded Canadian military historian, after years of fruitful work in Canadian social history. That was Bob – first, last, and always a teacher.

Bob Vogel never tired of examining the subjects discussed in this collection of essays dedicated to him. His history may have been passionate, but it was also empirical, analytical, and thoughtful. Bob would not stand for either careless praise or sloppy criticism, especially not for any unfair condemnation made in hindsight. But one of his own pet peeves was how frequently leaders lacked the most important kind of courage – moral courage – the strength to face up to their duty and to its consequences and to stand accountable for how they wielded their power. As is traditional, right, and proper for a Festschrift, these essays reflect the work of some of Bob's friends, colleagues, and students in areas related to those times, places, and events that so interested him.

NOTES

1 Biographical information was assembled by Aaron Krishtalka.

Robert Vogel:
A Career in Outline

PUBLICATIONS

Articles

"Sir Fairfax Cartwright and the Balkans." *New Review* (Sept. 1965), 9–16.
"No Lack of Rational Speed: The First Canadian Army, September 1944." *Journal of Canadian Studies* (fall/winter 1981).
"Some Reflections on the Teaching of Military History." *Canadian Military History* (autumn 1992).
"In the Tradition of Nelson: The Royal Navy in World War II" (review essay). *Canadian Military History* (spring 1993).
"Churchill and the Historians" (review essay). *Canadian Military History* (autumn 1993).
Reviews published in *Canadian Historical Review; Canadian Journal of History; Military Affairs; Orbis.*

Books

A Breviate of British Diplomatic Blue Books, 1919–1939. Montreal: McGill University Press, 1963.
with T.J. Copp: *Maple Leaf Route: Caen.* Alma, Out.: Laurier Centre for Military Strategic and Disarmament Studies, 1983.
– *Maple Leaf Route: Falaise.* Alma: LCMSDS, 1983.

– *Maple Leaf Route: Antwerp*. Alma: LCMSDS, 1984.
– *Maple Leaf Route: Scheldt*. Alma: LCMSDS, 1985.
– *Maple Leaf Route: Victory*. Alma: LCMSDS, 1988.
[These five volumes won the C.P. Stacey Award for 1990, granted for excellence in the study of Canadian military history.]

Invited Academic Papers

"The Warsaw Uprising of 1944." Dissenters' Club, Montreal.
"The Naval Arms Race and Disarmament." Graduate Seminar, Faculty of Law, McGill University.
"The Washington Treaties of 1922 and International Law." Graduate Seminar, Faculty of Law, McGill University.
with T.J. Copp: "Normandy Reconsidered." Ottawa Historical Society, Ottawa, 1983.
"Ultra and Allied Intelligence." Wilfrid Laurier University, Waterloo, Ontario.
"The Stalingrad Campaign." Wilfrid Laurier University, Waterloo, Ontario.
"Military History in the 20th Century." Graduate Society, McGill University.
"The Taste of Victory after Forty Years." McGill University.
"The German Army in Normandy." McGill University Staff/Student Seminars.
with T.J. Copp: "Anglo–Canadian Tactical Air Power in Normandy: A Reassessment." American Military Institute, Richmond, Virginia, 1987.
"The Summer of 1939." Graduate Society, McGill University, 1989.
"Britain at Bay, the Summer of 1940." McGill University, 1990.
"Britain and Russia: The 50th anniversary of the Grand Alliance of World War II." St James Literary Society, Montreal, 1991.
"The 50th Anniversary of the First Event in World History." University Club, Montreal, 1991.

WORK AT McGILL UNIVERSITY, 1959–1994

Administrative Positions

Secretary, Department of History, 1962–66
Secretary, Faculty of Arts and Science, 1964–66

Chairman, Department of History, 1966–71
Vice-Dean, Social Science Division, Faculty of Arts and Science, 1969–71
Dean, Faculty of Arts, 1971–81
Member of Senate (elected), 1968–69
Member of Senate (ex officio), 1969–81
Elected Member of Board of Governors (elected), 1978–81
Member of Senate (elected), 1989–95

Areas of History Taught

British History: Survey Course.
    Growth of the Welfare State.
    19th- and 20th-Century Britain.
    Seminars (including graduate seminars) in 20th-Century British History.
European History: "Plato to NATO," Introductory Survey Course.
German History: Survey of German History in the 19th and 20th Century.
Methods in History: Approaches and Methods in History
War and Society: Survey Course.
    History of the Second World War.
    Seminar in War and Society, 20th Century.
    Civil-Military Relations in 20th Century Europe.
    Military History in 20th Century: Graduate Seminars.

Graduate Students Supervised

* A contributor to this volume.

MA THESES
Aster, Sidney.* Anti-Soviet Tendencies in the British Press, 1937–1940."
    (1965)
Burridge, Trevor D.* "British Labour and the German Problem, 1945–
    1947." (1965)
Croydon, Reggy. "The Problem of Teschen at the Paris Peace Confer-
    ence, with Special Emphasis on British Policy." (1967)
DesRosiers, Edward. "British Naval Policy after the Washington Trea-
    ties." (1966)
D'Ombrain, Nicholas. "The Evolution of British Defence Strategy,
    1904–1914." (1966)

Drolet, Marc. "The Anatomy of British Battlecruiser and British Naval Policy, 1904–1920." (1993)

Durflinger, Serge M. "The Royal Canadian Navy and the Salvadorean Crisis of 1932." (1987)

Echenberg, Myron J. "The British Attitude towards the Congo Question, with Particular Reference to the Work of E.D. Morel." (1964)

Krishtalka, Aaron.* "The 'Old Tories' and Fascism." (1969)

Mikula, Benn. "The Economics of Shipbuilding and British Naval Strategy in the Period of Rearmament." (1988)

Mullen, Dennis Ian. "Concepts of Little England: A Study of Negative Reactions to the Growth of Empire." (1970)

Poupart, Ronald. "Les réactions des pays de l'axe face au pacte germano–russe de 1939." (1986)

Price, Karen. "The Phenomenon of War as Presented and Discussed in Secondary School Textbooks in England during the Inter-war Years, 1919–1939." (1968)

Proulx, Janet D.M. "Anglo–French Relations in 1940." (1966)

Purves, James Grant. "British Estimates of German Military Strength and Intentions, 1934–1939." (1966)

Ruiter, Glen. "The London 'Times' and the British Move towards Total War." (1970)

Sallans, Bonnie J. "'I am not Winston Smith': Orwell, the B.B.C., and '1984.'" (1992)

Sundaram, Chandar S. "The Indian National Army: A Preliminary Study of Its Formation and Campaigns." (1985)

Thompson, Diane Y. "The Attitude of the Church of England to World War I." (1968)

Tordjman, Gabriel. "The Scientific Origins of the British Eugenics Movement, 1859–1914." (1991)

Unsinger, Peter C. "The Place of the Dardanelles Campaign in British Strategy." (1964)

Woolner, David B. "Storm in the North Atlantic: The St. Pierre and Miquelon Affair of 1941." (1990)

PHD THESES

Burridge, Trevor D.* "The British Labour Party and the 'German Question' during the Second World War." (1973)

Cassar, George H. "The Dardanelles Operation: The French Role." (1968)

Farrell, Brian P.* "War by Consensus: Power, Perceptions and British Grand Strategy, 1940–1943." (1992)

Gerolymatos, Andre. "British Intelligence and Guerrilla Warfare Operations in the Second World War: Greece 1941–1944, A Case Study." (1991)

Krishtalka, Aaron.* "The Old Tories and British Foreign Policy, 1930–1939." (1983)

L'Esperance, Jeanne. "Prostitution, Purity, and Feminism: A Study of the Repeal of the Contagious Diseases Acts, 1864–1886." (1982)

McCollough, Edward E. "Labour's Policy in Africa, 1900–1951: The Theory and Practice of Trusteeship." (1971)

Millman, Brock. "The Anglo–Turkish Alliance, 1939–40: Anatomy of a failure." (1992)

Vallely, Lois M. "George Stephens and the Saar Basin Governing Commission." (1965)

In progress in 1994: four PhDs and 6 MAs.

PART ONE

Statesmen and Politicians

1

Chamberlain and Appeasement

ROBERT VOGEL

"The spirit of Munich," said Alexander Solzhenitsyn on receiving his Nobel Prize in 1972, "is an illness of will-power of rich people." U.S. President Dwight Eisenhower, on returning from the Geneva Conference in 1955, had to read his speech standing uncovered in the pouring rain, his vice-president having banned umbrellas at the airport because of their association with Chamberlain, which might remind people of Munich – although that day in September 1938 had been nice enough for the British prime minister to speak hatless. It is proper and legitimate to make every possible effort to avoid war, choosing the lesser evil over the greater in a variety of circumstances – even if that sometimes means coming to terms with leaders who are regarded as terribly immoral for any number of reasons, from mass murder to the banning of films. All policies that prevent war are generally regarded as legitimate and desirable, even if at times a little distasteful. The only reservation is that they may not be called policies of "appeasement."

Neville Chamberlain was prime minister from 28 May 1937 to 10 May 1940, less than three years, of which eight months was spent at war with Germany. For the last 60 years he, and the policy of appeasement that he symbolizes, have been under almost continuous attack. This is surely understandable, because the majority of his critics felt that the Second World War was not only a great tragedy but also one that could have been avoided. It was, in Winston Churchill's phrase, "the unnecessary war."[1] It was this idea that made the debate so bitter.

Human society really cannot function unless it believes that it can make choices, a process for which it provides itself with "leaders." These leaders may derive their power from an electorate, from divine right, or from the working out of the Hegelian world spirit, but, whatever the font of their legitimacy, posterity tends to judge them all by similar criteria. There may be debate about some of these criteria, but it is agreed that failure is not one of the coveted ones. Chamberlain's policy to prevent another European war failed. It was a failure of a policy he held to be so important that he thought the very survival of civilization dependent on its success. He may indeed have been right on the latter point, but the question remains whether he could have done anything to prevent the catastrophe. The excuse that he was prime minister for only a short time is not very convincing, because he had had considerable influence on British policy from the time he became chancellor of the exchequer in 1931. His influence stretched throughout the decade of the crisis that led to war and must therefore be judged in that light.

Historians usually recognize their obligation to try to depict the sequence of events as accurately as possible from the available evidence. Difficulties arise, however, from the natural tendency to fudge the difference between explaining the alternatives, the "what might have beens," and pursuing the more attractive "what ought to have beens," usually so clear in hindsight. Chamberlain's policy did not prevent war; therefore it was, as he himself was the first to recognize, a failure. It does not of course follow that any alternative policy would have led to better results; for instance, going to war in 1938 was no guarantee of a German defeat, or a faster Allied victory, or even a morally better world. Chamberlain saw all British declarations of war as a failure of his policy and did not believe that he could legitimately, or in any other way, engineer the overthrow of Hitler, any more than he could that of any other dictator active during the period. The world as Chamberlain saw it was not a particularly pleasant place, but war promised only to make it worse. In British domestic affairs there was some possibility for improvement, provided that no arms race destroyed the opportunity for a reasonable recovery from the Great War and the Great Depression. Certainly the United Kingdom in the 1930s was infinitely better off than those states that slipped into dictatorship or civil war. Chamberlain believed that another war would make things only worse for his country and possibly for everyone else as well. Wars were obviously even more unpredictable than peace, and, given the experience of the Great War, conventional wisdom seemed to suggest, in the face of all evidence to the contrary, that winning was hardly better than losing. The question nevertheless remains irresistible: was there not surely a better policy to handle the situation in the 1930s, one that could have prevented the Second World War?

It is unlikely that we shall again be treated to any great revelations about the diplomatic history of the interwar period, although, of course, one never knows for sure. Still, the outline and most details of British foreign policy of the era are now really rather well established. Germany's archives have surely by now given us the main outline of that nation's policy, and, while many of France's records were destroyed, the main outline of its policy is also clear, despite the endless quarrels of the post-1940 regimes. There have been some new points made regarding the Soviet Union, and we can probably expect more as the rewriting of its history continues with more open archives; but again, barring some startling new revelations, the outline of even its foreign policy seems fairly clear. Since the foreign policy of the United States of America was carried out as a kind of continuous and often acrimonious dialogue between the Senate and the White House, it is unlikely that there can be any more revelations from that source. In the absence of further revelations, is it possible to describe the 1930s without undue bitterness?

This study focuses not on what might have been done, but on what was done, in British foreign policy between the wars. The first section shows how deeply rooted the British instinct to appease became after the First World War and explains why this was so. The second section concentrates on Neville Chamberlain's role as prime minister in seeking to apply that policy with vigour and resolve in order to prevent war altogether. And it argues that the very strength that Chamberlain showed as prime minister made his policy all the more devastating a failure, for which he must stand largely responsible, despite the context in which he forged the policy.

A policy of appeasement, before it acquired its more negative reputation, simply meant a policy opposite to one that was bellicose. It was an attitude towards foreign affairs that, for Britain, certainly went back to William Ewart Gladstone in the 1870s and 1880s. In general terms it was a policy which assumed that international affairs, just like domestic affairs, would eventually be governed by reason rather than by passion and consequently by peaceful rather than by warlike actions.[2] It would of course be absurd to suggest that the British Empire had been acquired through a policy of appeasement or that the nineteenth century had marked the triumph of "reason" in this liberal sense in international affairs. Still, there had been relatively long periods when the great powers were not engaged in war with one another and attempted to settle disputes through a variety of mechanisms, not always successfully. It may be argued that the policy that led to the "end of isolation" for the British early in the twentieth century began as a policy of their trying to settle rationally their differences with the French and with the Russians, certainly to prevent a war over interests that were non-vital to all three powers.[3] Yet by acquiring Egypt, Sudan, and various other new possessions, by waging the Boer War, and finally by running a naval race with Germany, the British showed that they were not prepared to appease everyone to the same degree, that there were issues over which they would go to war – as indeed they did in 1914.

Whatever debate rages on about "old" and "new" diplomacy, the indisputable fact was that after 1918 the conduct of British foreign and imperial policy did change drastically, in many respects becoming very like the policies advocated by "liberals" before 1914. This was despite the fact that in 1918 the nation emerged from the war as undoubtedly the strongest of the victorious powers and therefore the strongest power in the world. Yet, despite this position, its policy almost from the moment of the armistice was one of appeasing first allies and then, within a remarkably short period, recent enemies. It is true that the British emerged from the war fatigued by four years of unimaginable effort, but it is also true that of the major belligerents it weathered the storm best. The Austro–Hungarian, Ottoman, and Russian empires had collapsed, the German Empire was beaten, and the French were so exhausted that it had been obvious in 1918 that the British Empire armies really sustained the Allies on the Western Front.

Japan and the United States did well out of the war economically, and the Japanese had scooped up former German colonies. After the United States entered the war in April 1917, it expanded its army rapidly to a peak of over two million men and sent some 41 divisions to France. But it had to transport them across the Atlantic largely in British ships and then equip them with French and British weapons not yet available at home. In raw numerical terms, in almost every category the British army and the Royal Navy (RN) were superior to the forces of all other powers.

The RN in particular was stronger in relation to the other powers than at any time since the Napoleonic Wars. In every category of warship the RN, after the surrender of the German fleet, was stronger than the next three largest navies. The Royal Air Force (RAF), formed as a separate service in the spring of 1918, had over 10,000 aircraft at the end of the war and was certainly the most formidable force of its kind in the world.[4] The British army was not only the largest but also the most successful in the world, the only one that appeared to have weathered the military devastation of 1917 without serious dislocation.

In terms of industry and finances the British economy survived the war in better shape than the other European powers, and, if indeed Germany was no longer a rival in overseas markets, then it faced little difficulty in recovering its pre-war position, or even in improving it substantially, particularly in its share of world trade. The United Kingdom borrowed some $4.2 billion from the United States during the war but was owed $8.7 billion by its European Allies – albeit that included some $2.8 billion loaned to Russia, now unlikely to be recovered.[5] These figures did not include the various reparation payments to be added to the British Treasury that would help reduce the very large national debt accumulated during the war.[6]

One final point about the British position in 1918: although the empire had shown some strain during the conflict, it emerged seemingly larger and more united than ever. Surely no one looking at the international scene in 1918 could predict that by 1950 Britain would be a second-class power, shedding its empire as quickly as possible. One can understand the anger and confusion of some historians who go from victory in 1918 to victory in 1945 and then come up with the much-reduced Britain of Margaret Thatcher in the 1980s.[7] Indeed, everyone looking at the apparent power of the British Empire in 1918 must regret that such power was not used to prevent the atrocities that occurred over the next 30 years. Is there a reasonable explanation for the rapid decline of British power after 1918 that in turn might shed some light on Chamberlain's policies? Was the British position in 1918 an illusion, a kind of brief postwar mirage?

It has been argued that Britain's pre-eminent position in 1918 was artificial, in the sense that the eclipse of Russia and the isolation of the United States were factors bound to pass rapidly, quickly revealing relative British weakness. But the world had to wait until 1942 for that revelation, and meanwhile apparently only the British could effectively take the lead in international affairs. It was a role for which the nation seemed quite unprepared in the 1920s. On the contrary, its immediate postwar posture was one of appeasement – of course, the kind of which everyone approves, but appeasement nevertheless.

The beginning of the interwar period was marked by the Peace Conference in Paris, the attempt by the Allied and Associated Powers to impose a settlement on Europe and the Ottoman Empire. But their treaties failed to pacify the world, despite the great ambitions and indeed the vision brought to Paris in 1919. No doubt that was part of the trouble, the attempt by the statesmen in Paris to be all things to all people – they tried to establish a permanent mechanism that would guarantee the future peace of the world, to satisfy wartime promises of territory and independence made during the war, to find means to deal specifically with German predominance in Europe (all the more difficult because of the elimination of Russian power), and at the same time to live up to many of the ideals proclaimed as Allied war aims. The victors were neither united nor determined enough to impose such an ambitious program, partly because of the misunderstanding at the very heart of the Versailles Treaty. The British and French had major differences in their approach to the settlement, but each was prepared to compromise in order to satisfy the ideals of the American president. They recognized that it was necessary above all to prevent the Americans from making their own peace and abandoning the alliance that they had so recently and reluctantly joined – as an "Associated Power," untainted by "secret treaties and imperialist ambitions."

The final version of the treaty contained all the contradictions inherent in trying to give birth to a new world through the creation of a League of Nations while still satisfying the old, and its discredited concepts of territorial adjustments and retribution. Even at that, the French agreed to sign only on the promise that the Americans and British would guarantee their borders. That promise and much else evaporated when the U.S. Senate threw out the whole treaty, forcing the United States to make a separate peace with Germany after all. This new complication in international affairs made an already difficult situation almost unmanageable. It also wrecked the very basis on which most compromises were made and thus left the victors almost as disgruntled as the vanquished.

Still, 52 months of uninterrupted slaughter was considerable incentive for putting some faith in ideas for maintaining peace in the world. So the settlement attempted to base itself at least in part on ideals that Wilson and others brought to Paris. The two fundamental ideas were of course the creation of the League of Nations and national self-determination. This last was the culmination of a hundred years of liberal idealism, during which the concept gained recognition and credibility. Various "national" committees were recognized before the Armistice as representing a number of "new nations." The ideal of national self-determination could not be denied, and although it started in Europe it spread rapidly to the world at large. The right to sovereignty seemed to belong to every group that could muster a fairy tale or two as proof positive of the existence of a "national culture," which was of course the foundation of another sovereign state. The fundamental contradiction between attempting to spread international law and creating numerous sovereign states did not escape everyone but seemed an ineluctable part of reality.

The Allies had ended the war without occupying many of the geographical areas discussed at the Paris conference. There was therefore no way for them to enforce decisions or often even to get a clear picture of the situation on the ground. People in many areas, accepting the legitimacy of violence for such causes as self-determination, began to follow national symbols, with many waving new flags and some eventually ready to fight even over the colour of their shirts. Although the guns were now silent in western Europe, much of the rest of the world erupted in conflict. The great powers struggled to decide where and on what basis they might intervene. Hesitation naturally made things worse, and rapid demobilization soon made intervention all but impossible.

There was for instance, absolute chaos on the borders as well as at the centre of the old Russian Empire. Here were indeed insoluble problems of violence. Bolsheviks and anti-Bolsheviks fought to gain power and to restore the territorial integrity of the empire. The Reds promised more self-determination to the old subject nationalities and so won the civil war essentially because they proved to be better liars than their opponents. The Allies first intervened to try to prevent the Bolsheviks from making a separate peace with Germany. After that happened, they stayed involved to pursue various contradictory commitments made to various White leaders, as well as to various independence movements in the nationalities on the borders of the empire.

The British, however, were not prepared to pursue this intervention in Russia once the war in Europe was truly over. "The evacuation of all Russian territory" by the Germans was after all number six of Wilson's famous Fourteen Points, but it was never clear whether that meant assisting the border states to gain independence. Poland was a separate case, meriting its own, the 13th, point. As soon as the Bolsheviks clearly gained the upper hand in Russia, the British cut and ran without much debate, principle notwithstanding.

Another indication of the tendency of British policy came at the Washington Conference of 1921–22 and in the treaties that it produced. The United Kingdom allowed its alliance with Japan to lapse and at the same time accepted naval parity with the United States. The Japanese alliance had been made in the first place in order to allow the British to retain their superior naval position in the Atlantic, the North Sea, and the Mediterranean, while still remaining secure in the Far East. And parity at the levels accepted in the treaties meant accepting the notion of parity in numbers and limits on ship size and on total tonnage of capital ships, with virtually no regard for the particular strategic demands placed on the RN. The RN would now be required to defend three oceans with the same number of ships that the U.S. navy used to defend two, while the Japanese fleet, now allowed to become as large as 40 per cent smaller, needed only to worry about one. It is clear that British policy at this conference attempted to appease practically everyone.

The agreements left the Japanese potentially able to dominate in the one ocean that concerned them – the Pacific – where lay vital regions of the British Empire. The British failed to oppose effectively at Washington any unfavourable position, even when their most vital interests were involved. For instance, British policy naturally demanded the abolition of the submarine – the most dangerous weapon that Britain had had to face during the war. Now it seemed not altogether unreasonable to suggest that if the world had become so civilized that it could abolish a substantial part of its weaponry – the treaties eventually called for the scrapping of nearly two million tons of warships – it should also be civilized enough to prevent the recurrence of unrestricted submarine warfare. But the French refused to agree either to abolish or even to limit smaller vessels, including submarines. They argued, in efffect, "guarantee us against another German attack and we will agree to your proposals; if not, then we have to look after ourselves however we see fit." Relations between the British and the French in fact later deteriorated to the point that in the 1920s the British saw the French Armee de l'Air (air force) as the biggest threat to its own security. Nevertheless, the British delegation signed agreements that hurt the RN more than any other, having persuaded the French to accept the ratio of capital ships. General appeasement was pursued in place of unilateral readiness.

Appeasing the United States seemed to make good sense, especially as by then there was no hope that the Americans would guarantee any provisions of the peace settlement, let alone French borders. Therefore it was certainly sensible not to get into disputes with the Americans that could only complicate British problems throughout the world. Equally, it could be argued that, as soon as it became clear that the Bolsheviks were likely to win Russia's civil war, the best policy was to make the best of the situation as it developed there. The crux of the matter for British policy was, however, this consideration: while there may well have been some calculation of concrete factors in their appeasing future great powers, appeasement was emerging as the policy to which the British would in the end resort in virtually every problem in which they became involved after 1919.

Again, for each individual problem one can make a good case for suggesting that such policy was in fact wise. Should an all-out effort have been made to destroy the Irish nationalists? Clearly not, but appeasement had its price even in the 1920s. The same observations held true over the imbroglio involving the Turkish settlement, which finally culminated in 1923 in agreement at Lausanne, which left the British more or less intact, even with a slight victory by retaining Mosul for Iraq.[8] The three new and precariously independent states in the Caucasus region were crushed between Turkish and Soviet power as soon as the English-speaking powers pulled out to cut their losses. If national self-determination was so right for the Irish, why was it so out of the question for the Armenians, who suffered more in the first twenty years of the century but had fewer friends in Boston or New York and less ability to cause trouble for the British?

In each case one can reasonably argue that any other policy would have led to even greater bloodshed. But each settlement did not stop the violence, it just extricated the British. British and French withdrawals from the Caucasus led to wholesale massacres that reduced the Armenian population from 3 million to 130,000 by the end of 1922.[9] From then to 1932 the Kurds staged three major revolts trying to establish their own state, but they were defeated by Iraq – helped on the last occasion by the British air patrol, which helped drive the Kurdish rebels across the Turkish border. The following year a revolt by Christian Assyrians led to another massacre, despite an attempt by the League to intervene. The French forced some 800 armed Assyrians out of Syria and back into Iraq, where their presence was used as an excuse by the Iraqi army to massacre unarmed villagers, without any interference from the British.

These discreditable incidents were typical of the whole period. The confusion about when to use force was part of the growing uncertainty, the loss of the Victorian vision of progress and sense of righteousness, that now dogged British leaders. Existing institutions could not match the new ideologies. By 1930 the British Empire covered a quarter of the world's surface and held a substantial part of its population, but imperialism was falling out of favour in an evolving British democracy. Great empires could hardly exist in a world that regarded national self-determination as the ultimate political good. Consequently the empire was fast becoming an anomaly that generated enormous defence burdens for Britain but added less certain reinforcements to its strength. The empire had really ceased to be a single unit during the Great War. The status of "Dominion" turned out to be the closest thing to independence, and the British found it harder to resist offering that status to all ready to ask for it. So even within the empire, British policy became ambiguous and uncertain. This dilemma was reflected in the debate in the House of Commons over the atrocity committed by General Dyer at Amritsar in 1919, when Secretary of State for India Edwin Montagu opened by asking, "Are you going to keep your hold upon India by terrorism, racial humiliation and frightfulness or are you going to rest it upon the growing goodwill of the people of your Indian Empire?"[10] Such an opening may not have helped Montagu at the time in a hostile House, but there was no doubt that in the long run the resounding "no" to the former would dominate British policy towards India.

Montagu ushered in reforms that continued a process of devolution in India, despite the vocal objection of some Conservative circles. And even that opposition called mostly for going slow, for not abandoning India to communal violence, which home rule would almost certainly unleash, and for not losing sight of British financial and commercial interests. Such interests could not readily be found by opponents of the Government of India Act of 1935.[11] The opposition rested, in the final analysis, on the notion that the British had a moral obligation not to allow India to fall into chaos. But against the moral certitudes of Mahatma Gandhi's *satyagraha* campaigns, that stance surely did not carry much conviction. British policy in India after 1918 was based on the concept of devolution, which in this context was appeasement.[12]

There was a special irony in the fact that when the Great Depression made it possible to abandon free trade, Joseph Chamberlain's son was chancellor of the exchequer and could wage and even win the fight for imperial preference. But as the Ottawa Conference of 1932 clearly demonstrated, it was too late to bring the dominions into any real economic union. The Depression made them, just like all other nations, so protectionist that there was no hope of getting them to work together. The Statute of Westminster in 1931 essentially confirmed their political independence, and nothing in the economic ideas presented at Ottawa could tempt them into any abbreviation of that new status. Neville Chamberlain might briefly believe that he had been given the chance to bring to fruition his father's most cherished dream – a great empire that was also a great economic union. But the reality at Ottawa was haggles over meat duties and wheat quotas, over the relative price of Russian fish and lumber – in short, dealing with a number of separate economies, all of them struggling. "We must open up the vision of a great Imperial policy, having within itself the mainspring which would continuously move us to closer unity."[13] But at a conference at which Chamberlain himself had to threaten to quit Prime Minister Stanley Baldwin's cabinet over meat duties, the great spirit of empire was apt to be trampled under the feet of vested interests. Chamberlain could console himself only by arguing, "The countries of the Empire have been drifting apart pretty rapidly. We have been in time to stop the rot." Of significance for his later dealings with Hitler, he believed that this had been achieved only because of "our unalterable patience."[14] But what had been won was hardly even a faint echo of his father's dream. Despite its size, the empire by the 1930s seemed more vulnerable than formidable.

Certainly by that time neither Japan nor Italy appeared to fear the consequences of taking actions that might provoke the displeasure of the British Empire. The Manchurian crisis of 1931–32 is often taken to be the first of the great crises that led to the Second World War. It is also often regarded as the critical one, because it demonstrated the ineffectiveness of the League of Nations, caused very greatly by the impotence of the British Empire and U.S. isolationism. By revealing that there was no effective mechanism to stop a determined aggressor, it encouraged other assaults. The weak response of the major powers moreover seemed to be the result of selfish and shortsighted policies rather than of specific military weakness or domestic problems. Even at the time Arnold Toynbee argued that the democratic powers were making a bad mistake in assuming that adventurism in China would satiate Japan rather than encourage it: "[T]hey were apparently inclined to regard the breakdown of the collective system of security as a cheap price to pay for the privilege, accorded in the myth to Odysseus by the Cyclops, of being eaten last."[15]

There can be no doubt that the British government appeased Japanese aggression in Manchuria in September 1931 and the related incidents in Shanghai in February and March 1932. But this should not be surprising. The period was one of the more traumatic in modern British history, encompassing the split and fall of the Labour government, the creation of the first National government, the loss of the gold standard, and the growing economic crisis spreading through the world, leaving millions unemployed. These were only the most obvious factors making the British government reluctant to take on any new burdens. Most dramatically, the Manchurian crisis began almost on the same day that a mutiny broke out among RN vessels at Invergordon; although this did not affect the RN's China Station, that force was already too weak to make much of an impression on the Japanese, and the incident did raise concerns about the navy as a whole. Moreover, the naval base at Singapore, the only possible base for a large British fleet east of Ceylon, was far from complete. A main fleet that had to interrupt its autumn cruise because of pay cuts for sailors was hardly likely to pose a serious threat to Japanese actions on the other side of the world.

The complicated diplomatic manoeuvres at Geneva that produced a condemnation of Japan were no substitute for physical pressure, economic or military, and merely gave Japan an excuse to quit the League. Other powers pursued similarly ineffective policies. The dilemma was clear: it was possible perhaps to stop Japanese aggression by a variety of means, including economic sanctions, provided that one was willing to risk war with Japan. There was clearly no policy that could stop Japan from pursuing its aggression without taking that risk, the very risk that neither Britain nor any other power was willing to accept.[16]

The crisis over Abyssinia involved similar problems. In this case the military options were simpler, in that Italy's operations in the area depended entirely on its ability to use the Suez Canal to reinforce and supply its forces. This meant crossing a sea and using a passage dominated by the RN. When all the debates over League resolutions and economic sanctions were over, the simple question remained: was the

British government prepared to risk war with Italy over its attack on Abyssinia? Perhaps the British pursued the worst possible diplomacy by publicly supporting League resolutions condemning and seeking to punish Italy while quietly trying to find a solution that might satisfy – appease – Benito Mussolini and, above all, avoid a naval confrontation. For there was no doubt that if diplomacy and sanctions failed, it would fall to the RN to enforce the will of the League.

And this at a time when the international pressure was greatly increasing because of the resurgence of German power in Europe. The British were in fact more aware now of their military weakness in face of potential threats than they had been during the Manchurian crisis. Partly because of that awareness they had begun to refurbish their armed forces, but that process would take a long time to change appreciably the balance of power. The Admiralty did not fear defeat in a clash with the Italian navy, but it did assume that the RN was likely to sustain losses high enough to tempt others, particularly Japan, into more adventurous policies.[17]

British policy with regard to the Italian crisis and support for the League at least in part reflected domestic issues. In 1935, the year in which Hitler abrogated the military clauses of the Treaty of Versailles, reintroduced conscription, and declared the existence of the German Luftwaffe (air force), the "peace movements" seemed at their strongest in the United Kingdom. The results of the Peace Ballot were proclaimed in June 1935. It was an enormous show of support for the League, with more than 11 million people participating. But the Abyssinian crisis that erupted four months later really put the issues in concrete form. The fifth question asked, "Do you consider that if a nation insists on attacking another the other nations should combine to compel it to stop by a) economic and non-military measures b) if necessary by military measures?" Only 6.7 million respondents answered "Yes" to that question, but this could nevertheless have been seen as a substantial endorsement for taking military action through collective security against an aggressor.[18] Was it?

There is a major difference between the abstract desire for peace and for the punishment of "aggressors" and the practical difficulties of international relations. One can see this in reaction to German rearmament from 1934 on. The Germans made little secret of their program to rearm after they withdrew from the League in late 1933. This, as well as the Far Eastern crisis, led the British government to reconsider its whole defence situation and issue a *Statement Relating to Defence* in March 1935.[19] When the Germans formally announced their rearmament program on 16 March 1935, the League condemned this unilateral abrogation of the Treaty of Versailles but went no further. There was certainly *no* sign of the British public being concerned enough to support any stronger British measures, which in any case were not forthcoming.

Quite the contrary. Apart from the first tentative steps towards rearmament, and diplomatic overtures to Italy at the Stresa Conference in April that bore little fruit, the most practical British move to prevent another naval arms race with Germany was to break ranks with their ally France in order to appease their adversary Germany. Without consulting the French, the British concluded on 18 June a Naval Agreement with the Germans that limited the size of the German navy but also acknowledged that that navy would be rebuilt and marked another departure from Versailles. The British were helping to dismantle their own settlement, rather than seeking to preserve it – appeasement.

An effort to handle the Abyssinian crisis in a similar, pragmatic fashion cost Stanley Baldwin's Conservative government its foreign secretary. Baldwin, prime minister again from June 1935, decided to call what turned out to be the last general election before the Second World War. The campaign was conducted with the enthusiasm generated by the Peace Ballot fresh in the public mind and in the midst of a crisis that had British diplomats leading the way at the League in condemning Italian aggression. With nearly everyone supporting upholding of the rules of proper behaviour in international relations for which the League stood – although *how* was a little unclear – the government presented itself as a champion of collective security, ready to lead the League in facing down the aggressor. But quietly Foreign Secretary Sir Samuel Hoare sought to find a political bargain, an old-style trade-off of territory, that would entice the Italians to cease and desist. When this activity became public knowledge, the howl of righteous indignation forced Baldwin to sacrifice Hoare to appease the anger of Parliament and the public.

Yet before the election Hoare made it clear that he did not want to risk war with Italy over the crisis – the very risk raised by any policy of imposing League sanctions – and he had good reason to think the public far from ready for war. Having failed to secure victory vis-à-vis Italy without being willing to take any risks, the British government did not really alter its policy. The next foreign secretary, Anthony

Eden, also opposed any course that would provoke a serious risk of war. In May 1936 all of Abyssinia duly fell under Italian control.

But another crisis had already arisen that made the whole situation seem even more complex. Taking advantage of the distraction caused by the crisis in Africa, the Germans marched into the Rhineland, symbolically re-establishing their full military rights in their western frontier districts. The Germans' occupation of "their own back yard" did not strike either the British government or public as grounds for serious reaction, but clearly the settlement of 1919 was all but dead and some new arrangement was necessary.

The question of what new arrangement, if any, could preserve order and stability in Europe now became the burning issue of the day – if it was not already – when civil war broke out in Spain in July 1936. The war divided the dictatorships, with Mussolini and Hitler supporting one side and Joseph Stalin in Moscow the other. It divided the democracies internally even more. This was probably the result more of the international clash of ideologies than of any grasp of the situation in Spain, but the division was bitter from the start and became progressively worse. That made it even more difficult for the democratic governments to find a sound policy, because the Spanish conflict took on the status of a morality play by which one could measure the goodness of one's own government through how it responded. Any attempt to stay out of the conflict was perceived by supporters of both sides to be a cynical move by their government to aid the other side. And many people came to see the conflict as a clear warning of the horrors of war, because of the atrocities committed by both sides and because of the devastation caused by modern industrial weapons. Try as it might, the British government seemed to be appeasing no one and settling nothing.

Chamberlain finally moved into centre stage when he became prime minister in May 1937. From the moment he took office, it was clear that foreign policy would form the major challenge for his government. This was itself ironic, because Chamberlain's greatest talents had always lain in social and domestic fields. His record there was formidable, not least in public housing, and as chancellor he had been part of, if not responsible for, the partial economic recovery from the Great Depression. Unemployment had dropped from a high of 22.1 per cent in 1932 to 10.8 per cent in 1937.[20] The new prime minister was reputed to be decisive and clear-headed, not one to suffer fools gladly. A somewhat forbidding figure at 68, he was very much the man in charge. Eden, his foreign secretary, was young and not very experienced, and Hoare had not really recovered from his débâcle in 1935. There were therefore few who could share the front bench in the House of Commons with Chamberlain in terms of prestige, particularly as he pointedly excluded Winston Churchill from the cabinet. Lord Halifax would emerge as the colleague closest to Chamberlain, and he of course sat in the House of Lords.

Chamberlain did *not* bring any new ideas to foreign policy. As a senior member of the British government from 1931 on he had had a major role in pursuing the direction of policy traced above – in effect, reflex appeasement. In such matters as imperial preferences and rearmament, his voice was decisive. No doubt as chancellor he had kept tight control over expenditure on arms because he had always believed that only a healthy economy could sustain any such program. To spend the nation into bankruptcy would be to invite ultimate disaster, so rearmament had to be tailored not to what the armed forces felt they needed but to what the chancellor thought the nation could afford. Nevertheless, expenditure on defence rose from £103 million in 1932 to £265 million in 1937, and to £700 million by 1939.[21] This did not match German, Japanese, or Soviet increases, but it was still a very substantial expansion.

Chamberlain is rarely considered a tragic figure, but if part of tragedy is to have one's actions always result in the opposite of what one intends, then there could hardly be a more tragic statesman in the twentieth century. Chamberlain's view of war was shaped by recent British experience. He subscribed to the conclusion that modern war was nothing but a tragic waste. He had been deeply affected by the death of his young cousin Norman and, after the first air raid on Birmingham, was moved to propose some very modern defences for the city.[22] In his view, any kind of war would lead only to ultimate disaster for the United Kingdom, and for the world, no matter who "won." Yet in 1937 he faced a world full of leaders who made warlike speeches at every opportunity; very soon, some went beyond speeches.

In July the Japanese instigated what turned out to be a full-scale war to dominate China, something bound to shatter all stability in Asia and jeopardize Western interests there. Chamberlain had long advocated reviving some accommodation with Japan – a policy that seemed all the more urgent to him after Japan and Germany concluded an Anti-Comintern Pact in November 1936 – a link that might grow into a combination aimed at more than just the communists.

While others in the British cabinet preferred to pursue an alliance with the United States, Chamberlain tried to build some kind of understanding with Japan. But he had little to offer. The Japanese could see that the British, without a major fleet in the region, could hardly contest their adventure in China. The incidents that occurred with growing frequency along the rivers of China between Japanese forces and British – and American – ships and citizens were all settled essentially on Japanese terms. There was no shortage of news regarding the bombing of cities and the terrible atrocities committed by the Imperial Japanese Army (IJA) after the fall of Nanking, but every examination of British defences tended to emphasize how weak they were.

The crisis in the Far East in fact brought to light some of the basic differences over policy within the British defence establishment. The Chiefs of Staff Committee (COS) might have been the most advanced planning organization to integrate views on national defence problems that then existed, but organization alone could not replace ships and men or prevent obvious and major differences between the services. For the Admiralty, Japan seemed to be the most dangerous threat. From India to Australia the empire was militarily most vulnerable, and Japanese aggression also directly menaced major British trade interests in China. The only possible response was to complete the naval base at Singapore and – after the failure of the Naval Conference of 1936, and the lapse of the naval treaties – to embark on a rapid buildup of capital ships. Since the Treasury insisted on keeping expenditures well under control, and since capital ships were among the most expensive items in the arsenal, giving the Admiralty priority could mean only less money for the RAF and the army.

The Treasury, led by Chamberlain, had insisted all along that a naval buildup should not be the main priority. That should instead be the protection of the homeland from air attack. Therefore the RAF should receive the lion's share of the available funds.[23] This also meant identifying Germany as the most likely and most dangerous enemy. As a result, between 1932 and 1939 the RN's share of overall defence spending dropped from nearly 50 per cent to less than 22 per cent. Although the RN's annual expenditures tripled in those same years, the RAF's went from £17 million to £248 million. Despite these enormous increases, the advice of the COS was consistent and unanimous: avoid military confrontation, above all one in which the empire would face a combination of Germany and Japan – or, worst of all, those two plus Italy. The COS clearly thought the empire in no position to enforce its will against any of the major powers.

Chamberlain was very definitely influenced by such professional military advice before he became prime minister. But it is simply wrong to suggest that his policy from 1937 on was fashioned exclusively by these considerations and that his whole object was to "buy time" to rearm the armed forces. The policy of appeasement was not meant to buy time. Chamberlain wanted to avoid a war, not to fight one at the time of his own choosing. He was utterly convinced that he could find a way to pacify Europe, including the Germans. He shared the view that the Treaty of Versailles had been somewhat unfair to the Germans and that a new settlement would have to take its place. This the prime minister felt could be done without war. Germany was only a special case in a generally chaotic world – special because it was growing powerful under the control of thoroughly unpleasant men who made much of the mishandling of 1919 and afterwards. It was therefore necessary to distinguish between genuine grievances and the purely aggressive tendencies of German policy and to persuade Hitler and his lieutenants to do the same.

This rationale for appeasement was widely shared by the prime minister's senior colleagues. Lord Halifax could trace his family back before the Tudors. His ancestor Robert Wood, the prior of Bodlington, had the distinction of being attainted for high treason and executed in 1537, the year of the Pilgrimage of Grace. His grandfather had been chancellor of the exchequer in Lord John Russell's ministry of 1846 and then served in India from 1852 to 1854 as president of the Board of Control; he had been secretary of state for India from 1859 to 1866, introducing some notable reforms in response to the Great Mutiny of 1857. He could hardly have imagined that his grandson would serve as viceroy of India under a Labour government and go even further than that government in seeking a peaceful solution to the Indian question. In 1931 Halifax took the great risk of negotiating with Gandhi himself, appeasing, at least briefly, his demands.[24] Halifax saw appeasement as the best way to satisfy what he regarded as the legitimate aspirations of the Indian leadership, even if there was some doubt about its representative nature. He had hoped to retire from public life when he returned from India but instead became president of the Board of Education and later secretary of state for war. By the time Chamberlain became prime minister, Halifax was lord president of the council and leader of the government in the House of Lords.

Along the way, Halifax joined the line of important visitors who made the trek to Hitler's eyrie at Berchtesgaden. Former Prime Minister

David Lloyd George went before him and hit it off well with Hitler, remarking, "[He] is indeed a great man."[25] More poignant surely was the meeting between Hitler and George Lansbury in April 1937; the Labour leader described Hitler as "a mixture of dreamer and fanatic, that he appeared free of personal ambition, that he was not ashamed of his humble start in life ... I felt that Christianity in its purest sense might have a chance with him."[26] Halifax went on his visit in November 1937. He of course was a senior member of the government, and therefore his mission can be seen as being more like Lord Haldane's to Berlin of 1912 – to seek a slowing of the arms race and to probe for any opportunity for reconciliation. Hoare believed Halifax to be well suited for the task, telling Chamberlain, "In India he had shown his wisdom in reconciling bitter differences. Communal troubles had become less acute under his mediating influence, Gandhi had become his personal friend. Might he not have the same success in Europe that he had won in Asia?"[27] Halifax had a three-hour discussion with Hitler, as well as lunch with Hermann Goering and tea with Josef Goebbels. He thought that it showed some moral defect in himself that he did not dislike these people more, seeing Goering as a great schoolboy. In any case, he said to Hitler that he thought that the major trouble spots in Europe – Danzig, Austria, Czechoslovakia – could all be settled amicably: "[I]f reasonable settlements could be reached with the free assent and goodwill of those primarily concerned we certainly had no desire to block them." Hitler replied to this invitation to dismantle what was left of the settlement of 1919 by asking Halifax, over lunch, why he had not had Gandhi shot.[28]

This meeting did not accomplish much, but it demonstrated that the British government as a whole was willing to accept those changes which fitted the concept of self-determination that they believed the Germans were most keen to make – no matter who else got hurt in the process. Such closeness of views must help to explain why Chamberlain overlooked the lack of results from such meetings and persuaded Halifax to succeed Eden as foreign secretary when the latter resigned in February 1938 – no longer able to stomach the prime minister's desire to go to some lengths to regain Mussolini's goodwill.[29]

1938: Height of Appeasement

That year, 1938, marked the culmination of the British attempt to appease Germany and thereby avoid another general war – an endeavour driven forward by the prime minister, but with the strong support of nearly all his colleagues and many others besides.

The "unalterable patience" that Chamberlain believed had brought him "success" at the Ottawa Conference now became the basis of his efforts to manage foreign policy in such a manner as to prevent another war. It meant treading a very fine line indeed, for Chamberlain, despite his "unalterable patience," was not a pacifist. Indeed, unlike all other major powers except France, in 1939 the United Kingdom declared war and did not wait to be attacked. The crucial question is not why the British did not go to war in 1938, but rather why they did so in 1939. After all, Chamberlain thought that war would bring massive casualties from air attacks, would ruin the economy of all of Europe, might well even destroy civilization. He was therefore not going to allow anything or anyone to stop him from doing everything possible to prevent another 1914. By that he understood the following: Europe must not again divide itself into two armed camps. Legitimate grievances must be rectified before they gave rise to international tensions that could provoke war. The arms race must be ended as quickly as possible. And the prime minister had no faith in the ability of the League of Nations to accomplish any of these goals, nor did he believe that the United States would add much to the process. He was of course not looking for an alliance with the United States or the Soviet Union, because he was convinced that such an alliance would provoke the very war that he wanted to avoid.

This was always the central core of the dilemma – the path that seemed the most hopeful in terms of peace was not necessarily the best one if war proved unavoidable. Chamberlain would do everything that he could to appease Italy in order to prevent it from becoming part of a hostile alliance system, but at the same time he wanted to avoid creating the friendly alliance system that seemed necessary to win a war if one came. A similar kind of contradiction dogged his policy towards France. This was partly also the result of another major difference of opinion between the services. The RAF wanted to ignore everything but "the knockout blow from the air" strategy, while the army maintained that the only way to beat Germany would be through a long war. Neither wanted a continental commitment, which, they feared, would entail the same stalemate as in 1914–18. Thus until 1939 there was no firm agreement, let alone any plan, to send a British army to France. The French found this peculiar, to say the least, not because they saw themselves as so much weaker than the other powers but because they believed that the British needed them as much as vice versa. The French leaders considered this mutual dependence self-evident, but it took the British government twenty years to realize it, because until 1939 it assumed that another Great War must be unthinkable. Not until after the Munich Crisis of 1938 was Chamberlain persuaded that another British continental commitment was crucial to maintaining any balance of power in Europe.[30] Before then, he led the way in searching for the settlement that could make the argument moot.

"No doubt much of human history consists in the more or less gracious acceptance of the ineluctable; but even the degree of grace is a matter of some interest."[31] In 1938, appeasement reached its apogee as the basis of British foreign policy. The British prime minister's zeal for peace and the German chancellor's ambition for war created a bizarre combination in the politics of Europe. Chamberlain was determined to find a lasting accommodation with Germany. Just as with imperial preferences, he may again have been on a kind of crusade to vindicate what his father had tried to achieve from 1898 to 1901 – an "Anglo–German understanding." He would carry it forward himself and if necessary shed colleagues along the way. The quarrel with Eden in February 1938 was really over the conduct of policy more than over its substance, but Eden caught the fundamental difference in beliefs when he said in Parliament that "of late the conviction has steadily grown upon me that there has been a keen desire on our part to make terms with others, rather than that others should make terms with us. This was never the attitude of this country in the past."[32]

Even in retrospect Eden did not see the threat to Austrian independence as anything but a warning of the coming of the next crisis – certainly not something to challenge a fight against.[33] This was in effect an accurate assessment of the general reaction: at the time "the Austrian crisis of 1938 appeared with the sureness of a Canadian winter and elicited as much surprise."[34] Here was an independent country, a member of the League of Nations, guaranteed by the treaties, simply invaded on the grounds that the Austrians were clearly part of the same ethnic nationality as the Germans and therefore not likely to oppose being annexed. And that also turned out to be correct. Certainly no one, not even the Austrians, seriously thought of going to war over this issue.

Nevertheless the means by which Hitler accomplished his ends did give Chamberlain pause. "It is perfectly evident, surely, now, that force is the only argument that Germany understands, and that collective security cannot offer any prospect of preventing such events," the prime minister wrote on 13 March. Chamberlain said "prevent," *not* "reverse," "such events." In that same note he drew the peculiar and surely false conclusion that "very possibly this might have been prevented if I had had Halifax at the Foreign Office instead of Anthony [Eden] at the time I wrote my letter to Mussolini [January 1938]." His next thought, however, showed that, while Chamberlain did grasp some consequences of the Anschluss, he had no intention of abandoning his policy: "for the moment we must abandon conversations with Germany, we must show our determination not to be bullied by announcing some increase or acceleration in rearmament, and we must quietly and steadily pursue our conversations with Italy. If we can avoid another violent coup in Czechoslovakia, which ought to be feasible, it may be possible for Europe to settle down again, and someday for us to start peace talks again with the Germans."[35]

It was of course not possible to avoid "another violent coup." The crisis in Czechoslovakia represented the culmination of all the trends of the interwar years, but the basic calculations remained essentially the same. The composition of the Czech state was testimony to the absurdities of the "national state" in eastern and central Europe. This is not to say that it was bound to fail. After all, the notion of the "racially or ethnically pure" state belongs to the world of political drug addicts. Yet it was an addiction so widely shared that it had an air of legitimacy. The "Bohemian-Germans" (Sudeten Germans) had proclaimed themselves to be part of Austria on 29 October 1918, one day after the proclamation of the Czech Republic.[36] They represented between 22 and 23 per cent of the population of the Czech Republic, and no doubt a lot of them believed in 1938 that they could best exercise their freedom by joining Nazi Germany. Certainly during 1938 the political party that first advocated autonomy in, then secession from, Czechoslovakia had gained so much enthusiastic support that many of the other smaller German parties dissolved themselves in order to join Heinlein's movement.[37]

Neither Chamberlain nor the vast majority of the critics of the Munich Agreement ever seemed to have questioned whether the wishes of the majority of Sudeten Germans had to be met no matter what the cost to Czechoslovakia, or indeed to Europe. The *Times* kept repeating that theme, "no solution should be considered too drastic which is desired by the overwhelming majority ... [T]he Germans of

Czechoslovakia ought to be allowed to decide their own future."[38] Throughout that summer of 1938 speeches by Chamberlain and Halifax reflected the basic dilemma of the British position with regard to the looming Czech crisis. There was no military commitment to Czechoslovakia, but there would be little hope of containing a war if one broke out. The best solution was obviously one that would please all parties, and the British government would do everything that it could to facilitate such an outcome – however unlikely. But Chamberlain's recurrent theme was the uselessness of war: "All the same, our object must always be to preserve these things which we consider essential without recourse to war, if that is possible, because we know that in war there are no winners. There is nothing but suffering and ruin for those who are involved." And again, "When I think of those four terrible years and I think of the seven millions [sic] of young men who were cut off in their prime ... then I am bound to say again what I have said before and what I say now, not only to you, but to all the world – in war, whichever side may call itself the victor, there are no winners, but all are losers."[39]

Nevertheless there was a crisis over Czechoslovakia. The balance of power was shifting in a manner that could not be ignored. Germany was rapidly becoming the dominant power, and Hitler's way of conducting foreign policy was anything but reassuring. If power was the only language understood by the leaders of the new Germany, then the British had better make it clear that they had such power and were prepared to use it. But did they in fact have such power? And perhaps even more critical, were they prepared to use it? Surely not over a question that seemed to be one of procedure rather than of substance. President Edward Benes of Czechoslovakia must come to some agreement with his restless German citizens, otherwise Hitler would have an excuse to move in with his army and "rescue" his "oppressed" fellow Germans.

The danger of war over Czechoslovakia came not only from Germany. Unlike the Austrian affair, the French government could not but take this issue very seriously. It had an alliance with the Czech state – one that it insisted it would honour. Prime Minister Edouard Daladier, despite his weak foreign minister, Bonnet, showed considerable reluctance about pressing the Czech government to negotiate with the "Bohemian-Germans." The French government was very aware that the choice confronting it was whether to retain its position in eastern Europe at the price of losing a possible British alliance or to bind the British to a continental commitment at the price of its failing to support its Czech ally.[40] Daladier chose the latter. It made France slightly more dependent on British initiatives but bound the British to the continent in an entirely new manner. That, however, was the result of the Czech crisis; meanwhile, there was the question of the German minority in the Czech state.

Chamberlain seems at first to have seen the mounting crisis as an opportunity to deal directly with Hitler. He had a plan for a dramatic move. He would fly to Germany and confront Hitler with the same cold logic that made him such a formidable debater in the House of Commons. There must not be a war over an issue with an obvious and equitable solution. A high degree of autonomy for the "Bohemian-Germans" within the Czech Republic should satisfy everyone. But autonomy was no more a solution for these "Germans" than it had been for the Austrians. By the late summer Hitler became convinced that he could press the issue so far that he could even launch a minor war to rescue his "beleaguered fellow Germans." He seemed prepared to risk a war with France over the question. But on the principle involved, Chamberlain was basically in the same position as every British prime minister since the idea that self-determination for "nationalities" was to be desired became widely accepted; the implied word was always of course "oppressed."

During Chamberlain's first visit to Germany in September, Hitler established that Chamberlain accepted the principle of self-determination, which, as Hitler pointed out, was not invented by him for the Czech problem but rather was brought into being to create a moral basis for the Treaty of Versailles.[41] Chamberlain hedged somewhat at this unhappy reminder of Versailles but said that he clearly held to that principle. He would try to get everyone else to agree to it also. It meant of course allowing the Germans of Czechoslovakia to join the German Reich, not just to get better terms within the Czech state. Having agreed to a principle, Chamberlain flew back home believing that the matter could be settled amicably, if the Czechs and the French agreed to this principle.

But the main difference now emerged between Hitler and Chamberlain. The British prime minister envisioned that once they agreed to the principle they could work out some fair and measured way to implement a transfer of power through properly supervised voting procedures and international conferences. Hitler had no time for such procedures. This was not just because he was in a hurry but because appearances were vital to him. What he wanted was an inspirational triumph with marching men and flying flags, not solemn international conferences. This difference very nearly led to war during the next week. When Chamberlain returned to Germany the conversations at Godesberg reflected Hitler's desire for drama and Chamberlain's demand for a decent and proper transfer of the lands and people in dispute. When Chamberlain left Germany the second time it looked as though there was going to be war over the manner of the transfer. That seemed sillier than ever, so at the Munich Conference all the parties compromised over the appearances, not the substance, of the Czech issue.

But of course it was not silly. That essentially was Chamberlain's mistake all along. He thought that he could win over Hitler to a general agreement to pacify Europe by accepting a basic principle, namely self-determination, and then finding the appropriate mechanisms to settle disputes. He believed that he had obtained from Hitler at their first meeting an assurance that the destruction of the rest of Czechoslovakia was not Hitler's aim, that Hitler had no further ambitions in Europe, but that, in any case, disputes would be settled without moving armies. That after all was the essence of the "piece of paper" that Chamberlain waved as the symbol of "peace in our time" when he returned from Munich. But the question of "appearances" was not so simple. The principle of national self-determination, like all other principles, seemed to work best when accompanied by sufficient force. Hitler's "triumphs" usually went hand in hand with the fanfare of power and lately of course also with its reality. The history of National Socialism is sometimes written as though Hitler invented the pageantry of power. All that he did was to take a tradition already old when the Egyptian pyramids were built and, like other successful leaders of political movements, adapt it to his own time. Hitler was deeply angry over the Munich Agreement surely because Chamberlain's persistence forced him to share the political stage with others and to give the appearance that a thing as elemental as German power could be regulated by international agreements.

The Munich Agreement therefore pleased no one. If Hitler was angry because he did not get sufficient prestige for annexing a small part of a small country pressed by its "allies" to give in without a fight, Chamberlain seems to have forgotten, in his zeal for peace, that prestige was a necessary part of the foreign policy of even the British Empire. It was ironic that while Munich was the culmination of

Britain's postwar foreign policy, it robbed the nation finally of that indefinable element of its position in the world – namely, prestige.[42] That is presumably why those in the United Kingdom who were ecstatic when Chamberlain returned waving his "piece of paper," and who seemed then to be the considerable majority, were quickly disillusioned when they discovered that the price of the agreement was a great loss of British prestige.

Chamberlain may well have regarded the loss of prestige as a price worth paying to preserve the peace. He described his government as being a "go-getter" for peace, in a speech made on 9 November 1938: "Now that the crisis is over, it is very easy to find fault with the solution, but the fact is that in the situation with which we had to deal it was not possible to present the ideal solution as the alternative to force. We were dealing with a situation which had arisen from forces which had been set in motion nearly twenty years before, and the surgeon who has to deal with long-neglected wounds or disease must cut more swiftly and more deeply than he who is dealing with the first symptoms. If the settlement at Munich imposed upon Czechoslovakia a fate which arouses our natural sympathy for a small state and a brave people, yet we cannot dismiss in silence the thought of what the alternative would have been to the peoples not only of Czechoslovakia, but all the nations that would have been involved."[43]

Blaming Versailles for the problems of Europe was no doubt a useful propaganda tool for the revisionist powers, but it was hardly likely to enhance the prestige of the powers that were the main authors of the treaty! Blaming Versailles of course had other consequences. The treaty no doubt incorporated many injustices, not least that of accusing the German government of being solely responsible for the outbreak of war in 1914. The logic did not escape Chamberlain: if the German government was not the author of the Great War, then the circumstances of 1914 were, so it was essential not to replicate those circumstances – no alliance system that could be construed as an attempt to surround Germany, no British continental military commitment, no ambiguity about British diplomatic commitments. The "go-getter" for peace avoided all these pitfalls in 1938. Would his policy succeed enough to allow him to go on avoiding them?

Although Chamberlain retained his ambition to be the peacemaker of Europe after Munich, he also drastically changed his foreign policy. If in 1938 he addressed the question of how the "legitimate" aspirations of the German government could reasonably be met, in 1939 he faced another question: how to prevent it from imposing its illegitimate claims on Europe. It was quite a different question, and the answers turned out to be suspiciously like those provided by the earlier policy of Sir Edward Grey in 1914. The difference in questions is also important to historians. If the only useful question about the Munich crisis is whether it would have been better to fight in 1938 than in 1939, then the military–economic issues deserve their pride of place in much of the literature.[44] One ends up earnestly comparing 30 Czech divisions with 50 Polish ones, weighing the possible benefits of a Soviet alliance against the British guarantee to Poland, all on the assumption – easy to make after 1945 – that it was both necessary and morally just to fight Hitler's Germany. Under this dispensation, Chamberlain should have asked only, "When was it best to do so?"

The answer was provided repeatedly by the COS, and its advice had been consistent for nearly 20 years: "[N]ot now ... some future time perhaps ... and not against Germany, Japan and Italy combined."[45] But Chamberlain did not want to figure out the best time to go to war with Hitler. He still wanted to know only whether it was necessary to fight him at all. He never of course seriously considered fighting Germany in order to change its domestic politics. The British had no major outstanding issue with Germany other than over its clearly expansionist foreign policy. If they could live with a Europe dominated by a single power, then they had no quarrel with Germany at all. Chamberlain pursued a policy which assumed that no one wanted to dominate Europe, that Hitler's demands were at least in part still the residue of the Great War, and that no one could possibly want another. So problems must be amenable to settlement by discussion and debate. But even his original biographer had to observe, "Many thousand pages of parliamentary debate could not muffle the sound of voices prophesying war."[46]

Chamberlain changed British foreign policy because he now believed that he needed to find another way to prevent war. He did not change it simply or even mainly to put himself in a better position to fight a war when and if it came. Although he sped up rearmament, now throwing financial discretion close to the winds, he still hoped that Britain would not have to use the new weapons. Moreover, because defending the home islands against air attack had taken priority, British moves in Europe did not have much military bite to them. Chamberlain did begin to harden British positions, but it was the final elimination of rump Czechoslovakia that led him on 17 March to denounce Hitler's move as a betrayal of all previous pledges.[47] British policy now moved towards a more traditional concept of the balance of power in Europe, opposing the power that seemed to be in a favourable position to bid for predominance on the continent.

In the end Baldwin said it best in a speech that neatly echoed Chamberlain's final, if reluctant, stance. At a lecture at the University of Toronto in April 1939, Baldwin summarized two of the major dilemmas of the postwar period: Victorian laissez-faire was dying if not dead, Marxism was powerless to be truly born. He pointed to the folly of a new war because of the destructive capacity of the new weapons – "enough to make Attila turn in his grave with envy" – and ended on a poignant note: "Civilization may perish as a result of war: it would certainly perish as a result of Nazism triumphant beyond the border of the country of its birth ... And now we know that should the challenge come, we shall be there. In Luther's words, 'we can do no other.' We were there when the Spanish galleons made for Plymouth; we were there on those bloody fields in the Netherlands when Louis XIV aimed at the domination of Europe; we were on duty when Napoleon bestrode the world like a demi-God, and we answered the roll call, as you did, in August 1914. We can do no other. So help us God."[48]

So the continental commitment was re-established, assuring France that the British–French alliance brought with it a British commitment that might be small at the beginning of a war but could, on the experience of the Great War, become very large indeed. In April, following Mussolini's coup on Good Friday against Albania, Britain introduced a measure of conscription for the first time in peacetime in its modern history. And as Hitler began to agitate against Poland, with which he had some grievances as "legitimate" as the ones against the Czechs, Chamberlain moved to make the British position crystal clear. At least in part to avoid what he saw as Grey's mistake of 1914 – making war more likely by keeping the British position ambiguous – Chamberlain guaranteed Poland and its territory unconditionally. Following the Italian move against Albania, he did the same for Greece and Romania. These moves were of course designed to warn Germany and Italy that the time of easy conquests was past and that the British, and presumably the French, would fight to protect the status quo in western and eastern Europe. But such a policy handed the initiative to the revisionist powers. Any one of them could now decide when and where to challenge the British guarantees.

Would revisionist powers take these guarantees seriously? Could the guarantees prevent further expansion? The answer provided by the events of 1939 illustrated that while Mussolini was intimidated enough to declare neutrality in September, Hitler showed considerable contempt for British warnings. British prestige was no longer great enough to deter his ambitions in eastern Europe. This was the first consequence of Chamberlain's actions in 1938. The second was the failure to forge a larger alliance system – this time to rebuild, not to avoid, the alignment of 1914. British prestige could hardly have stood very high in the Soviet Union, and the deep antagonisms between the two governments could not be overcome by a few months of cautious talks. With a good knowledge of the course and consequences of the Russian–German war from 1941 on, we can see how wrong Chamberlain was to hesitate in agreeing to Stalin's conditions for an alliance and we can assume that, with a little more understanding or a little more haste, that alliance should have been possible. Yet any fair evaluation of Chamberlain's calculations in his bid to restore the old anti-German alliance must take into account conditions and perceptions of the time.

It had taken the French more than three years to bring about a workable entente between Tsarist Russia and liberal England in 1907, and even then the real alliance remained between France and Russia. In moral terms, surely Chamberlain had every right to wonder who was the more repugnant dictator; up to 1939 Stalin had killed far more people than Hitler, and again it is only our awareness that Hitler began to catch up to him so dramatically during the war years that makes the choice easier in retrospect. But in any case Chamberlain's policy in 1939 was based almost exclusively on the balance of power, and, since the Soviet Union threatened that less than Nazi Germany, the British sought to make an alliance with it. But this was to be mainly a diplomatic alliance. After all, only the Soviet Union's apparent military weakness made it seem less of a threat to the status quo than Nazi Germany. In 1939 the Soviet Union seemed less formidable than the combination of Poland and Romania – again an absurd notion only in hindsight.

Nevertheless Hitler took Chamberlain's feelers seriously enough to dangle the suggestion of a fourth partition of Poland and went on to make a rapid alliance with Stalin on that basis. For both these two land powers the real issue was of course the French army – in their view, the strongest single piece on the board. Both dictators assumed, rightly, that the British were acting as spokesperson of the Western Allies and that the two powers could not be divided against each other. Therefore the pact with Stalin seemed to Hitler a master stroke, because it would surely make Chamberlain hesitate to meet Britain's relatively new obligations in central Europe. That in turn might keep France neutral long enough to allow the dictators to destroy Poland. With the Soviet Union involved, nothing could save Poland, and even Chamberlain would recognize that and not fight for a lost cause.

Hitler was almost right, but for the wrong reasons. It was not military calculation that made Chamberlain hesitate; it was still his personal quest for peace. Chamberlain took each step towards war with such a sense of personal failure and responsibility that when he finally confronted the British public and the House of Commons on 3 September, his speeches were all about "I," "me," "myself": "You can imagine what a bitter blow it is to me that all my long struggle to win the peace has failed ... everything that I have worked for, everything that I have hoped for, everything I have believed in ... I cannot tell what part I may be allowed to play myself ... I trust I may live to see the day when Hitlerism has been destroyed."[49] "And in this manner the greatest war in the history of the world began – not with a bang but with a whimper."[50]

It is hard to see what "cold logic" drove Chamberlain to meet his obligations and go to war. He knew that the Western Allies could not stop the German army from conquering Poland, just as he had assumed that nothing could stop it from conquering Czechoslovakia. These countries could be restored only after another victory. Yet the same logic said that there were no more victors in modern war. In his most private reflections Chamberlain believed that a military victory was not feasible at all, but he did feel that, if the Germans became convinced that they could not win, then they would overthrow Hitler.[51] He had hesitated until the last possible moment, hoping for some break. As late as 24 August 1939 there was the possibility that Goering himself would pay a secret visit to London. Many arrangements were made for such a visit. But, like many other "peace initiatives," it was still-born. There was really no way to avoid the commitments made to Poland, especially as it, unlike Czechoslovakia, would not allow itself to be conquered without a fight.

So the British went to war in September 1939 essentially over the question of the balance of power in Europe, just as Baldwin had predicted they would. There was no doubt a coincidence between the desire to dominate Europe and the general wickedness of the dictators. This coincidence united the British people behind their government, but it hardly produced a crusading atmosphere in Britain during the first winter of the war. The outbreak of the conflict did not even immediately end Chamberlain's hopes to avoid the kind of catastrophic war that he so feared. Both sides lived up to promises made on 2 September not to bomb each other's cities, at least in western Europe. Poland was crushed, but not without heroic resistance, and some news of the horrors committed by the occupying powers did reach London and Paris, but Dutch and Belgian neutrality was not violated. Above all, there was no bloodbath on the Western Front. This "false peace" was "an unutterably personal solace to him," and Chamberlain came to believe that Hitler had "missed the bus" and that Britain, by simply standing still, could see the war ended on Allied terms.[52] And "standing still" seemed to make good strategic and economic sense. Once the dominions joined in the war against Germany, the combined weight of the British and French empires seemed to promise that they could become strong enough to prevail.

By the same token, Chamberlain refused to agree to any negotiations without a previous German withdrawal from Poland. He really now believed that peace was impossible as long as Hitler stayed in power. His was the "fury of a patient man,"[53] and neither Hitler's "peace offensive" nor the other complications of the winter of 1939–40 moved him from this position. The war of the three major European powers seemed almost insulated from the rest of the world. The other powers pursued their own interests, each trying to take advantage of the preoccupation of the Western Allies. The Japanese carried on their war in China, which was not going all that well. The Japanese, like the Italians, were very unhappy at what they considered to be Hitler's betrayal of their agreements in making his alliance with the Soviet Union. There was a distinct coolness among the Axis powers, not helped by Germany's strictly neutral attitude during the Finnish war. The Soviet Union started that war to strengthen its position in eastern Europe. The United States, having in 1938 signed a very advantageous trade agreement with the United Kingdom, was moved in November 1939, by the combination of U.S. Congressional greed and presidential concern, to make a partial repeal of its ban on arms sales. The "cash and carry" policy allowed everyone the privilege of buying U.S. munitions, provided that they paid in cash and carried them off in their own ships. This was a clear advantage to those who had both – supposedly the Allies. But none of this did very much to further the Allied cause. Nor was the attitude of the smaller neutrals very encouraging. Quite to the contrary, they were very concerned not to give anyone any reason to intervene in their affairs, which was all perfectly normal.

But the war was anything but normal. The Allies' strategy was based largely on the notion that somehow, in the long term, they were bound to win; but meanwhile, since defence was so much stronger than attack, they would allow Germany to make the first move – which it did. The type of war that began with the invasion of Norway in April 1940 was the kind that Chamberlain had feared from the beginning. It was not one for which he could provide any real leadership. He was now 71 years old, and the growing list of defeats was blamed on him, not altogether unjustly. He was not a man of war even in wartime, but he remained stubborn until the end. Chamberlain led his country into the war with such obvious reluctance and repugnance that it could hardly be expected that he would enjoy running its war machine.

The gods arrange things in their own strange way. The angry debate in May in the House of Commons that destroyed Chamberlain began just two days before the German army launched its oft-postponed attack in the west. The outcome of the debate was somewhat ironic: Chamberlain was replaced by Windston Churchill, who had been his most severe and effective critic in the House for years, but who was also largely responsible for the débâcle in Norway. The result of the German attack was the defeat of France and the isolation of the British Empire. The events of the summer of 1940 in a sense represented the culmination of 20 years of dilemmas in Britain's foreign policy – dilemmas that arose from its efforts to apply its own political ideals to a postwar world in which many states rejected them. Sympathy for the ideal of national self-determination, hope for an international body to settle disputes without recourse to war, belief in disarmament as a way to minimize international tension – all these values arose in a world in which Britain was a satisfied power, ruling the largest empire in history. The British simply took too long to face the fact that newer political ideologies saw violence as not only necessary but desirable to change a status quo that they despised – and viewed disarmament as a plot to uphold that status quo and the position of those who gained from it. No Briton failed more completely to grasp this than Chamberlain, and unfortunately none had more authority over British policy than he.

In a way Chamberlain's appeasement policy was the most logical approach to the problem.[54] It was at least pressed with determination, as opposed to the aimless drift under MacDonald and Baldwin. And even though Chamberlain rejected the capacity of the League to help in the process, what he wanted his policy to achieve was within the boundaries of the ideals cherished by many League supporters. When Chamberlain saw that his policy had failed, he reverted to the age-old British instinct to act to uphold the balance of power. But the nine-teenth-century balance in which the British had the strongest economy and the strongest navy had vanished. There was just enough vigour, prestige, and confidence left in the empire for effective leadership to harness it in mid-1940 to fight for British survival. And in this new struggle Chamberlain, as a senior member of Churchill's war cabinet, gave his successor undivided loyalty and support, especially with regard to the British refusal to make a compromise peace with a tri-umphant Hitler.[55] But this stark dilemma itself underlined how com-plete Chamberlain's failure had been, however logical his policy might have seemed, given the mood of the nation and the situation facing it.

There was one final intervention by the gods. In late September 1940 surgery for throat cancer forced Chamberlain to resign; he died on 9 November. His ashes were interred at Westminster Abbey on 14 November. The members of the war cabinet were his pallbearers. The night of 14 November was obviously not the beginning of the Luftwaffe's attempt to force the British to surrender, but it was the moment for an attack so large that the target became a byword for aerial destruction. Chamberlain loved the music of Beethoven; the Germans' code name for their operation that night was Moonlight Sonata, and their target was Coventry. The raid was a fitting symbol of the destruction of the ideals that Chamberlain had set out with such determination to save in 1937. It was in this sense a very fitting accompaniment to his funeral.

NOTES

1 W.S. Churchill, *The Gathering Storm* (Boston, 1950), iv.

2 M. Howard, *War and the Liberal Conscience* (London, 1978); P. Kennedy, *The Realities behind Diplomacy: Background Influences on British External Policy 1865–1980* (London, 1981).

3 This is the argument made in the classic study by G.W. Monger, *The End of Isolation: British Foreign Policy 1900–1907* (London, 1963).

4 P. Kennedy, *The Rise and Fall of British Naval Mastery* (London, 1976), 332, says at least 20,000.

5 J.M. Keynes, *The Economic Consequences of the Peace* (London, 1919), 271.

6 G.C. Peden, *British Rearmament and the Treasury* (Edinburgh, 1979), 75, gives the debt as £650 million in 1914 and £7.8 billion by 1920. By 1939 the debt per head of population stood at £172, while in the United States it was £64, and in Germany, £33; ibid., 192.

7 See, for instance, Correlli Barnett, in *The Collapse of British Power*, *The Audit of War*, and *The Lost Victory*, who blames it all on the public schools, or Kennedy in *The Rise and Fall of British Naval Mastery* and in *The Rise and Fall of the Great Powers*, who says that it is all very complicated but that economic problems really seemed to predominate.

8 H. Nicolson, *Curzon: The Last Phase* (Boston, 1934), describes everything in detail, especially Curzon's position on Mosul and the petty triumph of the mighty empire over this piece of territory, tiny but full of oil.

9 Ibid, 317.

10 L.S. Amery, *My Political Life*, Vol. II (London, 1953), 204.

11 A. Krishtalka, "The Old Tories and British Foreign Policy 1930–1939," doctoral dissertation, 2 vols., McGill University, 1984, 426–527.

12 "But the heart had gone from the Raj. Gandhi held the moral lead. The British had only power. The Indian empire kept going largely from habit. The British sensed the notice to quit. The difference between them and the Congress was only over timing, not over the principle of 'Dominion status.'" A.J.P. Taylor, *English History 1914–1945* (Oxford, 1965), 133.

13 K. Feiling, *The Life of Neville Chamberlain* (London, 1946), 214.

14 Ibid., 215; K. Middlemas and J. Barnes, *Baldwin* (London, 1969), 675.

15 A.J. Toynbee, *Survey of International Affairs 1932* (London, 1933), 533.

16 S.W. Roskill, *British Naval Policy between the Wars*, Vol. II (London, 1976), 111.

17 Ibid., 248–84; A.J. Marder, *From the Dardanelles to Oran* (Oxford, 1974), 64–100.

18 R.A.C. Parker, *Chamberlain and Appeasement: British Policy and the Coming of the Second World War* (London, 1993), 46–7.

19 Cmd. 4827, *Statement Relating to Defence*, House of Commons, 1 March 1935.

20 Peden, *British Rearmament*, 208.

21 Ibid., 205.

22 Feiling, *Life of Neville Chamberlain*, 59.

23 See Peden, *British Rearmament*, passim; N. Gibbs, *Grand Strategy. Vol. 1. Rearmament 1919–1939* (London, 1976), part III; D. Dilks, "The Unnecessary War? Military Advisers and Foreign Policy in Great Britain 1931–1939," in A. Preston, ed., *General Staffs and Diplomacy before the Second World War* (London, 1978), 98–132.

24 Earl of Birkenhead, *Halifax: The Life of Lord Halifax* (London, 1965). He was Lord Irwin while viceroy, as his father lived to 95, long enough to see his son return from India.

25 P. Rowland, *David Lloyd George: A Biography* (New York, 1976), 732–7.

26 R. Blythe, *The Age of Illusion: England in the Twenties and Thirties* (Boston, 1964), 290–1. Vansittart, in *The Mist Procession* (London, 1958), 426, summed up Lansbury well: "He was one of those first class Christians who so nearly wrecked Christian civilization."

27 S. Hoare, *Nine Troubled Years* (London, 1954), 280; M. Gilbert and R. Gott, *The Appeasers* (Boston, 1963), 71.

28 Birkenhead, *Halifax*, 368–74; A. Eden, *Facing the Dictators* (London, 1962), 508–16.

29 Churchill might well have been demonstrating his grasp of Halifax's instinct for appeasing when, in order to get him out of the way in 1940, he sent him to, as ambassador, Washington, DC, where ingratiation was by then so sorely needed. Halifax held the post most successfully until 1946.

30 M. Howard, *The Continental Commitment* (Oxford, 1971); R.J. Young, *In Command of France* (Boston, Mass., 1978).

31 M. Beloff, *Imperial Sunset*, Vol. I (London, 1971), 7.

32 Eden, *Facing the Dictators*, 600.

33 Ibid., 5–8.

34 Young, *In Command of France*, 196.

35 Feiling, *Life of Neville Chamberlain*, 341–2.

36 J. Rothschild, *East Central Europe between Two World Wars* (Seattle, 1974), 79.

37 No doubt there was also much intimidation that the Czech authorities were reluctant to curb for fear of being "provocative" and giving Hitler an excuse to intervene.

38 J.E. Wrench, *Geoffrey Dawson and Our Times* (London, 1955), 370–1; Vansittart, *Mist Procession*, 470.

39 *House of Commons Debates*, 24 March, 2 July 1938.

40 Young, *In Command of France*, chap. 8.

41 *Documents on German Foreign Policy*, Series D, Vol. II, No. 487.

42 Nicolson, *Curzon*, 52–3, put it very well: "Prestige is founded on certain perfectly definable methods. Never to interfere unless your interference was decisive. Never to promise unless your promise could be fulfilled. Not to worry about what the other man might have in the back of his mind, but to make quite sure that he was in no doubt regarding the certainty of your own intentions. To be just, forgiving and above all reliable ... So long as our rule appeared inevitable [in India], it remained unquestioned. The slightest hint of hesitation and our prestige declined. The mere suggestion that we were ourselves uncertain of our own inevitability, and our prestige would disappear."

43 *Times*, 10 Nov. 1938; *Documents on International Affairs*, 1938, Vol. I, 116–17.

44 A good example is the marvellous assurance in P. Kennedy, *The Rise and Fall of the Great Powers* (New York, 1987), 318–19.

45 That surely is what it says in detail in 850 pages of Gibbs, *Grand Strategy.*

46 Feiling, *Life of Neville Chamberlain*, 47.

47 Ibid., 400.

48 Middlemas and Barnes, *Baldwin*, 1100.

49 Feiling, *Life of Neville Chamberlain*, 415–16. The response by the Able Seaman in the film *In Which We Serve* (1942) summed up the general feeling: "It ain't no bleedin' picnic for us neither."

50 Birkenhead, *Halifax*, 448.

51 Feiling, *Life of Neville Chamberlain*, 418.

52 Blythe, *Age of Illusion*, 295.

53 J. Wheeler-Bennett, *Munich: Prologue to Tragedy* (New York, 1948), 349.

54 [Editor's note: Robert Vogel did not have a chance to consult recent studies that bear on this analysis, including:] Frank MacDonough, *Neville Chamberlain, Appeasement, and the British Road to War* (Manchester, 1998), and R.J. Caputi, *Neville Chamberlain and Appeasement* (Pennsylvania, 2000).

55 H.N. Fieldhouse, "The Anglo–German War of 1939–42: Some Movements to End It by a Negotiated Peace," *Royal Society of Canada Transactions*, 4th series, 9 (1971), 285–312; D. Dilks, "The Twilight War and the Fall of France: Chamberlain and Churchill in 1940," in D. Dilks, ed., *Retreat from Power*, Vol. 2 (London, 1981), 53, 58–9.

2

Loyalty in Wartime:
The Old Tories and British War Policy,
1939–1940

AARON KRISHTALKA

Between the two world wars of the twentieth century the largest and most enduring back-bench group in the British Conservative parliamentary caucus was the "old tories," as they called themselves, or the "die-hards," as opponents called them.[1] They were the chief and very nearly the only rebels, independents, and consistent troublemakers in the party, whether it was in power (usually) or in opposition. They rarely numbered fewer than 20 or more than 60. They made their mark by dissidence and rebellion and by their advocacy of their own policies in every sphere of public affairs. Elections, deaths, and retirements slowly changed the names and faces among them. The general elections of 1929 and 1931 brought them the fresh political energies of about a dozen younger men, born near the turn of the century. But over half the old tories in 1931 had entered politics before the Great War or soon thereafter. What they had or would brook of leadership came from that older generation and remained largely unchanged during the two decades: exactly the state of affairs in their party. These older men, Sir William Davison, Colonel John Gretton, Sir Alfred Knox, Sir Henry Page-Croft, H.G. Williams, and a handful of others, made continuous this blue thread of tory dissidence across 22 years of meetings and rallies, leagues and committees, debates and divisions, and of parliamentary resolutions, private members' bills, motions, interjections, and questions, many of them left stranded, often intentionally, on the parliamentary order paper.

The fact that between the wars British electorates usually gave large majorities and a virtual monopoly of power to the Conservative Party magnified the importance of the old tories. It meant that they often functioned as a Conservative – they called it "genuine" – opposition to government and could stir up their fellow back-benchers or Conservatives at large, albeit usually not in sufficient numbers or soon enough to achieve their purposes. They did so most famously from 1931 to 1935, over India's political future and British disarmament, because the official Labour or Liberal oppositions wished to drive government policy further and faster, rather than halting or reversing it. They were not intellectuals or ideologues, proposed no theories of government or society, but were united by common – practical, they thought – ideas: about the fundamental goodness and health of British political and social institutions when properly exercised; about the evils of collectivist political or materialist faiths of every type; about the balance between state power and individual liberty, obligation and rights in a liberal democracy; about the limits to the competence of governments and the pretensions of special interests. Their support within the party and in Parliament varied with the cause. They pursued their several causes with independence, vigour, and resource, always keeping within the bounds of liberal parliamentary democratic political practice. One essential cause was imperial integrity and development, on which, they believed, depended Britain's security, position, and strength as a world power. Another basic cause was the integrity of their party's principles and its unity of purpose, over which they assumed a self-appointed guardianship. They sought to lead the party from its ranks. They rarely chose, therefore, to join or build political organizations opposed to the party either in or outside Parliament.

The old tories' record of dissidence and advocacy was rooted in issues that captured and divided their party before 1914: support for reform of the House of Lords, for the Unionist cause against home rule in Ireland, and for tariff reform to *protect* British industries and jobs and to give the United Kingdom a bargaining tool with other states in an increasingly protectionist world. They worked hard to rid their party of dogmatic adherence to free trade and to bring Conservatives to follow Joseph Chamberlain's dream of an imperial preferential tariff and economic integration – a cause that they pursued until the Second World War. They helped overthrow David Lloyd George's wartime coalition after they had opposed its policies: devolution in India, partition in Ireland, and independence for southern Ireland.

They pursued House of Lords reform to build a constitutional bulwark against the day when socialism or statism might possess the Commons. There they defended capitalism and individual liberty against the attacks of communists and socialists. In 1923 they could not forgive Prime Minister Stanley Baldwin for doing too much: for ruining the electoral chances of tariff reform by launching it precipitately and unprepared on the voters and for thus letting the Labour Party gain office (in power 1923–24). In 1929–30 they tried to oust him for having done too little, for thus causing the Conservative defeat and letting Labour in again. They embarrassed Baldwin by trying to abolish the closed shop, the immunity of trade unions to civil prosecution for losses caused by strikes, and the "political levy" – the automatic funding of the Labour Party from workers' union dues. They tried to limit the life of the National government coalition set up in September 1931 and wanted the Conservative Party to go independently to the electorate with its own policies – domestic, imperial, and foreign.

Although the old tories cared most for domestic and imperial economic recovery and development, the worsening international situation during the 1930s turned them increasingly towards issues of foreign policy. They opposed the second Labour government's and the new National government's policies on the League of Nations and disarmament as misguided and imprudent, disastrous for British interests and European peace alike. They never had slackened their suspicion of Germany; they criticized British aloofness from France during the Ruhr crisis of 1922–23, accepted the Locarno treaties as a return to Franco–British co-operation, warned about German evasion of the disarmament clauses of the Treaty of Versailles during the 1920s, and were among the first to denounce Hitler and the Nazis as a menace to Europe and to Christian civilization. Meanwhile, they were challenging official projects for the devolution of powers in India, amounting to home rule, from 1925 onward. They founded and led the India Defence Committee and League to fight the resulting legislation in Parliament and in the country and gingerly accepted Winston Churchill as an ally in that losing battle.

The old tories' foreign policy – if back-benchers may be said to have one – may be simply stated. For them, disarmament, the League of Nations, the Abyssinian and Spanish wars – however important – were but sideshows; the central issue was Germany, Germany resurgent, first in political chaos, then in Nazi hands, violent and arming for expansion. The problem of how to contain Germany shaped their policy: by negotiation and from a position of strength to meet the demands of Europe's dissatisfied powers – the appeasement of Europe – or by remaking the alliance of 1914, excluding Stalin's Soviet Union, to deter German expansion. They wanted early British rearmament, on a scale and design fitted to British interests, including a large army trained for continental warfare; steady political co-operation with France, and then with Italy in the "Stresa Front." This was a policy of following, not outrunning, France, of calculated reserve, not of aggressive diplomacy, and of limited commitments: Britain would achieve much by doing little in the right way. Events put this policy out of joint. British rearmament came too late; Stresa was abandoned; defence of the League Covenant came to rival co-operation with France; and France was increasingly reluctant to defend its continental position. The old tories then backed the policy that most resembled their own – Neville Chamberlain's, of appeasement. The reward was bitter. They preferred caution but cheered on the man of action. They dreamed of consolidating the empire in peace; Chamberlain was constrained to act in Europe and go to war. Blunders and delay before 1936, in their view, had made necessary a policy that stood theirs on its head. The United Kingdom was seen to deal with Germany from weakness, not from strength; to anticipate and lead, not to follow France; to alienate, then fawn on Italy; to undertake active diplomatic and political intervention, and then military commitments in central and eastern Europe; to have become in effect a continental power without an army. That the old tories explained and defended Chamberlain's policy with resolution and fair success merely added to the ironies, the capping instalment of which came in August 1939. They had spoken out against alliance with the untrustworthy Soviet Union, contrary to the declared policy of the leader whom they were defending. Proof of their arguments then appeared in the shape of strategic disaster, the Nazi–Soviet Pact. It made war inevitable and their leader's policy seem a failure. They insisted then and later that the failure was not Chamberlain's, but Europe's and especially Germany's, even when appeasement, like imperialism, became a term of reprobation and ignominy.

The eight months of Neville Chamberlain's war ministry (September 1939–May 1940) heralded the end of the old tories as a group. They had been steadily declining in number. Retirement and the fortunes of election thinned their ranks in 1935. Five years later the India rebels had dwindled down to about 25, just over half their former strength.[2] Until – and after – the political crisis of 1–9 May 1940 they remained Chamberlain's chief defenders and hence a considerable influence on the back benches. From September 1939 on the emergency of war called for political loyalty and unity. The degree to which some old tories defied that call – quietly during the autumn and more firmly, but still discretely, after the Soviet invasion of Finland in January 1940 – was also the measure of their division and dissolution, brought on by the political strains of war and defeat. They knew that in the politics of wartime their responsibility was to keep the party and country united behind the prime minister. But too many of them had been schooled in war by the Great War; not just by habit and temperament, but by experience, they would be independent judges of Chamberlain's capacity to direct an effective war effort. In May 1940, they took a part of his responsibility on themselves.

Conservative political divisions, which Croft saw effaced in the Commons on 3 September 1939, persisted in private. There were those few Conservatives, such as Sir Arnold Wilson, who did not want war with Germany and joined the Duke of Westminster's little group to discuss the means of ending it as soon as possible after the destruction of Poland.[3] After the group's second meeting, C.T. Culverwell, Conservative MP for West Bristol, another advocate of an early peace conference, called on the order paper for a secret sitting of the House to discuss the progress and conduct of the war and the general international situation.[4] Meanwhile the Conservative and Liberal oppositions to Chamberlain were disturbed that the Allies were doing nothing to help Poland and doubted the government's capacity to conduct war successfully. They returned to the idea that "Chamberlain must go" and to the wish for a genuine national government.[5] The Soviet intervention in Poland and the destruction of that state split these groups. Lloyd George began to doubt the likelihood of an Allied victory and contemplated a peace conference with American participation.[6] Robert Boothby, too, began to incline towards this view.[7] The grumbling at British inaction on the Western Front, suggested Lord Salisbury, might be stopped if a select group of politically independent privy councillors were formed, who would receive all confidential war information and be able to reassure the public without publishing details. Chamberlain dismissed the idea as futile: "To my mind we may have a much more formidable body of opinion demanding that we accept peace terms."[8]

The old tories determined to back the government and the war to wipe out Hitlerism. H.G. Williams's denunciation of the National Registration bill as cumbersome and unnecessary reflected his friends' and general Conservative opinion, but they would not dream of voting against something that the government wanted.[9] Sir William Davison wanted prompt action against Sir Oswald Mosley's fascist peace propaganda.[10] Croft urged the country to count its blessings while "stripping for the grim struggle ahead." The greatest blessing, according to Croft, was that the British strategic situation had greatly improved since mid-August. Then it had seemed as if the country would face three hostile navies across its communications – in the Far East, in the Mediterranean, and in home and Atlantic waters. The Nazi–Soviet pact averted this major peril now; Chamberlain and Halifax's wisdom had done so earlier by refusing involvement with Italy, Spain, and Japan on issues secondary to "the deadly menace of Germany." These three anti-Comintern powers were estranged from Germany over its pact with the Soviet Union – a "treachery so coldly calculated." "This enormity has swung world opinion right over to Britain who has become the leader of the world's crusade against evil as well as protector of the weak." There were more blessings: the support of the empire, of the dominions, of the Indian princes, and of Arab friends; and there was the national spirit of unity at home.[11]

Privately, however, Croft made known to the government that he and his friends were disturbed by Allied inaction during Germany's attack on Poland and by the likely effect of that stance on British public and foreign neutral opinion. He presented a plan of campaign to Chamberlain and to Sir Ernle Chatfield. The guarantee given Poland meant that it should be given maximum aid. British submarines should be sent into the Baltic. The Royal Air Force (RAF) should immediately attack German lines and airfields in the west, reinforcements and railway junctions serving the Western Front, German munitions factories within range, and military targets between Berlin and Poland. Croft could not believe that fear of reprisals was the cause of British inaction; nor did he hold out hopes for an early break in German morale.[12]

The most striking feature of Croft's plan was that it did not even mention a ground attack on Germany, particularly since he believed that wars were won by foot soldiers. Croft restricted himself to operations that British forces alone might undertake from home bases. Perhaps he took to heart now, as he had a year earlier, the defensive stance of the French army and ruled out an invasion of Germany for the moment. As we see below, Croft and the old tories did not wish to repeat the static fronts and huge casualties of the Great War. They therefore agreed with a strategy that forebore to pit the Allied armies against the fixed German frontier defences. They wished instead to engage and defeat the Germans in fluid battle after the enemy emerged from its defences to attack in the west. Croft therefore never tired of urging that the Territorial Army be designated and fully trained for continental war.[13] He and Gretton wanted action and, far from contemplating rebellion as in 1917, were still wholly loyal to Chamberlain, the man of action. But the old tories' whole career of independence, and their current uneasiness, served notice – if any were needed – that their support of the prime minister was not automatic.

It was easier for the old tories to uphold the honour of Poland than to defend its territory. Poland's defeat and Soviet–German co-operation led Lloyd George to question both privately and openly the wisdom of continuing the war. He argued in the press that Poland was not worth a war, that the British people did not wish to make colossal sacrifices to restore a Polish regime distinguished by its mediocrity and its appetite for ruling unwilling minorities by force.[14] The old tories turned to assault a compromise peace and the old foe who suggested it. Croft, Gretton, and their friends sent a public letter of regret, apology, and reassurance to the Polish ambassador in London, Count Raczinski.[15] In the House, Croft rose to condemn – with Duff Cooper and with David Grenfell of the Labour Party – Lloyd George's plea[16] for a secret session to weigh the chances of victory and to consider peace proposals. The understanding of the current situation, said Croft, did not require a secret session. The record of events and the nature of Hitler's regime were all too plain: "we are not prepared to consider the terms of Herr Hitler, but only the terms of a Government which represents the ideas of liberty and freedom."[17] Next day, C.T. Culverwell's impassioned plea for a negotiated peace fell on stony ground in the 1922 Committee.[18] At the end of the month the committee invited and applauded Lord Halifax's riposte.[19] Croft and Gretton's answers came sooner and illustrated their conception of British war aims: nothing less than the extinction of the Nazi state would do. In his constituency, while he watched with suspicion the activities of pacifists and communist aliens,[20] Croft loosed a rousing denunciation of the evils of Nazism and Hitler. The great British war aim was to destroy this evil, to win not territorial advantage but the right of nations to live in peace and freedom. Again Croft hailed Lloyd George's war speech of 3 September and condemned his peace speech of 3 October.[21] The unexplicated contrast between the two speeches implied, as Croft must surely have intended, a confusion of mind.

Gretton spoke similarly in his constituency and more pointedly in private to the government. He demanded that the RAF stop dropping propaganda leaflets over German cities. It was not worth the risk of casualties, although there had as yet been none. The leaflets were wrongly conceived, too long, badly drawn up, defective in translation into German, and in principle ineffectual: surely the intelligence service had reported in them what was public knowledge? The war could not be waged with such gentle means. Until the Germans suffered heavy reverses, propaganda meant to discredit Hitler would not work. He represented and held the loyalty of the German people. Only the defeat of Germany and the invasion of its territory – something not done in the last war – would teach that nation the habits of peace with its neighbours. If the leaflet campaign did continue, it should be directed by men who knew Germany well and "are skilled in setting out the facts which will present themselves later in the war."[22] In a strong plea in the Commons against schemes for a negotiated peace, Croft made the identical case – that the enemy was the German nation united behind Hitler, not simply his government.[23]

Gretton forbore to urge the substitution of bombs for leaflets; Croft did not demand an invasion of Germany immediately. But they made it clear that these steps would become necessary. In a letter to Chamberlain and in the House Croft attacked purely defensive thinking and dismissed as false and wrongheaded the theories of Captain Basil Liddell Hart about the relative superiority of modern defence, by which "the direction of the War Office appears to have been bemused." Croft exhorted the government to train and equip the British army for modern, fluid warfare so that it should be prepared to take the offensive at any moment.[24] Confident of victory, he agreed with the strategy of holding the Maginot Line to the sea. Supremacy at sea was a primary strategic goal in this scheme. The French army could not be destroyed; even if the land war were a stalemate, and the Royal Navy (RN) held the sea, the Allies would win. To avoid the stalemate, Germany would strike through Belgium and Holland in order to seek fluid battle. It was of supreme importance to be ready to meet a German thrust through the Low Countries and defeat it there: "[O]ur one great purpose would be to build and train at once an Army of manœuvre, with sufficient mechanised divisions to defeat the enemy in fluid battle ... [I]t would be a fatal mistake if we allowed a purely defensive complex to affect our military organisation."[25]

The government's foreign policy still found its strongest partisans among the old tories, even though they had outrun it in declaring their own war aims. Croft credited the diplomacy of Chamberlain and Halifax with keeping Turkey neutral and friendly; with drawing Italy, shocked by the Russo–German pact, "steadily back to her traditional friendship with Great Britain"; with securing Spain's neutrality; and with the apparent rapprochements between Italy and Greece, Italy and Turkey, Romania and Yugoslavia, Holland and Belgium. European states were "liberating their souls" behind the hedge of British and French bayonets. The United States was amending its neutrality acts and would become the arsenal of the Allies. Finally, in the Baltic region and elsewhere, the Soviet Union was double-crossing Germany, which for the sake of the Soviet alliance was ready to "sacrifice the very foundations of Nazi faith" – expansion to the east.[26]

Victor Raikes, old tory Conservative MP for Southeast Essex, stood by Chamberlain in rejecting demands to publish detailed war aims. The great aim in what promised to be a long war was victory and the destruction of Nazism and its leaders.[27] Charles Emmott, old tory Conservative MP for Surrey East, added that this aim stood unmoved by the obvious antagonism of German and Soviet interests in Poland, the Baltic, and the Balkans, the outcome of which lay in the future: "[W]hen that question is posed we will answer it." Meanwhile, the United Kingdom must devote all its energies to the fight.[28] Croft thought it premature to go beyond the government's general aims into schemes of European federation or other designs of a postwar settlement. Such ideas were an instance of the blithe arrogance of visionary Britons who presumed, to the acute annoyance of Europeans, that the British had a special dispensation to instruct them how to order their affairs. Croft put his war aims in "backbench phraseology": first, "Gangsterdom in Europe must end, and furthermore, the gangsters themselves must be not only disarmed, but prevented ever again from pursuing the terrible oppression of humanity and this blood feud against civilisation." Second, the "raped" nations of Europe must be liberated to decide freely their own fate. Talk of peace terms – "cooing words" – would not pry the German people away from their strong and united loyalty to Hitler. Only a supreme effort in war and an Allied victory could do that.[29]

In these ways the chief supporters of Neville Chamberlain made it clear that, Britain having gone to war, they meant to pursue it with the utmost energy, even though the country was not yet engaged in any land or air fighting in this "very peculiar war."[30] Furore over inefficiencies and muddle in the Ministry of Information[31] led seven old tories to join ten other Conservatives in the call for a select Commons committee to examine the system of appointments to national defence posts, both civil and military.[32]

They always remembered the imperial idea in the empire's war. Croft privately urged the government to have British skilled labour, not American, sent to Canada to help build facilities for training pilots and air crew.[33] Sir Herbert Williams thought twice about a parliamentary question on Lord Lothian's apparent references in Chicago to a future pooling of American and British naval power.[34] Williams instead told the Foreign Office that "federal union [with the United States], whatever that may mean ... is a form of vague nonsense which is now attracting the sloppy minds which previously thought that collective security meant something."[35]

The Soviet attack on Finland on 30 November 1939 and the Finns' initial successes provided another focus for the old tories' desire for vigorous prosecution of the war. Leo Amery pressed the government to send at least a small volunteer force to help Finland.[36] Sir Alfred Knox, Conservative MP, Wycombe, Bucks., thought it logically and morally right, and politically sound, to break off relations with the Soviet Union.[37] Both men had in mind encouraging neutral opinion. Croft, Knox, and others contemplated more warlike measures, as we see below, and Croft began drafting another memorandum to the prime minister. At the moment when Chamberlain was hesitating to intervene with force in Scandinavia, his most assiduous supporters and his sharpest critic were agreed that Britain should do so.

Meanwhile, during February 1940, Croft and his friends were alarmed at statements previously made in India by Lord Zetland and Congress Party members regarding India's acquisition of dominion status and independence after the war. In October 1939, Lord Wolmer, Conservative MP, Aldershot, Hampshire, to October 1940, before elevation to the House of Lords, had warned that such a step was fraught with danger because the problem of minorities, especially Muslim discontent with Hindu majority rule, was unsolved. But true to their decision of 1935, the old tories would do nothing to impede the working of the Government of India Act.[38] Instead they wrote to Zetland for private clarification of official intentions. His assurances to Croft and Knox did not satisfy them. Croft circulated the correspondence to four of his colleagues in the executive of the extinct India Defence League – Lord Salisbury, Lord Wolmer, Knox, and Sir Louis Stuart, secretary of the Indian Empire Society. For a moment they considered resurrecting the League, but Croft would not hear of it. His promise of loyalty to the government was sacrosanct. He and his friends instead assumed a watching brief, since for the moment the government seemed to have retained the political initiative in India.[39] In this way the first backbench Conservative "watching committee" to monitor the policy of Chamberlain's government in wartime was formed by the perennial, the India rebels, the old tories, his main supporters.[40] It was entirely in character that they did so over a great matter of imperial policy. Events would soon point their attention to questions closer to home. The fact that Croft led the watching committee meant that it would not easily become an engine of rebellion against Chamberlain but showed also that Chamberlain's chief backbench advocate had to acknowledge the direction in which his friends' opinions were inclining.

Back-bench sympathy for "little" Finland, fighting and losing alone against Soviet forces, now found voice among the old tories. Knox joined his to previous demands[41] that the United Kingdom immediately dispatch bombers, fighters, and air crew to aid the Finns.[42] Harold Macmillan, who had just returned from Finland, recommended that the government should send them materiel only, not troops.[43] Croft chafed at the government's and his own inaction. He continued to plead that the British army should be trained for the fluid warfare of fighting retreats and armoured attack. He made implicit his criticism of French defensive thinking by arguing that British armies had broken the German Western Front in 1918; with proper training they would do so again.[44] He yearned to serve in some capacity: the reward of office for his loyal services to the government was long due. But his own hints and Churchill's loyal advocacy[45] availed him nought. For a moment Croft lost patience with politics. He decided to volunteer to fight with the Finns and consulted a Harley Street doctor about his fitness for battle. Medical science recommended on 6 March that Croft stay in England. He was immensely disappointed.[46]

At the same time Croft sent to Chamberlain his memorandum, "Finland and after," with a covering letter, and copies to Churchill. None of these documents seem to have survived, but Churchill's reply illustrates their general argument. Croft contended that a British intervention in Finland, with materiel, fighter and bomber squadrons, and volunteer infantry, exemplified what might be done to engage the enemy at points where it was ill-placed to defend its supplies of ores and gasoline and its other vital interests. Croft contemplated air operations against the Soviet Union and Germany, across northern Scandinavia, in the Baltic, in the Caucasus, and perhaps in the Balkans. Churchill welcomed the attempt to stir Chamberlain into action and judged Croft's strategic ideas "very sound, though I am not sure that acting on them would involve official war with Russia, which I should prefer to avoid."[47]

Croft's position and opinions were important enough to elicit Chamberlain's immediate response and invitation to an interview.[48] He received Croft on 11 March. According to Croft's hurried memoir of their conversation,[49] the prime minister "agreed largely" with Croft's assessment of the Soviet Union and the Finnish War and pointed out possible repercussions of Croft's suggested anti-Soviet operations – in particular, attacks from the Labour opposition. Croft told him that the Soviet myth was exploded and that he rejoiced at Britain's official pledge to aid Finland – "Alas, too late!" noted Croft, when Finland agreed to Soviet terms on 13 March.[50]

None the less, he and Raikes rose to defend the government's policy and strategy in the Finland debate on 19 March. Raikes pointed out that, quite apart from the forbidding physical difficulties and tactical dangers involved, British intervention by land in Finland required the co-operation of the very unwilling neutrals, Norway and Sweden. British complacency and boredom bred of inaction were as dangerous as crackpot adventures born of the mere itch to act – as, for example, starting the bombing of German cities or launching an attack on the German western line. "Our task is ... to win this war without a Passchendaele or a Somme, if that can be done." This was Raikes's version of Croft's reiterated preference for fluid war; and he, like Croft a "good European," believed that the British war was against "the greatest forces of evil which have been known in the world for many years" – the combination of Nazi and communist empires. Even if the strain of war threatened to break up the British Empire he would fight on, because his purpose was morally higher than the preservation of the empire. If the government emphasized to the British people their great moral purpose, dealt frankly with them, and told them clearly the sacrifices required of them, the "Home front" would be kept sound.[51]

Croft answered Harold Macmillan's charge that the government had botched the task of supplying the Finns. However, he argued, perhaps it was necessary to distinguish now between true neutrals and those that supplied the enemy with war material. Swedish iron ore crossed Norway on its way to Germany. British action was called for if, after due warning, this traffic did not cease. Now Croft gingerly prodded the government to allay backbench anxieties: if Chamberlain decided to form a small war cabinet, as had been created in the last war, many of his supporters would agree that he was doing a wise thing.[52]

Croft's suggestion implied a true war coalition and the inclusion of Labour. This was the old tories' closest approach thus far to open criticism of Chamberlain's direction of the war. It issued not from a lack but from a surfeit of confidence in Britain's strategic position – so strong that it was free apparently to fight the Soviet Union as well as Germany. As they all but wished to go to war against the Soviet Union, so the old tories all but claimed the Nazi–Soviet Pact as a triumph for British diplomacy or, at any rate, the proof of its moral integrity: for now the moral exactly fitted the political alignment in this war, and evil – Nazism and communism – was gathered openly on the side of the enemy. In this sense the issues of the Great War, left unresolved after the victory of 1918, would be fought to conclusions: the geopolitical threat of the Greater Germany, the moral threat of Soviet communism. If Croft had doubts about Chamberlain's government, they arose from his own impatience to proceed with the task.

Chamberlain's cabinet reshuffle, announced on 3 April, failed to mollify his Conservative critics.[53] Once more Croft's hopes for office, and his advocate in the cabinet, were disappointed.[54] But he remained loyal to his leader, unlike some of his friends. They shared an anxiety "about the lack of drive in many of the departments of State."[55] That anxiety now drove Chamberlain's Conservative critics, following the precedent of the previous war, to form a "watching committee" of Conservative peers and MPs under Lord Salisbury. It had existed in embryo since February under an India label. Now its concern embraced the whole direction of the war and "whether concerted action or representations to the Government on any particular point would be advisable."[56] Besides Wolmer, Lord Lloyd, and Admiral Sir Roger Keyes, another India rebel and old tory, Sir Joseph Nall, Unionist MP, Hulme, Manchester, was a founding member of the committee. From its inception it had a formidable ally, Gretton.

During the last week of March, while the watching committee was being formed, Gretton strove, together with Lord Lloyd and S.S. Hammersley, Conservative MP for East Willesden, to rouse the cabinet to action regarding the sorry state of British tank development. This problem touched directly on Croft's and the old tories' notion of readying the British army for fluid warfare. Gretton spoke to Chamberlain at the end of the month. Lord Lloyd delivered his and Gretton's memorandum on the subject to 10 Downing Street on 2 April. Hammersley wrote to Chamberlain on the same day, having corresponded with the Ministry of Supply earlier. Gretton wrote again on 4 April to press for an answer. Chamberlain was at a loss for a reply and did not wish to be drawn into arguments on what his secretary called a highly technical matter.[57] Gretton and Hammersley insisted that the problem was in essence administrative, not technical, that tank design and production were in incompetent hands. They submitted a plan for the prompt overhaul of the administration of tank development. Should this reorganization be delayed, they promised to raise the matter in the secret Commons session scheduled for 11 April.[58] Chamberlain merely ordered their claims investigated. When Hammersley telephoned Chamberlain's office to hear whether any progress had been made, he was told that the matter was "fully engaging the ministers concerned."[59] Thus put off, Hammersley brought his complaint to the watching committee, which had had the relevant information all along from Lord Lloyd and Gretton. Neither Salisbury's private approaches to Chamberlain, nor a deputation to Lord Halifax on 29 April, fared any better than had Hammersley or Gretton.[60] The impression of bad management defended by political intransigence remained.

The Norwegian campaign was meanwhile being fought to its bitter close. The government's decision to evacuate all British troops from Norway, except from Narvik, raised the question of mismanagement – of cabinet indecision, administrative muddle, and tactical defeat – far more dramatically than could the question of tanks. By 1 May, while Keyes was still trying to convince the cabinet to take the offensive in Norway,[61] he and Amery were now organizing rebellion among their Conservative friends, to try in league with the opposition to unseat Chamberlain's government. But the overt Conservative opposition to Chamberlain was small. As Clement Attlee correctly understood, Conservative anxieties over the defeat in Norway required careful handling if they were to be transformed into a revolt against Chamberlain. To raise the issue of confidence was to push the Conservative back benches into Chamberlain's arms by arousing their instinct for loyalty in a crisis. In fact, that loyalty stood unquestioned, and it seemed intact. When they chose "open warfare" against Chamberlain, Amery and Keyes hoped at most to shake Conservatives.[62] As late as the Norway debate itself, which started 7 May, Harold Nicolson was so far from expecting to bring down the government as to contemplate voting with it, and Lord Salisbury told members of his watching committee not to vote against it.[63] On 1 May, before the committee had declared its position openly, Amery and his friends could expect to find arrayed against them Croft and most of the old tories, leading the back-bench defence of Neville Chamberlain.

The first signal that Chamberlain's most consistent supporters would not unite behind him was delivered by John Gretton on the evening of 1 May in his own constituency. He was speaking on the war situation to the annual meeting of the Burton Women's Unionist Association. He rejected in the bluntest terms any association with that "foul and immoral thing which contaminates all that it touches" – the Soviet communist state. He stressed the ruthlessness and skill of the German government, its evil and its aim of world domination. He warned against entertaining hopes of a Soviet–German split: the Soviet Union would cling to its alliance, not because it balked at betrayal, but because it was far weaker than Germany and feared it. Thus Britain's stake in the war was the very existence of Christian civilization: "We are fighting for our religion, our homes, morality and everything else, as well as for our existence as a nation. I am not putting it too high when I say this is a crusade of right against wrong – a war in which there must be no appeasement. It means one side or the other must have victory. It must be fought out." The total defeat of Germany – "a great and stupendous task" – called for "some more clear demonstration by the Government itself of its determination to win the war. Some of us are beginning to think that there must be elements who are weak and not in accord with the deep determined national will to win ... This is a time of trial for the Government, and by the way it handles the situation we shall judge whether it is to lead us or whether we shall have to look elsewhere for leaders in this great struggle."[64]

A full account of Gretton's speech appeared next day in the *Yorkshire Post*.[65] Word of it soon spread on the Conservative back benches.[66] Only for a moment was it merely the act of an independent old tory curmudgeon. For at the same time the details of the British defeat and withdrawal from Norway were becoming public knowledge.[67] The uneasiness on the Conservative back benches was only too apparent.[68] Various schemes for the reconstruction of the government from both Conservative and Labour sources appeared in the press. The most prominent was that of Salisbury's watching committee, which now came out in open revolt.[69] It suggested that Chamberlain should either form a coalition including Labour or resign. Since there could be little doubt that the Labour leaders would refuse to serve under Chamberlain, the watching committee's intervention was a clear call for rebellion.[70] The fact that Gretton had anticipated it and Nall had helped to frame it raised questions for Conservatives: how many of the perennial leaders of rebellion in the party were similarly inclined, and who would follow them?[71] Having deliberately shunned organization as a group, they could not readily meet at short notice to thrash out where they stood. Besides, they were themselves apparently divided, for Croft was still firmly loyal to his leader. The uncertainty of Conservative opinion was sufficiently great for Croft to try to clear the air around him on 7 May, the first day of the momentous Norway debate. The Speaker called him immediately after the leading opposition speakers. He was now the government's most prominent back-bench champion.[72]

Croft had a formidable task: more than just the detailed refutation of Attlee and Sir Archibald Sinclair's charges that the British had been strategically and tactically lame in Norway. Croft wished to lift the Commons out of its grim mood and buoy up his party's spirits. Perhaps he was bound to fail. He maintained that cool heads would not count as a disaster this first large engagement with the enemy in a long war. Indeed, a skilful and gallantly fought withdrawal had prevented a disaster "by mercy of Providence." The irruption of German power in Scandinavia did pose a great maritime and aerial danger to Britain; but, more to the point, the "so-called German victory in Norway" also extended Hitler's right flank by a thousand miles, cost him four-tenths of his surface fleet, apart from casualties, and would continue to cost him the large forces needed to guard it. Hitler's conquest of Norway, argued Croft, was a strategic blunder; but he did not say how the British might turn it to good account. Instead he insisted that neither the country nor the House should be unduly downcast by the "setbacks" in Norway. The press, he contended, which gave them prominence, was no reliable guide either in the assessment of military disasters or in the judgment of Neville Chamberlain's proven competence under great pressure. To Conservatives, and especially to the rebels, Croft put the matter simply in his appeal for unity and reasoned judgment: "[I]f you are convinced that you can find a better man then put him there."[73] There was no ambivalence in that challenge. Most old tories still believed in Chamberlain. Their doubts fell on his cabinet colleagues, as soon became clear, and thus they became involved in causing his downfall.

Croft had read the mood of the House sufficiently to avoid party animus. His avowed purpose was to deprecate it, difficult though this was; and he understood that the attack on the composition of the cabinet was an attack on Chamberlain. For the rest, his attempt to dispel the sense of disaster was unconvincing. It sounded like special pleading. If the German occupation of Norway had small strategic importance, then it was a strategic blunder for the British to have invaded Norway and fought there. The unspoken import of Croft's argument was that the defeat resided more in the interpretation than in the outcome of the Norwegian campaign – after six months of "queer war," the country had mistakenly magnified the very first into the crucial engagement of the war. But he could hardly tell the Commons that it was deluded, and so he could not meet the charges of muddle and incompetence. Josiah Wedgwood dismissed Croft's intervention as a display of the very species of "facile optimism" that might, if unchecked, compass British defeat.[74] The blunt speaking of Keyes, an admiral of the fleet,[75] and Leo Amery's relentless analysis of the government's failings in the prosecution of the war, capped by his famous invocation of Oliver Cromwell,[76] could not be undone by Croft's essay in loyalty and strategic reasonings.

Croft's own army now deserted him. On 8 May, the second day of the Norway debate, the 1922 Committee and the back-bench finance committee were to meet jointly at 5 p.m. to hear Sir John Simon on the budget.[77] A gathering of a different kind took place. Sir Herbert Williams arrived to find the assembled back-benchers in a harsh temper. They were angered most by Chamberlain's appeal that day – so different from Croft's – to their personal and party loyalties[78] in the hour of national crisis. Williams, still a Chamberlain supporter, carried with him his own version of the now widely held idea that the prime minister should form a genuine national war coalition and found wide support when he called for the elimination of inefficient ministers. This was precisely the step that Croft equated correctly with deserting the prime minister, who, to his own undoing, had flung the same equation at the Commons. Williams meant to save him. The chairman of the 1922 Committee, W.P. Spens, an observer within Salisbury's watching committee, and ever loyal to Chamberlain, was deputed to convey to his chief the demand for reconstructing the cabinet. It carried the threat that Williams and his friends, some 40 strong, many of them India rebels, would not support Chamberlain that night in the lobby.[79] How many more Conservatives would follow them was a matter for speculation. When Chamberlain, goaded by the opposition, had said, "I have friends in this House," he could not have predicted that these friends – the old tories, his most steadfast supporters – would think to desert him.

That evening, before the division, Chamberlain notified Spens that he would receive Williams and any of his friends the following afternoon and was ready to consider their representations. This message apparently convinced the would-be rebels to return to their loyalty. As Chamberlain was leaving the Commons' dining room, Williams told him the glad news.[80] No doubt Williams and his group were relieved, for they had no wish to oust Chamberlain. On the contrary, they clung to the idea – which Williams's delegation did put to Chamberlain next day – that he must stay in office but make sweeping changes in the government.[81] Another prominent old tory, Sir William Davison, Unionist MP for South Kensington, who abstained from voting on 8 May, insisted next day that Chamberlain be given the opportunity to reconstruct the government to include the Labour Party and trade union leaders.[82] Sir Patrick Hannon, who unconditionally supported Chamberlain, and begged him to stay in office, attested to this widespread but inexplicable understanding – Herbert Simon and Sir Samuel Hoare must go; Attlee, Arthur Greenwood, and Sir Archibald Sinclair would then be content to enter the cabinet.[83] The false assumption that the Labour Party would serve under Chamberlain permitted Williams and his 40 malcontents to kick at Chamberlain's better, unchanged ministers, while protesting their loyalty to him. Even as Williams spoke to him on 9 May, Chamberlain knew the truth.[84] Williams's conditional professions of loyalty must have seemed to Chamberlain ironic instruments of his own defeat.

The fateful division of 8 May reduced Chamberlain's majority to 80, the crucial fact being that 40 or more Conservative MPs, as he knew, insisted on a coalition that he could not construct.[85] Williams took pride that, but for his own efforts, Chamberlain's majority might have dropped to 40. He might have claimed with more plausibility to have helped procure the prime minister's resignation (on 10 May). For the truth was that Conservative conditional support did as much as the Conservative dissidents to force Chamberlain on the mercies of the Labour opposition for his political survival, and they drove him from office. Only the resolute, unconditional defence of Chamberlain, urged on the back-benchers by Croft and Sir Archibald Southby, might have enabled him to continue. If, as Williams believed, Chamberlain was unseated by intrigue,[86] then his own activities were a part of it. Of the India rebels, of this important section of his "friends," on whom Chamberlain had become accustomed to rely, some 25 still sat in the Commons on 8 May. Fourteen voted with the government;[87] seven were absent – four, perhaps all, deliberately: Davison, John Gretton, W.G. Howard Gritten (MP for Hartlepools), and Commander Arthur Marsden (Chertsey, Surrey).[88] Four voted with Amery against Chamberlain: Colonel H.W. Burton (Sudbury, West Suffolk), Keyes, A.R. Wise (Smethwick), and Lord Wolmer.

Thus did the strains of war split the old tories, who claimed always a moral leadership of their party. Thus did the Conservative rebels of two decades or more both encourage and decline to join a successful rebellion against a Conservative prime minister. They shared the responsibility but not the public credit for his fall. The irony went deeper. They had devoted 20 years to dragging the Conservative Party away from coalitions; now they helped to overthrow a Conservative leader because he would not or could not form a coalition. Paramount in their minds was the war: the war that they – and not they alone among Conservatives – thought the British and their empire were waging. It was not the war that posterity knows, which assumed much of its final strategic outline with the German attack on the Soviet Union in 1941. Rather, the old tories' war was the one that A.R. Wise saw in 1936,[89] and Gretton, Croft, and Raikes in 1939 and 1940: of good against evil, of Christianity against demonic paganism, of the light of Western liberal parliamentary democracy, on one side, against the darkness of collectivist, murderous tyranny, of the Soviet Union and Germany, communism and Nazism, on the other. This was the apocalyptic challenge against which some MPs measured Neville Chamberlain's government and found it wanting.

Croft soon experienced the irony of his position. From Paris, Lord Rothermere, now newspaperless, privately applauded Croft's defence of Chamberlain, while in Bournemouth the local newspaper sharply criticized it.[90] Croft had spent a career vexing Conservative leaders, unmolested by his constituency press. Now he got his first rap on the knuckles for unswerving loyalty. He was unrepentant, of course. To him Chamberlain remained the reorganizer of British power, and he felt chagrin and regret at his resignation. Even as he wrote in this sense to Chamberlain,[91] the new prime minister, Winston Churchill, offered him office and elevation to the peerage. Jimmy Maxton, Croft's former neighbour on the cross benches, sent him a rare tribute to his courage, independence, and steadfastness in sticking to his principles.[92] Churchill, his confrère in the India rebellion, rewarded these virtues by making certain that they would be exercised in a safer place[93] and in his own cause.

It was Gretton, in one of his now-rare speeches, who urged his friends and the Commons to give Churchill's new government a prompt and united vote of confidence.[94] The crisis of the war was on them.

NOTES

1 The genesis, career, ideas, political context, and influence of this group is studied in detail in A. Krishtalka, "The Old Tories and British Foreign Policy 1930–1939," doctoral dissertation, 2 vols., McGill University, 1984. After John Ramsden, *The Age of Balfour and Baldwin 1902–1940* (London, 1978), the most recent study of the pre-war Conservative Party is Anthony Selden and Stuart Ball, eds., *Conservative Century: The Conservative Party since 1900* (Oxford, 1994), in which John Barnes, "Ideology and Factions," 339–45, gives brief attention to party rebels and dissent. Larry L. Witherell, *Rebel on the Right: Henry Page Croft and the Crisis of British Conservatism, 1903–1914* (Newark, 1997), the only recent scholarly monograph on an old tory, concentrates on the earliest and formative part of his career.

2 J.R. Remer retired in August 1939. Seven of his colleagues died: Sir A. Boyd-Carpenter, Sir R. Craddock, and A.W. Goodman in 1937; Sir C. Cobb and Sir P. Dawson in 1938; F. Macquisten and Sir N.S. Sandeman in 1940. Michael Beaumont, who had not joined the India rebellion wholeheartedly, resigned his seat in 1938. The *Spectator* commented on "the little rump of die-hards" (7 Jan. 1938). After Chamberlain's fall, Croft and Wolmer went to the Lords and to office in Churchill's government; Keyes directed Combined Operations; Gretton drew near retirement.

3 The short career and the government's firm rebuff of this group may be
   traced in the Premier Papers, PREM1/379, and in FO800, Halifax Papers,
   vol. 216, H/XV/274, Lord Darnley to Halifax, 30 Aug. 1939; vol. 217,
   H/XV/280, Sir Maurice Hankey to Halifax, 12 Sept. 1939 – all held in
   the Public Record Office (PRO), London. Churchill wrote to Westminster
   separately, as a friend, that he was out of his depth and warned him of
   the "measureless odium and vexation" that persistence would earn
   him. The duke was absent from the group's second meeting in his
   house on 26 September. Its private attempt to approach King Leopold
   III of the Belgians concerning a joint appeal with Queen Wilhelmine of
   the Netherlands for a peace conference came to nothing, although that
   was hardly the end of the idea. See also Balliol College Library (BCL),
   Oxford, Harold Nicolson Ms. Diary, 6 Sept. 1939. The best recent
   survey of Conservative opinions and perturbations over British policy
   towards Germany and Italy is in N.J. Crowdon, *Facing Fascism: The
   Conservative Party and the European Dictators 1935–1940* (London, 1997),
   although it pays relatively little attention to the careers of particular
   factions. Frank MacDonough, *Neville Chamberlain, Appeasement, and the
   British Road to War* (Manchester, 1998), has a brief survey of "pro-
   appeasement" groups in the Conservative and other parties (95–9).
   R.A.C. Parker, *Chamberlain and Appeasement: British Policy and the
   Coming of the Second World War* (Hampshire, 1993), 316, 321–2, pays
   little attention to Chamberlain's main Conservative supporters, as does
   Paul W. Doerr, *British Foreign Policy 1919–1939* (Manchester, 1998).
   Robert J. Caputi, *Neville Chamberlain and Appeasement* (Pennsylvania,
   2000), is a historiographical survey and analysis of the literature
   on appeasement.
4 *Notices*, no. 170, p. 4454, 25 Sept. 1939. Three Labour MPs, who desired
   an immediate peace, signed this motion: A. McClaren (Burslem, Stoke-
   on-Trent), H.G. McGhee (Penistone, Yorkshire, West Riding), and
   R.R. Stokes (Ipswich): *Notices*, no. 172, p. 4490, 27 Sept. 1939. After that
   subject had been aired in the House by David Lloyd George, Geoffrey
   Mander and Colonel Baldwin-Webb (Conservative MP, The Wrekin,
   Salop) signed this motion, each with far different motives: *Notices*,
   no. 178, p. 4651, 5 Oct. 1939.
5 House of Lords Record Office (HLRO), London, Lloyd George Papers,
   G/3/13/10, Robert Boothby to Lloyd George, 10 Sept. 1939; Frances
   Stevenson to Boothby, 16 Sept. 1939 (copy); Nicolson Diary, 13 Sept.
   1939. N. Thompson, *The Anti-Appeasers* (London, 1971), 220 et seq.

6 BCL, Nicolson Diary, 20, 27, and 29 Sept. and 4 Oct. 1939.

7 HLRO, Lloyd George Papers, G/3/13/3, Boothby to Lloyd George, 29 Sept. 1939.

8 PRO, FO800, vol. 217, Halifax Papers, H/XV/288, Salisbury to Halifax, 22 Sept. 1939; Chamberlain's minute, no date. The large correspondence in FO800, vol. 326, H/XL/26 et seq., Dec. 1939–March 1940, and in the PREM Papers, 1/343 and 1/443, shows Halifax and Chamberlain's great patience and industry in replying to and rebutting all reasonable arguments for a negotiated peace.

9 *House of Commons Debates* (HC) 351, 382–3, 4 Sept. 1939; Sir Joseph Lamb's speech, 393, 4 Sept. 1939. Similar to this was Sir William Wayland's later opposition to coal rationing: HC 352, 378–9, 10 Oct. 1939.

10 HC 351, 953–4, 20 Sept. 1939.

11 Churchill College Archives Centre, Cambridge (CCAC), Sir Henry Page-Croft Papers (Croft Papers), 3/18, Address to the Bournemouth Rotary Club, 11 Sept. 1939, *Yorkshire Post*, 12 Sept. 1939.

12 CCAC, Croft Papers, CH 71, Croft to Neville Chamberlain, copy to Chatfield, 15 Sept. 1939; CH 71/2, "Memorandum on public opinion and the present situation." Chatfield politely dismissed Croft's views with the observation that many serious considerations other than sentiment must govern British strategy "in this peculiar war": CH 71/3, Chatfield to Croft, 18 Sept. 1939.

13 For example, HC 352, 350–1, 11 Oct. 1939. Recent monographs uphold the old tories' perception of France's strategic defensiveness and explicate the French position and official British views of it in some detail: Glyn Stone, "From Entente to Alliance: Anglo–French Relations 1935–1939," in A. Sharp and G. Stone, eds., *Anglo–French Relations in the Twentieth Century: Rivalry and Cooperation* (London, 2000), 180–204, and Michael L. Dockrill, "The Foreign Office and France during the Phoney War, September 1939–May 1940," in M.L. Dockrill and B. McKercher, eds., *Diplomacy and World Power: Studies in British Foreign Policy, 1890–1950* (New York, 1996), 171–96. The same case is placed in a somewhat broader British political context in M.L. Dockrill, *British Establishment Perspectives on France, 1936–40* (Hampshire, 1999), chap. 6.

14 *Sunday Express*, 24 Sept. 1939; P. Addison, "Lloyd George and Compromise Peace in the Second World War," in A.J.P. Taylor, ed., *Lloyd George, Twelve Essays* (London, 1971), 367.

15 *Yorkshire Post*, 30 Sept. 1939.

16 HC 351, 1870–4, 3 Oct. 1939.

17 Ibid., 1883–4, 3 Oct. 1939.

18 HLRO, Davidson Papers, J.C.C. Davidson to Stanley Baldwin, 6 Oct. 1939.

19 PRO, FO800, vol. 217, H/XV/335, Culverwell to Halifax, 31 Oct. 1939. Culverwell's arguments for a compromise peace are in this letter. He repeated his stand during the debate on the Address, HC 355, 377–83, 30 Nov. 1939.

20 CCAC, Croft Papers, AN/1, AN/2, Sir John Anderson to Croft, 16 Oct. and 19 Dec. 1939. These were replies to Croft's letters to Anderson, not in the file, of 4 October and 10 November 1939.

21 CCAC, Croft Papers, 3/18, *Bournemouth Daily Echo*, 10 Oct. 1939.

22 PRO, FO371/24101, C17326/13260/18, Gretton to Sir Kingsley Wood, 18 Oct. 1939. Wood sent Gretton's memorandum to the Foreign Office and the Ministry of Information: Wood to Gretton (copy), 23 Oct. 1939. The Foreign Office (J.M. Roberts, minute, 30 Oct. 1939) largely agreed with Gretton's criticism of the leaflet air raids.

23 HC 355, 337–9, 30 Nov. 1939.

24 HC 353, 1273–4, 22 Nov. 1939; CCAC, Croft Papers, CH 58, CH 58/3, Croft to Neville Chamberlain, 21 Oct. 1939; CH 58/3, "Memorandum on the Training of the Territorial Army"; CH 59, Chamberlain to Croft, 23 Oct. 1939 (acknowledgment and thanks); CH 60/1–7,War Office (WO), reply in detail to Croft's "Memorandum," no date, but prior to 1 Nov. 1939. Liddell Hart had suggested to Halifax that the Allies refrain from the attack and that a joint declaration "that we are renouncing military attacks as a means of combating would be a far-sighted move, strengthening our moral position, while forestalling the inevitable growth of derision abroad and disillusionment here." PRO, FO800, Halifax Papers, vol. 217, H/XV/279, Liddell Hart to Halifax, 8 Sept. 1939.

25 HC 355, 337, 30 Nov. 1939. Croft's ideas reflected his military experience of the Western Front in 1915–16 and the recommendations that he had then made in 1917 and 1918 to the War Cabinet through Lord Milner and the chief of the Imperial General Staff (CIGS), General Robertson, that tanks be organized and used in large, grand tactical formations, together with aircraft and specially trained and air-transported infantry, in order to break the German defences decisively: CCAC, Croft Papers, I/1, May 1917; I/2/1; I/2/1–8, Croft to Robertson, 20 May 1917; Robertson to Croft, 30 May 1917; I/2/9, Croft to Sir Douglas Haig, 1 June 1918.

26 CCAC, Croft Papers, 3/18, speech to his constituents, *Bournemouth Daily Echo*, 13 Nov. 1939.

27 HC 352, 579–82, 12 Oct. 1939.

28 Ibid., 612–15, 12 Oct. 1939.

29 HC 355, 331–3, 30 Nov. 1939. Leo Amery congratulated Croft on this speech – "a real breath of healthy fresh air": CCAC, Croft Papers, Amery to Croft, 2 Dec. 1939.

30 HLRO, Davidson Papers, J.C.C. Davidson's phrase, in a letter to Sir Esmond Ovey (British ambassador in Buenos Aires), 23 Oct. 1939.

31 See HC 352, 437–9, 11 Oct., and 515, 12 Oct. 1939.

32 Notices, no. 187, p. 4965, 25 Oct. 1939.

33 CCAC, Croft Papers, I/6/1–3, memorandum (copy), 30 Oct. 1939, sent to Neville Chamberlain, Kingsley Wood, Anthony Eden, and Ernest Brown. The memorandum is not in the Premier or FO papers; the copy in the Ministry of Labour files was not available to me for inspection.

34 New York Times, 5 Jan. 1940.

35 PRO, FO371/24227, A289/26/45, Williams to R.A. Butler, 10 Jan. 1940. Butler's reply was reassuring. Foreign Office officials agreed with Williams's opinion that "ambassadors ought not to make speeches except of a very ceremonial character" and that Lothian's remarks were imprudent.

36 Ibid., FO800, Halifax Papers, vol. 310, H/XII/243, Amery to Halifax, 23 Jan. 1940.

37 HC 356, 551, 24 Jan. 1940.

38 HC 352, 1667–73, 26 Oct. 1939; Croft confirmed this stand in an interjection.

39 CCAC, Croft Papers, ST/9–10, 11, 12, 13, 14/1–2, 2–26 Feb. 1940; SA/8/1–3, Lord Salisbury to Croft, 26 Feb. 1940; SA/9, Croft to Salisbury, 28 Feb. 1940.

40 In March, Croft and Raikes rose to the difficult task of defending the government's policy on Palestine. It was not easy to justify a policy that, despite the commonly known and appalling cruelties visited on the Jews by the Nazis, admitted no more than 10,000 refugees into Palestine in six months: HC 358, 471–80, 489–94, 6 March 1940.

41 The prospect of Finland's defeat drove Sir Oliver Locker-Lampson to call for the dispatch of a large army to Finland and for the appointment of a Commons committee drawn from all parties to get this done: Notices, no. 28, p. 919, 26 Feb. 1940. This reminder of the activities of the Long Parliament after 1642 was a curious anticipation of Amery's later, more famous invocation of Oliver Cromwell on 7 May 1940.

42 HC 357, 54, 6 Feb. 1940, and 187, 7 Feb. 1940. Amery too urged that this be done: PRO, FO800, Halifax Papers, vol. 310, H/XIII/260, Amery to Halifax, 8 March 1940.

43 PRO, FO800, Halifax Papers, vol. 310, H/XIII/253, memorandum by Halifax of a conversation with Macmillan, 4 March 1940; H/XIII/254 records Lord Hankey's identical recommendation.

44 HC 358, 1430–1, 14 March 1940.

45 CCAC, W.S. Churchill Papers, Churchill to Chamberlain, 31 Jan. 1940. Churchill suggested that Amery be appointed minister of food, to replace W.S. Morrison, and Croft his parliamentary secretary: "He has been waiting very long and very patiently."

46 CCAC, Croft Papers, GR/9, Frederick Grice to Croft, 6 March 1940; GR/10, note by Croft's son, 2nd Baron Croft.

47 Ibid., CH/89, Churchill to Croft, 11 March 1940, and CH/90, Churchill to Croft, 16 March 1940, thanking Croft for the memorandum.

48 Ibid., CH/63, PM's office to Croft, 7 March 1940.

49 Ibid., CH/64, evidently written a day later, with addenda written just after Finland made peace with Russia on 13 March 1940.

50 Ibid.

51 HC 358, 1881–5, 19 March 1940.

52 Ibid., 1900–4, 19 March 1940.

53 BCL, Nicolson Diary, 3 April 1940.

54 CCAC, W.S. Churchill Papers, Churchill to Chamberlain, 1 April 1940.

55 H.G. Williams, *Politics Grave and Gay* (London, 1949), 113.

56 CCAC, Keyes Papers, 15/66, Lord Wolmer to Keyes, 19 March 1940; L. Amery, *My Political Life* (London, 1953–5), vol. 3, 355. There is a brief account of the watching committee in the context of Conservative Party politics in 1939–40 in G.R. Searle, *Country before Party: Coalition and the Idea of "National Government" in Modern Britain 1885–1987* (London, 1995), 196–8.

57 PRO, PREM1/422, A.N. Rucker (Chamberlain's private secretary) to Sir Arthur Robinson (Ministry of Supply), 2 April 1940; Robinson to Rucker, 3 April; Rucker to Robinson, 4 April. Robinson wrote that the tank-development situation "is undeniably disturbing … the worst of our bad legacies from the War Office." J.P. Harris, *Men, Ideas and Tanks: British Military Thought and Armoured Forces 1903–1939* (Manchester, 1995), traces and analyses the problems and shortcomings of British tank and artillery design and armoured-warfare planning and bears out the worries of officials and the watching committees: see especially 299–303. A brief summary appears in David French, *Raising Churchill's Army: The British Army and the War against Germany 1919–1945* (Oxford, 2000), 96–8.

58 PRO, PREM1/422, Hammersley to Prime Minister, 8 April 1940. This secret session was postponed after the German invasion of Denmark and Norway: HC 359, 584, 10 April 1940.

59 PRO, PREM1/422, memorandum from PM's office to Rucker, 10 April 1940.

60 Amery, *My Political Life*, vol. 3, 356.

61 CCAC, Keyes Papers, 13/12, Keyes to Chamberlain (copy to Churchill), 1 May 1940; also 2/30, Keyes to Lady Keyes, 16 April 1940, his account of his attempt to win Churchill over to his plans to rush Trondheim and other Norwegian ports; 13/12, Keyes to Churchill, 16 April 1940, and memorandum.

62 Amery, *My Political Life*, vol. 3, 358.

63 BCL, Nicolson Diary, 7, 8, and 9 May 1940; Thompson, *The Anti-Appeasers*, 229.

64 *Burton Daily Mail*, 2 May 1940.

65 *Yorkshire Post*, 2 May 1940. Labour MP Ernest Bevin spoke in very similar terms the same evening in Stoke-on-Trent, *Daily Mail*, 2 May 1940.

66 My interview with Sir Victor Raikes, Carlton Club, London, 15 June 1972.

67 Neville Chamberlain delayed his statement on the Norwegian campaign for one day to 2 May: HC 360, 682, 1 May 1940; 906–13, 2 May 1940.

68 *Observer*, 5 May 1940; *Manchester Guardian*, 2–4 May 1940.

69 *Manchester Guardian*, 7 May 1940, reported also the schemes proposed by P.C. Loftus, Conservative MP for Lowestoft, and Robert Cary, Conservative MP for Eccles; Cary wished to reconstruct the French government as well. Hugh Dalton desired to scrap the British government altogether and get rid of Chamberlain and Sir John Simon. An anonymous "British politician" set out yet another design in the *Daily Mail*, 6 May 1940.

70 The process by which the watching committee came to act with the Labour and Liberal opposition parties and the Conservative dissidents is examined by D.M. Roberts, "Clement Davies and the Fall of Neville Chamberlain, 1939–1940," *Welsh Historical Review* 8, no. 2 (1976), 188–215; and by Thompson, *The Anti-Appeasers*, 223–30.

71 My interview with Sir Victor Raikes, Carlton Club, London, 15 June 1972.

72 The Norway debate (began 7 May 1940) has drawn many writers: it was a high political drama in a moment of crisis and gave a rare display of the power of Parliament, as distinct from government. See, for example, Roberts, "Clement Davies and the Fall of Neville Chamberlain," 224–9; R. Blythe, *The Age of Illusion* (London, 1963), 302–15; and Thompson, *The Anti-Appeasers*, 224–9.

73 HC 360, 1106–16, 7 May 1940.

74 Ibid., 1116, 7 May 1940.

75 Ibid., 1124–30, 7 May 1940.

76 Ibid., 1140–50, 7 May 1940.

77 HLRO, Davidson Papers, 3 s., vol. 5, insert at 97–8: notice of three-line whip (the most intense level), 8 May 1940.

78 HC 360, 1265–6, 8 May 1940.

79 Williams, *Politics Grave and Gay*, 113.

80 Ibid.

81 *Manchester Guardian*, 10 May 1940; Williams, *Politics Grave and Gay*, 113.

82 HC 360, 1438–9, 9 May 1940. P.C. Loftus, Conservative MP for Lowestoft – another abstainer, but not an old tory – made the same case: 1451–2.

83 CCAC, Hannon Papers, box 17, Hannon to Chamberlain, 9 May 1940. Chamberlain replied on 11 May that it had proved impossible for him to carry on, "however many of my late colleagues I had shed," since Labour had refused to serve under him. "Perhaps I may consider myself well-treated in that they [i.e., Labour] have now consented at least to sit in the same room with me." See also Chamberlain's letter to Hannon, 8 May 1940, thanking him for his letter of support on behalf of Birmingham's Conservative MPs. Half of this group could not be included in Hannon's message of support: Amery (Sparkbrook) and J.A.C. Wright (Erdington) voted against the government on 8 May; J.R.H. Cartland (King's Norton), E. Kellet (Aston), and Locker-Lampson (Handsworth) abstained.

84 This is evident from the time of the meeting and from Williams's description of Chamberlain: shaken, "unable to get out of his chair." Williams, *Politics Grave and Gay*, 113.

85 The division a year earlier on the government's Palestine policy – HC 347, 2189–98, 23 May 1939 – drove its majority down to 89, but none of those 89 MPs was threatening Chamberlain with rebellion if he did not meet their conditions. The old tories unanimously supported him.

86 Southby made clear that he and other Conservatives believed this: HC 360, 1160, 7 May 1940; Williams, *Politics Grave and Gay*, 113; my interview with Sir Victor Raikes, Carlton Club, London, 15 June 1972.

87 Of the 365 Conservative MPs, 252 voted with the government, 34 voted against, and 79 were absent. Of the last, 15 were "paired" and 33 were known to have abstained deliberately: HC 360, division lists, 8 May 1940; *Times*, leading article, 10 May 1940; *Manchester Guardian*, 9 and 10 May 1940.

88 These were present in the House that day; there is no evidence that the others abstained through deliberate absence, although they probably did.

89 HC 309, 169–71, 24 Feb. 1936.

90 CCAC, Croft Papers, RO/9, Rothermere to Croft (telegram), 9 May 1940;
3/18, *Bournemouth Times and Directory*, 10 May 1940. The *Bournemouth Daily Echo* was silent.

91 CCAC, Croft Papers, CH/66, Croft to Chamberlain (draft copy), 12 May
1940; CH/67, Chamberlain to Croft, 13 May 1940: Chamberlain wrote
that he would put Croft's letter "among my most treasured possessions ... a tribute from a man whom I am proud to count among my
oldest friends." After he died, Croft wrote to his widow in condolence
and praise of her husband. The terms of praise were extravagant even
for Croft: CH/68, 17 Nov. 1940, and acknowledgment.

92 CCAC, Croft Papers, MA/32, Maxton to Croft, 14 May 1940. Croft
replied that he did not want the peerage and preferred to stay in the
Commons, now that "I was not driving members out to the smoking
room ... where they could escape the infliction."

93 Croft still itched to be as close to war service as possible – in civil
defence, the fighting services, the War Office, or helping to raise new
armies: ibid., MA/14, Croft to David Margesson, Conservative Chief
Whip, 7 Sept. 1940.

94 HC 360, 1516–17, 13 May 1940.

3

Clement Attlee Reconsidered

TREVOR BURRIDGE

If survival and the attainment of high office were sufficient proofs of outstanding political leadership this paper would be superfluous. Clement Attlee's record of 20 years (1935–55) as leader of a major British party was unsurpassed in the twentieth century. Similarly, his five years as a wartime cabinet minister second only to Churchill, followed by six as prime minister, speak for themselves. To many of his contemporaries, however, Attlee was to politics as *Lucky Jim* would become to the novel – the apotheosis of the anti-hero. His personality, declared one commentator, was the least impressive among those who had held the highest post in the land.[1] Journalists used to write about his extraordinary ordinariness. His unprepossessing physical appearance was on a par with his minimal qualities as an orator. He made no striking contributions to political theory, nor had he any talent as a political organizer. Bad enough in a prime minister, these shortcomings in the leader of a mass movement devoted to drastic social change defied all expectations. Just as Disraeli was called "the Asian mystery," pronounced one newspaper, so Attlee might be called "the English mystery."[2] He would remain, concluded another journalist, the great enigma who would fascinate historians and biographers of the future, although the writer implied that "baffle" might be as appropriate as "fascinate."[3]

Unlike most British prime ministers after they leave office, Attlee's reputation grew considerably. His name was used to describe British

wartime policy towards Germany[4] and to characterize the predominant public mood of the 1940s.[5] But the historian who seeks to eval-
uate his career, and the quality of his leadership, has still to reckon
with three special difficulties. One is the relative paucity of his archival record, which Kenneth Morgan found to be "typically reticent and
unpenetrable."[6] A second is Attlee's singularly elusive type of leadership. Henry Pelling has referred to him as "a master of the *coup de
repos*."[7] Even after producing over 600 pages on Attlee's life, his sympathetic and authorized biographer, Kenneth Harris, felt obliged in
his final paragraphs to stress the element of luck in his subject's
career.[8] A good question about that career, put by a distinguished
American observer in 1954, retains much validity. "Was he the real,
the natural leader of the party, or did he rise because of incurable
rivalries among abler men ... [W]ere Bevin, Morrison, Cripps, perhaps
even Laski, the great men, Attlee merely Prime Minister by default?"[9]
The almost-half-century that has elapsed since he relinquished the
party leadership ought at least to provide a useful perspective from
which to answer that question.

Of course, chance does play a part in every successful political
career, perhaps especially in democracies. Attlee himself had no doubt
that he had been very fortunate.[10] The way for his accession to the
party leadership was paved by the decimation of the Parliamentary
Labour Party (PLP) at the 1931 election; and Adolf Hitler can be said
to have contributed significantly to Attlee's national promotion. Personal incompatibilities within the Labour Party did help Attlee maintain his position, although such tensions are not unusual in politics.
More generally, Attlee's rise reflected his party's rise during the first
half of the century – he grew as Labour's servant, not, as did Ramsay
MacDonald, as its creator.[11] But in politics there is no immaculate
conception of success;[12] nor is there any foolproof formula for remaining a leader as long as Attlee did. R.T. Mackenzie remarked aptly:
"Attlee's success after he won the leadership in 1935, and the authority he wielded without overt challenge can hardly be dismissed as
the record of a misfit who stumbled into the leadership by accident."[13]
The cabinets over which he presided from 1945 to 1951 were composed of the most heterogeneous group that had ever attempted to
govern the country. That he was able to draw together, hold together,
and produce a collective effort from people of such disparate opinions, temperaments, social backgrounds, ambitions, and abilities was
also not merely fortuitous.

The third difficulty inevitably brings to mind the well-known wise-crack about "a modest man with much to be modest about." Perhaps the main reason why Attlee has been so underestimated, and his career misunderstood, is because of his invincible modesty. No one of his importance in British political history has exceeded him in this particular. Not only was its extent almost incomprehensible, but he seemed to go out of his way to display it. When Winston Churchill invited him in May 1940 to join a coalition government, Attlee intimated that he would, but quite needlessly added that he would do so not as an individual, only as the leader of his party.[14] When Harold Laski criticized the style of his leadership in January 1944, Attlee disarmingly replied: "As you have so well pointed out, I have neither the personality nor the distinction to tempt me to think that I should have any value apart from the party which I serve."[15] When prime minister, he astounded people by such actions as sometimes fetching his own cup of tea on the absurd grounds that the messenger was "probably busy."[16] But Attlee's modesty was both a personal trait and a fundamental aspect of the socialism that underlay his whole approach to political leadership. It turned out to be an enormous advantage and is a key to understanding his career. A certain amount of modesty at the top was what his party needed after 1935 and his country after 1945. This study argues that Clement Attlee was indeed the right man, in the right places, at the right times.

Attlee was uncommonly shy from childhood – whether on account of being the seventh in a family of eight children, or because of his mother's family possessiveness, or from his lack of exceptional ability at games, or simply because of his late Victorian upbringing as a whole is a matter of speculation. And although a basically happy child, he never outgrew his youthful shyness. It was compounded by many of his adult experiences, which set him apart from his immediate companions and made of him an intensely introspective, private individual.

Born in 1883, he became a middle-class social worker with a small independent income in the pre-1914 London slums and an older infantry officer in the war. His political apprenticeship lasted more than a decade: he was a non-pacifist member of the Independent Labour Party (ILP); the first Labour member of Parliament (MP), elected 1922, with an Oxford education; one of Prime Minister's Ramsay MacDonald's parliamentary private secretaries (PPSS), 1923–4; and one of a handful of Labour (junior) ministers to survive the 1931 general election. As party leader he was a left-leaning leader of the opposition from 1935 to 1940, who sided, on the main issue of the day – rearmament – with right-wing trade-union leaders, and a taciturn deputy to Churchill during the Second World War. He served as prime minister in a postwar cabinet of Labour prima donnas and finally as leader of a wrangling party from 1951 to 1955.

All these experiences tended to push him into a nearly watertight compartment of his own. He became, in the words of Francis Williams, who observed Attlee closely when he was prime minister, "a true solitary who required less than most men the support [and the friendship] of others."[17] Yet far from hamstringing Attlee's leadership role, this solitariness enhanced it.

His combination of modesty and introspection with socialist convictions made of Attlee an exceptionally self-sufficient, self-controlled, and strong personality, at his best in difficult situations. The military made no mistake in choosing him to command the rear-guard during the evacuation of Suvla Bay in December 1915. The bombastic Hugh Dalton, who sneered at Attlee's election as leader of the Labour Party in 1935 – "and a little mouse shall lead them" – came in 1941 to confess to his diary: "Whenever the pressure in the pipe gets too great, I go to see this little man."[18] Attlee's decisiveness, his ability to get things done with a minimum of fuss, were remarked on by overworked and exhausted colleagues in the Second World War.[19] Referring to the postwar period, the often-critical Aneurin Bevan remembered, "[I]t was a constant source of wonder how he was able to bear the strain … with crisis piled upon crisis, and no sign of letting up, and in the end emerged fresher, or so it seemed, than the rest of us."[20] Around him, several of his ministers were breaking down physically, never to recover. In particular, Attlee had two precious assets for leadership: acute judgment of character and the ability to delegate. Perfectly aware of his own limitations, he had a keen eye for those of others. He could make up his mind about people, quickly and without sentimentality. Attlee's zest for delegation was comparable with some men's yearning for power, but there was no other way to carry out the immense legislative program and administrative burden of 1945 to 1951.

In any case, Attlee, as a socialist, was not in politics to glorify his ego; he was there to serve. Not an intellectual, he came to socialism by way of ethical conviction. To him it was a moral creed, not a doctrine; it gave a sense of purpose, not a blueprint for action. Its ultimate goal was fellowship, which could neither be legislated nor

imposed. It could not be achieved until there was a majority of socialists. The democratic process was absolutely fundamental to it, and
democracy meant establishing a wide consensus of opinion, which
had to begin in the Labour Party. "I am not prepared," Attlee wrote
in 1937, "to arrogate to myself a superiority to the rest of the movement. I am prepared to submit to their will, even if I disagree. I shall
do all I can to get my views accepted, but, unless acquiescence in the
views of the majority conflicts with my conscience, I shall fall into
line, for I have great faith in the rank and file."[21] By rank and file, he
did not mean "that small proportion of people who are continually
interested and active in politics."[22] He was referring rather to the
broad mass of people who were content with nominal membership
and support of the Labour Party. As leader of his party, Attlee derived
his strength from the representativeness of his opinions, not from
their originality, nor from his non-existent charisma. The kind of political atmosphere that he could create was that of calm reasonableness,
not of spurious excitement. To him, politics was just a job, a prosaic
business of qualified judgments, compromises, and questions of priorities. Exercising political authority meant making decisions that
affected people's lives, but so did exercising authority in other professions. Government was merely the art of the possible – but, in
Attlee's case, what was possible for reform and improvement.

Virtually alone among middle-class university-educated socialist
leaders in Britain, Attlee began his political apprenticeship at the
lowest level of activity, on the street corners. For several years, in the
most unpromising field, he worked as a rank-and-file member of the
ILP. He carried the (wooden) platform, called the crowd, buttered
bread, and collected money in aid of strikers. Although he soon grad-
uated to the role of speaker, Attlee had few, if any, career ambitions.
He saw his task as one of propaganda. What counted for him, politically, before the Great War was the comradeship and the "apostolic
enthusiasm."[23] But if he lacked the burning itch for power, Attlee had
a great longing to do something immediately, however limited, to
relieve the distress of poverty. Hence his social work took precedence
over his politics – with the unexpected result that he eventually
acquired his only power base – a safe parliamentary seat. Even in
1931, when Labour lost two of its three seats in Stepney, Attlee, thanks
to his local reputation, managed to hang on.[24]

To understand Attlee's later career, it is necessary to know something of his political experience before he became an MP and how he

obtained his seat. During the Great War, Attlee discovered that he had some capacity for leadership. "This soldiering business," he wrote to his brother Tom in 1918, "is only tolerable when one has a definite unit under one's command."[25] He also refined his ideas about socialism and how it might be brought about, remarking in the same letter, "We were too Webby [Sidney and Beatrice Webb were leading Fabians] … I am sure I was having a fatal love of statistics and a neat structure of society. I think we shall have to allow for greater variety." Attlee thought in particular that wartime patriotism, which had affected socialists such as him and conservatives alike, might be mobilized for the cause, provided that the socialists were more tolerant.

This idea received a setback in the party's return to internal strife after 1918, but Attlee was able to put the gist of it into effect in a Labour framework. On his return to the East End of London, he found that the pre-war rivalries between ethnic English Cockneys, Irish Catholics, and Jews, which helped frustrate Labour's prospects, remained. Indeed, despite structural and ideological changes in the party, these rivalries were exacerbated by Stepney's division into three local party factions. In this situation, Attlee's capacity for devotion and detachment, impartiality and efficiency, was invaluable. He was rapidly adopted as parliamentary candidate for Limehouse and then, pending a general election, co-opted as mayor of Stepney, where, in November 1919, Labour gained its first victory – Attlee having written the election address and led the campaign.

Attlee as mayor at once demonstrated his value to the odd assortment of Labour councillors. Within the limits of the local authority's jurisdiction, he presided with remarkable success over the implementation of a municipal welfare state.[26] He found his perfect political niche at the very beginning of his career. The local newspaper noted his style: his decisions on any statement not in order were rendered in "intensely concentrated, almost curt, precise and unmistakeable sentences, like the slamming of a railway carriage door."[27] Attlee later explained that the hardest and most valuable work of a borough councillor was done in committees. The man who thought that he could make a show of speeches in full meetings reported by the press would find himself disillusioned.[28] For Attlee, the object of gaining power was "to get on with the job" of improving the quality of life for others.[29] His method once in office was to cut the cackle, master the details, make the decisions. To all intents and purposes, this was the technique that he later followed as prime minister. It reflected his

earlier approach to social work, where the need for limited and immediate objectives formed part of "a scheme of social life which one is
striving to attain."[30]

Attlee's much longer parliamentary apprenticeship reinforced his
ideas about Labour Party leadership. Soon after he become an ILP MP
in 1922, Ramsay MacDonald in 1923 made him an unpaid PPS –
mainly because he was one of the few "respectable" Labour MPs with
a university degree, officer status, and administrative experience. He
was obliged to consider politics and policies from the angle of
Labour's national leadership, rather than as a back-bencher. He again
saw that compromise was essential once abstract ideas had to be
translated into practical politics. One's loyalty to the Labour movement as a whole had to take precedence over affiliation with minor
coteries, otherwise one could or would achieve nothing. By 1927,
again in opposition, Attlee transferred his own parliamentary candidature from the ILP to the Parliamentary Labour Party (PLP). In the
early 1920s he also acquired a specialist knowledge of how the Commons functioned and enlarged the scope of his political interests. As
a parliamentary performer, he distinguished himself by his moderate
tone, brevity, succinctness, simplicity of language, and common sense
– enlivened occasionally by a cutting or sarcastic remark – and his
concentration on the subject. Not remarkable in themselves, these
qualities were rather rare in the PLP of that period.

After Attlee's first brief stint in 1924 in a national government, as
under-secretary of state for war, he found a regular place in the PLP
hierarchy and increased his reputation by his expertise on local government and electricity topics. In defence matters, he broached in 1926
two themes that he was to repeat many times in the 1930s: defence
policy ought to be linked to foreign policy, and the military services
must be co-ordinated.[31] As well, Attlee's nomination to the Simon
Commission in 1927 not only led him to become his party's leading
authority on India, it also revealed three other qualities that he would
eventually bring to the party leadership: willingness to accept responsibility, realism, and pragmatism. In terms of personal advancement
it was a totally unpromising assignment, but Attlee squared up to it.
To the radicals who demanded immediate independence for India, he
argued that without an Indian-officered army that country could not
exist as a politically viable entity; and what would be the point of
handing the masses there over to their own exploiters? All in all,
Attlee made an important contribution to the Simon Report, which,

though overtaken by events, represented a definite advance in the subcontinent's road to self-government.

Attlee's experience in the Labour government from 1929 to 1931, including six months as postmaster general, added to his leadership apprenticeship in several other respects. Like many in the party, he was brought forcefully to recognize the huge gap between socialist aspirations and what a Labour government could reasonably expect to accomplish in a five-year parliamentary mandate. More particularly, his work at the Post Office persuaded him that nationalized industries should be removed from direct political control, especially from interference from the Treasury, for reasons of efficiency and morale. He was also reminded of how much he personally yearned to do something rather than theorize, and when he did theorize it was always with a view to action. In 1930 Attlee spent some time preparing a memorandum on the problems of British industry, on which the economist Colin Clark assisted him, and to which he could bring the insights derived from his membership of the government's Economic Advisory Council – which also included John Maynard Keynes, trade unionists, and businessmen. Attlee's paper was never used, but its most interesting feature, as Kenneth Harris indicated, was its insistence on action.[32]

Yet Attlee's economic views remained fairly orthodox, even if he was not predisposed to suspect the political motives of the ILP, to distrust Lloyd George, and to be much too loyal to the Labour Party to follow Oswald Mosley into the wilderness. Its programs would have entailed unbalanced budgets, which Attlee would have accepted only if absolutely unavoidable. He collaborated instead on Labour's 1931 election manifesto, *Labour's Call to Action*, which declared that a balanced budget was the first consideration of sound national finance. There is no evidence to suggest that he was among the handful of people who advocated abandoning the gold standard. His advocacy of rather drastic measures in the early 1930s to deal with what appeared then to be the total collapse of the capitalist system was basically a pragmatic reaction on his part. Once the crisis passed, and became overshadowed by international political developments, Attlee returned to his former gradualism – although Labour's Short Programme of 1937 marked a sharp break with traditional economic thinking and was quite acceptable to Labour's left wing.

The political aspect of the 1931 crisis also underlined two of Attlee's most valuable qualifications for party leadership – his integrity and his grasp of practicalities. He rejected contemptuously any move that threatened to reduce the unemployed worker's standard of living, while leaving the rentier relatively untouched. For Attlee, this was the main *socialist* issue of 1931, and in this regard he was never a moderate socialist. MacDonald's proposition – to cut unemployment benefit payments – struck at the very roots of his moral being. The speed with which Attlee resigned emphasized his absolute loyalty to the Labour cause – in contrast, for example, with Herbert Morrison, who hesitated to return to opposition, or with those cabinet members who accepted cuts but refused to put them into effect, for party political reasons and because of the hostility of the Trades Union Congress (TUC).[33]

And of all the Labour theorizing about "MacDonaldism," it was Attlee's analysis of the role of a future Labour prime minister that turned out to be the most prescient: "a good Chairman, able to get others to work." The prime minister's job, Attlee explained in 1932, would be to reconcile differences of opinion and to be the ultimate arbiter of decisions in the light of the interim socialist plan that had been accepted by the electorate.[34] What a Labour government would require in its leader was a catalyst, not a stimulant, a co-ordinator, rather than someone who would provoke, a team leader rather than a one-man band. This was nothing other than the Stepney recipe, although in the same paper Attlee also expounded his views on the organization and use of cabinet committees – an area in which he would prove himself an expert.

Nevertheless, Attlee could hardly have imagined in 1932 that he would be that hypothetical prime minister. Being made a member of the PLP's triumvirate in 1931 was no great distinction. Power in the movement at large had shifted from the PLP into the hands of the TUC.[35] He was not elected to the party's National Executive Council (NEC) at the 1933 annual conference, where the trade-union votes predominated. Stafford Cripps, George Lansbury, and Attlee were chosen as the leading spokesmen for the PLP mainly because of their seniority.[36] Lansbury was the only former cabinet minister to retain his seat in the Commons, and Cripps and Attlee were the only former junior ministers to do so. In selecting Cripps and Lansbury, faute de mieux, the PLP repeated to some extent the mistake that it had made with MacDonald. Both Cripps and Lansbury were leonine characters and, as such, almost by definition unsuitable as Labour leaders, even if the climate of the time hid that reality. In addition they each had particular shortcomings. Lansbury was as heart-strong as Cripps was head-strong; and Cripps was as irresponsible as Lansbury was naive. Cripps refused to take over from an ailing Lansbury in December 1933 and resigned from the NEC in 1935, as Lansbury did from the party leadership. But Attlee still had his own leadership claim to make.

With the party in opposition again in 1931, an enormous parliamentary burden fell on Attlee's shoulders. In 1932 his speeches filled more columns of Hansard than those of any other MP, laconic as they were. He proved conscientious, assiduous, and, in the end, indispensable. He replaced Lansbury in 1933 and again, in 1935, for the general election. He became Labour's parliamentary maid-of-all-work. By 1934 he had secured election to the NEC,[37] which indicated that, despite his rather strong extra-parliamentary language from 1931 on, he had begun to find support among the unions. He had further opportunity to learn not only that any major departure from the advice of the TUC was impossible for the Labour Party – a major lesson of 1931 – but also that, within the party, a bridge between idealists and pragmatists could be built only on the strength of organized labour.

Thus, although Attlee owed his election to the PLP's leadership at the annual conference in 1935 partly to the fact that he was not MacDonald, or Lansbury, or Cripps – and Morrison was also suspected of being egotistical[38] – he owed it even more to his work in the Commons from 1931 on. His participation in the remodelled National Council of Labour and various NEC committees from 1934 on did not hinder his candidature, especially given his speech at the 1935 annual conference. This speech has been largely ignored by historians, yet it was Attlee who provoked Lansbury to the pathetic expression of his utopianism that in turn brought down Ernest Bevin's celebrated wrath.[39] Attlee began by reminding the delegates that in the Commons "you can't take up a negative attitude, you have to deal with realities" – a generalization that must have gone down well with trade unionists! He then tackled the burning realities of foreign and defence policy, both demolishing the pure pacifists such as Lansbury and giving the definitive reply to Cripps's position on these questions.[40] The other two contenders for the leadership – Morrison and Greenwood – had flaws comparable in degree to Lansbury and Cripps. Each had alienated a number of influential trade-union leaders, Morrison lacked parliamentary experience and Greenwood was known to be too fond of drink. Attlee's victory on the second ballot[41] (most of Greenwood's votes went over to him) did not seem inevitable at the time – for one reason, he was such a public-school, middle-class figure – but in retrospect it appears otherwise. Afterwards, the loss of the 1935 general election was not held against Attlee – the NEC had been worried for months about the electoral situation.[42]

Attlee's new job had proved to be a difficult position from the inception of the PLP in 1900. As a federal body it had originally opted for a chairman and not, as did the other parties, for a leader at all. Keir Hardie was elected by a single vote, and the post was thereupon made non-permanent. The first person actually to want the job was MacDonald, who held it from 1911 to 1914. In 1917 Arthur Henderson had few qualms about giving up the chairmanship, and he was followed by William Adamson, who, though "obviously incompetent,"[43] served until 1921. The postwar constitutional changes and the electoral gains of 1922 saw the return of MacDonald – by a mere five-vote majority in a PLP caucus of 142 – in just the second contest for the post. He was called chairman and leader but turned out to be far more leader than chairman. What this checkered history indicated by 1935 was the need for someone at the top who could combine both functions. Attlee's record as a sort of political social worker, with demonstrated convictions, experience, and executive ability, meant that he came closer than anyone else to meeting these requirements.

Attlee's adroitness, patience, and realism were perhaps never needed more by the Labour Party than between 1935 and 1940. The heady delights of hopeless opposition and great issues positively invited dissension among the 150-odd MPs. So too did the party's internal structure, which permitted the expression of dissenting opinion at all levels. Attlee's main party task was to try to keep his colleagues from flying apart over foreign and defence policy. As leader of the opposition, he also considered it his duty to present a coherent alternative to the government's policies. He was obliged to concern himself politically with both tactics and grand strategy. The proof of his ultimate success is that in 1940 he was able to take a nearly united party into Churchill's coalition on equal terms with the far more numerous Conservative Party. He owed his success, as well, to the fact that he happened to be correct on the main issues of the day.

Despite the hesitations and ambiguities in 1935 in the government's attitude, in his own party, and in public opinion generally, Attlee had always recognized the implications of a collective security policy. Warning the Commons in April 1933 that the rise to power of the Nazi Party in Germany had added a new dimension to the international situation, he stated that, although Labour believed in reducing armaments, an essential preliminary of disarmament was security. Belief in a collective security system, he said in February 1934, meant meeting obligations: "[Y]ou had to be prepared to act." The following month he repeated that there could be no disarmament without security; the possibility of war must be faced if commitments to the League of Nations were to be carried out.[44] To his party's 1935 showdown annual conference, as odd-man-out in the Labour triumvirate, he acknowledged that the League could be viewed as just an alliance, but it was a "very big alliance."[45] Perhaps the best tribute to Attlee's pre-leadership articulation of his, and majority Labour, opinion on the subject was Stanley Baldwin's decision in 1935 to call an election. One of the prime minister's slogans was, "The Socialist Policy Means War";[46] he, in contrast, pledged his word that there would be no great increase in armaments.[47]

It has to be conceeded – Attlee later did so himself –[48] that the weight of his argument about collective security was somewhat reduced by Labour's votes against the Service Estimates. Yet he had solid grounds for supporting those votes. In parliamentary terms, a vote against the Service Estimates was nothing more than a convenient and customary way of registering lack of confidence in the government's defence policy as a whole and in the foreign policy on which it was based. That the Labour votes also served to disguise party differences on the subject was a perfectly normal political ploy. An opposition is not required to divulge the details of its policy were it in office. Attlee had to take into account the pure pacifists, who were overrepresented in the PLP, and the ideological left. The pacifists may have been down after 1935, but they were not out. The left wing's position – distrust of any arms in the hands of capitalist governments and a view of the League as an imperialist conspiracy – received a boost after the fiasco of the Hoare–Laval Plan and again with the outbreak of the Spanish Civil War. No doubt, had Labour been in power, as Dalton loudly proclaimed to the party's 1935 conference, it would have been compelled to provide armaments.[49] Attlee knew this perfectly well; one of his first actions as leader had been to set up a NEC committee to get "an informed opinion" about defence.[50] But Labour was not in power, and the types of alternatives in the Commons – to vote with the government or to abstain – are rarely attractive to any leader of the opposition.

This problem could have led the PLP, Attlee pointed out, to cease voting against any Supply Estimates. Nor could the dilemma be resolved, he added to the NEC in 1936, by moving token reductions, as that would indicate that Labour wanted less spent on the services, "although we really desire more."[51] In March 1936, a majority of the PLP ignored Attlee's advice, moving token reductions in the individual Service Estimates and abstaining on the main one. Less than five months later, with the onset of war in Spain, the PLP reversed itself, thus proving Attlee's tactical point. His preoccupation was to try to prevent hardening of Labour's divisions, so as to ensure maximum party unity when the proper moment for decision arrived. He did not have to wait long. With the deepening of the international crisis in 1937, the armament issue faded and the left wing split. In July 1937 the PLP opted to abstain a second time on the Service Estimates, still against Attlee's advice. But although the vote in favour was only 45 to 29, with half the PLP not participating, Attlee "scrupulously refused to entertain a manœuvre to reconsider the decision."[52] The conscription issue, in contrast, was relatively insignificant. Allies abroad rather than men were required, and Attlee could correctly claim in 1939 that conscription at that stage would be actually detrimental to national strength.[53]

During the war, Attlee quietly perfected his qualifications for the premiership. The circumstances were ideal. As a founding member of the coalition war cabinet, he was irremovable; only he and Churchill sat in it from beginning to end. Apart from a brief period as dominions secretary when the role of that department was critical, he alone among cabinet ministers had no departmental responsibilities. He operated freely over the full range of affairs, domestic, foreign, military, and imperial; he sat on every committee of importance, creating several of them himself. The powerful committee was his natural element. His first job, with Greenwood, was to review the entire machinery of government. They found a great mass of committees and proceeded to scrap most of them. They substituted a few ministerial bodies, of which two became paramount: the Defence Committee and the Lord President's Committee. Attlee sat on both. He was deputy chairman of the former, often replacing an absent or ill Churchill. He took over the chairmanship of the latter – which co-ordinated all aspects of home affairs – from Sir John Anderson in September 1943. With the single exception of Chamberlain, who died in November 1940, Attlee was the only cabinet minister to sit on both these bodies.

Another of Attlee's functions was of great future importance: he chaired the three successive subcommittees of the war cabinet that dealt with the formulation of British postwar foreign policy. To the last of these, the Armistice and Postwar Committee, reported the British representative on the European Advisory Commission, the various specialized, interdepartmental committees of officials, the Foreign Office, and the chiefs of staff. Altogether, no better apprenticeship for a future prime minister could have been devised. Attlee could well recall that he was acquainted "not only with all the outstanding problems but with the course of events out of which they had developed. I ... understood the machinery of government, and knew personally the leading figures in the Civil Service and in the Fighting Services."[54] He had also built up a close working relationship with Ernest Bevin and had taken especial care to bring forward younger Labour politicians.

Some members of the Labour left, however, were not impressed by Attlee's self-effacing style of leadership and did not understand his aims. They thought instead of an open, direct confrontation with the status quo forces, despite, or because of, the often-desperate war situation. Laski's strictures provoked Attlee in January 1941 into a vivid explanation of his technique. "I am sufficiently experienced in warfare to know that the frontal assault with a flourish of trumpets, heartening as it is, is not the best way to capture a position."[55]

He had early considered that the war could not be won without "a good deal of practical socialism,"[56] but he also feared that the cost of victory might threaten the accomplishment of many of Labour's social goals for some time afterwards.[57] Attlee's main political concern was to ensure that the great change in public opinion on domestic matters did not suddenly fade away, as had happened following the First World War. He aimed to permeate political life with reformist ideas, to smooth the way for permanent change – for which the formation of the wartime coalition presented a historic opportunity and in comparison with which the engineering of specific measures during the war was of secondary importance. To him, the inter-party harmony that came to prevail during the war over a wide range of domestic issues was an essential preliminary to any lasting institutional reform. The accord has been fittingly called "the Attlee consensus."[58] Attlee possessed what the extremists lacked – a two-dimensional view of British society. If he saw the injustice and inequality, he was also conscious of the underlying unity and stability. The revolution he sought aimed to take into account both dimensions, so as to be the more effective.

In retrospect, the most striking feature of Attlee's postwar government was its executive efficiency. No British ministry in modern history has faced problems of comparable magnitude, at home and abroad. Equally, none has enacted a comparable body of social-reform measures, besides putting the nation on the road to economic recovery. Attlee's government also began, in a decisive manner, the peaceful dismantlement of the empire. So great was its success that Kenneth Morgan warned seriously that from a historical point of view it is "in grave danger of retreating from reality into the half-world of legend and fantasy," although Henry Pelling's study mitigated that danger.[59]

As prime minister, at any rate, Attlee possessed definite advantages: Labour's possession of a detailed program, the partial spillover of the wartime sense of solidarity, the selfless character of all his senior ministers except Morrison, the "ghost of the 1931 split,"[60] the support of organized labour, the disarray of the Conservative opposition, and the crisis atmosphere that prevailed until at least 1947. To these advantages, he added his unrivalled experience of affairs, his proven wartime record, and the self-confidence that went with them. His leadership contributions, if unheroic, were as varied as they were continuous. But it is possible to be more specific. As prime minister, Attlee ran his own show.

Even during the election campaign in 1945, Attlee made it clear he would brook no interference from the Labour movement at large, especially not from theorists with tactical independence from the government and the PLP.[61] Prime ministers, he considered, had to deal in priorities.[62] Although he aimed to conciliate, that is not a sufficient description of his chairmanship of the cabinet. He controlled the agenda and made sure to extract the opinions that he wanted when he wanted them. He told his ministers that the cabinet's time was not to be wasted by unconsidered policies or parochial controversies.[63] His summing up of discussions was masterly. He made his appointments without "fear or favour" – not hesitating, for example, to surprise and initially disappoint people of the stature of Bevin and Dalton. He remodelled the cabinet structure "as no one had done since Lloyd George, and with far more permanent effect."[64] He sat at the apex of a series of committees that unquestionably magnified his influence. He kept the selection of chairmen and members firmly in his own hands and, by the end of 1947, chaired the most important committees – Economic Policy, Defence, and India and Burma – himself.

Attlee led by both precept and example, probably setting a prime ministerial record for brevity in the process. His own office was organized on a wartime basis, his Map Room being converted into an operational economic headquarters. The first prime minister to address the TUC's annual conference was also the last to use troops to break unofficial strikes.[65] He was not afraid to risk clashes on occasion with his leading ministers – with Morrison over bread rationing, with Bevin over India[66] – and anytime with the left wing. In the Commons, his debating superiority over Churchill astonished and delighted his supporters.[67] There is no need to stress his predominant role over India, but the extent of his influence on British foreign policy in general is often overlooked. Bevin may have been the mouthpiece and leading negotiator, but Attlee's self-control, restraint, and concentration on the global situation were Bevin's points of reference – and Bevin at first had nothing to negotiate. It was Attlee, too, who carried the ultimate responsibility and took the major decisions over the atomic bomb.[68] When Morrison wanted to send troops into Iran, Attlee simply overruled him.[69]

From the party political point of view, Attlee was little short of a godsend, the most redoubtable Labour leader that the Conservatives have faced – before Tony Blair. He made no major mistakes and had the inestimable value of not arousing the middle class. He could have stood up in the Commons and announced "the revolution," ruefully remarked an opponent, and made it sound like a change in a regional railway timetable. Another protested that he had effected a revolution but people had not realized it. They had been hypnotized by "the most successful political dentist in history."[70] Attlee's popularity in the opinion polls consistently outran that of his party.[71] Despite austerity and shortages, Labour increased its vote in 1950 by 1.25 million and in 1951 secured the highest number of votes obtained by any party until 1992, by which time the electorate was nearly 10 million people larger. And while his respectability and patriotism frustrated criticism from outside Labour ranks, his socialist views disarmed organized conspiracy from within. Above all, Attlee showed his party how to adjust to the realities of power at the highest level.

After 1951 Attlee perforce continued with the lesson. He was ready to give up the leadership but had good reason to think that his probable successor, Morrison, would split the party. Thus he soldiered on, trying for a last time to preserve unity. To govern effectively meant taking decisions with a minimum of talk; return to opposition called for different tactics. Unable to choose his colleagues, Attlee's only recourse was to attempt to get Labour to suspend judgment until opinions had time to work themselves out. He was obliged, for example, in the Commons debate on West German rearmament in 1954 to recommend abstention to any Labour MPs who did not wish to vote in favour – rather like Churchill had done to Tories in 1946 over the American loan, but with better results.[72] Until the spring of 1954, indeed, Attlee succeeded in keeping Labour in electoral contention. It was not to be expected at his age – 70 in January 1953 – that he could provide any new ideas. In any case, he did not believe that they were needed. He thought – correctly – that the Bevanite issue did not raise any fundamental principles, and he was careful to distinguish between Aneurin Bevan and his followers. However, though detached, Attlee was neither a passive spectator nor entirely neutral in the dispute. For some time he continued to hope that Bevan would succeed him.[73] He reprimanded both left and right but feared a right split more than a left because left-wing deviations were normal Labour Party occurrences. Who today can say that he was wrong?

In the retrospect of nearly 50 years later, it is abundantly clear that Clement Attlee was "the real, the natural leader" of his party in his time. Despite the luck, circumstances, and rivalries that contributed to his promotion and helped keep him in the leadership, he proved to be "a great administrator of political ideas"[74] – the necessary counterpoise to Labour emotionalism and the vital catalyst who best held the party together in opposition and made it function superbly in office. He also very nearly achieved a lasting consensus in the nation. Though a modest man, there was absolutely nothing in his career for him to be modest about.

NOTES

1 Harry Broadman, in the *Manchester Guardian*, 12 April 1954.
2 *News Chronicle*, 15 May 1952.
3 J.D. Margach, "You'd Never Think That Clem Had It in Him," 8 Dec. 1955.
4 "The Attlee Plan," in T. Sharp, *The Wartime Alliance and the Zonal Division of Germany* (Oxford, 1975), 52.
5 "Attlee's Consensus," in P. Addison, *The Road to 1945: British Politics and the Second World War* (London, 1975), 270.
6 K.O. Morgan, *Labour in Power 1945–1951* (Oxford, 1984), 6.
7 H.A. Pelling, *A Short History of the Labour Party* (London, 1962), 125.
8 K. Harris, *Attlee* (London, 1982), 568–9. Other recent and favourable biographies include T. Burridge, *Clement Attlee: A Political Biography*

(London, 1985); J.H. Brookshire, *Clement Attlee* (Manchester, 1995); and F. Beckett, *Clem Attlee* (London, 1997).

9 Crane Brinton, in the *Manchester Guardian*, 24 May 1954.

10 C.R. Attlee, *As It Happened* (Oxford, 1954), 217.

11 R. Rose, "Clement Attlee," in H. Van Thal, ed., *The Prime Ministers: From Sir Robert Walpole to Edward Heath* (London, 1975), 692.

12 F. Williams, *The Triple Challenge* (London, 1948), 50.

13 R.T. Mackenzie, *British Political Parties* (– 1963), 357.

14 Labour Party, *Report of the Annual Conference, 1940*, 123.

15 Attlee to Laski, 1 May 1944, quoted in K. Martin, *Harold Laski: A Biographical Memoir* (New York, 1953), 152–3.

16 D. Jay, "The Quiet Master at No. 10," *Times*, 26 April 1980.

17 Williams, *Triple Challenge*, 57.

18 London School of Economics Library (LSE), Hugh Dalton Diary, 26 Nov. 1935, 8 May 1941.

19 Lord Chandos, *The Memoirs* (London, 1962), 293; Lord Ismay, *The Memoirs* (London, 1960), 133.

20 Aneurin Bevan in *Tribune*, 16 Dec. 1955.

21 C.R. Attlee, *The Labour Party in Perspective* (London, 1937), 136.

22 Ibid., 103.

23 CCAC, Attlee Papers, Draft Autobiography.

24 His batman recalled, "[I]f anyone having a drink of an evening in a pub dared to say a word out of place about the Major there wasn't no argument, someone 'ud just bash him. Quick, before he got into worse trouble from others." Quoted in Williams, *Triple Alliance*, 54.

25 Bodleian Library, Oxford, Attlee Papers, C.R. Attlee to T. Attlee, April 1918.

26 W. Golant, "The Political Development of C.R. Attlee to 1935," BLitt. thesis, Oxford University, Ms. d1263, 102–4.

27 *East London Observer*, 6 Dec. 1919.

28 C.R. Attlee, *Metropolitan Borough Councils: Their Constitution, Power and Duties*, Fabian Tract No. 190, March 1920, 14.

29 F. Williams, *A P.M. Remembers* (London, 1961), 81.

30 C.R. Attlee, *The Social Worker* (London, 1920), 150.

31 *House of Commons Debates* (HC) 192, 782–8, 25 Feb. 1926.

32 Harris, *Attlee*, 88. The memorandum appears in full (570–84).

33 D. Marquand, *Ramsay MacDonald* (London, 1977), 645; B. Donoughue and G.W. Jones, *Herbert Morrison: Portrait of a Politician* (London, 1974), 164–8.

34 C.R. Attlee, "Cabinet Reconstruction," 12 Oct. 1932, quoted in Golant, "Political Development," 289–91.

35 Pelling, *Short History*, 71.
36 W. Golant, "The Emergence of C.R. Attlee as Leader of the Parliamentary Labour Party in 1935," *Historical Journal* 13, 2 (1970), 319.
37 The voting figures were: Morrison: 2.134 million, Dalton: 1.893 million, Attlee: 1.563 million, Dallas: 1.255 million, and Cripps: 1.187 million.
38 Donoughue and Jones, *Herbert Morrison*, 241.
39 Bevin charged Lansbury with "taking [his] conscience round from body to body asking to be told what … to do with it." Labour Party, *Report of the Annual Conference*, 1935, 179.
40 Ibid, 173–4.
41 The votes on the first ballot were: Attlee, 58, Morrison, 44, and Greenwood, 33. On the second ballot: Attlee, 88, and Morrison, 48.
42 Labour Party, NEC Minutes and Papers, 2 May 1935.
43 Pelling, *Short History*, 49.
44 HC 276, 2740–7, April 1933; 285, 1000–4, 6 Feb. 1934; 287, 465–6, 14 March.
45 Labour Party, *Report of the Annual Conference*, 1935, 173–4.
46 J.F. Naylor, *Labour's International Policy: The Labour Party in the 1930s* (London, 1969), 115.
47 A.J.P. Taylor, *English History 1914–1945* (Oxford, 1965), 383.
48 Attlee, *As It Happened*, 98.
49 Labour Party, *Report of the Annual Conference*, 1936, 182–4.
50 Attlee, *As It Happened* and "The Nation's Defence," *Socialist Commentary* (June 1956).
51 LSE, Dalton Papers, Part II, Section 2, 3/1, Attlee, "Votes in Supply," Labour Party Memorandum, 1936.
52 Naylor, *Labour's International Policy*, 194–5.
53 Ibid., 284. Attlee thought afterwards that to oppose conscription in 1939 had been "a mistake"; *As It Happened*, 103. Even so, when conscription was considerably enlarged in scope during the war, it was found that many highly skilled men essential to the war effort had been swept into the net, and efforts had to be made to demobilize them.
54 Attlee, *As It Happened*, 151.
55 Hull University, Laski Papers, Attlee to Laski, 29 Jan. 1941.
56 HC 355, 22–3, 28 Nov. 1939.
57 *Foreign Relations of the United States, 1940*, Vol. 1, 81.
58 Addison, *Road to 1945*, 270.
59 Morgan, *Labour in Power*, 1; H. Pelling, *The Labour Governments 1945–1951* (London, 1984).
60 J.P. Mackintosh, *The British Cabinet* (London, 1977), 503.
61 Pelling, *Short History*, 93.

62 *Times*, 15 Jan. 1957.

63 Public Records Office (PRO), CAB128/1, Conclusions, 9 Oct. and 29 Nov. 1945.

64 Morgan, *Labour in Power*, 48; J. Brookshire, "Clement Attlee and Cabinet Reform 1930–1945," *Historical Journal* 24, no. 1 (1981).

65 In 1945 and 1949. See PRO, CAB128/1, Conclusions, 16 Aug. 1945; P. Hennessy, "Waterfront Troubles plagued Attlee from 1945," *Times*, 3 Jan. 1980.

66 PRO, CAB128/8, Conclusions, 21 July and 31 Dec. 1946; PREM8/502.

67 J.D. Hoffman, *The Conservative Party in Opposition 1945–1951* (London, 1964), 230.

68 M. Gowing, *Independence and Deterrence: Britain and Atomic Energy 1945–1952, Vol. 1, Decision Making* (London, 1974), 27.

69 Williams, *A P.M. Remembers*, 254–5. The depth and extent of Attlee's clash with Bevin over the Middle East is now much clearer: R. Smith and J. Zametica, "The Cold Warrior: Clement Attlee Reconsidered 1945–47," *International Affairs*, 61, no. 2 (spring 1985), 237–52; J. Saville, *The Politics of Continuity: British Foreign Policy and the Labour Government 1945–46* (London, 1993), 112–48.

70 R.J. Cruikshank, in the *News Chronicle*, 28 March 1953.

71 Ibid., 24 Sept. 1951.

72 In the debate over West German rearmament only six Labour MPs voted against Attlee's advice; Harris, *Attlee*, 524. In the American loan debate 71 Conservatives voted against and eight voted with the government, despite Churchill's recommendation to abstain; Hoffman, *Conservative Party*, 231.

73 Perhaps until 1954. But in 1955 Attlee used all his skill in committee tactics to prevent Bevan being expelled from the Labour Party. P.M. Williams, *Hugh Gaitskell: A Political Biography* (London, 1979), 337–47; M. Foot, *Aneurin Bevan 1945–1960* (London, 1973), 455–80; J. Morgan, ed., *The Backbench Diaries of Richard Crossman* (London, 1981), 385–414. In 1955, the party whip was withdrawn from Bevan – temporarily, thanks to Attlee's intervention – after 62 Labour MPs abstained in a vote on Labour's amendment to the Conservative government's Defence White Paper.

74 Williams, *The Triple Challenge*, 63.

PART TWO

Officials and Diplomats

4

The Frustration of A.V. Hill: British War Science and the Baconian Paradox

NEIL CAMERON

Biographies and histories of the British scientific elite between 1919 and 1945 first appeared in quantity in the 1960s, concentrating on the celebrated Lindemann–Tizard quarrel in the Committee for the Scientific Study of Air Defence (CSSAD), or the Tizard Committee, in the late 1930s. Most still reflected the political perspectives and controversies of two decades earlier. In the years since 1970, two of the most influential wartime scientists – R.V. Jones and Solly Zuckerman – have published their memoirs, and some additional documents became available, such as the papers of Nobel laureate Patrick Blackett (Physics, 1948). More important, the release after 1970 of secret code-breaking transcripts from Ultra necessitated a broader reinterpretation of the general British conduct of the war.[1]

Nevertheless, the 1960s' view of British science and politics from 1933 through 1945, especially that popularized by the novelist and science journalist C.P. Snow, is still widely influential. By being first with an account of the CCSAD, in U.S. lectures quickly converted into a highly accessible book, Snow made his version widely known, and even hostile biographers had to respond to it. Snow concentrated on wartime Prime Minister Winston Churchill's scientific adviser Frederick Lindemann (Lord Cherwell), on the scientist–administrator Henry Tizard, and on the physicist and later operational research specialist Patrick Blackett, who had also provided Snow with his oral recollections.[2]

But the most instructive commentary on science and power in the Depression and war years comes from another independent scientist on the original Tizard Committee – Archibald Vivian ("A.V.") Hill, Cambridge don and Nobel laureate.[3] After 1940, Hill, like Tizard, was largely shunted aside. But even Lindemann wound up being far more important as part of Churchill's inner circle of advisers than as his intermediary with the war scientists. Hill was not exactly a rival of either Tizard or Lindemann. Though highly qualified to be a scientific *éminence grise*, he was passed over. This was not only a consequence of Lindemann's special relationship with Churchill, it also reflected a more general change in government–science relations, which had been evolving since the turn of the century.

This study argues that Hill's ambiguous status created, and then exposed, a growing divergence between the characteristics of the political and of the scientific elites. It begins with a look at Snow's account, outlines the Tizard–Lindemann quarrel and its wartime aftermath, sketches the sociology of science in Britain between 1900 and 1940 as background to wartime science, and then shows the side-lining of A.V. Hill as a new relationship between science and politics finally found expression during the war.

THE BACONIAN SCIENTISM OF C.P. SNOW

About 1960, C.P. Snow, a Cambridge physicist who had achieved fame as a journalist and novelist, gave two sets of lectures later published as small books: *The Two Cultures and the Scientific Revolution* (1960) and *Science and Government* (1961).[4] Both volumes occasioned considerable controversy, drawing both admiring and fiercely critical reviews and correspondence in leading journals of opinion on both sides of the Atlantic.

The Two Cultures argued that natural scientists constituted a distinct "culture" of men and women who "thought alike," irrespective of their views on religion, philosophy, or politics. All of them, unlike members of the "literary culture," had "the future in their bones." For Snow, like Francis Bacon, science, even when seemingly a pure exercise in intellectual curiosity that yielded discoveries of no immediate practical consequence, was a sort of elevated form of technological advance: an enterprise serving humankind by effecting all things possible. And like H.G. Wells, he also treated the entire scientific community and its enterprise as part of a broader movement of modern industrial society towards socialism. Furthermore, he believed that the creators and critics of literature, particularly in Britain, were preventing this trend, while inexorable, from having its fullest possible desirable influence on education and social policy. Writers and university dons, scandalously rejoicing in their complete ignorance of even such basic scientific concepts as the second law of thermodynamics, were guilty of a futile and reactionary snobbery, depriving science of the level of recognition and respect that it deserved and holding back its full potentialities to enrich and improve society.

This argument had considerable appeal for men and women working in science and technology and living in a country where Oxford and Cambridge graduates in disciplines such as classics, history, and literature made up most of the political, administrative, and industrial elites. As might be expected, it brought forth a hostile response from many of these, especially from the famous and acid-tongued literary critic F.R. Leavis, already angry at Snow for having portrayed him unsympathetically as a thinly veiled, fictionalized character in one of his works. His own counterblast to *The Two Cultures* in the Richmond Lectures was so extreme in its language that Cambridge University Press consulted Snow and took legal advice before publishing it, for fear of a libel suit.[5] Other praise and condemnation of Snow was of sufficient volume to fill an entire student reader for American college students. Snow also republished the lectures with a reply to his critics.[6]

Science and Government drew an almost equally heated response from Lord Birkenhead in his biography of Frederick Lindemann, and a more measured one from Ronald Clark in his biography of Tizard.[7] Originally a set of lectures to an American university audience, it was not only an account of the Tizard–Lindemann quarrel, but also an extension of Snow's more general argument in *The Two Cultures*. Snow ended his story of the eccentric Lindemann's wartime influence on Churchill with the solemn declaration that such an arrangement "must never occur again," implying that it had arisen from the British preference for amateurism and for keeping scientists "on tap but not on top."

Snow went from Leicester College in the 1920s to study spectroscopy at Cambridge, which endeavour did not go particularly well, partly because Ernest Rutherford was concentrating almost all the energies of physicists at the Cavendish Laboratory on the study of atomic particles. Snow always had literary ambitions, however. In 1934 he published his first serious novel, *The Search*, an account of the scientific life notable mainly for its portrait of a character called Constantine, an only slightly fictionalized version of John Desmond Bernal, a Marxist–Leninist crystallographer and polymath and Snow's friend and mentor. The book was not a great initial success, however, and through most of the 1930s Snow mostly wrote scientific journalism.

The views expressed in his journalism – which changed only mildly even during the Cold War – were those of a conventional British intellectual of the left. He was distressed by the economic misery widely found in pre-war Britain, highly sympathetic to the Soviet Union without ever showing much interest in Marxism–Leninism, and both resentful of bastions of privilege and ambitious to enter them. He displayed a firm conviction of socialism's inevitability and superiority, less for it as a revolutionary and egalitarian ideal than for its rational planning and allocation of resources to replace inefficient and chaotic British capitalism. During the war, as a bureaucrat overseeing placement of scientists, he saw partial fulfilment of such ambitions, much as John Kenneth Galbraith did as a wartime U.S. administrator of price controls.

After the war, Snow started to receive considerable critical and popular success as a novelist. The individual novels in his long cycle, *Strangers and Brothers*, were at least partial *romans à clef*, with scientists and other Cambridge dons appearing recognizable to many English readers. The popular success of his books, not only in England but in other English-speaking countries, his marriage to the novelist Pamela Hansford Johnson, and his knighthood, in combination with a persona of considerable *gravitas*, made him something of an august public figure by the early 1960s, when both *The Two Cultures* and *Science and Government* appeared in quick succession. By the end of the decade he was a Labour peer.

Snow's two little books remained influential for years, being used widely in survey courses in the liberal arts and social sciences. The "two cultures" became a cliché. Although the vogue for the term declined, it was still shaping undergraduate education for many scientists, sociologists, and journalists in the 1990s. Snow's interpretation of the Tizard–Lindemann quarrel received an almost equally central position in courses on "science policy," "humanities of science," and the like. Snow, and most of his admiring imitators, implicitly assumed that science, society, and progressive or socialist politics were all moving in a single, permanent, and irresistible direction – even though his own portrait of the British scientific elite challenged this notion.

Other developments – most notably, the fall of communism and the enduring Thatcherite reversal of statism in Britain – have also scarcely borne out this once-confident scientism. Snow's thesis was occasionally recognized as something of a bed of Procrustes, even when it was intellectually fashionable, but it has never had to contend with a fully worked out alternative view. Hence, while Snow's own novels have not found much lasting favour – most of them are now out of print – his Baconian portrait of British science to the mid-century has lived on. But it has always been a portrait that revealed more about Snow than it did about science.

THE TIZARD–LINDEMANN QUARREL

The Tizard Committee, 1935–1940

In *Science and Government*, Snow drew on the then freshly available papers of Sir Henry Tizard and on the oral recollections of the brilliant physicist and socialist Patrick Blackett to reconstruct the story of what happened in Tizard's CSSAD, formed in 1935, especially after pressure by Winston Churchill on Prime Minister Stanley Baldwin brought Churchill's close friend Frederick Lindemann on to the committee. This story, told many times, needs to be briefly recapitulated here.[8]

The committee was originally the brainchild of a Royal Air Force (RAF) engineering officer, Harry Wimperis, who had in mind serious research into the possibility of some kind of "death ray" or electronic interference beam to deal with the threat posed by bomber attack. This was in 1934, when Baldwin made his gloomy comment in the House of Commons that "the bomber will always get through," and this bleak pessimism had also inspired a letter from Lindemann to *The Times*, advocating the creation of a scientific group to address the problem. This double initiative was itself one of the causes of later friction, since Churchill and Lindemann immediately saw the committee, launched in early 1935 without Lindemann, as merely "departmental" and an inadequate response to their own agitation. Their own efforts led eventually to creation of a more politically powerful but less efficient Air Defence Research Committee (ADRC), reporting directly to the Committee of Imperial Defence (CID).

Tizard was then the rector of the science- and technology-focused Imperial College in the University of London. From a naval family, he rejected a naval career only because of a minor eyesight problem, studying chemistry at Oxford and Berlin. In the First World War, like Lindemann and many other scientists of his generation, he served in the Farnborough Research Establishment of the Royal Flying Corps. Quite friendly in those days with Lindemann, he helped him to become head of the Clarendon Physics Laboratory at Oxford after the war. He was not in the front rank of British scientists but had already shown outstanding talent as a scientist–administrator. He chose with remarkable care the members of the CSSAD (Tizard Committee), who varied in number between five and eight. The two independent scientist members each had strong claims to membership. A.V. Hill started off studying mathematics and physics but later switched to physiology, winning a Nobel Prize (1922) in the latter. The same age as Tizard, he had been an artillery officer in the First World War and was now biological secretary of the Royal Society. Patrick Blackett had served as a very young naval officer in the First World War and was later one of Rutherford's most brilliant physics students at the Cavendish. He was specializing in cosmic rays, work for which he too received a Nobel Prize after the Second World War.

While political views were not an explicit concern, Tizard, Hill, and Blackett were quite representative of the dominant political currents of the time. Tizard was a sort of Baldwinian conservative, Hill an extremely forceful independent, and Blackett a very leftish and pro–Soviet Union radical. They could also claim to speak for all three armed services – Tizard, for the RAF; Hill, for the army; and Blackett, for the Royal Navy. As well, they represented variously the Royal Society, Cambridge, Oxford, and Imperial College; physics, chemistry, and physiology; physiological physics; calculated artillery fire; flying experience; and cosmic-ray research. As well, Tizard could draw on Robert Watson-Watt, a specialist in the physics of radio beams, to carry out experiments for the committee at the National Physical Laboratory at Teddington, and was on excellent terms with senior RAF officers. His little group of outstanding talents took in a very wide range of both abilities and connections. If anybody could come up with a working "death ray" on demand, it was surely the group to do it. Furthermore, while they rapidly concluded that nothing practical could be done in that quarter, Watson-Watt's initial experiments led him quickly to the idea of radar, and they were all able to recognize its potential and to see the need to integrate it into the whole system of aerial defence.

Lindemann, to Churchill and other friends, was always "the Prof." He arrived late and ill-humoured on the Tizard Committee and was very different from all the others. Even his enemies, who were legion, would generally grant that he had an outstandingly powerful intellect and great courage, and he had also shown initial brilliant promise as a physicist. In addition, the son of a highly successful Alsatian engineer-entrepreneur, he was immensely wealthy, with a private income of £20,000 a year, almost ten times his Clarendon stipend, and far higher than the professional income of any British scientist, even Ernest Rutherford. He moved in high society, became one of Churchill's closest friends, was an ultra-conservative in politics to an extent that even Churchill occasionally found somewhat hair-raising, and despite, or because of, a partial education in Germany and fluency in the German language, was bitterly anti-Nazi and a Germanophobe. He was a man of fierce loyalties, convictions, dislikes, and grudges. He also had a highly deductive, a priori inclination in his thinking. At best, this gave him a gift for succinct and forceful explanations of scientific and technical problems, just the sort of thing that Churchill felt he needed, whether as journalist, parliamentary debater, or war-time leader. At worst, it put "the Prof" at odds with Oxford dons, establishment political leaders, and top civil servants, and with many of his own scientific colleagues, nearly all of whom were far more empirical and cautious in temperament.[9]

In addition to his very close friendship with Churchill, Lindemann won the respect and affection of many leading figures, including some of the more politically conservative scientists, such as Sir George Paget Thomson. But even his close friends found him a singular and eccentric figure. His aristocratic and unconventional parents had sent him to a Scottish public school; his university education was German; he was a lifetime bachelor, a vegetarian by choice with no admiration for vegetarianism; a champion tennis player who had played with the Kaiser and the Tsar; a charmer in high society; a mentor and hero to many Oxford undergraduates, including Churchill's son, Randolph; a friend of Einstein's who had done disappointingly little original work at the Clarendon, but who turned that facility into a top laboratory anyway by travelling around Nazi Germany in his chauffeur-driven Rolls-Royce and recruiting such brilliant Jewish scientists as Francis Simon. He was not a man with much patience for committees of any kind.

When Lindemann joined the Tizard Committee, he brought additional causes for trouble. He and Churchill were both preoccupied with the idea that the best way to stop attacking bombers would be with aerial mines, fired up by rockets or attached to barrage balloon cables. The other members were willing to give this idea a hearing, but calculations by Hill and initial experiments gave no more encouraging results than they had found with death rays. Lindemann, however, would not be swayed. He and Churchill continued to pound away about aerial mines inside and outside the committee. They also cheered on Watson-Watt's radar experiments but, unlike Tizard, did not fully grasp that what was so crucial was not the discovery itself – soon to be duplicated in other countries, including Germany – but getting the ground-control radio operators and RAF fighter pilots to understand how "radiolocation" would transform air warfare.

Before long, Tizard and Lindemann had not only ended their former friendship, but were quarreling bitterly in the committee. Hill and Blackett sided entirely with Tizard and wrote letters of resignation, forcing Lord Swinton, the air minister, to reconstitute the committee without Lindemann; Tizard, to demonstrate his clout, also brought in Rutherford, though never as an active member.

Lindemann Ascendant, 1940–1945

Rutherford died in 1937, leaving what could be called a vacant throne in British science. I consider his own importance in science–government relations below. The Tizard Committee functioned happily till 1940, having to deal also with the ADRC, on which Hill, Lindemann, and Tizard also sat, along with Churchill and the service chiefs. Blackett eventually became a major developer of operational research for the Admiralty. Hill and Tizard in 1940 carried out two missions to the United States, which helped launch British–American wartime collaboration.[10] But they participated little in major war work after 1940, with Churchill in office and Lindemann, now Lord Cherwell, his close cabinet adviser.

Churchill as sponsor and Cherwell continued largely futile research on aerial mines to 1943. Cherwell played a role, though not always decisive, in several major scientific–technical decisions, including the area bombing offensive on Germany launched after March 1942; timing of the introduction of radar-jamming metal foil, code-named "Window"; and bombing priorities and targets in response to the V-weapons in 1944. Blackett thought Cherwell almost unfailingly wrong – he was known around the Admiralty as the ALD (anti-Lindemann device) – and Snow took much the same view in *Science and Government*. The disagreements were not only "scientific" or "political," in the sense of strategic policy, but also ideological. Snow, Blackett, and many other scientists on the left were strong supporters of an early "Second Front" on the continent, to relieve pressure on the Soviet Union. This stance affected their general view of war priorities, especially the bombing offensive, since they would have much preferred to see many of the four-engined bombers diverted to the Battle of the Atlantic, easing the way for a continental invasion in 1942 or 1943.

Controversies about some of these issues live on, unresolved even by the belated documentary revelations of the Ultra transcripts. For example, Cherwell, by his own admission, was a nay-sayer who preferred looking for objections to any proposed course of action. He underestimated radar partly because he realized very early that filling the air with simple microfoil dipoles could jam or fool it. The British used the "Window" technique on D-Day to help convince the Germans that the main attack was at the Pas de Calais rather than at Normandy. Cherwell delayed introduction of Window till less than a year earlier, because he assumed that the Germans would quickly get the point, hence rendering British radar ineffective. Had the British "opened the Window" much earlier, that might have saved the lives of many bomber crews, but both the Allies and the Germans might have been thwarting each other's radar for an extended period, and the D-Day deception might have been jeopardized. Cherwell may have made the wrong choice, but we cannot be certain.

Cherwell's support for the bombing offensive raises similar problems. It was far from being his exclusive responsibility, but he did provide an influential memorandum in March 1942, drawing on research provided by Bernal and Zuckerman. After the war, the bombing was found to have had little effect on German industrial production, but it necessitated a large defensive effort by Germany. Had the large bombers been diverted to the Battle of the Atlantic, the Germans might have switched from producing night fighters to making long-range fighters for the Atlantic as well. The famous dual-purpose 88-mm guns and their crews would have gone to the Russian front rather than ringing German cities, and so on.

Cherwell was often unequivocally wrong, but even then he did not invariably get his way. His defenders, such as Sir Roy Harrod, the

Oxford economist who worked closely with him in his own small statistical department, and R.V. Jones, his Oxford pupil who became head of scientific intelligence in the war, could point out that he was right about some rather major issues. He had told Churchill in the 1920s about the possibility of an atomic bomb; he fully recognized the menace posed by the Nazis from the start; he supported area bombing because he doubted the accuracy of the specific target-bombing strategy used earlier in the war; and he annoyed Churchill by refusing to share his enthusiasm for operation *Habbakuk*[11] – Geoffrey Pyke's proposal to build a million-ton aircraft carrier out of specially modified ice. Even Snow conceded these instances, while still holding that Cherwell's technical judgments were almost invariably poor. Many other scientists agreed with him. But Snow did not attribute bad decisions to Cherwell's idiosyncrasies, or to Churchill's. His more general argument was that Churchill's method of obtaining scientific advice from trusted cronies was wrong in principle and should never be repeated. He does not offer a more suitable alternative but seems to assume, as in *The Two Cultures and the Scientific Revolution*, that collectively and collaboratively functioning committees of government scientists should offer such advice to policital leaders.

Science and Government, however, rather than being a cautionary tale about the bad effects of the Churchill–Lindemann combination, revealed the difficulties of Snow's own model. In *The Two Cultures* he had even included Lindemann among those who had "the future in their bones." But he failed to realize that scientific professionalization and growing statism were limiting the top-level impact of scientific advice by 1940. Scientists were increasing in number and status, but British politics had changed since 1900. The man at the centre of this story was A.V. Hill.

ARISTOCRATIC SCIENTISTS AND SCIENTIFIC ARISTOCRATS, 1900–1940

Two centuries after Newton published the *Principia*, science was only beginning to achieve consistent institutionalization through changes in the universities. The very words "scientist" and "physicist," with their attendant implication of a professional occupation, were not even coined until well into the nineteenth century. Only university chairs in mathematics provided regular professional employment for men of scientific interests, many of whom, like Michael Faraday, still preferred to be known as "natural philosophers." The rise of chemistry, the creation of red-brick universities in the new cities of the industrial revolution, and the competition of Germany all led to the gradual introduction of undergraduate university degrees in natural sciences in British universities. Integration of engineering into the universities as well, along with industrial demand for chemists, opened the prospects of teaching jobs for science graduates.

But professionalization developed slowly and arose alongside the older tradition of aristocratic amateurism. The dons of Oxford and Cambridge, even some of the mathematician–scientists, resisted introduction of science degrees until quite late in the nineteenth century. James Clerk Maxwell, for example, the brilliant first director of the Cavendish in the 1870s, was a Scottish laird who thought that there was no better training for a young potential scientist than a good classical education. His successor, Lord Rayleigh, was another independently wealthy scientist–aristocrat, a brother-in-law of Arthur Balfour. When he became the first British Nobel Prize winner in physics (1904), he donated the prize money to the Cavendish. J.J. Thomson, Nobel Prize winner (physics, 1906) for his discovery of the electron and Cavendish director from Rayleigh's departure till Ernest Rutherford's accession in 1919, was of middle-class background, but Richard Bellamy Clifton, director of the Clarendon Laboratory at Oxford from 1870 to 1920, was a Lincolnshire landowner who spent more of his youthful and potentially productive years worrying about the effects of the agricultural depression of the 1870s on his tenants than on the newest developments in physics.

It was Rutherford who became the prototype and eventual leading figure of British professional science from the early 1900s to his death in 1937. But even he, as an undergraduate in New Zealand, had studied liberal arts, including mathematics and a particularly stimulating general science course. His studies at the Cavendish and at Trinity College, Cambridge, were made possible by a scholarship provided throughout the British Empire, but his lack of public school and Oxbridge undergraduate background denied him an immediate post as a don. His work at McGill University in Montreal with Frederick Soddy on radioactive disintegration brought him a Nobel Prize and world recognition, but Arthur Shuster, another independently wealthy physicist, resigned his chair at Manchester and richly endowed it, to bring Rutherford back (in 1907).[12]

Knighted before the First World War, Rutherford became Baron Rutherford of Nelson in the 1920s, president of the Royal Society by the 1930s, and a friend of Prime Minister Stanley Baldwin's.

Co-discoverer with Niels Bohr of the planetary model of the atom, head of the world's leading experimental physics laboratory, and a man of superabundant personal energy and ebullient optimism, Rutherford was a sort of constitutional monarch of a feudal community of elite scientists, headed by Nobel laureates, winners of other prestigious awards such as the Royal Society's Copley Medal and Bakerian Lectures, and fellows of the Royal Society, especially members of its executive council.

The Royal Society, while it had had considerable ups and downs since its creation in the seventeenth century, had become a very prestigious club of fewer than 500 fellows (FRSs), including occasional foreign members such as Albert Einstein – and Eamonn de Valera, seldom now remembered as a distinguished mathematician. The older fellows included numerous "extinct volcanoes," but many others were admitted at the peak of their career. Many scientists, not exclusively British, were said to treasure their FRS even more than their Nobel Prize. At meetings they not only encountered the elite among their colleagues in different branches of science, but special appointees from the worlds of industry and politics, such as the auto-maker Lord Nuffield and Arthur Balfour, who after the First World War, as lord president of the council, was minister responsible for science.

Even in the 1930s and 1940s, Lindemann, who was an FRS, was singular only in his background and temperament, not in being a wealthy scientist-amateur. Of the two Royal Society secretaries, A.V. Hill, the biological secretary, was middle class in origin, but the physical secretary, the chemist Sir Alfred Egerton, was an aristocrat directly descended from a high courtier to the Stuart monarchy. Thomas Merton, another Oxford chemist who served on the society's executive council and who provided valuable technological devices in both world wars, came from a rich and distinguished family. Aristocrats and independently wealthy scientists were not, between 1900 and 1940, a small elite of birth within a larger elite of scientific talent; they were still as significant a group as the middle-class professionals.

This aspect of British scientific life in the first half of the twentieth century has been underestimated in many accounts, especially by historians as "future-oriented" as Snow. In the spirit of "history from below," for example, much scholarly attention has gone to the Association of Scientific Workers (ASCW), a more syndical type of organization set up in the 1930s to unite scientists and technicians and joined and supported by radicals such as Bernal and Blackett. The ASCW grew rapidly during the war, eventually reaching 16,000 members, and later evolved into a major white-collar union, the Association of Scientific, Technical, and Managerial Staffs. But it drew in only the most radical members of the scientific elite. Throughout the years 1933–45, apart from competing with the long-established and less politicized British Association for the Advancement of Science (BAAS), its attempted "horizontal" organization lost it in elite access and influence what it eventually gained in numerical clout.

Victorians, Edwardians, and Scientific Radicals in the 1930s

By the 1930s, most of the British scientists who could be described as late Victorians – those born well before 1880 – had moved into offices that were mainly honorific, including even Rutherford, who was Royal Society president until his sudden and unexpected death in 1937, which shocked the British and even the international scientific community. His successors were Sir William Bragg, a gentle and somewhat unworldly Christian who shared the 1915 Nobel Prize in physics with his son Lawrence for their work on X-ray crystallography and who died in 1942, and then Sir Henry Hallett Dale, a top medical scientist. Bragg, who had lost another son in the Great War, was horrified by the prospect of another war and broadly supported the politics of appeasement; Dale, who had some of the shrewd practicality of a working physician, was more in tune with the waspish A.V. Hill.

Late Victorians such as Rutherford and Bragg, untroubled and uninstructed by political life, were contemporaries more of Bertrand Russell and H.G. Wells than of Churchill. The same was true of Sir Richard Gregory, the editor of *Nature* and long president of the BAAS. But the real leading figures of British science in the 1930s were quite different. Just below the still-forceful Rutherford, most of the dominant figures had been born around the mid-1880s. James Chadwick, Egerton, Hill, Lindemann, Merton, and Tizard were contemporaries of T.S. Eliot, James Joyce, and the European dictators. Unlike the Victorians, they grew up in the world of automobiles, airplanes, dreadnoughts, and submarines. All had fought the Germans in the First World War in various capacities; Merton, most romantically, had secret duties for MI-5. Yet they were as accustomed as the older generation to careers and preferments determined mainly in university departments and laboratories. All had been familiar with the unique prestige and authority of Rutherford, a 20-year reign with, it rapidly

became evident, no obvious successor. All as well had been consult-
ants on bodies such as the Aeronautical Research Council, rather than
being direct employees of government.

Within the scientific community, professionalization and occupa-
tional opportunities had expanded in their lifetime, but still at a leisurely pace. While pharmaceuticals, fabric dyes, and other industrial
demands had produced several thousand chemists by the 1930s, there
were still only about 530 physicists in Britain, even including those
who taught in secondary schools. Sir George Paget Thomson, the man
who started work on the very earliest atomic bomb project in 1940,
once commented that he and his colleagues were regarded as having
the same combination of high intellectual status and low practical
utility as professors of Greek.

Bernal and some other radical and Marxist scientists and science
journalists tried to alter this situation with the Social Relations of
Science (SRS) Movement. This effort included a 1939 book by Bernal,
The Social Function of Science, which attempted a sort of Marxist sociology of science. Several similar volumes, and a large number of
newspaper and periodical articles, appeared throughout the 1930s.
The radicals made a great deal of noise – enough, for example, to
cause George Orwell to publish an essay denouncing British scientists
in general, apparently under the impression that all or nearly all of
them represented the same mixture of Stalinism and utopianism as
Bernal.[13] But the SRS was as limited in its intellectual influence on the
scientific community as the ASCW was in organizational. A vigorous
counterattack soon emerged from the émigre Hungarian chemist
Michael Polanyi, who launched an anti-Marxist Society for Freedom
in Science.[14]

SRS enthusiasts held up the "planned" science of the Soviet Union
as a model for emulation. Most members of the scientific elite were
not very impressed, even if they held mildly leftish views. That several had visited the Soviet Union and formed friendships among
Soviet scientists did not help. All but the communists and fellow
travellers were profoundly shocked and disgusted when the Russian
physicist Peter Kapitza, who had been working with Rutherford, took
a trip to the Soviet Union and was prevented by Stalin from returning
to England. Rutherford, who regarded Kapitza almost as a son, never
forgave the Soviet Union. Biologists in Britain grew steadily more
concerned about the meteoric rise of the crackpot Ukrainian plant
breeder Trofim Lysenko, who had the ear of Stalin. The full impact
of Lysenkoism, which destroyed Soviet genetics, came in the war

years and later, but its growing shadow was already clearly visible in the 1930s.[15]

It is possible that British scientists, or scientists more widely, were less moved by the purely political betrayals and atrocities of communism than were literary intellectuals. Certainly scientists, even those who became disillusioned about the Soviet Union, did not produce the sorts of cries of anguish that came from writers such as Arthur Koestler. But the non-Marxists, leftish or not, did recognize in Soviet science another mixture of bad philosophy, superstitious nonsense, and thuggish politics similar to what the Nazis were introducing in Germany. Bernal was a sufficiently loyal communist to tie himself in knots of explanation for decades, but Lysenkoism eventually drove J.B.S. Haldane from the Communist Party and ended the fellow travelling of Julian Huxley and a host of other vaguely progressive scientists and science journalists. Dialectical materialism seemed baffling to most of them in any case. The intellectual history of the British scientific community is another reminder, if any further one be needed, that hostility to communism, even as early as the 1930s, required no campaign of reactionary capitalists. For all but the most starry-eyed readers of the publications of the Left Book Club, the Soviet Union was already a most unappealing argument for Marxist socialism. Even the avowed leftists of the British scientific community showed a strong attachment to liberal individualism in both theory and practice. Several scientists besides Lindemann were conservative, even arch-conservative, and many more could best be described as apolitical.

Rebellions of sorts within the hierarchical structure of science were not unknown: Blackett, Chadwick, Mark Oliphant, and some other bright physicists eventually chafed under Rutherford's benevolent rule at the Cavendish and scattered to other university departments, where they could run their own ship. But this is a common tale in all professions. There were rebellions within the professional associations several times, not only in the 1930s. But not even the radicals rebelled against the elite of the Royal Society, who were, after all, at the meritocratic pinnacle of the most purely meritocratic of all professions.

A . V . HILL AND THE END OF AN ERA

The Uniqueness of A.V. Hill

The presidential position being largely honorary, the top of the Royal Society was represented in practical affairs by its two secretaries, physical and biological. Of these two, the aristocratic Egerton always deferred to A.V. Hill (1933–45), brilliant, forceful, and superbly articulate. A 1922 Nobel Prize winner for his postwar work on physiology, which followed initial studies at Trinity in mathematics and physics, Hill had won all the other top scientific prizes as well. With his other impressive distinctions, qualifications, and connections – the latter included marriage to the sister of John Maynard Keynes – he seemed the logical man to be the voice of British science and frequently assumed that he was so entitled. In peacetime, he was assuming this position. If he was not Rutherford's heir apparent, by the early 1930s he was certainly a forceful spokesman for the next generation of scientists. For example, in 1933 he gave a characteristically sharp and unequivocal Romanes Lecture, in which he argued that general abilities such as good judgment were scattered as uncertainly among scientists as within any other group. Among those scientists whom he did not consider well-equipped was Einstein, who had recently proposed that young mathematicians could be given employment as keepers of lighthouses. "Pity the poor sailors who would depend on their lights," was Hill's comment.[16]

In the same address Hill attacked both the dialectical materialism of the Soviet Union and the "German physics" of the Nazis. Johannes Stark, a German physicist and Nobel Prize winner (1919) who was also a Nazi Party member, wrote an angry letter to Rutherford, with whom Stark had some past personal contact, rather naively calling on him to silence Hill. The letter not only showed how little Stark understood British freedom, but how little he understood Rutherford, who agreed in substance with everything that Hill said. None the less, age and august position apart, Rutherford would have been unlikely to deliver the same kind of speech. He had something of the same caution in all public matters as his friend Stanley Baldwin. Hill, although he and Churchill wound up bitterly at odds, was in many ways the "Churchillian" scientist of the 1930s. But both the strength and the limitations of his position came from what had been happening to aristocratic amateurism and professionalism in both the science and politics of the first three decades of the century.

At the time Hill was born (1886), Lord Salisbury could still wear all the hats of Victorian amateurism at once. Conservative prime minister, philosopher, and theologian, he also maintained his own scientific laboratory at his Hatfield estate. There would never be another British leader quite like him, but such a remarkably close integration of science and political leadership continued with his nephew Arthur Balfour. Balfour was the brother-in-law of Lord Rayleigh, Cavendish director in the first years of the century, and was on close and friendly terms with his immediate successor, J.J. Thomson, and with Rutherford. He was scientifically literate, recognized the role of science and scientists in both peacetime and war, and spent his last years in politics as in effect minister responsible for scientific affairs. When the Liberals were in power, they managed something similar by depending on the rather windier Richard Burden Haldane.

But while both politics and science from the 1880s to the 1930s mixed the contributions of aristocrats and middle-class professionals, their mixtures were evolving differently. In politics, the steady advance of mass democracy from the 1880s on made the professionalization of political activity necessary for all ambitious men, irrespective of their origins. Neither Balfour nor any other aristocrat in politics could live the leisurely and polymath existence of Salisbury by the turn of the century. That odd pair of friends in the British Liberal Party of a decade later – Churchill and David Lloyd George – came from entirely different social origins and early careers, but Churchill had to engage in the same kind of party work and electoral campaigning as Lloyd George, the solicitor's clerk from Wales. Furthermore, both of them, like almost all the politicians of their time, were in the process of greatly expanding the permanent machinery of the state.

The statist expansion of the early twentieth century did not go nearly as far in the United Kingdom as it did in Germany, although some social critics pressed for British imitation and a drive for "national efficiency" – a buzzword of the time. The creation of the National Physical Laboratory, though fairly important for testing of various kinds, set up no serious rivalry to the physics of the Cavendish. Even the more ambitious science–government institutions that came out of the First World War – the Department of Scientific and Industrial Research and Research Councils to aid agriculture and medicine – did not bring major scientific research under even partial government direction. More significant for long-term relations, the latter simply came steadily more under the influence of democratic mass politics, and permanent government departments, notably including the armed services, all moved a long way from Victorian individualism.

Aristocratic participation in politics did not fade away after Balfour; Lord Swinton, the capable air minister of the mid-1930s, is only one of several examples. Furthermore, Cherwell was also not the only wartime cabinet member with scientific background and connections. Sir John Anderson, the Whitehall professional turned minister of home security, had studied science as an undergraduate in Scotland. His field was the chemistry of uranium, one reason he was given responsibility for Tube Alloys, the British atomic bomb project. He also brought Bernal into scientific advisory work; Bernal and J.B.S. Haldane, originally in the service of communist propaganda, had applied their energies to close study of aerial bombing in the latter 1930s, and Anderson decided that he wanted Bernal even if he was, as he put it, red as the fires of hell.[17] But by well before 1940, neither the presence of aristocrats nor that of scientifically literate politicians indicated preservation of the original aristocratic ideal of versatile amateurism and integrated individual thought and action at the top. Cabinet government, not the mind of a Salisbury or a Balfour, was the instrument of integration. In brief, aristocrats were adapting to the democratic politics of middle-class professionals.

In the scientific community itself, the situation was almost the reverse. Scientists advanced to top positions originally on the basis of individual achievement, not of birth or numerical support, and the Royal Society turned even those of relatively humble origin into holders of a kind of special life peerage. This markedly different direction from the world of ordinary British politics was compounded by the lukewarm involvement of most British scientists, including Rutherford, in politics and government. Lindemann was not just eccentric in temperament, but eccentric in political intensity. He was the *only* interwar scientist of privileged background who made use of his personal wealth and social advantages to involve himself heavily in politics. Churchill had found himself a special friend in more ways than one. Conservative, Liberal, and even Labour politicians of the 1930s and 1940s had frequent contacts with aristocrats and men of independent wealth, but not with men of science; aristocratic and independently wealthy scientists such as Egerton and Merton had upper-class social connections, but no political ambitions.

This is one of the reasons why Rutherford's sudden death in 1937 not only was a shock but produced a difficult situation for the scientific professionals who were being drawn into determined opposition to Hitler and into preparation for war. Rutherford himself had been "political" only in the sense of ruling his Cavendish dominion and maintaining a friendly but not intimate relationship with Baldwin. He was not very enthusiastic about scientists' close peacetime involvement with government, even for the purpose of getting research money. Yet he had done anti-submarine research for the Admiralty in the First World War, and his loathing for Nazism had been evident when he gave his support to the Academic Assistance Council, which helped German Jewish academic refugees. Had he lived a few years longer, he would almost certainly have taken his guidance on science–government relations from Hill and Tizard.

Rutherford clearly approved of Hill and Tizard's more direct work in preparing for war: Tizard, as we saw above, had no difficulty in bringing him on to his committee for added clout after the quarrel with Lindemann. But in activities from helping Jewish refugees to supporting secret war research, Rutherford in the mid-1930s had tended to react, rather than to initiate; the initiatives came from Hill. None the less, the New Zealander simply had far more prestige and influence than any other scientist in the country, amateur or professional, aristocratic or middle-class. Furthermore, he was director of the Cavendish, which, under an unbroken succession of outstanding directors for almost 70 years, had come to be regarded as the greatest centre of experimental science in the world. Rutherford presided over a spectacular range of discoveries by his students, proliferating again in the 1930s after the somewhat slower 1920s. He used to tell his colleagues that they were living in "the heroic age of physics," and most of them, including the non-physicists, agreed – although some must have felt at least mild irritation at his famous, cheery declaration that science was made up of physics and "stamp collecting," or those disciplines devoted more to identification and classification than to seeking powerful explanations.

Rutherford had created an expectation among both scientists and laymen that any single figure who might become the dominant voice of British science would probably be a physicist. But the closest thing to a Cavendish heir apparent had been the Russian, Peter Kapitza. There was a galaxy of brilliant talent in physics in the United Kingdom in 1937, composed of both Cavendish researchers and former Cavendish people now at other university departments. But none was seen as standing head and shoulders above the rest, which is possibly why the laboratory chose Lawrence Bragg, a crystallographer, rather than an atomic researcher, to succeed Rutherford.

So while A.V. Hill was brilliant, distinguished, well-connected, and heavily involved in both openly anti-Nazi politics and secret defence preparations, he could not simply assume Rutherford's mantle. Not only that: Lindemann *was* a physicist and director of Oxford's Clarendon. He was not very highly regarded by Rutherford and the other professional physicists, not having much followed up his early promise in his first decade at Clarendon. The one book that he published was on quantum theory – respectable, but put in the shade by the work of Werner Heisenberg. But to Churchill and his circle, and probably to most other Conservative politicians and powerful members of English society as well, these distinctions did not mean very much. Lindemann could claim the personal friendship of Albert Einstein, whose highly theoretical general theory of relativity had not overwhelmed empirical British scientists, but whom most non-scientists regarded as having almost superhuman intelligence. Lindemann also had a gift for explaining complex modern physical theories to non-scientists – a sufficient qualification in itself to have him taken more seriously than many scientists, who were somewhat unjustly but widely assumed to be incomprehensible to outsiders.

Hill and Attempts to Assert the Royal Society's Authority, 1939–1942

That a would-be scientific grey eminence would gain a useful step up with a seat in the Commons occurred to both Lindemann and Hill, who stood for the special seats still provided for the ancient universities. Lindemann ran as an independent Conservative at Oxford in 1936 but was defeated. Hill stood, also as an independent Conservative, at Cambridge in a 1940 by-election and was elected, serving in the House until 1945. From the mid-1930s until May 1940, Hill, Tizard, and Lindemann had roughly equal political influence, Tizard having in addition his great administrative influence with the RAF. Once Churchill moved in May 1940 from being First Lord of the Admiralty in the war cabinet to prime minister, however, Tizard and Hill were gradually excluded from all influence. Churchill brought Lindemann into his cabinet by making him a peer, but that was not a crucial factor: he had started using "the Prof" as an adviser as soon as the war began, having him set up a small statistical department that he continued to run as Lord Cherwell. Churchill also set up his own department to develop war inventions – MD 1, often referred to by the service professionals as "Churchill's toyshop."[18]

Hill still carried out important activities until late in 1940. He helped create a Royal Society register of scientific talent, to prevent what had happened in the First World War, when young scientists readily volunteered for the same kind of war service as the rest of their generation, wasting their talent in the trenches. The Royal Society fellows had never forgotten that H.G.J. Moseley, creator of the modern atomic-number periodic table, died from a Turkish sniper's bullet at Gallipoli when only 26. Hill also carried out a very useful scientific mission to Canada and the United States, which laid the groundwork for Tizard's mission shortly afterwards. The Tizard mission was not only a great step forward in scientific co-operation between the British and the Americans; Britain's willingness to provide the Americans with its single most important scientific advance – the cavity magnetron, which would provide vastly superior short-wave radar – did much to strengthen co-operation on the most general level.[19] Lindemann grudgingly accepted this decision, but certainly would not have done the same thing. On the organizational side, Hill pressed hard, and with superficial success, for the creation of a strong Scientific Advisory Committee (SAC) to the war cabinet. This SAC, composed essentially of the top members of the Royal Society, sat throughout the war. It successfully recommended that the British transfer their atomic project work to the Americans but otherwise was largely ignored.

Hill kept up all the pressure that he could for another two years. His major secondary project was to get additional SACs for each of the armed services. This initiative also had partial success by 1942, in the creation of such a committee to serve the Ministry of Supply with the application of the committee's scientific brainpower. He also tried to convince various influential figures in government to revive a long-extinct office, master-general of ordnance. He probably hoped that either he or Tizard would fill this office. His correspondence provided no suggested candidate from politics or the services, and he was probably thinking of himself, perhaps less administratively skilled than Tizard, but more pugnacious and imaginative, and with a seat in the Commons.

The problem was that all Hill's proposals, however persuasively and forcefully argued, would have had to win the unified support of the service chiefs or of the whole war cabinet – the only kind of pressure likely to move Churchill. Hill was quite unable to muster this kind of support; in fact he was as likely to be gently chided by a correspondent for not getting solidly behind the war effort. From his Commons seat, Hill sometimes sniped at the government. Most of his criticisms were quite valid, though to little effect. Churchill's bitterest wartime critics on the left dreamt that Labour's Stafford

Cripps could actually dislodge Churchill, in a sort of 1942 reprise of Lloyd George's overthrow of Asquith's government during the First World War. But whether or not Cripps could have been another Lloyd George, Churchill was no Asquith, and many MPs, whatever their reservations about some of Churchill's decisions, were unlikely to consider Cripps a great improvement. Cripps did know something about science. He almost became a chemist, and his sister was married to Egerton. Blackett, whose political views were almost identical to those of Cripps, would probably have welcomed a Cripps-led cabinet, but Hill, for all his frustrations, was much less attracted to the idea.

After 1942, the organizational structure and main activities of British science were largely fixed. Cherwell managed to work success-fully with some scientists, especially Oxford ones such as R.V. Jones and Solly Zuckerman. The demands of radar and ultra-high-frequency (UHF) radio snapped up young physicists and electrical engineers throughout the services, so rapidly that neither the Royal Society's register nor Cherwell's nay-saying much determined where they went. Thomas Merton actually provided a major war invention – the nitrous-oxide boost that gave a brief extra burst of speed to British fighter aircraft. Tizard and Hill, however, largely sat out the last years of the war, although Tizard had another stint of advisory influence afterwards.[20]

CONCLUSION:
THE PARADOX OF WAR BACONIANISM

Francis Bacon created a visionary utopia of science in *Novum Organum* and *The New Atlantis*, imagining scientists as organized into a pre-eminent state institution, dedicated to the service of humanity and the effecting of all things possible. Something of the Baconian dream clearly persisted in the hopes of Bernal and Snow. But the Royal Society owed far more to the example of Isaac Newton, the natural philosopher engaged in a "pure" pursuit of truth. The outstanding British scientists of the next two and a half centuries made their dis-coveries by following what appeared to them to be the most fruitful paths for investigation, not by taking much interest in the paths favoured by popular opinion, commercial advantage, or national interest. Rutherford, Hill, and nearly all the other FRSs of over 60 years ago identified with this tradition of research. But the renewed threat of war posed by Nazi Germany convinced them of the need to adopt what might be called a "war Baconianism." Germany presented a very special kind of challenge, not just as a deadly foe, but as the other European nation in which science had been most highly developed – the country that in the First World War introduced Fritz Haber's poison gas and was expected under the Nazis to combine ruthlessness towards civilians with application of its scientific brainpower to warfare, especially to attack from the air.

Nevertheless, the FRSS' scepticism about Baconianism came not just from the political utopianism of its most ambitious incarnations. All "applied research," even for a narrowly focused purpose, is supposed to draw on original scientific thought; it is not a mere extension of technology. Major discoveries may generate an immense range of practical uses, but immediate uses can not be produced to order, even given the exceptional urgency of war. During the First World War, the British government was ready and willing to throw a million pounds into science; it was hoping that scientists would hand it a weapon or weapons that could win the war. But J.J. Thomson, the sceptical and hard-headed Cavendish director whom it asked for guidance, commented that it could do little more than give more support to the best laboratories and students. He compared what would have happened if the government had asked for a better method of probing for bullets or shrapnel in war wounds: an immense expenditure on resources and researchers might come up with something like a metal probe with a light on it, but the real life-saver of wounded soldiers turned out to be X-rays, discovered and studied by scientists giving no original thought to the medical applications.

The Second World War ended with the most spectacular and terrifying demonstration imaginable that "pure" science could yield immense practical consequences. Still, the atomic bomb can be better described as a "war-ending" rather than as a "war-winning" weapon: even given the vast resources that the Americans could devote to the Manhattan Project, and even though they drew on an international community of the top physicists from half a dozen countries including the United Kingdom, the weapon was not ready in time to use against Germany. Furthermore, most of the fundamental research that led scientists to believe the bomb possible was actually completed by the outbreak of the war, carried out by researchers such as Otto Hahn who were trying to understand the nature of matter, not to create a super-weapon. The giant effort in men and resources took place because of the very great subtlety and complexity of the engineering details. In other words, even the success of the Manhattan Project does not exactly prove what many people think that it does – that Baconian projects can always succeed, so long as they are provided with sufficient resources.

Even a half-century that has seen even more resources expended on both military and civilian science of all kinds has not diminished the inherent unpredictability and the uncertainty of the whole scientific enterprise. These factors constituted the insuperable problem of the "planned" science of the Soviet Union, which led simply to a new version of Potemkin villages. If economic resources, laboratory facilities, and scientific talent were all that was necessary to surmount a problem, a cure for cancer would have been discovered decades ago, and the Tizard Committee would have provided Britain in the 1930s with a death ray.

However, atomic physicists did succeed in building a bomb, applied cancer research has greatly lowered its incidence of fatality, and the first testing requirements of the Tizard Committee put Watson-Watt on to radar. What the Royal Society executives believed, with considerable justification, was that their knowledge of where the very best scientific talent was to be found, and their capacity for recognizing and quickly exploiting the military potential in various lines of research, provided the most likely form of "war Baconianism" with any prospect of success. But they had several factors working against them. They did not have the prestige of Rutherford – so great that it could actually be translated into ordinary political clout. None of them could claim to be personally responsible for a crucial war weapon. They were not, like Watson-Watt – or like Randall and Boot, the younger physicists who developed the cavity magnetron – the actual inventors of radar, or nuclear physicists – and even the latter could not promise a bomb in short order, or any other special weapon. Their accustomed political impact had been based on influence, not on power, and even the influence had to be applied individually. The charter of the Royal Society actually prohibited the organization itself from direct involvement in politics.

These men found themselves in Churchill's line of fire not just because of his own obstinate conviction, shared by Lindemann, that aerial mines would be the great solution to the problem of British defence if only a lethargic establishment could be driven to throwing enough resources into their development. Like Maurice Hankey and several other talented public figures of the interwar years, the Royal

Society men were also the victims of Conservative Prime Minister Neville Chamberlain's perceived failure in foreign policy and his initial conduct of the war. The apparatus of consultative committees for which Hill continued to press, even for the first two years that Churchill was in power, was almost exactly the kind of governmental machinery against which Churchill and Cherwell were reacting. This rebellion had a number of unsatisfactory consequences, but Hill could not get around the indispensability of Churchill as a democratic war lord. Even in a speculative and counterfactual argument, the most that can be imagined is a government led by Lord Halifax, with Churchill still in the cabinet, and this improbable combination, while giving less power to Lindemann, would not be all that likely to have given reverent attention to the SAC. Men in power, an American president once remarked, listen to the advisers whom they want to hear.

Most exasperating to Hill, even given wartime censorship, he received an alarming idea of the kind of advice, "scientific" or not, that Cherwell was providing. As we saw above, if there was one thing about which Snow was right, it was that Cherwell gave a considerable amount of bad counsel. But aristocratic amateurism did not have much to do with this failing, except for his lack of broad or deep familiarity with the scientific community, his knowledge and approval being confined largely to a small group of Oxford colleagues. As well, even his mistaken judgments were commonly shared by others and were based on sufficiently cogent reasons. His real frailty was a combination of dogmatic obstinacy and personalization of disagreements. Churchill always found this temperament congenial, and a valuable source of strength, and it is hard to imagine his giving much weight to an "adviser" of more conventional kind. In Hill's ideal world, the nation would have found a war lord as inspiring as Churchill who also either had Balfour-like scientific literacy or would have seized on Hill or Tizard rather than on Lindemann to be his intermediary to science. But Hill was not a utopian, in either his overall political convictions or his organizational schemes, the failure of which disappointed but did not much surprise him.

The problem of scientific advice to political leaders in a democracy was not solved entirely satisfactorily in interwar and wartime Britain, but aristocratic survivals, either in the political leadership or in the cultural system of science, were not to blame. What happened can best be understood as the consequence of an unrevolutionary society, attempting a continuing reconciliation of rival meritocracies of intellectual achievement, hereditary advantage, and political power, but suddenly confronted by a revolutionary foreign threat.

The leading scientific figures of the time – whether they wound up in directing positions, as did Blackett, Jones, and Zuckerman; in the Los Alamos laboratory, as did Cockcroft and Oliphant; or on the outside for the latter part of the war, as did Hill and Tizard – all, including Cherwell, combined great powers of intellect with strong character. But all, again including Cherwell, could only to a very limited degree impose their will on either the overall nature of pre-war and wartime political leadership or the actual development of militarily applicable science and technology. Cherwell's frailties and strengths were almost a logical extension of Churchill's, not of his own privileged background or of his particular scientific abilities. The scientific eminence of Hill and his Royal Society colleagues never provided in themselves any guarantee of executive power in the state, any more than did the achievements of, for example, an R.G. Collingwood or a Ludwig Wittgenstein. What they could really claim credit for was their role in creating the quality of the British science that could produce the discoveries and developments that did so much to help the Allies win the Second World War. That was distinction enough.

NOTES

1 R.V. Jones, *Most Secret War* (London, 1978) and *Reflections on Intelligence* (London, 1990). S. Zuckerman, *From Apes to Warlords* (London, 1978); F.H. Hinsley and A. Stripp, eds., *Codebreakers: The Inside Story of Bletchley Park* (Oxford, 1994). The papers of most major British scientists of the 1933–45 period are held at Churchill College Archives, Cambridge (CCAC). A systematic treatment of the impact of the wartime decoders on Cherwell's decisions remains to be done.

2 C.P. Snow, *Science and Government* (Cambridge, Mass, 1961); *Appendix* (Cambridge, Mass, 1962).

3 The Hill Papers are at CCAC. On Hill, see B. Katz, "Archibald Vivian Hill," *Biographical Memoirs of Fellows of the Royal Society*, vol. 24 (1978), 71–149. See also Hill's own collection of essays and miscellaneous papers, *The Ethical Dilemma of Science* (London, 1960). Hill also receives considerable attention in R. Clark, *Tizard* (London, 1965). His general importance, especially in his liaison trip of 1940 to Canada and the United States, is covered in D.H. Avery, *The Science of War: Canadian Scientists and Allied Military Technology during the Second World War*

(Toronto, 1998), and D. Zimmerman, *Top Secret Exchange: The Tizard Mission and the Scientific War* (Montreal, 1996).

4 C.P. Snow, *The Two Cultures and the Scientific Revolution* (Cambridge, 1960), and *Science and Government*. Harold Macmillan's Conservatives were in power when both books appeared, and the volumes provided ammunition for their Labour opponents. Harold Wilson brought Labour to power in 1964, presenting his party as the one that understood the "white-hot technological revolution" and appealing to "the man in the white [laboratory] coat."

5 F.R. Leavis, *Two Cultures? An Answer to C.P. Snow* (Cambridge, 1961). Leavis argued that Snow had no talent as a novelist and that what he regarded as a "culture of science" was merely an assemblage of the conventional prejudices of *New Statesman* readers. His counterattack was not "conservative," but rooted in his own passionate belief that great novelists such as D.H. Lawrence, and critical readers of his own level of discrimination and intense engagement, were the proper tutors of a single culture. But he was able to cite some scientific allies and, for all his immoderate language, made some telling points; he was particularly devastating on Snow's bland assertion that a "culture" was defined by a group of people who all "thought alike."

6 C.P. Snow, *The Two Cultures and a Second Look* (Cambridge, 1962). Snow did not respond to Leavis, nor very much to more polite critics from what he called the "literary" culture. He came close to allowing a "third" culture for the social scientists.

7 Lord Birkenhead, *The Prof in Two Worlds* (London, 1961); see also Sir Roy Harrod, *The Prof* (London, 1960), and Clark, *Tizard*.

8 Snow, *Science and Government*; Clark, *Tizard*; P.M.S. Blackett, *Tizard and the Science of War*, Institute of Strategic Studies Tizard Memorial Lecture (London, 1960; *Studies of War* (London, 1961); R. Watson-Watt, *Three Steps to Victory* (London, 1957). Almost all histories dealing with British science during the war give some version of what happened in the Tizard Committee, but Clark's remains the most detailed and balanced.

9 Birkenhead, *The Prof*, passim. This biography and Harrod's shorter memoir (*The Prof*) are both strongly partisan defences, not detached studies, but show that Lindemann could inspire as much admiration and affection among Oxford Conservatives as he did scepticism and alarm among Cambridge professional scientists. Both his attackers and his defenders agree, however, on his highly deductivist turn of mind. He published two papers on the theory of numbers when fully involved in early war duties for Churchill.

10 Zimmerman, *Top Secret Exchange*, passim; Avery, *The Science of War*,
    passim. On the crucial cavity magnetron developed by H.A.H. Boot
    and J.T. Randall, see J.T. Randall, "The Cavity Magnetron," *Proceedings
    of the Physical Society of London* 58, part 3 (1946), 247–52.
11 Churchill played down the intensity of his enthusiasm for aerial mines
    in his postwar memoirs, listing them as just one of several interests –
    for example, in *Their Finest Hour* (Boston, 1949), 336–7. The Cherwell
    Papers tell another story. Various kinds of research on aerial mines
    received top priority in the first four years of the war, including the
    use of a squadron of *Havoc* fighter-bombers to test a trailing version.
    Correspondence between Churchill and Cherwell also gave consider-
    able attention to the even odder *Habbakuk* project – a scheme put for-
    ward by Louis Mountbatten's near-crackpot adviser, Geoffrey Pyke,
    to build a one million–ton aircraft carrier out of specially modified ice,
    which led to Bernal's doing experiments on icy lakes in Canada. In this
    case the enthusiasm was Churchill's, Cherwell being highly sceptical.
    However, Churchill supported two almost equally far-fetched devices –
    Mulberry artificial harbours and PLUTO (pipe line under the ocean)
    fuel-transmission lines, which were both used successfully in the
    D-Day invasion in 1944.
12 On the aristocracy in general political life, see W.L. Guttsman, "The
    Changing Structure of the British Political Elite 1886–1935," in *British
    Journal of Sociology* 2 (1951), 122–34. Guttsman's table of 193 cabinet
    members in the years of his study gives 70 as coming from the
    aristocracy, 99 from the middle class, and 24 from the working class.
    On Arthur Balfour as the uniquely successful integrator of aristocracy
    and science, see Lord Rayleigh, *Lord Balfour in His Relation to Science*
    (Cambridge, 1930).
        The most aristocratic scientist in the exact sense of the term was the
    physical secretary of the Royal Society in the 1930s and war years, Sir
    Alfred Egerton. He was descended from the Earl of Bridgewater on his
    father's side, while his mother was an Ormsby-Gore. He was married
    to the sister of Stafford Cripps. See Lady Egerton, *Sir Alfred Egerton*
    (London, 1963).
        Other noted scientists had hereditary or marital connections to what
    Noel Annan has called the "intellectual aristocracy." The mathematical
    physicist Charles Galton Darwin, for example, was a grandson of the
    famous evolutionist and a godson of both Galton and Lord Kelvin. On
    Arthur Shuster, Rutherford's return to England, and his 12 years in the
    chair that Shuster endowed, see the memorial tribute, including papers

by Blackett and others: J.B. Birks, ed., *Rutherford at Manchester* (Manchester, 1962). Rutherford was well paid at McGill and was quite happy living in Montreal. He moved probably more to be closer to the Cavendish than because of financial considerations. In any case, the very man who symbolized the new "professional" science thus had an important part of his career shaped by the action of a wealthy scientist–patron.

13 J.D. Bernal, *The Social Function of Science* (London, 1939). Orwell, Editorial in *Polemic* (May 1946), reprinted in his *Collected Essays, Journalism and Letters, Vol. 4, 1945–59* (London, 1968), 185–92. Orwell was aware that there were scientists with quite different views from Bernal's, but thought that "scientists as a body ... are much more subject to totalitarian habits of thought than writers, and have more popular prestige"; Orwell to Arthur Koestler, 31 March 1946, 155–6. See also S. Hook, *Reason, Social Myths, and Democracy* (New York, 1940). Influential left-wing but anti-Stalin intellectuals, Orwell and Sidney Hook were savage critics of Bernal's Stalinist scientism and may have helped to limit its impact. The revelations just after the Second World War of the nuclear espionage of Klaus Fuchs and other scientists led to a widespread popular perception that communist influence had been very large among scientists. It was a frequent theme of both British and American films of the Cold War era. As in the case of diplomacy and the intelligence services, even individual communists, if they were scientists working on the atomic bomb or other defence weapons, could have great impact. But the actual number of communists and fellow travellers in such areas now appears to have been quite small, no higher proportionately than among literary intellectuals. However, some non-Marxist but radical scientists were pro–Soviet Union in the 1930s, such as the biologist and wartime operational researcher C.H. Waddington; see his *The Scientific Attitude* (London, 1941). A 1964 Festschrift for Bernal included contributions by a couple of front-rank British scientists who shared Bernal's views, but even this group of friendly contributors included some sceptics about his vision of planned science. See M. Goldsmith, ed., *The Science of Science* (London, 1964).

14 See J.R. Baker, *The Scientific Life* (London, 1942), and *Science and the Planned State* (London, 1945); M. Polanyi, *Rights and Duties of Science* (Manchester, 1939), *The Contempt of Freedom* (London, 1940), and *Science, Faith and Society* (Chicago, 1946). Polanyi, a distinguished chemist, never won a Nobel Prize, but several of his students did, and his son John became a Canadian Nobel laureate (chemistry, 1986). Somewhat

like Karl Popper and other intellectual émigrés from the former
Austro–Hungarian Empire, Polanyi tried to give the freedom that he
found in England a more philosophically rigorous defence than native
defenders such as Hill found necessary. But Hill and nearly all his colleagues, in their various memoirs and non-scientific writings, almost
invariably sound far more like Baker and Polanyi than like Bernal or
even Snow.

15 On Lysenkoism and its impact on British scientists, see J. Huxley,
    Science on Trial (London, 1948); J. Langdon-Davies, *Russia Puts the
    Clock Back* (London, 1948); and R. Clark, *J.B.S.: The Life and Work of
    J.B.S. Haldane* (London, 1968). As celebrity assets for communism, both
    Bernal and Haldane received far more latitude in speech and writing
    than did ordinary party members; and Haldane used this latitude to
    the full. Despite almost two decades of professed Marxism–Leninism,
    including a weekly science column for the *Daily Worker*, he was more
    of a great English eccentric than a typical Marxist radical of his time.
    With characteristic obduracy, he continued to claim that Lysenko's the-
    ories might have some good points even after he left the party. When
    he deplored the absence of adequate liaison between scientists and
    government at the outset of the war, it was the past role of Balfour that
    he held up as an ideal, not that of the Liberal R.B. Haldane, his uncle.

16 Hill, "The International Status and Obligations of Science," Huxley
    Memorial Lecture, 1933, reprinted in full in his *The Ethical Dilemma of
    Science* (London, 1960), 205–21. As well as Einstein, Bernard Shaw was
    a target, but in both these cases Hill was humorous and quite mild. He
    was much fiercer on both Nazis and communists, also noting that the
    sensible people who hated war were still quite capable of fighting it.

17 On Bernal, see B. Swann and F. Aprahamian, ed., *J.D. Bernal: A Life in
    Science and Politics* (London, 1999). As a good example of the kind of
    pre-war bombing research carried out by Bernal and Haldane, see
    Bernal's *The Freedom of Necessity* (London, 1949), composed largely of
    articles that he published in the 1930s and early 1940s, and Haldane's
    A.R.P. (London, 1938). On Anderson, see J.W. Wheeler-Bennett, *Sir John
    Anderson* (London, 1966).

18 See R.S. Macrae, *Winston Churchill's Toyshop* (Kineton, 1971). MD 1
    produced two notable successes: the rocket projectiles that saw consid-
    erable use late in the war – in the D-Day bombardment, for example –
    and the PIAT infantry anti-tank weapon. It expended considerable
    resources on outright flops, such as several different versions of aerial
    mines, and a partial flop, the photoelectric fuse that was a predecessor

of the more successful, and very important, radio proximity fuse,
developed by the Americans but drawing on British advances in radar.
It also produced the sticky bomb, another infantry weapon that worked
after a fashion but was disliked by troops required to use it. Even the
successes were relatively minor. Certainly none came near to being
the kind of war-winning weapon that Churchill wanted. MD 1 was
nowhere near as valuable a component in either British defence or the
Allied victory as were more orthodox government bodies such as the
Telecommunications Research Establishment (TRE). Its career high-
lights the difficulty of what this study calls "war Baconianism" and
Churchill's sometimes-wild flights of imagination.

19 Zimmerman, *Top Secret Exchange*, passim. Robert Buderi's recent,
comprehensive history of radar, *The Invention That Changed the World*
(New York, 1996), opens with an account of the Tizard mission, and
most earlier histories of American war science also recognize the
crucial role of British provision of the cavity magnetron. All three of
Britain's most crucial scientific contributions to war technology relate to
its collaboration with the United States: its giving the Americans an
early start in developing centimetric radar and related electronic
devices; its contribution of nuclear physicists to the Manhattan Project;
and its sharing of information gleaned from Ultra decodings. British
and American relations with the Soviet Union, even in the warmest
period of the Big Three alliance, never had the same character.

20 Shorter accounts of science in modern war sometimes refer to the First
World War as "the chemists' war" and the Second as "the physicists'."
For Britain, however, given its decision not to undertake an atomic
bomb project, it may best be described as belonging to the electrical
engineers. See G. Hartcup, *The Challenge of War* (New York, 1970), and
Buderi, *Invention*. Engineers, even scientist–engineers, had much less
prestige and government influence in the United Kingdom than in the
United States. There was no British figure to compare to Vannevar
Bush. Rutherford did not really come to appreciate the usefulness of
engineering applied to physics until the very last years of his life,
demonstrated by his students Kapitza and John Cockcroft, and it took
electronic warfare to raise up engineering's overall importance.

Members of the scientific elite were not, however, contemptuous of
technology and technologists. Their outlook was partly a consequence
of their own versatility. Most British physicists of the first four decades
of the century, even Lindemann, were quite adept at the design of
laboratory instruments. Similarly, British biologists could readily be

deployed on wartime operational research because nearly all of them
were familiar with sophisticated mathematics and statistics. On Merton,
the independently wealthy elite scientist who was also a very competent practical technologist, see H. Hartley and D. Gabor, "Thomas
Ralph Merton," *Biographical Memoirs of Fellows of the Royal Society,*
Vol. 15 (1969), 421–40. On Tizard's postwar role, see Clark, *Tizard,* and
also M. Gowing, *Independence and Deterrence: Britain and Atomic Energy
1945–1952* (London, 1974).

5

Sir William Seeds:
The Diplomat as Scapegoat?

SIDNEY ASTER

The *Foreign Office List* for 1940 concluded its entry for the British diplomat Sir William Seeds with the notation "unemployed." This was the intriguing end to a mission in Moscow that Seeds had begun in January 1939. He arrived to take up the position of British ambassador to the Union of Soviet Socialist Republics with high expectations of a fruitful culmination to a 35-year foreign-service career. In what proved to be the final months of peace, his assessments of the political and military strengths of the Soviet Union, of its commitment to the "peace front" against Nazi Germany, and of leading Soviet personalities were all used in the Foreign Office's formulation of policy towards the Soviet Union. On his shoulders, too, rested the primary negotiating role in the three-phase search for a British–French–Soviet treaty of mutual assistance, which Germany's seizure of Prague on 15 March 1939 spurred and which ultimately failed with the surprise signing on 23 August 1939 of the Nazi–Soviet Pact. In January 1940, after only 12 months in Moscow, Seeds returned to London, his mission abandoned in the aftershock of the outbreak of war.

Seeds's mission, self-contained and dramatic as it was, presents a case study in leadership, personality, and responsibility at the ambassadorial level, in the little-examined context of an authoritarian environment.[1] What reasonable expectations can one have of a diplomat circumscribed by censorship, limited freedom of manoeuvre, and restricted movement? What information and perceptions informed the evaluations made by Seeds and his embassy staff, and how accurate could they have been? What effect did they have on the negotiations for the "peace front" in 1939? Given that Seeds, while on active service, never had any direct communication with Prime Minister Neville Chamberlain – in contrast to other ambassadors, such as Sir Nevile Henderson in Berlin – what weight was attached to his views when presented at cabinet and committee levels? After the signing of the Nazi–Soviet Pact on 23 August, and with Soviet neutrality declared after the outbreak of war on 3 September, was Seeds's position in Moscow so undercut by events as to leave him immobilized? In January 1940 or earlier was Seeds held culpable for the failure of the tripartite negotiations? Was his leave of absence a rebuke, was it a recall dictated by other considerations, or did he accept responsibility, realize that the war presented new challenges, and step aside to let another person face them?[2]

Seeds was born in 1882 in Dublin, though of an Ulster Protestant family, was educated at Rugby, and from an early age aimed for a foreign-service career that would include Russia. He spent the period from September 1899 to June 1900 in St Petersburg, where he lived with several Russian families, studying the language and culture. He was there again from July to October 1900 and, as he recalled, grew to love the "real old Russia like a story or play by Chekhov."[3] In 1904 he entered the diplomatic service, and he was posted to Washington, DC, and later to capitals in Europe, the Far East, and South America. His last appointment prior to Moscow was in 1930, when he became ambassador to Brazil. He was already known as a difficult taskmaster who "did not suffer fools gladly, nor always sufficiently restrain his brilliant wit."[4] In March 1935 Seeds applied for sick leave. Instead he was asked to take on a three-year appointment as ambassador to Portugal, which he refused to do. He insisted on being placed *en disponibilité*, and this was finally agreed.[5] Seeds then returned to England to his estate, Fairfield, near Lymington.

The prospect that Viscount Chilston, ambassador to the Soviet Union since 1933, was to retire gave Seeds hope of fulfilling his lifetime ambition. In February 1937 he started lessons to refresh his knowledge of Russian. He arranged for an interview at the Foreign Office and asked to be sent to Moscow. On 2 April 1938 the secretary of state for foreign affairs, Lord Halifax, wrote to Seeds offering him the Moscow position, which he accepted the next day.[6] The appointment, formally announced

Sir William Seeds (centre) with Soviet Foreign Minister Maxim Litvinov (left) and Mikhail Kalinin, chairman of the Presidium of the Supreme Soviet (right), on 28 January 1939, when the new British ambassador presented his credentials.

on 16 August, was favourably received in the press, with comments directed at the fact that Seeds, though not well known, was "methodical," "efficient," "reliable," and "unobtrusive." *The Times* added that he had "all the Ulsterman's liveliness, fluency and wit."[7] Seeds did the rounds in London, consulting with Halifax, several Foreign Office officials, Soviet Ambassador Ivan Maisky, and Chilston, "for 'coaching' re Moscow."[8]

He arrived in the Soviet capital on 21 January 1939 and began his social and diplomatic contacts, meeting first with Maxim Litvinov, commissar for foreign affairs, and his deputy, Vladimir Potemkin.[9] On 28 January, accompanied by senior members of the embassy, he officially presented his credentials to President M. Kalinin. Seeds reported to the Foreign Office that during the interview he produced a "visible sensation" by speaking in Russian, saying how pleased he was to return to the Soviet Union after such a long time.[10] In his diary he noted with evident pleasure: "I was taken to Kremlin in a Rolls-Royce car by Barkoff, the Chef du Protocol Ceremony and long interview afterwards with Kalinin and Litvinov a great success, and my little Russian speech created delighted surprise."[11]

Seeds was thrilled with the appointment. "He is the only English-man I have met who really wanted to live in Moscow," Halifax later observed.[12] However, conditions in Moscow were another matter. The Bolshevik revolution and Stalinism had changed the face of the country and made the work of all foreign ambassadors trying and frustrating in the extreme. Moreover, the Soviet post was especially lacking in facilities for tapping "unofficial" sources of information. Seeds pointed out to Halifax that foreigners in Moscow "have practically no personal contacts with official or private Russians beyond those of a purely formal or business nature." Any attempt to establish covert contacts would also have been unsuccessful. Soon after arriving in Moscow Seeds lamented: "I am precluded by my guardian-devils of the police who dog my every movement abroad from any possibility of acquiring first-hand knowledge, or even impressions."[13] With intimate knowledge and contacts impossible, he had to gather information mainly from a judicious reading of the Moscow and provincial press. From these, Seeds kept up a steady flow of extracts with commentaries, always with awareness of the limitations involved. Not surprisingly, a visitor to the British embassy in 1939 later commented, "I did not envy the Ambassador his task of representing Great Britain in the Soviet capital."[14]

Seeds's dealings with Soviet officialdom were at the outset friendly. His relationship with Litvinov was especially warm, and he genuinely regretted the latter's "resignation" on 4 May 1939.[15] As for Vyacheslav Molotov, Litvinov's successor, the pressure of the ensuing negotiations strained their relationship. Seeds later observed that "there was never any 'negotiation' in the ordinary sense with Molotov," who merely acted as the messenger for the "rigid plans" approved by his bosses.[16] A mutual dissonance emerged after their first encounter. None the less, Seeds was generally well disposed towards the communist state. "I am not amongst those who seem incurably suspicious of this country," he later observed. His view of the desirable in British–Soviet negotiations was "friendliness and contacts but no obligations." However, he confessed on several occasions "to not being at all sure what these people are actually up to." And in the earlier stages of the negotiations he concluded, "I see no option but to continue to take them at their word."[17] His relations with other heads of foreign missions in Moscow, however, were amicable, reinforced by a social

life where the diplomatic community had to rely on itself for enter-
tainment and mutual support. In particular, Seeds had high praise for
the French ambassador, Paul Emile Naggiar, who was also new to
Moscow, and with whom he was to collaborate intimately during the
tripartite negotiations.[18]

Seeds was fortunate that, on his official assumption of duties, British–
Soviet relations were in a state of flux. First, the Soviet Union was
flirting with a policy of isolation, having been left on the sidelines
during the resolution of the German–Czech crisis in September 1938.
Britain was preoccupied with its relations with Germany, France, and
Italy but had increasingly to reconsider its policy towards the Soviet
Union. Second, of the particular problems that the Moscow embassy
dealt with during the winter of 1939, one concerned the stir caused
by rumours at the end of January that Karl Schnurre, of the Economic
Department of the German Foreign Ministry, would journey to Moscow
to negotiate a new German–Soviet commercial agreement. The Soviet
government, Seeds felt, was "not averse from encouraging rumours
of a Russo–German flirtation," but there was "as yet no indication of
any impending political or military contacts."[19] Later Seeds was able
to report that the visit had been cancelled. The reservations with
which Seeds covered these reports of German–Soviet contacts characterized the view that he was to take on several future occasions.
Third, Germany reputedly wanted to expand into the Soviet Ukraine.
Seeds reported that the Soviet Union professed indifference towards
these reports.[20] Furthermore, he did mention several times that Soviet
officials had hinted at a possible retreat into isolation. This was confirmed in interviews between officials in London and Maisky, the
records of which were regularly forwarded to Seeds.[21]

It was the problem of British–Soviet trade, and British complaints
that the Soviet Union was not buying enough British exports, that
produced some spirited debate and activity. Britain's Board of Trade
regarded the 1934 temporary trade agreement as "unsatisfactory" and
wished to negotiate a new one.[22] While some officials in the Foreign
Office agreed that "Russia is no friend of ours" and that "the Soviets
are … entirely opportunist and could not be relied upon," they
equally understood that the prevailing perception of British policy
as "biased, for 'ideological reasons,' against collaboration with the
Soviet Union" had to be changed. By mid-February, as one official
put it, the British were prepared to make "a special effort to play
ball with the Russians." One idea floated was for Seeds to seek an

audience with Joseph Stalin. This was vetoed on the grounds that the newly appointed envoy "would be riddled with a number of questions which he would be unable to answer in any satisfactory manner."[23]

However, out of these discussions and their linkage with the ongoing commercial negotiations finally emerged a commercial mission to Moscow in late March led by Robert Hudson of the Department of Overseas Trade. Among Seeds's first tasks in Moscow, therefore, was the daunting prospect of trying to convince Soviet officials that British policy was not one of cold-shouldering their country. He was not optimistic, writing that the Soviet Union, "sitting on velvet, has every intention of continuing to do so, and will not be moved by fair words or vague arguments." None the less, he was prepared to espouse any "constructive proposal" to lure it into co-operation.[24]

Within six weeks of his arrival, Seeds wrote a long preface to four memoranda prepared by embassy staff, analysing what he termed "the vitality, or instability, of the Soviet regime."[25] In the preface, he concurred with the views of his staff that the government was "as firmly established as any regime can reasonably expect to be" and that, while the possibility of internal stress might surface in case of war, the regime would prove stronger than tsarist Russia, as it had "stronger moral stamina." Seeds compared the Russia of his student days with the new situation. He observed that the political and intellectual elite fully supported the regime, which offered it limitless opportunities. With regard to the "humbler classes," he admitted that first-hand information was lacking, but he suspected that these too supported the government. He concluded his personal observations with some remarks on the efficiency of Soviet persuasion techniques – cinema and wireless for propaganda, the firing squad for dissenters.

The views of some of the embassy staff, clearly developed under the previous ambassador, then followed. First, "it would be a grave mistake, in the event of war, to count on a consistent and reasonably stable policy on the part of the Soviet Government." Soviet policy was essentially opportunist, and Soviet leaders would not hesitate overmuch "to change horses in mid-stream." Second, both the Red Army and the air force, though loyal, had "suffered severely" from the purges. While they could be counted on to defend Soviet territory, neither seemed to have any offensive power.[26] Finally, embassy officials had little confidence in Soviet industry's ability to sustain wartime production.[27]

One further document that Seeds produced before the tripartite negotiations was a lengthy analysis of Stalin's speech on 10 March to the 18th Congress of the Communist Party of the Soviet Union. He observed that it contained "little that was new or unexpected." Rather, he wrote, it confirmed the prevailing Soviet tendencies to condemn the British and French for trying to push Germany eastwards and to emphasize that the Soviet Union would not be drawn into a conflict that did not concern it. Seeds surmised that, given the existing condition of the Red Army, the Soviet economy, and the transportation system, the Soviet Union was going to avoid intervention in a conflict between the capitalist powers. Hence Stalin's repeated assertions of his readiness to mount an impregnable defence of the Soviet Union if attacked, but his desire to avoid being dragged into the "second imperialist war." Seeds referred to Stalin's assurance of support for the victims of aggression, warning that this should be interpreted as "assistance in the form of war materials, provisions and technical help after aggression was in full swing." Seeds's final comment is poignant in retrospect: "Those innocents at home who believe that Soviet Russia is only awaiting an invitation to join the Western democracies should be advised to ponder M. Stalin's advice to his party: 'To be cautious and not allow Soviet Russia to be drawn into conflicts by warmongers who are accustomed to have others pull the chestnuts out of the fire.'"[28]

With the German seizure of Prague on 15 March, the roles of Seeds and his embassy staff became pivotal. In reaction to this event, the British government shifted from minimal involvement with the Soviet Union to pursuing it as a partner to deter Germany.[29] British efforts in this direction fall into three periods: 17–31 March, 1 April–25 May, and 25 May–25 August. The first phase began on 17 March when Halifax, acting on fears that Germany was poised to attack Romania, instructed Seeds to inquire of the Soviet government "whether they can give any indication that they would, if requested by the Roumanian Government, actively help the latter to resist German aggression."[30] The Soviet Union replied with a suggestion to summon a conference to meet in Bucharest. While not specifically rejecting this idea, Halifax in turn instructed Seeds on 20 March to seek Soviet adherence to a declaration by Britain, France, the Soviet Union, and Poland to consult together as to joint resistance in case of further European aggression. In a discussion with Litvinov the following day, Seeds pushed the British proposal as being a "clearer warning to potential aggressors" and "easier to decide on owing to the smaller number of Powers concerned at the outset." The Soviet Union agreed to a declaration, but on 24 March Polish opposition scuttled it.[31] The first attempt at closer British–Soviet political collaboration had foundered.

The parallel exercise in British–Soviet commercial diplomacy fared no better. Hudson, who had arrived in Moscow on 23 March, spent several days in the company of Seeds conferring with Soviet officials. The two, however, made no headway on trade questions. As well, they strayed into political discussions and tried to convince Soviet officials that British policy had firmed up, and so the mission ended in some controversy.[32] Seeds's activity during this period gives abundant evidence of his attempts to improve British–Soviet relations. His cordial contacts with Litvinov enabled him to carry out his instructions with a minimum of difficulty but, unfortunately, with a paucity of results. His efforts were matched by Halifax, who cautioned in the wake of the failure of the four-power declaration that it was "important not to reinforce their [Soviet] tendency towards isolation" and it would be dangerous to give the Soviet government "the idea that we were pushing her to one side." Halifax proposed, on the basis of similar advice from Seeds, to work towards retaining Soviet "close interest" in the crisis.[33]

The second period of attempted British–Soviet collaboration began in the wake of the British guarantee to Poland on 31 March and lasted until 25 May, when for the first time the British cast a proposal in the form of a tripartite treaty of mutual assistance. Momentous as the 31 March guarantee was, it was also critical for Seeds in the following weeks. The Soviet Union directed its resentment at its exclusion from the picture prior to the British–Polish guarantee at Seeds when he was called to see Litvinov on 1 April. The latter pointed out that his government had suggested a six-power conference and had then agreed to sign a four-power declaration and that both had been "summarily dropped." Seeds failed to mollify Litivinov, who then warned that his country "would henceforth stand apart free of any commitments." Seeds had to report that the guarantee had been "misunderstood and not at all appreciated." Litvinov recorded how "very coldly" he had treated Seeds.[34]

Seeds continued to exercise some personal influence as he urged on Halifax the necessity of consultation with the Soviet Union on future co-operation. Certainly the head of the Central Department, William Strang, later referred to the "advice from the Ambassador at

Moscow" as one of the factors driving the British government, "step by step ... to move towards the Soviet position."[35] The fact that similar advice came from some members of the cabinet, sections of the House of Commons, the British military, and public opinion also helped. On 6 April Seeds thought that Litvinov's pride might be boosted by a hint that Britain was still open to the idea of a "conference of sorts" or to some form of collective agreement. Halifax saw Maisky, on 6 and 11 April, but could report little progress. On both occasions Halifax defended British policy, while Maisky reaffirmed Soviet commitment to resist aggression.[36]

On 13 April Seeds cautioned, with some considerable foresight, that the situation as it was developing posed a temptation for the Soviet Union "to stand aloof." On this and on several other occasions during this phase of the negotiations, he stressed that he "emphatically" agreed with Maisky, who had commented to Halifax that the British must find "some means" "to prevail on Poland and Romania to accept the idea of some form of Soviet military assistance." He suggested to Halifax that a way of bypassing the difficulty would be for the French, first of all, to ensure to themselves Soviet assistance, on the basis of the 1935 Franco–Soviet pact of mutual assistance. Thereupon France would make it clear to Poland and Romania that if they wanted French assistance, they must be willing to accept some manner of aid from France's ally.[37] This suggestion never was acted upon, but it indicates how committed Seeds was at this stage to hastening Soviet inclusion in Western defence planning.

Seeds also continued to caution against any action that would estrange the Soviet Union or feed its suspicions about British foreign policy. Thus on 14 April Halifax instructed him to seek from the Soviet government "a public declaration ... that in the event of any act of aggression against a European neighbour of the Soviet Union ... the assistance of the Soviet Union would be available, if desired."[38] Litvinov's reply three days later amounted to a proposal for a mutual assistance agreement between Britain, France, and the Soviet Union, as well as a complementary military convention. Seeds confided to his diary on 17 April: "Intense diplomatic activity reigning for about a week. I saw Litvinoff day before yesterday and yesterday. To-night at theatre (*Much Ado About Nothing*) I was dragged out to go see him & receive Soviet proposal for a [sic] Anglo–Franco–Soviet pact of mutual defence and protection for Soviet neighbours menaced by German aggression: the resultant telegram kept my poor staff working till 3.45 a.m. Interesting feature of my being whisked out of theatre was that I thereby gave my police followers (who were sitting quite fairly close to me) the slip!"[39]

Initially, Halifax contemplated repeating the suggestion of 14 April, believing that the Soviet proposal ignored "practical difficulties." Seeds, however, advised him that doing so would only confirm Soviet suspicions "that we are trying to evade association with this country's efforts."[40]

Another vital point when Seeds's views prevailed concerned the dismissal of Litvinov. On 4 May Seeds telegraphed to the Foreign Office that an "inconspicuous four-line notice on back page" in the press stated that Litvinov had been dismissed. Whether it presaged a Soviet retreat into isolation, he observed, it was impossible for him, or any of his diplomatic colleagues, to predict with "any pretense of knowledge."[41] In his diary Seeds wrote that the news was a "Bombshell … I had an interview yesterday with Litvinov who gave me no inkling of this startling development." Halifax replied two days later with the government's response to the Soviet proposals – a modified restatement of the request for a declaration. Halifax instructed the ambassador that he should ask Molotov whether the change of personnel implied a shift in outlook or policy. If Molotov admitted that the situation had changed or if, as Halifax put it, "you feel doubts as to present policy of the Soviet, you should suspend actions and inform me by telegraph." Halifax was himself reassured by Maisky that "no change of policy was to be assumed from the recent departure of M. Litvinov."[42]

There was insufficient evidence for Britain to alter course, even simply to mark time. Seeds would have wished for a more accommodating response from home. But acting according to instructions, on 8 May he gave Molotov the revised British proposal for a Soviet declaration, which he had altered slightly for purposes of clarification, as well as providing the requisite Russian translation. The document provoked a "relentless cross-examination," which on one item subjected the ambassador to a "most unpleasant ten minutes." Nevertheless, Molotov said twice that there was no change in Soviet policy "but added cryptic remark that it was liable to be altered if other states changed theirs." In his usual understated style, Seeds described the whole hour-long interview as "somewhat trying." In his diary he wrote: "Terrible day of work for me preparing and carrying out delicate, and in the upshot – very trying, interview with Molotov on anti-aggression business."[43]

Seeds returned to the subject of Litvinov's dismissal on 12 May. He stressed to London that there was "no real evidence" that the Soviet Union intended to retreat from its proposals of 18 April, to enter into a policy of isolation, or to come to terms with the Axis – although he considered each a possibility. Instead, he argued that "all the evidence which has been accumulating in the past week would seem to show that the Soviet Government are for the moment still prepared to pursue a policy of collaboration." Seeds deplored Litvinov's departure: "I fear that his replacement by M. Molotov will make matters difficult for myself and my colleagues."[44] Seeds favoured continuing a policy of seeking Soviet collaboration. The Foreign Office noted his caution that the extreme Soviet demands might be a preparation for a retreat into isolation.[45]

Seeds soon unburdened himself to a colleague at the Foreign Office: "I am very sad at Litvinov's disappearance … We had got to understand each other very well, whereas Molotov is still an enigma and I shall have to walk very warily … For the moment my impression is that Litvinov's disappearance means chiefly the loss of an admirable technician or perhaps shock-absorber, and that we are faced with a more truly Bolshevik – as opposed to diplomatic or cosmopolitan – *modus operandi*. Reactions to what we say or do not say will be more violent and the great men in the Kremlin will be more apt to plunge off into the deep end if disappointed or indignant." Seeds wrote this after his second meeting with Molotov and interpreted Molotov's "stream of questions … [as] more a desire for information than an intention of letting us down." Seeds further observed, given the advanced state of the negotiations: "I see no option but to continue to take them at their word and to believe that they are not manœuvring to let us down with a sudden bump." However, more wary, he decided that he would now defer to Potemkin to act as interpreter. Seeds's prognosis of the coming temper of the negotiations was accurate, and he also found this reflected in what he termed "unpleasant" Soviet press coverage.[46]

On 14 May Molotov replied with, as expected, a flat rejection of British proposals. He reiterated his government's demand, made first on 18 April, for a British–French–Soviet pact of mutual assistance, a guarantee of some states of eastern Europe, now to include Latvia, Estonia, and Finland, and agreement on forms of material assistance. Seeds at once pointed out that reference to Finland was problematic. Molotov seemed unimpressed and argued that the entire proposal was based on what he called "the need for 'reciprocity.'"[47]

The impasse required major decisions from the Chamberlain government. As a consequence, between 14 and 24 May the locus of the negotiations shifted to London, briefly to Geneva for a meeting of the Council of the League of Nations, and then back to London. In these, Seeds played little role, but he confided to his diary that the negotiations were causing him "considerable nervousness & strain." He urged an early riposte to the Soviets, whom he described as being "in a somewhat impetuous mood." He reassured a Soviet official that he was "personally optimistic," that Britain was trying to be accommodating, and that he was "personally disgusted" with the flood of inaccurate press reporting about the negotiations.[48] Behind the scenes, however, a dramatic struggle was going on to win over Chamberlain. As each level of the policy-making elite – the cabinet, its Foreign Policy Committee, the cos, and diplomatic advisers – fell into line in favour of a mutual assistance pact with the Soviet Union, the prime minister kept up a stout resistance.[49] At last on 23 May the permanent under-secretary of state at the Foreign Office, Sir Alexander Cadogan, signalled the volte-face: "P.M. apparently resigned to idea of Soviet alliance, but depressed." The cabinet approved the principle of a triple alliance and, in accordance with Chamberlain's specific wishes, linked the draft alliance to Article XVI of the League's Covenant. The text of the draft agreement and an explanatory memorandum were sent to Seeds on 25 May, with instructions for its joint presentation with the French ambassador.[50]

Thus did the third and final phase of the tripartite negotiations begin. The role that Seeds played, as this proposal and others were redrafted and broadened both in their diplomatic and their military implications, was central. He argued the merits of the British case with astuteness and tenacity. On occasion he was dumbfounded by the "suspicious mind" of Soviet officials and by the tendency of Soviet negotiators to read their own misgivings into statements that they had imperfectly understood. This necessitated repetitive arguments that taxed Seeds's patience and led him to complain of being "irritated to be interrogated."[51] In some areas Seeds exercised considerable personal influence, with various degrees of success. He acted as primary negotiator as refinements of the various complex articles of a draft treaty of mutual assistance were hammered out in the Kremlin. The nature of the negotiations now changed and began to exhibit signs of severe strain. His relationship with Molotov degenerated into polite antipathy. He found the foreign minister "totally ignorant of foreign affairs," with "a rather foolish cunning of the type of a peasant." Their interviews sometimes consisted of harangues and endless repetitions, which "relapsed into wranglings," as the Russian engaged in relentless cross-examinations. With Molotov, Seeds observed, "the idea of negotiation – as distinct from imposing the will of his party leader – is utterly alien."[52]

When Seeds and the French chargé d'affaires, Jean Payart, saw Molotov on 27 May to present the joint proposal for a triple alliance, they discovered that a copy was already in his hands, received directly from Paris. What followed was a turning point in the negotiations and for Seeds personally. The ambassador described how he was "astounded" to hear Molotov's negative reaction. Afterwards in his diary Seeds noted: "Payart & I to see Molotov in Kremlin in order to present generous & far-reaching draft of agreement for reciprocal assistance. Were turned down in manner which savoured of the grotesque and the insulting." Another interview a day later on the same set of proposals proceeded on what Seeds called "sadly familiar lines." Allusions to the League Covenant, the complexity of a military planning exercise, and indirect aggression were again fought over, with little progress.[53]

Seeds used the impasse to submit to the Foreign Office what he termed his "considered views" on the negotiations.[54] First, he asserted that the draft proposal gave the Soviet Union "all reciprocity that they are entitled to expect and offers them terms quite sufficiently generous – in fact almost more generous than the Soviet Union's possible assistance is in practice worth." Second, he expressed confidence that the Soviet Union was willing to ally with Britain but wanted "to extract the maximum terms." He noted that if "as many observers here believe, they are playing with us and are really out for isolation," then no further concessions would be useful. Seeds concluded, however, with the view that the risk of a Soviet political agreement with Germany was "never … more than just a possibility at any time." In any case, he claimed the Soviet Union was so well covered by British commitments to Poland, Romania, and Turkey as "to remove any serious temptation to indulge in so remarkable a *volte face*" if the negotiations broke down.

The scope for Seeds's initiative increased appreciably during the third phase of negotiations. The sensitivity of the issues, and the role of the negotiations in British grand strategy, meant that general principles and policy directives always emanated from London. However,

Halifax several times allowed some discretion to Seeds on matters that might be better calculated, as he put it, "to lead to early progress." What Halifax envisaged were details – minor drafting changes and tactics – rather than anything of principle. In points of drafting, the Foreign Office would usually provide Seeds with several alternatives, sometimes leaving the final choice to his initiative. Unfortunately Seeds, while offering Molotov the minimum, would often have to provide the maximum. From time to time he conceded on "mere questions of drafting ... as M. Molotov will suspect a trap in every amendment we propose."[55] As for future problem areas, Seeds anticipated that these would include the definition of indirect aggression, guarantees to the Baltic states, and reference to the League. While he was fully aware of the military importance that the Baltic states had for Soviet security, he declared himself "bound to draw attention to a (?less) praiseworthy motive on their part."[56]

In a speech on 31 May to the Supreme Council of the Soviet Union, Molotov surveyed the tripartite negotiations and laid down what he called the "necessary minimum" conditions. These included a guarantee against attack on all states of central and eastern Europe bordering on the Soviet Union, guarantees of assistance against indirect attack, and a concrete military agreement.[57] The Soviet reply came on 2 June in the form of modifications to the British–French proposal to include Soviet desiderata. The major changes, noticed immediately by Seeds, were the attempt to downplay the reference to the League of Nations; the specific mention of Belgium, Greece, Turkey, Romania, Poland, Latvia, Estonia, and Finland; and a new Article 6 that would make the political and military agreements enter into force simultaneously. Seeds targeted the last as a change "of considerable importance."[58]

The Soviet counterproposals rankled in the Foreign Office, which felt that the British had made sufficient concessions to sign a treaty. The prospect of continuing delays and ongoing telegraphic exchanges convinced Halifax to recall Seeds for consultation. A thorough briefing, Halifax informed Seeds on 6 June, would arm the ambassador "with the necessary arguments" for an "expeditious" conclusion. Seeds answered the recall with the news that he was confined to bed with a temperature that would delay his departure for several days.[59] This quite incidental setback led to one of the most controversial decisions of the tripartite negotiations. Rather than await Seeds's recovery, or take up one of the several offers of help from politicians, diplomats, or other public figures, the foreign secretary chose William

Strang, head of the Central Department of the Foreign Office, who had served in Moscow from 1930 to 1933, to journey there on a special mission to assist the ambassador. An announcement to this effect was made in the House of Commons by the prime minister.

Such were the precise origins of the "Strang Mission."[60] It did not represent any lack of confidence in Seeds. The records to this point reveal almost no critical comments about him. When the Foreign Policy Committee met on 5 June, an unnamed member accused Seeds of not using "any close or sustained argument" when presenting the British case. In contrast, Cadogan empathized with the ambassador, noting, "I am sorry for Sir W. Seeds, who did his best in difficult circumstances" and "kept up his end fairly well."[61] Halifax went on record to say, when Maisky suggested that he journey to Moscow, that he regarded "this kind of business as better handled by Ambassadors."[62]

Strang arrived in Moscow on 14 June and carried with him papers prepared by the Foreign Office and approved by the prime minister.[63] These documents included instructions to be used in conversations with Molotov, a draft treaty, and notes on individual articles. Seeds was "given discretion to modify its expression, though he would leave the substance unchanged." Any draft articles proposed by Molotov, or by the British and French ambassadors in concert, were to be referred to London. The strategy was to end the negotiations quickly.

The question of the Baltic states now stood as the major, but not the only, stumbling block. The position in Moscow, as far as Seeds was concerned, was somewhat eased by the agreement of the French ambassador to act not only in concert, but also "jointly and simultaneously," and to encourage Paris to centre the negotiations in the Soviet capital.[64] An additional technical difficulty remained. Seeds reminded the Foreign Office that the negotiations required constant translation of documents into French. The oral translation at interviews was provided by Potemkin, who knew French, while the actual conversations led to what Seeds described as "misunderstandings inevitably to be expected both from the cumbrous procedure of a conversation in two languages [French and Russian] and from the tendency of Soviet negotiators to read their suspicions into imperfectly understood verbal statements."[65]

On 15 June, in a meeting that lasted two and three-quarter hours, Seeds, Strang, and Naggiar presented to Molotov, who was assisted by Potemkin, some of the materials brought from London. Whereas previously, Seeds observed, the two sides had exchanged entire draft treaties, he now proposed to examine contentious points "round the table one by one." Molotov again indicated that the discussion of the Baltic states did not meet the Soviet view. Indeed, when he recalled the two ambassadors on the following day, he warned them against treating the Soviet government as "naive and foolish" and placing it in a "humiliating position." At the conclusion, Molotov produced a written reply to the latest British–French representations, with the main emphasis on the guarantee to the Baltic states.[66] Seeds's impression, as conveyed in his diary, was that without receiving that guarantee Molotov would settle for nothing more than "a plain tripartite treaty providing only for indirect aggression on our three states."[67]

The French ambassador afterwards told Seeds that they should meet Soviet wishes on the issue.[68] Halifax telegraphed to Seeds that the reference to the Covenant could be dropped. For his part Seeds advised that there would be no point in continuing without a "review" of British proposals. Halifax's reaction was to reiterate the British perspective, exhorting Seeds to make "early and rapid progress" but to remain reluctant to divulge some vital British concession, unless Seeds was under pressure to do so. In other respects, Halifax left Seeds discretion regarding minor points of drafting.[69] The reality was that Seeds, helped by Strang, Roberts, Naggiar, and, from a distance, Sir William Malkin, principal legal adviser to the Foreign Office, was trying to meet the Soviet position, but always with the intention of allaying suspicions.[70] Strang privately observed how difficult were the "mechanics of the negotiations" and hence the ambassador's position. He found Molotov "stiff and hostile," ignorant of the outside world, and "impervious to argument." Strang observed cogently, "Nor can it be said that our negotiating position is a strong one." Nevertheless, he was confident that an agreement would finally emerge.

The negotiations resumed on 21 and 22 June, and so too did the haggling. Molotov demanded guarantees for the Baltic states and stated that no progress was evident in any of the British–French proposals, which he rejected as "unacceptable." In his diary Seeds commented that Molotov had "put us definitely in a take-it-or-leave-it position." Halifax confessed that he was "bewildered," reassured Seeds that he realized "the difficulty of dealing with a man of such inarticulate obstinacy," and asked for advice. Seeds replied that "argumentation and skillful formulae" were exhausted. He noted that Soviet suspicions were insurmountable and counselled meeting the Soviet demand of 2 June with its list of states to be guaranteed against aggression.[71]

During the following days, the negotiations again became the subject of intensive debate at the highest levels of government in London.[72] Another series of concessions, moulded by Halifax in consultation with the French government and Seeds, was developed. Seeds was given latitude to decide at what point to reveal these, but he himself believed that it was time to draw up a draft of the entire treaty.[73] When the two ambassadors met with Molotov on 1 and 3 July they were taken, yet again, by surprise. They had come prepared to see a list of guaranteed states included, as a secret annex, in the treaty, deletion of references to the League, and agreement to a no-separate-peace clause. Instead, they were met with some new twists. Molotov baulked at the inclusion of Luxembourg, the Netherlands, and Switzerland among the states to be guaranteed. Then he pointed out that the draft treaty made no provision for "indirect aggression" – the kind that had brought down Czechoslovakia in March. He proposed a secret protocol listing Estonia, Finland, Latvia, Poland, Romania, Turkey, Greece, and Belgium and defining indirect aggression as "an internal coup d'état or a reversal of policy in the interests of the aggressor."[74]

Seeds's reports of these developments precipitated another round of discussion in London. The possibility of breaking off the negotiations was rejected because of the massive amount of intelligence, not necessarily accurate, accumulating about secret contacts between the Soviet Union and Germany. As Halifax then put it, "our main object in the negotiations was to prevent Russia from engaging herself with Germany."[75] Moscow was not of course the easiest place to gather intelligence. By observing the activity at the German embassy, however, Seeds had concluded accurately that commercial negotiations were indeed in progress.[76] This was the same conclusion reached on 4 July in the Foreign Office. The discussions in London may have been marked by fatigue and growing cynicism, but this all led in one direction – continuation, with toughness.[77]

The "limit of concessions" was cabled on 6 July to Seeds. The British government was prepared to forgo guarantees to Luxembourg, the Netherlands and Switzerland, provided that Molotov abandoned his "completely unacceptable" definition of indirect aggression and substituted a British alternative which emphasized that there had to a be a clear threat of force. Again Halifax exhorted his ambassador to show, "in the near future, some result of our protracted negotiations."

Naggiar had asked for, but been denied, complete plenipotentiary powers to complete the negotiations. Such a request was never made by Seeds, who had previously received restricted powers. Now at last he was given permission to tidy up some of the outstanding issues, with some exceptions. "You realize of course," Halifax wrote on 6 July, "that we cannot agree to make entry into force of Agreement dependent on conclusion of military conversations."[78] It then took the British–French negotiating team in Moscow two days – 8 and 9 July – to carry out these instructions, without success. Molotov proposed a new definition of indirect aggression – an issue never resolved, despite strenuous efforts during the following weeks. Then came the latest sticking point. He insisted that the entry into force of the diplomatic agreement would depend on prior conclusion of a military agreement and on their simultaneous signature. "I think we can carry the negotiations no further without further instructions," Seeds wearily concluded in the early hours of the morning.[79]

With the negotiations having reached a crisis point, Halifax canvassed Seeds's view on 12 July about Soviet reaction to either a breakdown or to reverting to a tripartite agreement of mutual assistance. Seeds advised meeting this latest Soviet demand, as he opposed falling back to a treaty of mutual assistance or indeed breaking off the negotiations, "because there is no knowing whether there is not a party in Soviet Government ready to seize opportunity for securing a breakdown." However, in the event of a breakdown, Seeds preferred that it should come on the definition of indirect aggression, rather than on Article 6 of the draft treaty – that is, provision for simultaneous entry of the political and military agreements. In response, Halifax laid down a much tougher line for the ambassador to pursue. He set out why Britain could accept neither the loose definition of indirect aggression offered by Molotov nor the "completely abnormal procedure" proposed by the Soviet Union regarding Article 6. "I appreciate the fact that I am setting you an arduous task in instructing you to reject the two chief proposals which M. Molotov made to you at your last interview," Halifax observed, "but we are nearing the point where we clearly cannot continue the process of conceding each fresh demand put forward by the Soviet Government." Halifax concluded, "Our patience is well-nigh exhausted."[80]

Matters of high principle became yet more bargaining chips when discussions resumed on 17 July. Seeds had been instructed to trade, at a suitable moment, the immediate opening of military talks for the

Soviet Union's meeting British concerns on indirect aggression. Instead, Molotov demanded as a sine qua non the simultaneous entry into force of the political and military agreements. Otherwise, "there was no point in pursuing the present conversations."[81] London took this as an ultimatum, and it spurred some very cynical discussions about issuing a counterthreat.

Equally significant, the irritation in cabinet circles led to an unseemly search for scapegoats. The Foreign Policy Committee on 19 July questioned Seeds's competence for the second time. Sir Samuel Hoare, the home secretary, criticized Seeds for "not arguing the case as fully and exhaustively as it might be desirable to do. No doubt the local circumstances and conditions made this difficult, but he thought that His Majesty's Ambassador might be given a hint that he should go into all the points in greater detail and argue out each subject exhaustively." Halifax said "that he had derived much the same impression from the telegrams. He did not think any blame could rest on Sir W. Seeds and Mr. Strang who had no doubt done their best in most difficult and disagreeable circumstances." Sir Thomas Inskip, secretary of state for dominion affairs, felt that Seeds's position "had been a very difficult one because he had never been given definite instructions to stand fast on any particular point. He would have been in a much stronger position if he had been able to tell M. Molotov that the insistence of the Soviet Government on a particular matter would involve a breakdown of the negotiations." Chamberlain agreed "but felt that the telegrams gave the impression, no doubt quite wrongly, that we had been feeble and weak kneed in the discussions with M. Molotov." R.A. Butler, parliamentary under-secretary for foreign affairs, "reminded the Committee that … whenever the Ambassadors attempted to maintain a sustained argument M. Molotov interrupted them by saying that the Soviet Government had given their decision and demanding that they should pass on to the next item on the Agenda." Chancellor of the Exchequer Sir John Simon "did not agree with the view that had been expressed that our representatives in Moscow had been unable to argue our case exhaustively."

Chamberlain favoured calling the Soviet bluff, even at the risk of a breakdown.[82] Yet, in a startling turnabout, caused largely by pressure from the French government, the instructions sent to Seeds on 21 July indicated that the British were prepared to meet Soviet demands regarding Article 6 and open military talks even before finalizing the political agreement.[83]

Seeds's position appeared not to be at all harmed. Halifax continued to ask for his advice on strategy and also urged the ambassador "not [to] be unduly deterred either by modesty or the desire for brevity and economy from setting forth at length the part which you yourselves [i.e., including Strang] played in the discussion."[84] Seeds wrote privately that he was "somewhat hurt, in my pride as a well-trained diplomatist," by such advice. He believed that a diplomat "must speak to his brief but, in reporting home, must not yield to the fatal temptation of 'hearing himself speak' but must concentrate on reporting the reactions and views of the other side. A fatal temptation … [is] not to listen to the other side but to devote oneself entirely to planning one's next brilliant remark." Seeds went on: "And now let me get off my chest a grouse against certain sinners amongst whom I strongly suspect your friends the C*b***t M*n**t**s [sic] to be leading culprits. Can nothing be done to make people at home KEEP THEIR MOUTHS SHUT?" He complained that "indiscretions and leakages" had undermined his position as negotiator, making the talks "a heart-breaking experience … a fruitful source of misunderstandings and delays, and often a free gift to the German propagandist."[85]

The British concessions were well timed. On 21 July Moscow Radio announced the renewal of commercial discussions between the Soviet Union and Germany. Seeds and the French ambassador did not get to see Molotov until 23 July, when the latter announced his "keen satisfaction" with the news that the Soviet version of Article 6 was acceptable. Then Molotov declared that the definition of indirect aggression, the focus of such bitter contention for weeks, would no longer "raise insuperable difficulties." Why "waste time upon points of detail"?, he asked, and he added that military talks should start at once in Moscow. On 27 July Seeds brought Molotov news of British concurrence, which he received as a matter of course. The rest of the discussion returned to the definition of indirect aggression, but Seeds could report no progress.[86] Halifax felt assured that, with military talks imminent, there was no danger of a breakdown during the next critical weeks. On 29 July he ordered Seeds to take no further action "without further instructions from me."[87]

When Seeds went to the Kremlin on 2 August primed to tackle indirect aggression, he found Molotov unhelpful in the extreme. "M. Molotov was a different man from what he had been at our last interview," Seeds telegraphed, "and I feel our negotiations have received severe set-back." He anticipated a "pause" in the negotiations as the military mission took centre stage. On 4 August, Strang, on Seeds's suggestion, was recalled to London, where he arrived on 8 August.[88] The political negotiations never resumed, despite Strang's spending some time after his return, as he put it, "preparing a whole lot of new formulae to try and tempt M. Molotov."[89]

As much as anyone else, Seeds was aware of how dangerous it was to begin military talks without a political agreement. He had already alerted Halifax to the problems that lay ahead, indicating that he was pessimistic about the outcome. However, an early start would deliver "a healthy shock to the Axis Powers and a fillip to our friends." In addition, Seeds warned, the problem of passage rights for the Red Army through Poland would have to be resolved.[90]

The British and French military missions arrived in Moscow on 11 August, and talks opened the next day. Seeds took no direct part in these negotiations, except for one decisive but ultimately futile intervention. On 14 August the Soviet chief negotiator, Defence Minister Marshal K. Voroshilov, demanded that the Red Army have passage rights across Poland and Romania to engage with Germany. Seeds had already on his own initiative urged London to abandon the restricted instructions given to the head of the British mission, Admiral Drax. He wished to see the talks progress beyond these "vague generalities" because "the Soviet military negotiators are really out for business."

Seeds's intervention was successful, and he was no doubt relieved to read on 15 August new instructions for "bringing the military negotiations to a conclusion as soon as possible."[91] That was not to be. On 17 August, Voroshilov asked that the talks be suspended until Poland returned its reply. Both the British and the French applied enormous pressure on the Polish authorities. However, even as a compromise was reached with Poland, the Soviet press announced on 21 August conclusion of the commercial credit agreement between the Soviet Union and Germany and on the 22nd the impending visit to Moscow of the German foreign minister, Joachim von Ribbentrop, to conclude a non-aggression agreement.[92] Within hours of the latter's arrival on 23 August a Nazi–Soviet non-aggression treaty and a secret protocol dividing eastern Europe into spheres of influence were signed.

The Foreign Office shared Seeds's scepticism about possible Soviet–German political collaboration.[93] Consequently, Halifax instructed Seeds to get confirmation of the press communiqués and, if he confirmed them, to accuse Molotov of "an act of bad faith." It is not hard

to imagine Seeds's discomfiture as he and Molotov exchanged recriminations on the evening of 22 August. The Russian accused the British
of a "lack of sincerity." Seeds's diary recorded: "At 8 p.m. I had interview with Molotov when he pretended that it was our insincerity
which had forced Russians to treat with Germany and I had at any
rate satisfaction of talking to him of Russian 'bad faith' which
annoyed him extremely."[94] When the terms of the Nazi–Soviet Pact
appeared in the press, as well as the Soviet version of the reasons for
the breakdown in the military conversations, Seeds forwarded these
to the Foreign Office without comment. On 25 August, the day the
military mission left Moscow, Molotov told Seeds that the Soviet
government regarded the tripartite talks as ended.[95]

Several days later Seeds offered Halifax his views on these events.
He wrote that foreign circles in Moscow had been prepared for a
commercial agreement between Germany and the Soviet Union. He
admitted that he could foresee a breakdown and "an eventual decision of Soviet neutrality." However, the announcement on 22 August
of Ribbentrop's visit to conclude a political pact "came as a veritable
bombshell." He continued, "I must frankly confess that I did not
contemplate that the Soviet government ... could have the duplicity
to reach out the hand of friendship to the prime mover in the anti-
Comintern and, what might be called, aggression front." Finally,
Seeds expressed his gratification that "after months of patience and
self-control" he had instructions "to accuse the Soviet Prime Minister
to his face of 'bad faith,' a charge which an accuser cannot usually
make and survive."[96]

The fact of the matter is that Seeds did not long survive as ambassador. With the outbreak of war on 3 September, the position that he
occupied in Moscow was central, but only for a short time.[97] He early
on conceded that speculation about Soviet intentions could "only be
based on intuition." He predicted, wrongly, that the Soviet Union
would break off relations and, rightly, offered the first warning of the
forthcoming Soviet invasion of Poland.[98] The fate of Poland was a
bitter pill to swallow. In the Foreign Office, opinions divided between
those who would encourage genuine Soviet neutrality and the sceptics who argued that the Soviet Union's only objective was to "further
their own nefarious ends."[99]

However, British policy at this point was to maintain good relations
with the Soviet Union. In this, Seeds provided firm and consistent
support. On 17 September he observed that, despite the invasion of

Poland, "I do not myself see what advantage war with the Soviet Union would be to us." He then added candidly, "though it would please me personally to declare it on M. Molotov." He believed that a British–Soviet war would be playing into German hands and therefore favoured the "greatest possible moderation." Seeds also urged that negotiations be opened for an early war trade agreement with the Soviet Union and that these talks take place in London, "because our recent political and military negotiations here suffered from effect produced on these people's suspicious minds by delays arising from inevitable references home on our part." His views on locale were accepted, and negotiations proceeded.[100] Under wartime conditions, exports of such products as rubber and tin, ordered by the Soviet Union from Britain, had military value, with the same holding true for Soviet exports such as timber.[101] On 19 October an ad hoc barter agreement for these specific products was reached.

The intense activity at the Moscow embassy since the spring and the pace of events in Europe since the Nazi–Soviet Pact had taken their physical toll on Seeds. His diary records details of his several ailments, the anxieties that he felt, his sadness as colleagues departed, the increasing discomfort of an early winter in Moscow, the loss of embassy staff, and dwindling food supplies.[102] At the end of September and in early October Seeds briefly lost his composure. He feared that Soviet forces might seize British ships at Archangel and Murmansk and speculated that the Soviet Union might "at any time come into the war against us." His anxieties were aired in cabinet on 30 September and hastened the commercial negotiations. However, they also evoked the comment from Collier that Seeds "is misreading the Bolshevik character."[103] Asked to explain his pessimism, Seeds replied: "I have not reached a conclusion that Russia is coming into the war against us in the immediate future. But I think the chance is perhaps fifty–fifty that she may do so."[104] It was perhaps not coincidental, but the question of Seeds's future was already being discussed. On 13 October Anthony Eden, the secretary of state for the dominions, broached with Maisky the question of representation in Moscow and inquired what sort of person would work best with the regime, adding: "The position did not seem to be a very pleasant one for a diplomat." Collier also noted: "As regards the Moscow Embassy, I venture to suggest (and I know this view is shared by Mr. Strang) that the best sort of representation in present circumstances would be a solid, well-known peer, in the confidence of leading members of

H.M. Government." Cadogan and Halifax also had considered the question, but without reaching any conclusion.[105] Seeds polled his military attachés on possible Soviet entry into the war, and the reply, now supported by Seeds, was that this was not in Soviet interests. It is not surprising that it was Strang who recommended that the embassy be thanked for the materials, adding, "Sir W. Seeds would I am sure much appreciate a kind word."[106]

During October and November, the British government would have preferred continuing its campaign to improve Soviet relations, but obstacles persisted. The Soviet Union imposed mutual-assistance pacts on Estonia, Latvia, and Lithuania, and Seeds offered what little information he could glean from the press and official communiqués.[107] From Scandinavian ambassadors, he was able to provide information on the ominous Soviet–Finnish negotiations that were proceeding in Moscow.[108] On 25 October Molotov gave Seeds a note protesting against British contraband regulations and the methods used to examine neutral shipping. Britain resolved that issue later in November by relaxing the applications against the Soviet Union.[109]

The fact remained, however, that events were pressing on Seeds. On 19 November, in a letter to Strang, he confessed that Soviet intentions "have got me hopelessly beat." He concurred with diplomatic opinion in Moscow that the Soviet Union would develop closer relations with Germany. He now rejected his previous view that war would come between Britain and the Soviet Union. He lashed out against the communist press in Britain and at the freedom of expression enjoyed by "every anti-patriot, crank and half-wit," all of whose views were reproduced in the Soviet press. Seeds concluded: "Finally, to end this long screed, I would tell you who know this place that with a hostile press, small boys jeering at the flag on my car when I drive out, very few servants, nothing doing by way of entertaining by my colleagues, greatly reduced supplies from home, etc, etc, life for His Majesty's Ambassador in Moscow is even more [?] than usual." Fitzroy Maclean, a former embassy member, commented that Seeds "takes rather too gloomy a view of the dangers to us of Soviet–German cooperation; but he seems altogether rather depressed." To which Lascelles added, "And no wonder!"[110]

The Soviet invasion of Finland on 30 November put on hold any further attempts to improve British–Soviet relations. It also added to Seeds's ongoing discomfiture in Moscow. On 6 December he advised the Foreign Office that he no longer believed that British interests were served by the Soviet Union's remaining neutral. It was now apparent, he wrote, that "the Soviet Union has settled down definitely into an undeclared war against us" and that a German–Soviet rift was unlikely. He related, in great confidence, that the U.S. ambassador, Laurence A. Steinhardt, had suggested a Soviet blockade. "I confessed," wrote Seeds, "that my mind had lately been working on a somewhat similar line but that I was not at all clear that the moment had yet come." This telegram evoked some puzzlement as to what exactly the ambassador had in mind and a request to the cos to assess the consequences of going to war against the Soviet Union. Among the reasons cited was that "for Sir W. Seeds' guidance, we ought I think to explain to him why we don't agree with his analysis." So great was the burden of work for the cos that a response was completed and forwarded to the cabinet only on 8 March 1940.[111]

Seeds's telegram of 6 December evoked this observation: "For months now Sir W. Seeds has been unable to do any serious business with the Soviet Government, and it must now be admitted that the value of the Embassy as a listening post is very slight." Perhaps it was not sheer coincidence that Seeds was also exploring the possibility of the United States's looking after British interests in Moscow in the event of a breakdown in relations.[112] Such concerns were undercut by this brief telegram that Seeds sent to London on 22 December. "Having spent a year in Moscow in somewhat trying conditions I would be grateful if I could be granted a leave of absence in England starting early next month and leaving Mr. Le Rougetel in charge of His Majesty's Embassy." The leave of absence was approved at once.[113]

That, however, was *not* the full story. Seeds's diary for 22 December reveals the background: "Received this morning tel. from Sir A. Cadogan suggesting I shd go home on leave as they intend to publish a White Book on Anglo–Franco–Soviet pact negotiations, which might make my position here difficult for a time at least!" Soviet policy towards Finland and the Baltic states had indeed convinced the British government to lift the veil of secrecy about the tripartite negotiations and Soviet demands made relating to those areas. Chamberlain announced the proposal for a white paper in the House of Commons on 13 December.[114] Seeds's leave therefore potentially served a variety of purposes – including the question of his future.

On 31 December Seeds made his farewell visit to Molotov and expressed "his personal regrets at the present unsatisfactory relations between our two countries." After the collapse of the tripartite talks,

Seeds continued, he was prepared for a Soviet policy of strict neutrality, but he had been "distressed" by the attacks in the press and in speeches despite British attempts "to show goodwill." Could Molotov give him a message to carry back to London to help "relieve the tension?" What followed was a catalogue of alleged British misdeeds towards the Soviet Union, which included its hostile press, its supplying munitions to the Finns, and its spearheading the exclusion of the Soviet Union from the League of Nations. Seeds concluded his report: "Monsieur Molotov was personally friendly and spoke without heat but quite definitely." The interview confirmed that attempts to improve British–Soviet relations were unpromising. "Sir William Seeds was extremely forthcoming," Maclean observed, "but was rebuffed at every step by M. Molotov."[115] On 2 January 1940 Seeds and his wife, Lady Seeds, left Moscow, seen off by what he described as "[q]uite a lot of unfortunates [who] came to station to say farewell in bitterly cold weather." They travelled via Odessa and Bucharest to London, where they arrived after a strenuous eight-day train journey.[116]

Before his departure Seeds contributed to the 1939 annual report on political developments in the Soviet Union. This he did with a great deal of equanimity, despite his disappointments, and not without his usual sense of humour. Seeds recalled that he came to Moscow at an opportune time. While it was true that the Soviet Union was "sulking" over its being sidelined in 1938, possibilities existed to allay Soviet suspicions, to improve relations, and to convince that nation of Britain's serious resolve to improve relations. Such was the background against which he worked for the first three months of his mission.

Then he turned to "the ensuing and ill-fated negotiations" and indicated that there were: "certain fundamental factors which were present throughout and which rendered the success of the negotiations more than problematical ... I would beg not to be taken as condemning the policy of His Majesty's Government ... (for that would be both presumption on my part and also contrary to universal and my own conviction that an attempt had to be made), nor as criticizing certain errors of procedure (which were largely inevitable in the circumstances), nor ... as inviting censure for the certain degree of optimism which I may have shown during the negotiations (for a negotiator without hope is best deprived of his job)."

Of these "factors," Seeds considered personalities of the "foremost importance." After the removal of "that astute cosmopolitan, M. Litvinov," Soviet policy was in the hands of Stalin and his inner circle, who were provincial, regarded compromise as a sign of insincerity, and were "hard bargainers because they demand what they expect to receive." Seeds continued: "It was, indeed, one of the most unfortunate results of our position during all the negotiations that, although we were, in fact, the petitioners asking for the favour of Soviet assistance, we were compelled to refuse the far-reaching treaty offered us as early as the 2nd June and grudgingly to accept it only bit by bit." The second factor was Soviet suspicion and the belief that "Great Britain is ideologically and historically something very close to 'Enemy No. 1' in Soviet eyes." The "most heartbreaking feature of the negotiations" was the Soviet conviction that Britain was always working towards an agreement with Germany at Soviet expense.

Seeds then turned his attention, in a more outspoken manner, to "specific obstacles" to an agreement. He faulted the Poles for refusing to co-operate but pointed more to the "maddening efforts" to arrive at a definition of indirect aggression and the opening of military talks before a political agreement was concluded. He speculated that historians might "wonder at the persistence shown by the British and French Governments in carrying on these ill-fated negotiations for so many months and in the face of such obvious difficulties." He believed that "the remarkable wave of pro-Russian enthusiasm which swept Great Britain" compelled the negotiations to continue – whether it was "credulous believers in Stalin's selflessness," the "defeatists who saw in the Russian steamroller the answer to British defence," or that "the professional friends of the Soviet Union, press and public, worked themselves into a veritable fever." Under such circumstances, a democratic country had no option but to persist. Seeds concluded with a personal opinion that time and events would inform the public as "to the verities of the problem, to the patient pertinacity of His Majesty's Government and, I venture to add, to the grievous task imposed on myself and my most devoted and skillful collaborator, Mr. William Strang."[117]

As soon as Seeds's request for leave had been approved on 24 December, it was widely rumoured that he had been recalled, including suggestions that this was connected to the proposed white paper.[118] The Foreign Office tried to counter the impression that his departure was related to the deterioration in Soviet relations. On 3 January 1940 *The Times* reported from "well-informed quarters" that Seeds's return was not connected with the white paper, that he had a leave coming to him, and that his absence from Moscow would not be prolonged indefinitely.[119] On 27 January Lady Seeds gave a newspaper interview that was very critical of Soviet conditions. This led to some further speculation that Seeds would not return.[120]

In the ensuing months, when otherwise not in ill-health, Seeds consulted with the Foreign Office and maintained his belief that the Soviet Union did not want war with Britain.[121] He also spoke to various groups, including directors of Lloyds Bank, the Thirty Club, leading members of the Labour Party, and *The Times*. From 8 to 11 April he joined other British envoys from Hungary, Italy, and southeastern Europe at a conference on political and economic issues, presided over by Halifax at the Foreign Office. The occasion allowed Seeds to have his first tête-à-tête with Chamberlain.[122] Meanwhile, parliamentary questions and press speculation queried the future of British representation in Moscow. On 4 April Halifax minuted: "No date has at present been fixed for the return to Moscow of His Majesty's Ambassador now on leave in this country." This was repeated on 24 April and 8 May in the House of Commons. However, the parlous nature of British–Soviet relations, and Soviet pressure, hastened a resolution. The war cabinet began discussions on returning "an Ambassador to Moscow."

The end, which came suddenly for Seeds on 20 May, is recorded in his diary: "Bella and I by morning train to London. I called on Sir Alexander Cadogan (Perm. Under Sec. at F.O.) who informed me that I am not to go back to Moscow but that Sir Stafford Cripps, the extreme Left-Winger M.P., is to go there on Special Mission as with New National Govt. (which includes all prominent Labourites) it is hoped that the Kremlin may prove more amenable than it did to me as representing the infamous (!) Chamberlain."

Cadogan noted in his diary: "5.30 Seeds. Broke it to him that he wouldn't go back to Moscow and that there would be a 'special mission' there also! I can't agree to anymore. He took it very well."[123] Some last-minute complications regarding Cripps's status led to cabinet approval on 31 May for his appointment as ambassador. This was announced in the Commons on 5 June, and with it came public realization that Seeds had been replaced. He retired from the Foreign Office on 10 April 1941.[124]

For the most part, Seeds subsequently kept his silence. He lectured occasionally on tsarist Russia and life under the Bolsheviks. From 1943 to 1962 he served as the Foreign Office's representative on the Council of the School of Slavonic and East European Studies in

London. In an interview with the *Irish Times* after the war he stated that he did not regard the time ripe yet for him to talk of the events leading to the Nazi–Soviet Pact. In a rare exception, he wrote to *The Times* about "our toilsome negotiations in 1939," the "yelps" of the British press eager to ally with the Soviet Union, while "one Russian hand was kept firmly along the seam of his trousers while the other, behind his back, was groping for gifts from Hitler." From 1958 onwards he gave several interviews, but only to historians whom he regarded as serious students of the pre-war period.[125]

The short period of active service that Sir William Seeds gave as British ambassador to the Soviet Union, from January 1939 until January 1940, embraced one of the most crucial episodes in British–Soviet relations and in the immediate origins of the Second World War. On him fell the primary role in forging a British–French–Soviet alliance. This task was complex in the extreme. It demanded extraordinary diplomatic skills, patience, and perseverance. The talks were all the more difficult because they were carried on in three languages. As well, negotiations changed from the exchange of whole draft texts to on-site debates about specific articles and phrasing that required legal input. What was lacking was any kind of informal forum where participants could make contacts, iron out misunderstandings, and reach compromises. The process also demanded close co-ordination between Paris and London, which was not always possible, especially when the French ran ahead of the British. Continuous leaks to the press, mainly from Soviet diplomats in Western capitals, often cut the ground from under the principal negotiators in Moscow.[126] Certainly the intelligence dimension worked to Soviet advantage. It is likely that the Soviet spy in the Communications Department of the Foreign Office, exposed in September 1939, helped Soviet negotiators. In contrast, intelligence about Soviet–German contacts, leaked to the U.S. embassy in Moscow, was not shared with Seeds until very late.[127] Finally, the talks took place under the glare of international attention, subject to leaks and indiscretions, which made the notion of "behind-the-scenes" diplomacy a mockery.

Would a more sceptical approach by the ambassador have altered the course of the tripartite negotiations? In his final report for 1939, Seeds had answered that charge, noting that some optimism was required of every negotiator. His experience in Moscow in 1939 certainly provides evidence of the tenacity with which he pursued his mandate. There were occasions when his initiatives influenced the talks, and others when his views were disregarded. At times he was given some latitude to negotiate; other times his hands were tied. The authoritarian context within which Seeds had to operate, and the severe limitations placed thereby on an ambassador's freedom to manoeuvre, must have affected Seeds's efforts. However, in the final analysis, the role that he played and the assessments that he relayed to London were only two factors in an enormously complex multi-power decision-making process. The constraints imposed on him by politicians and a Foreign Office divided about the wisdom of a British–Soviet–French pact were also crucial, especially given that the tripartite negotiations were ultimately lost not in Moscow, but by the policy-making process in London and Paris.

Within the limits prescribed by his functions as a professional diplomat, and the inherently difficult nature of the Moscow post, a very adept emissary served the British government well. With the outbreak of war, and the subsequent deterioration in British–Soviet relations, there remained little scope for the exercise of any influence by the ambassador. By May 1940 it was time for Seeds to step aside, and he did. Within weeks the new ambassador, Sir Stafford Cripps, was already experiencing the humiliation of being kept waiting on the doormat. The Foreign Office advised him "to cultivate the virtues of patience and long-suffering, as indeed all British Ambassadors in Moscow are bound to do."[128]

NOTES

1 Sir William Seeds has received little attention from historians other than in S. Aster, *1939: The Making of the Second World War* (London, 1973). Some of Neville Chamberlain's other ambassadors during this period have been studied. See P. Neville, *Appeasing Hitler: The Diplomacy of Sir Nevile Henderson* (London, 2000) and "Nevile Henderson and Basil Newton: Two British Envoys in the Czech Crisis 1938," in I. Lukes and E. Goldstein, eds., *The Munich Crisis, 1938* (London, 1999), 258–75; D. Gillies, *Radical Diplomat: The Life of Archibald Clark Kerr, Lord Inverchapel, 1882–1951* (New York, 1999); J. Herman, *The Paris Embassy of Sir Eric Phipps: Anglo–French Relations and the Foreign Office, 1937–1939* (London, 1998); D.C. Watt, "Chamberlain's Ambassadors," in M. Dockrill and B. McKercher, eds., *Diplomacy and World Power: Studies in British Foreign Policy 1890–1950* (Cambridge, 1996), 136–70, on

Sir Nevile Henderson, Sir Eric Phipps, and Sir Robert Craigie;
B. Strang, "Two Unequal Tempers: Sir George Ogilvy-Forbes, Sir Nevile
Henderson and British Foreign Policy, 1938–1939," *Diplomacy and
Statecraft* 5 (1994), 107–37; B.D. Rhodes, "Sir Ronald Lindsay and
the British View from Washington, 1930–1939," in C.L. Egan and
A.W. Knott, eds., *Essays in Twentieth Century American Diplomatic
History Dedicated to Professor Daniel M. Smith* (Washington, DC, 1982),
62–83; V.B. Baker, "Nevile Henderson in Berlin: A Re-evaluation,"
Red River Valley Historical Journal of World History 2 (1977), 341–57;
G. Waterfield, *Professional Diplomat* (London, 1973), on Sir Percy
Loraine; and F. Gilbert, "Two British Ambassadors: Perth and
Henderson," in F. Gilbert and G. Craig, eds., *The Diplomats 1919–1939*,
Vol. 2, *The Thirties* (New York, 1965), 537–54.

2 The British–French–Soviet negotiations have been the subject of intense
historical examination. A full-scale study is M.J. Carley, *1939: The
Alliance That Never Was and the Coming of World War II* (Chicago, 1999).
Its bibliography lists many of the previous articles on the matter. See
also S. Aster, *British Foreign Policy 1918–1945: A Guide to Research and
Research Materials* (Wilmington, Del., 1991), 304–10.

3 Seeds to the author, 17 and 29 Sept. 1972; author's interview with
Seeds, 18 Sept. 1968. Seeds discussed his experiences in Moscow with
the author in interviews and correspondence from 1968 until before his
death on 2 November 1973.

4 Obituary by "A.N.N.," *The Times*, 17 Nov. 1973.

5 Sir William Seeds Papers, Diaries, 23 March, 6 and 24 April, 8 May
1935. I am very grateful to Corinna Seeds, of Hydra, Greece, for permission to consult the Seeds's family papers, which are in her possession. I am also indebted to her for sharing with me her recollections of
her grandfather Sir William Seeds and for enriching my understanding
of both the person and the personality.

6 Seeds Papers, Diaries, 20 Feb. 1937, 2 and 3 April 1938.

7 Ibid., Press Cuttings File for 1938–40; *The Times*, 16 Aug. 1938, 9 Jan.
1939.

8 Seeds Papers, Diaries, 27 Oct., 17 AND 29 Nov., 10 and 14 Dec. 1939.

9 Public Record Office (PRO), London, FO371/23683, N105, 326, 333, and
371/105/38, provide details of Seeds's appointment, salary, and so on.
An oversight regarding his official credentials and the letters of recall of
Lord Chilston almost delayed his assuming charge of the embassy:
FO372/3324, T1163, 1280, 1283/1120/377. Seeds's evident distress at this
episode is chronicled in Seeds Papers, Diaries, 25, 26, and 28 Jan. 1939.

10 PRO, FO371/23683, N751/105/38, Seeds to Halifax, 28 Jan. 1939;
    Documents on British Foreign Policy (DBFP), Third Series, Vol. IV, 45–6.
    Minutes in FO371/23683, N751/105/38, indicate that the Foreign Office
    regarded Seeds's audience as "undoubtedly a success" and that Seeds's
    Russian "is proving an asset."

11 Seeds Papers, Diaries, 28 Jan. 1939.

12 London School of Economics (LSE), Hugh Dalton Papers, Diaries,
    12 July 1939.

13 PRO, FO371/22980, C12678/15/18, Seeds to Halifax, 29 Aug. 1939; *DBFP*,
    Vol. VII, 383; FO371/23684, N1292/233/38, Seeds to Halifax, 6 March
    1939; *DBFP*, Vol. IV, 189. On the problems of relying on the Soviet press,
    see also FO371/23696, N1006/1006/38, Seeds to Halifax, 17 Feb. 1939.
    Seeds later lamented that he "nearly wept tears of boredom over a daily
    perusal of the Soviet press with its masses of statistics anent the pro-
    duction, say, of pig iron"; Letter to the Editor, *The Times*, 6 Oct. 1942.

14 E. Wrench, *I Loved Germany* (London, 1940), 228–9.

15 PRO, FO371/23685, N2547/233/38, Seeds to Halifax, 12 May 1939; *DBFP*,
    Vol. V, 545–6.

16 LSE, Dalton Papers, Diaries, 13 Feb. 1940.

17 PRO, FO371/23681, N1683/92/38, Seeds to Halifax, 28 March 1939;
    DBFP, Vol. IV, 524; FO371/23066, C7614/3356/18, Seeds to Oliphant,
    16 May 1939; *DBFP*, Vol. V, 572; FO371/23060, C514/3356/18, Seeds to
    Halifax, 13 April 1939; *DBFP*, Vol. V, 104.

18 PRO, FO371/23686, N3287/281/38, Seeds to Halifax, Report on Heads
    of Foreign Missions at Moscow, 5 July 1939. Seeds wrote of Naggiar:
    "A tiny swarthy little man with a prominent nose, looking like a
    Levantine sparrow, M. Naggiar is brimming over with intelligence,
    activity and cynical wit. I could not have wished for a more helpful
    and loyal colleague in the current negotiations with the Soviet Govern-
    ment. He has a good knowledge of English." Arabella, Lady Seeds
    confirmed this impression, writing that "[t]he French Ambassador
    both Willie & Strang like very much, he is very clever & an interesting
    talker, is never dull." Seeds Papers, Diaries, Lady Seeds to Theobald
    Butler, 5 Aug. 1939.

19 PRO, FO371/23686, Seeds to Halifax, 2 Feb. 1939; FO371/23687, N513/
    411/38, Seeds to Halifax, 27 Jan. 1939; *DBFP*, Vol. IV, 34. See also the
    minutes on this telegram in FO371/23687, N513/411/38, minutes by
    Laurence Collier in FO371/23686, N464/243/38, 24, 27, and 28 Jan.
    1939, FO371/23687, N453/411/38, 30 Jan. 1939, FO371/23680, N511/92/
    38, and FO371/23686, N464/243/38, Vereker to Collier, 14 Jan. 1939.

20 PRO, FO371/23683, N750/105/38, Seeds to Halifax, 26 Jan. 1939; *DBFP*, Vol. IV, 24–5.

21 PRO, FO371/23677, N902/57/38, Seeds to Halifax, 19 Feb. 1939; *DBFP*, Vol. IV, 123–4; FO371/23677, N669/57/38, Halifax to Seeds, 14 Feb. 1939; *DBFP*, Vol. IV, 106–7.

22 The British position is summarized in PRO, FO371/23680, N375/92/39, memorandum by Oliver Stanley, Board of Trade, 1 Feb. 1939. Halifax to Seeds, 2 March 1939, with notes by Collier, 2 February 1939, gave Seeds the rationale for using trade negotiations to improve British–Soviet diplomatic relations.

23 PRO, FO371/23677, N57, 1029/57/38, minutes by Caccia, Lascelles, Collier, Ashton-Gwatkin, Cadogan, and Vansittart, and by Oliphant and Cadogan, in FO371/23697, N1459/1459/38, provide evidence on the variety of opinions in the Foreign Office on the Soviet Union at the time Seeds was appointed.

24 PRO, FO371/23677, N902/57/38, Seeds to Halifax, 19 Feb. 1939; *DBFP*, Vol. IV, 123–4; FO371/23697, N1459/1459/38, Seeds to Oliphant, 21 Feb., Oliphant to Seeds, 20 March 1939.

25 PRO, FO371/23684, N1292/233/38, 6 March 1939; *DBFP*, Vol. IV, 188–99. The personnel included in the exercise, who had not been in the Soviet Union much longer than Seeds, were F.H.R. Maclean, 2nd secretary, February 1937–April 1939; Colonel R.C.W.G. Firebrace, military attaché, April 1937–December 1939; Wing Commander C. Hallawell, air attaché, March 1937–November 1941; and F.H. Todd, commercial secretary, August 1938–May 1940. The only one to have published an account of his experiences in Moscow was Fitzroy Maclean, *Eastern Approaches* (London, 1961). See also F. McLynn, *Fitzroy Maclean* (London, 1992). The Foreign Office's Northern Department, otherwise silent on the personnel of the British embassy, singled out Todd for his poor command of English, while Collier noted, "the chancery as a whole are not strong on the literary side." Minutes by Lascelles, 29 July, and Collier, 27 July 1939, in FO371/23688, N3507/478/38.

26 Firebrace, who spoke Russian, told the author that his ability to assess the Soviet military at first hand was negligible. He was always followed by the Soviet police and thus had to rely on the press and other military attachés. The only Soviet officer whom he ever met was Marshal Voroshilov. Author's interview with Colonel Firebrace, 6 Aug. 1968. His isolation is confirmed in PRO, FO371/23688, N485, 489, 1014/ 485/38. The comments of MI-2 are in FO371/23688, N1542/484/38, Brownjohn to Collier, 16 March 1939. See also K. Neilson, "Pursued by

a Bear: British Estimates of Soviet Military Strength and Anglo–Soviet Relations 1922–1939," *Canadian Journal of History* 28 (1993), 216–21; J.J. Herndon, "British Perceptions of Soviet Military Capability 1935–1939," in W. Mommsen and L. Kettenacker, eds., *The Fascist Challenge and the Policy of Appeasement* (London, 1983), 308–19; and FO371/23688, N1014/485/38, Firebrace to Seeds, 7 Feb. 1939. Seeds later discovered that for almost two years his military attachés "had been given no facilities for carrying on their work." FO371/23677, N1895/57/38, Seeds to Oliphant, 4 April 1939; FO371/23678, N2546/57/38, Seeds to Halifax, 16 May 1939.

27 The Northern Department found the document "of great value and interest" and recommended its distribution – "King, Cabinet, Dominions." Sir Lancelot Oliphant, deputy under-secretary of state for foreign affairs, observed: "[B]oth the dispatch from Sir William Seeds himself – with only a few weeks personal experience of Soviet life but with abundant knowledge of Imperial Russia – and the memoranda from more experienced members of his staff, make extremely interesting reading." PRO, FO371/23684, N1292/233/38, minutes by Lascelles, 15 March, and Oliphant, 17 March 1939.

28 PRO, FO371/23684, N1598/233/38, Seeds to Halifax, 20 March 1939; DBFP, Vol. IV, 411–19. Foreign Office minutes raised concern that the speech did not provide much encouragement for Hudson's mission to Moscow: FO371/23684, N1320/233/38, Minutes by Collier and Oliphant, 13 March 1939.

29 PRO, FO371/23065, C7010/3356/18, provides a narrative of British–Soviet relations, March–May 1939.

30 PRO, FO371/23060, C3356/3356/18, Halifax to Seeds, 17 March 1939; DBFP, Vol. IV, 360–1. In a highly praised personal appraisal, Seeds doubted that the Soviet Union would actively help Romania: minutes in FO371/23061, C3968/3356/18.

31 PRO, FO371/23060, C3598/3356/18, Halifax to Phipps, Seeds, and Kennard, 20 March 1939; DBFP, Vol. IV, 400–1; FO371/23061, C3683/3356/18, Seeds to Halifax, 21 March 1939; DBFP, Vol. IV, 429; FO371/23061, C3821/3356/18, Seeds to Halifax, 22 March 1939; DBFP, Vol. IV, 467.

32 Carley, *1939*, 108–12. The venture into political discussions, supported by Seeds, was also approved by Collier, who minuted on 29 March, "We may have our doubts as to the positive value of Soviet help ... [but] Soviet goodwill is of advantage to us"; PRO, FO371/23681, N1683/92/38. In his diary Seeds wrote of the "strain of ... keeping Hudson within bounds ... all spoilt by inexplicable action of FO in

refusing at last moment to allow publication of a communiqué containing vague references to political talks, as a result of which Hudson &
I and staff spent miserable hours trying to get hold of Litvinoff who,
when we got him, told us it was too late. So that communiqué was
published by Soviet agency, and Hudson left for Helsingfors [Helsinki]
with conviction that his political career had been ruined." Seeds
Papers, Diaries, 27 March 1939. The commercial discussions, tied by
Britain's Board of Trade to the outcome of the tripartite negotiations,
were eventually overcome by events. See minutes in FO371/23682,
N3503, 3517, 3605, 3710, 3861/92/38.

33 Aster, *1939*, 88–95; PRO, FO371/23063, C5144/3356/18, Seeds to Halifax,
14 April 1939; DBFP, Vol. V, 205.

34 PRO, FO371/230/16, C4575/54/18, Seeds to Halifax, 1 April 1939; DBFP,
Vol. IV, 574–5; A.A. Gromyko, ed., *Soviet Peace Efforts on the Eve of World
War II, September 1938–August 1939, Documents and Records* (Moscow,
1973), 234.

35 Lord Strang, *The Moscow Negotiations 1939* (Leeds, 1968), 10.

36 PRO, FO371/23016, C4864/54/18, Seeds to Halifax, 6 April 1939; DBFP,
Vol. V, 45–6; FO371/23016, C4884/54/18, C5068/3356/18, Halifax to
Seeds, 6 and 11 April 1939; DBFP, Vol. V, 53–4, 82–4.

37 PRO, FO371/23063, C5144/3356/18, Seeds to Halifax, 13 April 1939;
DBFP, Vol. V, 104; FO371/23063, C5330/3356/18, Seeds to Halifax,
14 April 1939; DBFP, Vol. V, 198–9.

38 PRO, FO371/23063, C5144/3356/18, Halifax to Seeds, 14 April 1939;
DBFP, Vol. V, 205; FO371/22969, C5460/15/18, Seeds to Halifax, 18 April
1939; DBFP, Vol. V, 228–9.

39 Seeds Papers, Diaries, 17 April 1939.

40 PRO, FO371/22969, C5460/15/18, Halifax to Phipps, 21 April 1939;
DBFP, Vol. V, 267; FO371/23741, R3287/661/67, Seeds to Halifax,
25 April 1939; DBFP, Vol. V, 319.

41 PRO, FO371/23685, N2253/233/38, Seeds to Halifax, 4 May 1939; DBFP,
Vol. V, 410, 412–13.

42 Seeds Papers, Diaries, 4 May 1939; PRO, FO371/23065, C6705/3356/18,
Halifax to Seeds, 6 May 1939; DBFP, Vol. V, 443, 448–50, 453–4.

43 PRO, FO371/23065, C6804/3356/18, Seeds to Halifax, 9 May 1939; DBFP,
Vol. V, 469–71; Seeds Papers, Diaries, 8 May 1939.

44 PRO, FO371/23685, N2547/233/38, Seeds to Halifax, 12 May 1939; DBFP,
Vol. V, 542–6.

45 The significance of Litvinov's dismissal, as analysed by Foreign Office
personnel, was summarized by the comment: "The outlook is dark

whatever the explanation ... and Molotov himself is both ignorant and crude." PRO, FO371/23685, N2282/233/38, minute by Lascelles, 5 May 1939. Further discussion in FO371/23685, N2253, N2282, 2547/233/38; FO371/23697, N2752/1459/38; and FO371/23678, N254657/38, Seeds to Halifax, 16 May 1939.

46 PRO, FO371/23066, C7614, 3356/18, Seeds to Oliphant, 16 May 1939; DBFP, Vol. V, 571–2; FO371/23685, N2346/233/38, Seeds to Halifax, 9 May 1939; DBFP, Vol. V, 471; Seeds Papers, Diaries, 9 and 11 May 1939. Strang affirmed that Potemkin did his job well: PRO, FO371/23069, C9010/3356/18, Strang to Sargent, 21 June 1939; DBFP, Vol. VI, 138. Seeds found him "somewhat of a poseur and maker of phrases." FO371/23103, C15398/13953/18, Seeds to Halifax, 25 Sept. 1939.

47 PRO, FO371/23066, C7065/3356/18, Seeds to Halifax, 15 May 1939; DBFP, Vol. V, 558–9.

48 Seeds Papers, Diaries, 19 May 1939; PRO, FO371/23066, C7280/3356/18, Seeds to Halifax, 18 May 1939; DBFP, Vol. V, 590; FO371/23067, C7935/3356/18, Seeds to Halifax, 22 May 1939; DBFP, Vol. V, 647–8.

49 See Aster, 1939, 174–84, R. Manne, "The British Decision for Alliance with Russia, May 1939," Journal of Contemporary History 9 (1974), 3–26, and L.G. Grace, The British Political Elite and the Soviet Union, 1937–1939 (London, 2003), 117–42.

50 PRO, FO371/23066, C7469/3356/18, Cadogan to Halifax, 23 May 1939; D. Dilks, ed., The Diaries of Sir Alexander Cadogan 1938–1945 (London, 1971), 182; FO371/23066, C7661/3356/18, Halifax to Seeds, 25 and 26 May 1939; DBFP, Vol. V, 678–81, 688.

51 PRO, FO371/23068, C8598/3356/18, Seeds to Halifax, 17 June 1939; DBFP, Vol. V, 89–91; FO371/23069, C8840/3356/18, Seeds to Halifax, 20 June 1939; DBFP, Vol. V, 115–20.

52 PRO, FO371/23067, C7758/3356/18, C7939/3356/18, Seeds to Halifax, 30 May 1939; DBFP, Vol. V, 722.

53 Seeds Papers, Diaries, 27 May 1939; PRO, FO371/23066, C7682/3356/18, Seeds to Halifax, 27 May 1939; DBFP, Vol. V, 701–2. Even the Soviet record refers to Seeds's "look of extreme amazement" at reaction to the British–French proposals: Gromyko, ed., Soviet Peace Efforts on the Eve of World War II, 345.

54 PRO, FO371/23067, C7895/3356/18, Seeds to Halifax, 1 June 1939; DBFP, Vol. V, 736.

55 PRO, FO371/23069, C8661/3356/18, Halifax to Phipps, 19 June 1939; DBFP, Vol. VI, 106; FO371/23069, C9182/3356/18, Seeds to Halifax, 30 June 1939; DBFP, Vol. VI, 209–10.

56 PRO, FO371/23067, C7939/3356/18, Seeds to Halifax, 30 May 1939; DBFP, Vol. V, 725–7; FO371/23069, C8928/3356/18, Seeds to Halifax, 24 June 1939; DBFP, Vol. VI, 160–3.

57 PRO, FO371/23067, C7886/3356/18, Seeds to Halifax, 1 June 1939; DBFP, Vol. V, 743–6. It was possibly a sign of displeasure that neither Seeds nor Naggiar, who had returned to Moscow, attended. Seeds Papers, Diaries, 31 May 1939.

58 PRO, FO371/23067, C7970/3356/18, Seeds to Halifax, 2 June 1939; DBFP, Vol. V, 753–4.

59 PRO, FO371/23067, C7970/3356/18, Halifax to Seeds, 6 June 1939; DBFP, Vol. V, 776–7; FO371/23067, C8097/3356/18, Halifax to Seeds, 7 June 1939; DBFP, Vol. V, 787. Seeds Papers, Diary, 3 and 7 June 1939, suggests that Seeds may not have been displeased to be spared the return trip.

60 For details see Aster, 1939, 264–8. Strang's recollections are in his Home and Abroad (London, 1956), 173–98, and The Moscow Negotiations, 1939 (Leeds, 1968). From 14 to 22 June he was joined by Frank Roberts, a member of the Foreign Office's Central Department and ambassador to Moscow 1960–62. See Frank Roberts, Dealing with Dictators: The Destruction and Revival of Europe 1930–70 (London, 1991), 36–8. Another guest at the Moscow embassy at this time was John Dilke, sent by The Times as special correspondent to cover the negotiations. He was in fact Seeds's son-in-law. Noting this in his diary, Seeds wrote that "we are not giving any information whatever to press!" Seeds Papers, Diaries, 19 June 1939. On Dilke, see also entry of 5 April 1939 in G. Martel, ed., The Times and Appeasement: The Journals of A.L. Kennedy, 1932–1939 (London, 2000), 288.

61 PRO, CAB27/625, Minutes, Foreign Policy Committee (FPC), 5 June 1939; FO371/23067, C7936, 7937/3356/18, minute by Cadogan, 10 June 1939, and by R.A. Butler, who wrote on 12 June, "Sir W. Seeds seems to do better than he himself makes out."

62 PRO, FO371/23068, C8214/3356/18, Halifax to Seeds, 8 June 1939; DBFP, Vol. VI, 6.

63 PRO, FO371/23068, C8440/3356/18, FO memorandum 12 June 1939; DBFP, Vol. VI, 33–41; FO371/23068, C8565/3356/18, minute by Cadogan, 15 June 1939.

64 PRO, FO371/23068, C8436/3778/18, Seeds to Halifax, 13 June 1939; DBFP, Vol. VI, 54–6; FO371/23068, C8461/3356/18, Seeds to Halifax, 14 June 1939; DBFP, Vol. VI, 65.

65 PRO, FO371/23069, C8840/3356/18, Seeds to Halifax, 20 June 1939; DBFP, Vol. VI, 116.

66 PRO, FO371/23068, C8506/3356/18, Seeds to Halifax, 15 June 1939;
    DBFP, Vol. VI, 79; FO371/23068, C8599/3356/18, Seeds to Halifax,
    16 June 1939; *DBFP*, Vol. VI, 85–7; FO371/23068, C8598/3356/18, Seeds
    to Halifax, 17 June 1939; *DBFP*, Vol. VI, 89–91.

67 Seeds Papers, Diaries, 15 and 16 June 1939.

68 PRO, FO371/23068, C8595/3356/18, Seeds to Halifax, 17 June 1939;
    DBFP, Vol. VI, 91.

69 PRO, FO371/23068, C8565/3356/18, Halifax to Seeds, 17 June 1939;
    DBFP, Vol. VI, 92; FO371/23068, C8644/3356/18, Seeds to Halifax, 18
    June 1939; *DBFP*, Vol. VI, 98; FO371/23069, C8661/3356/18, Halifax to
    Seeds, 19 June 1939; *DBFP*, Vol. VI, 103–5; FO371/23068, C8710, 8711/
    3356/18, Halifax to Seeds, 21 June 1939; *DBFP*, Vol. VI, 128–9.

70 PRO, FO371/23068, C8704, 8710, 8711/3356/18, Seeds to Halifax,
    20 June 1939; *DBFP*, Vol. VI, 109–12; FO371/23069, C9010/3356/18,
    Strang to Sargent, 21 June 1939; *DBFP*, Vol. VI, 138–40.

71 Seeds Papers, Diaries, 22 June 1939; PRO, FO371/23068, C8769/3356/18,
    Seeds to Halifax, 22 June 1939; *DBFP*, Vol. VI, 140–3; FO371/23068,
    C8769/3356/18, Halifax to Seeds, 22 June 1939; *DBFP*, Vol. VI, 144–5;
    FO371/23069/C8928/3356/18, Seeds to Halifax, 24 June 1939; *DBFP*,
    Vol. VI, 160–3.

72 Aster, *1939*, 269–71.

73 PRO, FO371/23069, C8928/3356/18, Halifax to Seeds, 27 June 1939;
    DBFP, Vol. VI, 173; FO371/23069, C9084/3356/18, Seeds to Halifax,
    29 June 1939; *DBFP*, Vol. VI, 179; FO371/23069, C9084/3356/18, Halifax
    to Seeds, 29 June 1939; *DBFP*, Vol. VI, 193–4; FO371/23069, C9154/3356/
    18, Seeds to Halifax, 30 June, 1 July 1939; *DBFP*, Vol. VI, 208–9; FO371/
    23069, C9182/3356/18, Seeds to Halifax, 30 June 1939; *DBFP*, Vol. VI,
    209–12.

74 PRO, FO371/23069, C9229/3356/18, Seeds to Halifax, 1 July 1939; *DBFP*,
    Vol. VI, 230–2; FO371/23069, C9293, 9286, 9295/3356/18, Seeds to
    Halifax, 4 July 1939; *DBFP*, Vol. VI, 251–2.

75 PRO, CAB27/625, Minutes, FPC, 4 July 1939.

76 PRO, FO371/23068, C8265/3356/18, Seeds to Halifax, 10 June 1939;
    DBFP, Vol. VI, 22; FO371/23068, C8489/3356/18, Seeds to Halifax,
    15 June 1939; *DBFP*, Vol. VI, 77.

77 PRO, CAB27/625, Minutes, FPC, 4 July, 1939; CAB23/100, Cabinet
    Minutes, 5 July 1939; FO371/23686, N3335/243/38, MI2, "The
    Possibilities of a Soviet–German Rapprochement," 4 July 1939.

78 PRO, FO371/23069, C9295/3356/18, Halifax to Seeds, 6 July 1939; *DBFP*,
    Vol. VI, 275–8; Carley, *1939*, 170–1.

79 Molotov defined "indirect aggression" as action accepted by any of the
states in the secret annex "under threat of force by another Power, or
without any such threat, involving the use of territory and forces of the
State in question for purposes of aggression against that State or
against one of the contracting parties, and consequently involving the
loss of, by that State, its independence or violation of its neutrality."
PRO, FO371/23070, C9599/3356/18, Seeds to Halifax, 10 July 1939; DBFP,
Vol. VI, 313.

80 PRO, FO371/23070, C9709/3356/18, Halifax to Seeds, 11 July 1939; DBFP,
Vol. VI, 319–20; FO371/23070, C9755/3356/18, Seeds to Halifax, 12 July
1939; DBFP, Vol. VI, 332; FO371/23070, C9709/3356/18, Halifax to Seeds,
12 July 1939; DBFP, Vol. VI, 333–6.

81 PRO, FO371/23070, C9889/3356/18, Halifax to Seeds, 15 July 1939; DBFP,
Vol. VI, 360; FO371/23070, C10054/3356/18, Seeds to Halifax, 18 July
1939; DBFP, Vol. VI, 375–7.

82 PRO, CAB27/625, Minutes, FPC, 19 July 1939.

83 PRO, FO371/23070, C10054/3356/18, Halifax to Seeds, 21 July 1939;
DBFP, Vol. VI, 427–9. On 20 July Strang described the negotiations as a
"humiliating experience … We could probably have got a better agreement by closing quickly with the substance of the Soviet draft of the
2nd June than we shall get today … The Ambassador has read this
letter and agrees with it." FO371/23071, C10507/3356/18, Strang to
Sargent, 20 July 1939; DBFP, Vol. VI, 422–6.

84 PRO, FO371/23070, C10054/3356/18, Halifax to Seeds, 2 and 22 July
1939; DBFP, Vol. VI, 430–1, 448.

85 PRO, FO371/23073, C11927/3356/18, Seeds to Sargent, 3 Aug. 1939.

86 PRO, FO371/23071, C10319/3356/18, Seeds to Halifax, 24 July 1939;
DBFP, Vol. VI, 456–60; FO371/23071, C10316/3356/18, Halifax to Seeds,
25 July 1939; DBFP, Vol. VI, 478; FO371/23071, C10580/3356/18, Seeds
to Halifax, 28 July 1939; DBFP, Vol. VI, 521–5.

87 PRO, FO371/23071, C10277/3356/18, Halifax to Seeds, 28 July 1939;
DBFP, Vol. VI, 525; FO371/23682, N3503/92/38, Halifax to Seeds, 29 July
1939; DBFP, Vol. VI, 533.

88 PRO, FO371/23072, C10821, 10886/3356/18, Seeds to Halifax, 3 Aug.
1939; DBFP, Vol. VI, 570–4, 575–6, 592; FO371/23072, C10886/3356/18,
Halifax to Seeds, 4 Aug. 1939; DBFP, Vol. VI, 592; Gromyko, ed., Soviet
Peace Efforts on the Eve of World War II, 458–9. On 12 August a new formula for "indirect aggression," almost coinciding with the Soviet definition, was approved by Chamberlain. It never saw the light of day in
Moscow. It was certainly Lady Seeds's impression that the ambassador

and Strang had enjoyed a very good working relationship. See Seeds
Papers, Diaries, Lady Seeds to Charlotte Elizabeth Butler, 21 June,
13 July, and 5 Aug. 1939, and Lady Seeds to Theobald Butler,
5 Aug. 1939.

89 Seeds Papers, Diaries, Strang to Lady Seeds, 10 Aug. 1939.

90 PRO, FO371/23071, C10325/3356/18, Seeds to Halifax, 24 July 1939;
   DBFP, Vol. VI, 460–1; FO371/23071, C10496/3356/18, 26 July 1939; *DBFP*,
   Vol. VI, 493–4.

91 PRO, FO371/23072, C11275/3356/18, Seeds to Halifax, 13 Aug. 1939;
   DBFP, Vol. VI, 682–3; FO371/23072, C11275/3356/18, Halifax to Seeds,
   15 Aug. 1939; *DBFP*, Vol. VII, 8–9.

92 PRO, FO371/23687, N3880/411/38, Seeds to Halifax, 21 Aug. 1939; *DBFP*,
   Vol. VII, 99; FO371/23073, C11718/15/18, 22 Aug. 1939; *DBFP*, Vol. VII,
   118.

93 Foreign Office intelligence on the Nazi-Soviet negotiations was
   analysed in: PRO, FO371/23686, N4146/243/38, memorandum by
   Collier, 25 Aug. 1939. See also D.C. Watt, "An Intelligence Surprise:
   The Failure of the Foreign Office to Anticipate the Nazi–Soviet Pact,"
   Intelligence and National Security 4 (1989), 512–34.

94 Seeds Papers, Diaries, 22 Aug. 1939; PRO, FO371/23073, C11778/3356/
   18, Halifax to Seeds, 22 Aug. 1939; *DBFP*, Vol. VII, 121–2, 126–7; FO371/
   23073/C11740/3356/18, Seeds to Halifax, 23 Aug. 1939; *DBFP*, Vol. VII,
   142–3.

95 PRO, FO371/23073, C11856/3356/18, Seeds to Halifax, 23 Aug. 1939;
   DBFP, Vol. VII, 154–5; FO371/23080, C11946/3778/18, Seeds to Halifax,
   24 Aug. 1939; *DBFP*, Vol. VII, 197; FO371/23073, C12060/3356/18, Seeds
   to Halifax, 25 Aug. 1939, *DBFP*, Vol. VII, 237; FO371/23070, C12154/
   3356/18, Seeds to Halifax, 27 Aug. 1939; *DBFP*, Vol. VII, 305–6.

96 PRO, FO371/22980, C12678/15/18, Seeds to Halifax, 29 Aug. 1939; *DBFP*,
   Vol. VII, 383–5; minutes from the same file by Roberts on 6 September,
   and by Strang and Collier on 7 September, expressed sympathy for
   Seeds's views. On 11 September, Seeds further argued that the Nazi–
   Soviet political negotiations were very "last minute" and poorly pre-
   pared: FO371/22983/C13871/15/18, Seeds to Halifax, 11 Sept. 1939.
   G. Roberts, "The Alliance That Failed: Moscow and the Triple Alliance
   Negotiations 1939," *European History Quarterly* 26 (1996), 383–414, suggests that Soviet evidence confirms that a triple alliance was feasible
   until early August.

97 British–Soviet relations for this early period of the war can be followed
   in P.W. Doerr, "'Frigid but Unprovocative': British Policy towards the
   USSR from the Nazi–Soviet Pact to the Winter War, 1939," *Journal of*

Contemporary History 36 (2001), 423–9; G. Roberts, *The Unholy Alliance: Stalin's Pact with Hitler* (London, 1989); S.M. Miner, *Between Churchill and Stalin: The Soviet Union, Great Britain, and the Origins of the Grand Alliance* (Chapel Hill, NC, 1988); M. Kitchen, *British Policy towards the Soviet Union during the Second World War* (London, 1986); and G. Gorodetsky, *Stafford Cripps' Mission to Moscow 1940–1942* (Cambridge, 1984).

98 PRO, FO371/22983, C13871/15/18, Seeds to Halifax, 11 Sept. 1939; FO371/23699, N4282, 4287, 4295/4030/38, Seeds to Halifax, 9 and 10 Sept. 1939.

99 PRO, FO371/23682, N4510/92/38, minutes by Collier and Oliphant, 14 Sept. 1939.

100 PRO, FO371/23103, C14003, 14247/13953/18, Seeds to Halifax, 17 and 19 Sept. 1939. For a detailed account of the German invasion of Poland as seen from Moscow, see FO371/23103, C15398/13953/18, Seeds to Halifax, 25 Sept. 1939.

101 PRO, FO371/23682, N4510/92/38, memorandum by Stanley, 13 Sept. 1939; FO371/23682, N5434/92/38, memorandum, "Trade with Russia," Board of Trade, 18 Oct. 1939.

102 Seeds Papers, Diaries, 25 and 31 Aug., 6, 16, 23, and 28 Sept., 9 Oct. 1939. Noel Coward, on a visit to Moscow that summer, which included a meeting with Seeds, noted that the ambassador "looked frail and strained, for he ... for a long time had had the unenviable task of dealing with the complex Russian mentality." N. Coward, *Autobiography* (London, 1986), 303.

103 PRO, FO371/23700, N4839/4427/38 Seeds to Halifax, 29 Sept. 1939; FO371/23678, N5131/57/38, Seeds to Halifax, 9 Oct. 1939; FO371/23682, N4939/92/38, War Cabinet Conclusions, 30 Sept. 1939; FO371/23678, N5131/57/38, minute by Collier, 11 Oct. 1939.

104 PRO, FO371/23678, N5131/57/38, Halifax to Seeds, 11 Oct. 1939; FO371/23678, N5240/57/38, Seeds to Halifax, 13 Oct. 1939. At the same time Seeds also had to admit that "reliable information" on what was happening in the Soviet Union was impossible to obtain: FO371/23698, N5359/2035/38, Seeds to Halifax, 8 Oct. 1939.

105 PRO, FO371, 23682, N5426/92/38, Eden to Halifax, 13 Oct., minutes by Collier, Oliphant, and Cadogan, 19 and 20 Oct. 1939. Cripps affirmed that he was approached at this time by Churchill to fill the Moscow post. C. Cooke, *The Life of Richard Stafford Cripps* (London, 1957), 251.

106 PRO, FO371/23678, N5778/57/38, Seeds to Halifax, 20 Oct. 1939, with reports by Clanchy, Firebrace, and Hallawell, and minute by Strang, 5 Nov. 1939.

107 See miscellaneous files in PRO, FO371/23689, and FO371/23690, N5714/
518/38, Seeds to Halifax, 20 Oct. 1939.

108 PRO, FO371/23693, N5732/991/38, Seeds to Halifax, 28 Oct. 1939.
FO371/24791, N183/1/56, provides an account of events leading to the
Soviet attack on Finland on 30 November 1939, and FO371/24791,
N191/1/56, Seeds to Halifax, 20 Dec. 1939, continues the analysis.

109 See PRO, FO371/23071, N5637, 5638, 5853, 6584, 7215/5637/38.

110 PRO, FO371/23698, N6979/1459/38, Seeds to Strang, 19 Nov., minutes
by Maclean, 6 Dec. and by Lascelles, 7 Dec. 1939. Seeds's last telegram
from Moscow related that censorship had been imposed on the dis-
patches of foreign correspondents, and postal censorship legalized,
thereby making the embassy's work even harder: FO371/24854, N853/
821/38, Seeds to Halifax, 2 Jan. 1940.

111 PRO, FO371/23678, N7134/57/38, Seeds to Halifax, 6 Dec., minutes by
Maclean, Lascelles, and Sargent, 8 Dec., and by Halifax, 17 Dec.,
Sargent to Ismay, 22 Dec. 1939, and materials in FO371/24845, N2709/
40/38, FO371/24846, N3313/40/38. It is misleading to suggest that the
notion of breaking relations and imposing a blockade came first from
Seeds. Cf. Carley, 1939, 237, and J. Colville, The Fringes of Power:
10 Downing Street Diaries 1939–1955 (London, 1985), 56.

112 PPRO, FO371/23678, N7540/57/38, Seeds to Halifax, 17 Dec. 1939;
FO371/24845, N193/40/38, Seeds to Collier, 20 Dec. 1939.

113 PRO, FO371/23683, N7861/105/38, Seeds to Halifax, 22 Dec., Halifax to
Seeds, 24 Dec. 1939. John H. Le Rougetel joined the embassy from his
previous position in Bucharest in January and stayed until November
1939. Naggiar also left Moscow at this time and was not replaced until
June.

114 Seeds Papers, Diaries, 22 Dec. 1939. Thus Seeds was not "recalled for
consultations," Gorodetsky, Stafford Cripps' Mission, 17, or "withdrawn
because of the Finnish War," Miner, Between Churchill and Stalin, 13, or
"recalled," Kitchen, British Policy, 5, or "withdrawn … in preparation
for the official rupture," E. Estorick, Stafford Cripps: Master Statesman
(London, 1949), 225.

115 PRO, FO371/24845, N40/40/40, Seeds to Halifax, 1 Jan., minute by
Maclean, 2 Jan. 1940.

116 Seeds Papers, Diaries, 2–10 Jan. 1940; PRO, FO371/24849, N93/93/38,
Le Rougetel to Halifax, 2 Jan. 1940.

117 PRO, FO371/24850, N1500/132/38, Le Rougetel to Halifax, 27 Jan. 1940,
with enclosure Political Review of the Year 1939. Seeds wrote sections 1
and 2, covering the period from January to August, before he departed.

The document received no further distribution, beyond the Northern Department, but it did become part of the Confidential Print.

118 Seeds Papers, Diaries, Press Cuttings File for 1938–1940; *New York Times*, 3 Jan. 1940. On 3 January 1940 *The Times* and the *New York Times* reported that Seeds would take a two-month leave. On 11 January *The Times* quoted Seeds as saying that "he might stay a month or even two months."

119 PRO, FO371/24845, N40/40/38, minute by Maclean, 2 Jan. 1940, and *The Times*, 11 Jan. 1940. By 1 January 1940 "Papers Regarding the Anglo–Soviet Negotiations 1939" was completed. Seeds was consulted about the exercise. The white paper contained a 15-page "Summary of Contents," prepared by Frank Roberts, and 95 documents, including telegrams – "subject to a few minor excisions" – and public statements. French and Polish reservations, Maisky's protests, and uncertainty about the British case led to the announcement on 6 March 1940 that the document would not be published. See files in PRO, FO371/23678, 24395, 24396, and PREM1/409. All copies were officially withdrawn, but the American journalist William Kuh obtained one. See *World Telegram*, 11 Jan. 1940, and *Nation*, 16 March 1940.

120 *New Milton and District Advertiser and Lymington Times*, 27 Jan. 1940; *Daily Worker*, 2 Feb. 1940; *New York Herald Tribune*, 16 Feb. 1940.

121 Seeds Papers, Diaries, 16 Jan. 1940; PRO, FO371/24839, N3706/5/38, Seeds to Sargent, 29 March 1940.

122 Seeds Papers, Diaries, 16 Feb., 4, 8 and 10 April 1940.

123 Ibid., 20 May 1940; Churchill Archives Centre, Cadogan Diaries, ACAD 1/9, 20 May 1940.

124 PRO, FO371/24849, N93/93/38, minute by Halifax, 4 April 1940, W.M. 127(40), 13, W.M. 129(40), 6, W.M. 141(40), 6, W.M. 149(40), 9. The first choice to replace Seeds was Sir Maurice Peterson. The events that finally resulted in Cripps succeeding Seeds can be followed in ibid. and in FO371/24840, N5499, 5672/5/38, FO371/24841, N5807/5/38, FO371/24847, N5689/40/38, as well as in Miner, 20–47, Kitchen, 26–32; Gorodetsky, 16–34; H. Hanak, "Sir Stafford Cripps as British Ambassador in Moscow May 1940 to June 1941," *English Historical Review* 94 (1979), 48–70; P. Clarke, *The Cripps Version: The Life of Sir Stafford Cripps 1889–1952* (London, 2002), 183–9; and S. Burgess, *Stafford Cripps: A Political Life* (London, 1999), 136–9.

125 *Irish Times*, 13 Sept. 1946; *The Times*, Letter to the Editor, 14 Aug. 1953. Seeds post–1940 activities can be followed in his diaries, which he kept until 27 June 1972, when ill-health forced him to abandon them. The

historians who interviewed Seeds were V.I. Popov, Stuart R. Schram, Gottfried Niedhart, J.C. Doherty, and the author.

126 S. Aster, "Ivan Maisky and Parliamentary Anti-Appeasement 1938–1939," in A.J.P. Taylor, ed., *Lloyd George: Twelve Essays* (London, 1971), 317–57.

127 Aster, *1939*, 314–18; D.C. Watt, "John Herbert King," *Intelligence and National Security* 3 (1988), 62–82; N. West and O. Tsarev, *The Crown Jewels: The British Secrets at the Heart of the KGB Archives* (London, 1998), 80–95, 281–2; J. von Herwarth, *Against Two Evils: Memoirs of a Diplomat Soldier during the Third Reich* (London, 1987), 140–67; and C.E. Bohlen, *Witness to History, 1929–1969* (New York, 1973), 67–87. Herwath's contact at the British embassy was a 2nd secretary, Armine R. Dew.

128 PRO, FO371/24844, N5807/5/38, minute by Sargent, 28 June 1940. A minute by Maclean on 1 August 1940, in FO371/N6072/30/38, suggested that the difficulties experienced by Cripps paled next to those faced by his predecessors such as Seeds.

PART THREE

Military Commanders

6

Claus von Stauffenberg and the Military Ethos

PETER HOFFMANN

Claus von Stauffenberg was born in 1907, the youngest son of Count Alfred Schenk von Stauffenberg, lord chamberlain of the last king of Württemberg. On his mother's side, Claus had Gneisenau among his ancestors. At the age of 11, he was deeply shocked when the First World War ended with Germany's defeat, the collapse of the monarchy, and the emergence of a republic. In the following five years he made a revolutionary commitment to a classless – but not unranked – national community, Volksgemeinschaft, and to the "fight," Kampf, for the fatherland, as he wrote in a school essay in January 1923. The need to fight was made clear to him that year by a vengeful French army occupying the Ruhr. At 15½ Stauffenberg was inducted by the poet Stefan George into the master's esoteric circle and began a life-long commitment to the ideal Germany of the future, which George envisioned in a poem entitled "Secret Germany."[1] In 1926, Stauffenberg joined a cavalry regiment, and he spent the second half of his life as a professional soldier, helping to create and then serving in modern armoured divisions and in a related position in General Staff Headquarters. He could justly be described as one of the least likely army officers to attempt to overthrow a head of state. When he did begin to work actively for Hitler's demise, he made it a condition that none of the politicians of the Weimar era be returned to power afterwards.[2]

After his own efforts to persuade military leaders to help overthrow Hitler failed in the autumn of 1942, Stauffenberg had himself posted to the front. He served as senior staff officer, now with the rank of lieutenant-colonel, in the 10th Panzer Division in Tunisia, where he got badly shot up, losing an eye, a hand, two fingers on the other, and a kneecap. It was too late to try to salvage the German nation-state from the war: German forces had been evicted from North Africa, had lost the initiative on the Eastern Front with the failed Kursk offensive in July 1943, and had also lost their Italian ally in September. Yet, despite his disappointment with the senior front-line commanders before all of these setbacks, Stauffenberg was persuaded to join a group of conspirators – most were civilians, had been attempting since 1938 to subvert the regime, and were, he thought, far too garrulous. Through his appointment to a key staff position in the Home Army Command in Berlin, in autumn 1943, he was now close enough to the centre of power to make available some armoured training battalions for a coup d'état, the planning of which he could now directly assist.

Mainly through his own energy, Stauffenberg organized the civil-ian and military plotters and began the long search for an assassin to kill Hitler. Finally, expecting the momentary collapse of both major fronts in the summer of 1944, as Army Group Centre in the east was being annihilated and the western Allies were breaking out of their bridgehead in France, Stauffenberg, crippled though he was, undertook the desperate attempt to act as both assassin and coup leader. This required the impossible – namely, his simultaneous pres-ence in two places more than 500 kilometres apart: in Berlin and at Hitler's headquarters, either near Salzburg or near Rastenburg in East Prussia. Stauffenberg was shot on the evening of 20 July 1944, not yet 37 years old, after the narrow failure of his attempt to assassinate Hitler. Perhaps his end was predictable in view of what he attempted. But on the whole the unexpected rather than the predictable dominated Stauffenberg's life. This study examines the principal roots of Stauffenberg's direct action. It proposes that they lie in his understanding of the place of the German army in the German state, his view of the military leader's responsibility, and his reaction to crimes committed by the National Socialist regime during the Second World War. Stauffenberg was a career army officer, and an exceptionally well-educated one, but not a philoso-pher; nor was he much concerned to record his thoughts for poster-ity. Those of his pragmatic views that are on record I present as he expressed them.

After January 1933, when Adolf Hitler was appointed chancellor of Germany, Stauffenberg continued to believe that he was following his purpose of serving his fatherland, in spite of his reservations about the coarse politicians who now claimed to be the nation's guardians. But he soon began to think about an intervention by military leaders against the National Socialists. Two letters have survived in which Stauffenberg expressed this thought.

Late in 1937 Brigadier Georg von Sodenstern, chief of the General Staff of Army Group 2 at Frankfurt on Main, wrote an article on "The Essence of Being a Soldier."[3] He was concerned by the trivialization of the military ethos through the massive expansion of the army, through the general pre-military training of millions of youths, and through shallow national-defence propaganda. Sodenstern declared that the soldier's readiness to die set him apart from all other communities. Men and officers must abandon all personal interests; officers must be exemplars to their men in life and death. Devotion to the commander-in-chief, and death on the battlefield, were the fulfilment of a soldier's life. Sodenstern concluded that the ethos of soldierly duty was the nation's most noble possession. Therefore it must not be allowed to become an everyday topic of trivial propaganda but must be kept as a secret. War was an action not comparable to any other expression of the nation's will. War bore a stern countenance; the horror of battle made men silent. Sodenstern's article openly criticized Hitler's nation-in-arms policy, which portended the sacrifice of the flower of German youth in frivolous military adventures.

Stauffenberg read the article when it was published in the *Militärwissenschaftliche Rundschau* in January 1939 and wrote to Sodenstern, on 6 February and again on 13 March, to thank him for expressing the principles of the soldier's existential commitment and for rejecting the vulgar hue and cry for a nation-in-arms. He added that he wanted to be "led by men whose attitude commanded his respect." Many people believed, Stauffenberg wrote further, that only the "powerful effectiveness of [National Socialist] forces outside our own ranks" had rebuilt the armed forces, so that military men could withdraw into a narrow professionalism. But they were wrong. "To be a soldier, especially a military leader, an officer, means to be a servant of the state, and this includes overall responsibility." Therefore: "We must know not only how to fight for the Army itself, no, we must fight for our nation, even for the state, in the knowledge that the military forces and its pillar, the officer corps, represent the most essential support of the state and the true embodiment of the nation." In the "great battle, the national battle which decides the existence or non-existence of the nation," the responsibility would fall to the military forces. No political organization could take responsibility away from the military forces, which could not confine themselves to their own narrowly defined domain. Stauffenberg meant for the army to assume the leadership of the nation without Hitler and without the National Socialists.[4]

It is clear that Stauffenberg was no adherent of the two-pillar theory, which sought to co-opt the army into an alliance with the National Socialist Party. In January 1943 he again told a fellow officer who mentioned the responsibility of the military leadership: "We are indeed the leadership of the Army and also of the nation and we shall seize this leadership."[5] Stauffenberg was accustomed to identifying the existence of a military officer with what he called "the aristocratic principle." Although he himself came from a long line of noblemen, he did not mean the formal nobility of birth. Ability and commitment were the important qualities, "beyond descent and individual interests," as he put it.[6] To Stauffenberg "the aristocratic principle" required that the man who dedicated his life to the army felt wholly "co-responsible" and included his private life, his family, and his children in this responsibility. What Stauffenberg called "co-responsibility" had political dimensions, as he noted in the letter to Sodenstern of 13 March 1939: "To be a soldier, especially a military leader, an officer, means to be a servant of the state, to be part of the state, and that includes overall responsibility."[7] Stauffenberg was here referring to the Sudeten Crisis, in which the army leadership had not been a decision-making factor, as it ought to have been. In his view, seeking success by bluffing was a frivolous, irresponsible gamble with the lives of the nation's youth.[8]

During the war Stauffenberg did not change his view on the "overall responsibility" of the army. He cited it in 1944 when he appealed to brother-officers for support in the uprising against Hitler's regime: once Hitler was overthrown, the army – the most conservative institution in the state, and the one institution rooted in the people – had to maintain order. Hitler had betrayed the army by sacrificing millions of lives to his own vanity and for frivolous purposes, and he had dishonoured the nation by the crimes committed under the cover of war.[9]

Stauffenberg embraced the existential situation of the soldier. He certainly agreed "that the soldier's readiness to die set him apart from all other communities." But he was appalled, to be sure, by a nihilist equation of life and death and by talk of a "Germanic" notion of "sacrificial death on the field of honour" and, failing it, of murder or suicide for the survivors, so that they too might join Odin's company of heroes. He was repulsed by declarations that Christian ethics had not valued sacrificial death, but that the humanists of the Renaissance had restored it to its proper place. In Stauffenberg's view these shocking gushings had nothing in common with the soldier's ethos.[10] Death on the battlefield in fulfilment of the soldier's duty was indeed the consummation of the soldier's existence.[11] But it was, Stauffenberg agreed with Sodenstern, "the nation's noblest possession": it could be justified only in the necessary service of the nation, and it must not be bandied about but "kept as a secret." Not many soldiers confronted the prospect of death on the battlefield as seriously and soberly as Stauffenberg. During the war he received high decorations for bravery.[12]

It followed logically from a serious, moral rationalization of the soldier's sacrifice of his life that this sacrifice had to be morally justified by its purpose. Reflections on the place of the army in the nation and on the "overall responsibility" of soldiers and officers were therefore the theoretical frame of reference for Stauffenberg's action against the head of state and supreme commander. Soldiers had to swear an oath of enlistment and of loyalty to Hitler personally. To many this was not a mere formality, but an existential commitment, which they honoured as long as the leader to whom they had sworn allegiance was alive. Military commanders frequently cited it to justify obeying Hitler's orders to the last day. Stauffenberg for his part roundly declared that loyalty had to be mutual, that Hitler had betrayed the army and the nation, and that the oath of loyalty sworn to Hitler was therefore invalid.[13] The essential commitment for him lay not in a formality, but in what he called "overall responsibility" to the nation: "As General Staff officers we must all share the responsibility."[14]

While theoretical reflections provided the basis for taking a position against the political leadership, the direct impetus for Stauffenberg to act to overthrow Hitler came from his outrage at the brutal treatment of the civilian population in the German-occupied areas of the Soviet Union, at the mass starvation of prisoners-of-war, and at the mass murder of "racially inferior" persons, especially Jews.[15] Of the total of 5.7 million Soviet prisoners-of-war in German custody during the war, 2 million were dead before 28 February 1942, 3.3 million had perished by the end of the war; mobile killing squads operated in the

Soviet Union from 22 June 1941, killing 700,000 Jews; the methodical stationary extermination of Jews and others had just begun.[16]

At the time when Stauffenberg was certainly informed of mass
murders of Jews and prisoners-of-war – between 26 and 30 April 1942
– at which time he condemned Hitler's genocidal policies in a conversation with his former divisional commander, Brigadier Friedrich-
Wilhelm Baron von Loeper, he still approved of Hitler's military strategy. He still believed that it had been right and correct to try to
capture Moscow in 1941, despite the double calamity of an early
Russian winter and the insufficient resources of the German army.
His military professional verdict against Hitler came later.

In May 1942 Lieutenant (Reserve) Hans Herwarth von Bittenfeld,
who worked in the Foreign Office section for the occupied and unoc-
cupied Soviet Union, informed Stauffenberg of the mass murder of
Jews and found that he already knew. Also in May 1942 Stauffenberg
and Herwarth both received a report from an officer who had been an
eye-witness as ss men rounded up the Jews in a Ukrainian town, led
them to a field, had them dig their own mass grave, and shot them. On
hearing this report, Stauffenberg said that Hitler must be removed.[17]

In August 1942 Stauffenberg and Major (General Staff) Oskar-Alfred
Berger, who worked with him, often rode together for two hours early
in the morning before they began their day's duties in the General
Staff. During the second or third outing in August 1942 Stauffenberg
said suddenly: "They are shooting Jews in masses. These crimes must
not be allowed to continue."[18] Stauffenberg still singled out the
murder of the Jews as his reasoning for his verdict against the regime.

A particularly valuable piece of evidence of the kind adduced in
these three episodes has recently come to light. It is important not only
because of its content, but also because it was generated and recorded
chronologically very close to the event, and because it was recorded
by agents who must be regarded as disinterested in the salient point
and therefore reliable on it. A close friend of Stauffenberg's, Major
Joachim Kuhn, who was captured by Soviet forces in July 1944,
revealed to his captors that Stauffenberg had told him, in August 1942,
that German treatment of people in the Soviet Union, especially of
Jews, proved that Hitler's war was monstrous, that he had lied about
the cause of the war, and that therefore he must be removed.[19]

Stauffenberg believed that he must act on his convictions. He was
unorthodox enough to think that he, though only a major, must try
to bring about the regime's overthrow. But he knew that the principle

of military subordination and hierarchy could not simply be overturned by a major. He believed that the senior commanders had the duty to carry out his verdict that Hitler must be removed, and he knew of course that only the most senior commanders had the power to remove the regime and keep its ss army in check.

Stauffenberg's duties in General Staff Headquarters took him to a number of army group and army headquarters at the front in Russia. After a visit to Sixth Army Command Headquarters at Kharkov and to a large number of its divisional headquarters at the front in the last days of May 1942, Stauffenberg was unable to take his leave personally from Lieutenant-General Friedrich Paulus, Sixth Army commander, because of a conflict of schedules. On 12 June 1942 Stauffenberg wrote Paulus to thank him for his hospitality. He said that his visit to the front had been "refreshing," where "the supreme commitment is made without hesitation, where life is sacrificed without grumbling, whereas the leaders and exemplars bicker for prestige or have not the courage to stand up for a view, not even for a conviction, that affects the lives of thousands."[20] These leaders were evidently not "men whose attitude commanded his respect," as he had demanded in his letter of 6 March 1939 to Sodenstern. While he appealed to Paulus as a senior leader to recognize his right and responsibility to resist Hitler, he criticized leaders who failed to act on their responsibility. More disappointments followed.

Between 11 and 20 September 1942 Stauffenberg visited Lieutenant-General von Sodenstern, now chief of the General Staff of Army Group B – commanded by General Maximilian von Weichs – in Starobjelsk. He spoke with Sodenstern for two hours to win his support for action against Hitler. He hoped that in face of the criminal character of the supreme commander Sodenstern would agree that soldierly loyalty must be set aside. But it was not possible for Sodenstern to accept Stauffenberg's reasoning as superseding his "devotion to the commander-in-chief." Sodenstern declined because he could not reconcile mutiny in the face of the enemy with his understanding of the military ethos.[21] In the same month, Stauffenberg visited XXXX Panzer Corps Command Headquarters in a hut on the Terek between the Black Sea and the Caspian. The corps, part of the First Panzer Army in Army Group A, was commanded by Lieutenant-General Geyr von Schweppenburg from June to 27 September. Stauffenberg's elder brother, Alexander, had served under Geyr's command in 1923, Geyr was a family friend, and Stauffenberg had visited him in 1936 in

London when Geyr was military attaché there.[22] But Stauffenberg had no more success with Geyr than he had had with Sodenstern.[23]

After these visits, at the end of September, just days after the dismissal of the chief of the General Staff, General Halder, the chief of the General Staff Organization Branch in which Stauffenberg headed a section, Lieutenant-Colonel (General Staff) Mueller-Hillebrand, held a meeting in his office. Present were Stauffenberg and Captain (General Staff) Otto Hinrich Bleicken of Quartermaster General War Administration Branch. Stauffenberg presented the subjects for the meeting and described the situation of field-army personnel, which was appalling. The immediate occasion was Hitler's order to constitute ten air force mechanized-infantry "field divisions" and, on Hermann Goering's intervention and contrary to original plans, Hitler's further order not to use the new divisions as replacements on the Eastern Front. But the army had to equip fully the new divisions with vehicles equivalent to the needs of four or five armoured divisions. Bleicken demanded to know who was responsible for withholding the badly needed replacements from the field army and requested that Hitler be told "the truth." Stauffenberg jumped to his feet and shouted: "Hitler is responsible. A fundamental change is possible only if he is removed. I am ready to do it."[24]

It was physically dangerous to fail to report persons who uttered such sentiments. Courts-martial killed over 1,000 German soldiers in 1942 alone.[27] Stauffenberg's superior officer, Mueller-Hillebrand, was a witness to Stauffenberg's threat. It is not known whether or not he reported the incident to the new chief of the General Staff, Lieutenant-General Kurt Zeitzler, or whether Bleicken reported it to his superior officer. Bleicken immediately gave his special missions staff officer, 2nd Lieutenant (Reserve) Walther Bussmann, a historian in civil life, an account of the meeting "in order to be able to refer to it later." Bussmann did the same by giving his academic teacher an account.[26] Bleicken and Bussmann's reactions indicate that both men took the threat seriously, and also the danger to themselves from having heard it.

Through his subversive efforts in September 1942, Stauffenberg became so dangerous to himself and to his interlocutors that he had to remove himself to the front. His promotion to lieutenant-colonel and posting as senior staff officer to the 10th Panzer Division in Tunisia was decided before the end of December 1942.[27] He deferred it to make one more effort – namely, to try to persuade Field Marshal Erich von Manstein to take the lead in a revolt of senior commanders against Hitler. Manstein was the most respected strategist in the army and in prestige perhaps second only to the much more senior Field Marshal Gerd von Rundstedt.

Stauffenberg took the same position as General Ludwig Beck, who resigned as chief of the General Staff in August 1938 in protest against Hitler's war policy. Beck had declared that senior commanders had a responsibility to the soldiers, the people, and the nation – an "overall responsibility" that superseded mere military obedience.[28] Manstein took a much narrower view of his duties: he insisted on being only a soldier and on leaving all political decisions and all political responsibility to Hitler. This is illustrated by an exchange between Beck and Manstein during the Sudeten Crisis in 1938.

In July 1938, when Beck had decided to resign, he informed Manstein, who had until recently been his deputy chief of the General Staff. Manstein wrote Beck a letter of 18 pages to persuade him to reconsider. He argued that it was the split between the leadership of the armed forces overall and of the army that had resulted in Beck's negative assessment of the situation and that it was only necessary to persuade Hitler to create a unified overall command and one chief of the general staff for the entire Wehrmacht. Concerning a German attack on Czechoslovakia and the threat of French and British intervention, Manstein said that military responsibility was confined to advising Hitler on whether or when French intervention could be accepted, whereas British intervention could not at all be an acceptable contingency. He maintained that "military responsibility" would be concerned only if the political and the military leadership did not agree on this question. Manstein evidently implied that Hitler would have to be informed that British intervention was "unacceptable" – that is, militarily unmanageable. But then Manstein had another way out; he continued: "The decision, on the other hand, *whether* the political situation would result in an intervention of the Western Powers, that decision is subject in my view only to the responsibility of the *political* leadership. The military leadership was responsible only for securing a quick success against Czechoslovakia, and for doing militarily everything to deter the French. The risk without which in politics as in warfare a great success cannot be achieved, that remains the risk of the political leadership, which, however, as I may explain later, must allow the military leaders full freedom to keep this risk as low as possible. In any case, the final responsibility can only be the *Führer's*. At least to-date he always proved to have assessed the political situation correctly."[29]

Having essentially agreed with Beck on the responsibility of military leaders, Manstein had proceeded to contradict himself by abdicating this responsibility and deferring to Hitler's judgment. The contradictions and inconsistencies in Manstein's argument betray an uneasiness about Beck's position and an uncertainty about his own. Manstein was in fact arguing against his own better judgment. He withdrew "into a narrow professionalism."[30] Beck wanted to avoid an unjustified war; Manstein was prepared to have one and to put the burden of responsibility on the political leadership. The military leadership had only to provide expert craftsmanship.

When it was suggested to Manstein in 1943 that if he became chief of the General Staff he could save the situation, Manstein agreed that Hitler's leadership was disastrous. But although he himself no longer had confidence in Hitler's leadership, he believed, as he wrote in his private diary, that Hitler was the only person who had the confidence of the people and the soldiers, and he, Manstein, would serve him if he were asked. Hitler of course was most unlikely to ask for help. Thus the course leading to the inevitable catastrophe would have to continue. But Manstein maintained that any interference with the political leadership by military leaders would mean that they abandoned the principle of military subordination, and that would always work against them; the army would be destroyed by internal strife.[31] This was equivalent to the position that in the interest of internal unity the army must continue aiding Hitler in the commission of his crimes. Manstein, of course, would have vehemently rejected this interpretation. He maintained – evidently against his better judgment, because he believed that Hitler's leadership was disastrous – that the war could still end in a draw. He must be considered too intelligent not to have understood that the Allied Powers were winning and that, as they had publicly announced on several occasions, they were going to disarm Germany completely.

When Stauffenberg briefed Manstein on 26 January 1943, Manstein agreed that "a change in leadership" was urgently desirable because of Hitler's poor generalship. He said after the war that he had told Stauffenberg that he would try to persuade Hitler to agree to a change. But Stauffenberg was not looking for a "change in the leadership structure" while Hitler as dictator remained in place. Stauffenberg wanted Manstein to lead the army and the nation to overthrow Hitler and to end the wanton slaughter and generally the crimes of Hitler's war. Stauffenberg's position was a fundamental one, similar to the one that Beck had taken in 1938. Manstein later claimed to have "warned" Stauffenberg against such talk. In fact, Manstein threatened to have Stauffenberg arrested.[32]

Stauffenberg's views of the place of the army in the nation provided him with the theoretical foundation for action against the government. He held to the hierarchical order, but when his appeals to senior commanders failed he applied a theory of devolution: since the senior generals had failed to act, the imperative to act had devolved upon the colonels.[33] The question of how a new government would be formed was moot in view of the principal Allied war aim: Germany's unconditional surrender. Had it been left to the soldiers, the question would simply not have arisen because the hierarchical principle of seniority and qualification would have applied. Stauffenberg committed himself to elections – after the return of the soldiers, who must have a voice in forming a new constitution – and to the restoration of guaranteed civil liberties.[34] It would be absurd to expect Stauffenberg to have developed "democratic" convictions in the army. He used the term "aristocratic" for the role of officers but adhered to a meritocratic view. He also insisted on a statement being drafted that documented his commitment to justice and to the rule of law for all, but which also scorned "the lie of equality" and expressed his confidence in "the natural ranks" of human beings.[35]

The crimes of Hitler's regime against Soviet prisoners-of-war, Jews, and others gave Stauffenberg the first impetus to demand and consider action against Hitler, supreme commander of the Wehrmacht. As a result, long before the Stalingrad catastrophe, and long before he considered the war lost, Stauffenberg sought direct action against the regime. Stauffenberg's cousin Peter Yorck von Wartenburg spoke for both of them when on trial for his life in the "People's Court" of Roland Freisler, Hitler's notorious hanging judge. When Freisler said that Yorck and Stauffenberg had not approved of the extermination of the Jews – Freisler's term was Judenausrottung – Yorck calmly confirmed it.[36]

Once Stauffenberg had decided that action against Hitler was required, he acted more radically than other opponents. Stauffenberg's military ethos provided the theoretical framework for action. While still a major in the General Staff, he sought personally to induce senior commanders to initiate a revolt. Failing in this, he applied a theory of devolution: if the generals did not act, the colonels must act. Driven by his perceptions of the soldier's commitment, the "overall responsibility" of the soldier and officer, and his military ethos, he staked his own life on doing what the situation demanded. That decision led Stauffenberg to a responsibility squarely faced. In the failed uprising of 20 July 1944 he ultimately sacrificed his life for the honour of his nation and his family.

NOTES

1 S. George, *Gesamt-Ausgabe der Werke*, Vol. 9 (Berlin, 1937), 59–65.

2 Stauffenberg said to Major Dietz Baron von Thüngen in 1942 or January 1943 that there must not be "restoration," history could not be turned back, and the "change" had to produce something "new"; Dietz Freiherr von Thüngen, Notes on Stauffenberg, typescript, Thüngen, 25 Jan. 1946, Institut fur Zeitgeschichte, Munich, ED 88; Stauffenberg to Jakob Kaiser in the spring of 1944: "Herr Kaiser, es darf aber nicht zu einer Restauration kommen." Elfriede Nebgen, *Jakob Kaiser, Der Widerstandskämpfer* (Stuttgart, 1978), 173–4.

3 For this and the following, G. von Sodenstern, "Vom Wesen des Soldatentums," *Militärwissenschaftliche Rundschau* 4, no. 1 (1939), 42–60; G. von Sodenstern, Zur Vorgeschichte des 20. Juli 1944, typescript, Frankfurt/M. 1947, National Archives, Washington, DC, RG338 MS B-499; K-V. Giessler, "Briefwechsel zwischen Claus Graf von Stauffenberg und Georg von Sodenstern von Februar/März 1939. Gedanken zum Wesen des Soldatentums," in F.P. Kahlenberg, ed., *Aus der Arbeit der Archive. Beiträge zum Archivwesen, zur Quellenkunde und zur Geschichte, Festschrift fur Hans Booms* (Boppard am Rhein, 1989), 552–4.

4 Stauffenberg to Sodenstern, 13 March 1939, printed in P. Hoffmann, *Stauffenberg: A Family History, 1905–1944* (Cambridge, 1995), 288–90; also R. Fahrner, *Gneisenau* (Munich, 1942), 17–19; Rede von Hans Christoph Freiherr von Stauffenberg am 2. August 1963 [in Bad Boll], mimeographed, n.p., n.d., 125–6.

5 Thüngen, Notes.

6 See Stauffenberg's letter to his father of 27 April 1926 in Hoffmann, *Stauffenberg: A Family History,* 287; Stauffenberg, letter to his wife's cousin Rudolf Baron von Lerchenfeld, 6 March 1934, Lerchenfeld Papers; Bernd von Pezold, interview, 1 July 1972; Stauffenberg, ms. letter to his fellow-student in the War Academy Hermann Teske,

29 Aug. 1937, copy in the author's possession; Stauffenberg's "Oath" of July 1944, printed in Hoffmann, *Stauffenberg: A Family History*, 293–4.

7 Stauffenberg to Sodenstern, 13 March 1939.

8 Hoffmann, *Stauffenberg: A Family History*, 104.

9 Ibid., 203, 212.

10 Ibid., 49–50.

11 Stauffenberg to Clemens and Elisabeth Count Stauffenberg, 13 December 1941 upon the death of Karl Berthold Count Stauffenberg in combat before Moscow; Stauffenberg to Ruth von Blomberg, 25 Dec. 1942, Blomberg Papers; facsimile in J. Kramarz, *Claus Graf Stauffenberg 15. November 1907–20. Juli 1944. Das Leben eines Offiziers* (Frankfurt am Main, 1965), 112–13.

12 Hoffmann, *Stauffenberg: A Family History*, 298.

13 P. Sauerbruch, "Bericht eines ehemaligen Generalstabsoffiziers über seine Motive zur Beteiligung am militärischen Widerstand," in *Vorträge zur Militärgeschichte 5. Der militärische Widerstand gegen Hitler und das NS-Regime 1933–1945* (Bonn, 1984), 139–49.

14 Kramarz, *Claus Graf Stauffenberg*, 132.

15 Heinz Danko Herre, interview, 7 Dec. 1986; J. Thorwald, *Wen sie verderben wollen. Bericht des grossen Verrats* (Stuttgart, 1952), 54–65, 70–3; Major (General Staff) Heinz Hoppe, in J.J. McCloy II, *Die Verschwörung gegen Hitler. Ein Geschenk an die deutsche Zukunft* (Stuttgart, 1963), 67; H. Herwarth von Bittenfeld, "Meine Verbindung mit Graf Stauffenberg," *Stuttgarter Zeitung* no. 162, 18 July 1969; H. von Herwarth, *Zwischen Hitler und Stalin. Erlebte Zeitgeschichte 1931 bis 1945* (Frankfurt am Main, 1982), 250; Herwarth, interview, 3 Jan. 1985, letter 8 May 1986; W. Loos, *Oberkommando des Heeres/Generalstab des Heeres. Bestand RH 2. Teil 2* (Koblenz, 1988), 39; R.-C. Freiherr von Gersdorff, *Soldat im Untergang* (Frankfurt/M, 1977), 97–99; D. Irving, *Hitler's War* (London, 1977), 325, and note on 850 quoting from Lahousen's report on a conversation with Army Group Centre G-2 (Gersdorff), 28 Oct. 1941; cf. F. Halder, *Kriegstagebuch, Band III* (Stuttgart, 1964), 221, 242, 252, 264, 276, 280, 289, concerning mistreatment of prisoners-of-war.

16 C. Streit, *Keine Kameraden. Die Wehrmacht und die sowjetischen Kriegsgefangenen 1941–1945* (Stuttgart, 1978), 9–10; H. Krausnick and H-H. Wilhelm, *Die Truppe des Weltanschauungskrieges. Die Einsatzgruppen der Sicherheitspolizei und des SD 1938–1942* (Stuttgart, 1981), 620, for the figure of 700,000 Jews killed on the territory of the Soviet Union; R. Hilberg's 1,300,000 in *The Destruction of the European Jews* (New York, 1985), 1219, includes other territories and prisoners-of-war;

I. Arndt and W. Scheffler, "Organisierter Massenmord an Juden in nationalsozialistischen Vernichtungslagern," *Vierteljahrshefte für Zeitgeschichte* 24 (1976), 105–35.

17 Herwarth, *Zwischen*, 250; Herwarth, interview, 3 Jan. 1985; Karl Michel, interview, 23 Aug. 1979.

18 Oskar-Alfred Berger, letter, 7 May, and interview, 12 July 1984.

19 Transcript of interrogation of Major Joachim Kuhn on 2 September 1944, Central Archives of the Federal Security Service (FSB) of the Russian Federation, Moscow; also Bundesarchiv-Militärarchiv Freiburg i.Br. President Boris Yeltsin presented a copy of the transcript to Chancellor Helmut Kohl on 30 November 1997 during the chancellor's visit to Russia. See also P. Hoffmann, "Tresckow und Stauffenberg. Ein Zeugnis aus dem Archiv des russischen Geheimdienstes," *Frankfurter Allgemeine Zeitung*, 20 July 1998.

20 Stauffenberg to Paulus, 12 June 1942, printed in P. Hoffmann, *Claus Schenk Graf von Stauffenberg und seine Brüder* (Stuttgart, 1992), 462–3.

21 Sodenstern, Vorgeschichte; W. Keilig, *Das deutsche Heer 1939–1945. Gliederung-Einsatz-Stellenbesetzung* (Bad Nauheim, 1956-[1970]), 211/359; see above, p. 169.

22 Hoffmann, *Claus Graf von Stauffenberg*, 49; Hoffmann, *Stauffenberg: A Family History*, 79.

23 J.-D. von Hassell, letters, 9 and 14 Aug. and 5 Sept. 1990; J.-D. von Hassell, Aus dem Kaukasusfeldzug 1942/43, typescript, n.p. [1943]; Herwarth, 3 Feb. 1963; Friedrich Freiherr von Broich, letters to Joachim Kramarz, 14 and 20 June 1962, Gedenkstätte Deutscher Widerstand, Berlin.

24 Kriegstagebuch Org. Abteilung, 11–30 Sept., 11–20 and 25 Oct. 1942, Bundesarchiv-Militärarchiv RH2/82; Otto Hinrich Bleicken, Bewegte Jahre-Erinnerungen eines Generalstabsoffiziers, typescript, Hamburg, 1990, 80; Bleicken, letter, 15 Sept. 1990; Walter Bussmann, interviews, 27 Aug. 1974, 24 April 1985, and 17 Aug. 1990; W. Bussmann, *Die innere Entwicklung des deutschen Widerstandes gegen Hitler* (Berlin, 1964), 29; W. Bussmann, "Politik und Kriegführung. Erlebte Geschichte und der Beruf des Historikers," *Fridericiana*, Zeitschrift der Universität Karlsruhe, Heft 32 (1983), 10.

25 W. Wagner, *Der Volksgerichtshof in nationalsozialistischen Staat* (Stuttgart, 1974), 945; M. Messerschmidt, F. Wullner, *Die Wehrmachtjustiz im Dienste des Nationalsozialismus. Zerstörung einer Legende* (Baden-Baden, 1987), 49–50, 70, 73.

26 Bleicken did not answer the author's question "in which situation he expected 'to be able to refer to it'"; Bleicken, interview, 25 Dec. 1990; Bussmann, interviews, 27 Aug. 1974, 24 April 1985, and 17 Aug. 1990.

27 Hoffmann, *Stauffenberg: A Family History*, 152–7.

28 Beck's memorandum of 16 July 1938 in Bundesarchiv-Militärarchiv Freiburg i.Br. H 08–28/4.

29 Manstein to Beck, 21 July 1938, typed with ms. amendments, Bundesarchiv-Militärarchiv N 28/4.

30 See page 170.

31 Hoffmann, *Stauffenberg: A Family History*, 159–62, 188–9.

32 Ibid., 159–61. Stauffenberg's conversation with Manstein was a little more complex, but in the essential matter – action to remove Hitler – Manstein was no more accommodating than that.

33 Bürklin, in Kramarz, *Claus Graf Stauffenberg*, 131. Stauffenberg probably did not know the treatise by Theodore de Bèze, *Du Droit des magistrat sur leur subjets* ([n.p.], 1574).

34 *Spiegelbild einer Verschwörung. Die Kaltenbrunner-Berichte an Bormann und Hitler über das Attentat vom 20. Juli 1944. Geheime Dokumente aus dem ehemaligen Reichssicherheitshauptamt* (Stuttgart, 1961), 152.

35 Hoffmann, *Stauffenberg: A Family History*, 243–6.

36 *Spiegelbild einer Verschwörung*, 110; *Der Prozess gegen die Hauptkriegsverbrecher vor dem Internationalen Militärgerichtshof Nürnberg 14. November 1945–1. Oktober 1946*, Band XXXIII (Nürnberg, 1949), 424.

7

The Dice Were Rather Heavily Loaded: Wavell and the Fall of Singapore

BRIAN P. FARRELL

Field Marshal Earl Wavell emerged in good shape from the gauntlet of historical scrutiny regarding his role in the Second World War. Notwithstanding his accomplishments, much of this good press results from a tendency to acknowledge – even compensate for? – the bad luck that Wavell faced being in a position of high command early in a war for which the British Empire was not prepared. Wavell had four wartime positions of very great authority and responsibility, finishing up as viceroy of India. But his conduct of one post in particular has all but been placed beyond criticism, so dire were the straits into which he was thrust. In a futile bid to stop the Japanese onslaught in Southeast Asia, the Allies hastily organized in January 1942 a unified command for the region. Wavell was named the first Allied supreme commander, responsible for directing the operations of all Allied forces in the American–British–Dutch–Australian (ABDA) theatre. His new command ranged from Burma through northern Australia to the Philippines. Wavell's orders were to hold at least the "Malay Barrier" – the line running from Rangoon through Singapore and Java to Australia. The received wisdom is clear. Given an all but impossible job, Wavell did his soldierly best. Working from so poor a starting point, receiving so little support, no blame could be assigned to him for the loss of Southeast Asia – which included the disastrous fall of Singapore, the British Empire's largest surrender of the war.

It would indeed be unfair to blame Wavell for the fall of Singapore *per se*. But as the military commander directly responsible to the Allied governments for its defence when it came under direct attack, Wavell brought in certain attitudes and made certain decisions that had an effect on the final stage of the campaign, including the defence of the island itself. Just because he took over late in the day, Wavell should not be excused from all scrutiny as to whether he took responsibility for the moves that he made and for their consequences. This essay examines Wavell's perceptions of the Japanese, his evaluations of subordinate commanders, and his command decisions that directly affected the defence of Singapore. It addresses three questions. To what extent did Wavell stiffen or weaken the defence of Singapore? On what basis did he assign responsibility for its fall? Finally, did the field marshal accept any responsibility for his own part in the final result, and does it matter?

When he took over as supreme commander, ABDA Command, Wavell's chances of preventing the Japanese from conquering Singapore ranged from slim to none. The defence of Singapore was jeopardized by, in the words of the British official historian, a "chain of disasters" ranging from the initial and poorly conceived "Singapore strategy," through the calculated risks in grand strategy taken by Prime Minister Churchill and his advisers after the fall of France in June 1940, to a series of command errors made by theatre commanders trying to defend Malaya (see Map 7.1) against a Japanese assault that began on 8 December 1941.[1] The decision to base strategy for defending the British Empire in a war against Japan on despatching the Royal Navy (RN) to the Far East in a time of emergency was never sound. Critics rightly pointed out that it was only a substitute for the better alternative that the British could no longer afford: maintaining a large battle fleet in the area. Worse, some warned all too presciently that Japan would not challenge the empire unless it was already hard pressed closer to home and had to make a hard choice about where the greatest danger lay. Worse still, the naval base built on Singapore island to house the fleet suffered from years of being used as a political football in British politics and as a target of chancellors of the exchequer, including Churchill in the latter 1920s, determined to limit expenditure. The end result was that the base was not even large enough to maintain the minimum-size fleet deemed necessary to handle any attack by the Imperial Japanese Navy (IJN) – but now it

Map 7.1   Location of forces, 8 December 1941–31 January 1942.

was there, an obvious crucial target for the Japanese in any attack that they might one day launch. Nevertheless, the "Singapore strategy" held sway as the war plan for imperial defence against Japan. The RN would deploy as soon as possible to lead the countercharge to the Japanese attack; in order to make sure that its crucial base in Singapore was available as and when required, the other services were charged to hold it until the navy could arrive.[2]

For a variety of reasons, both the army and the Royal Air Force (RAF) were in hardly better shape than the RN to defend Singapore. They suffered from the same excess of threats over resources, the problem of overstretch, that kept the battle fleet close to home. Worse, they made local defence plans in isolation, failing badly to co-ordinate their efforts. The army's Malaya Command was less culpable here; it at least sorted out once and for all by 1939 a most basic fact: the only realistic way to hold Singapore was to defend it at arm's length, to meet and hold any invader up country, on the Malay peninsula. The fixed defences of the island itself, based on an impressive array of coastal artillery, would face any direct assault. But the enemy might invade overland and come from the north, moving along the good road network that now made Malaya's jungles far from impenetrable. If it did so, it had to be kept out of air-attack and especially artillery range of the naval base, or it could be rendered unusable. But Malaya Command had only one brigade of regulars when war broke out in Europe in September 1939 and received only one brigade from India in reinforcement. This was not enough to hold a large enough portion of the peninsula to guarantee the safety of the base.[3] Unfortunately, there was no choice.

From 1936 on, RAF Far East Command assumed correctly that it would be relied on to meet the brunt of any enemy invasion, in the absence of the battle fleet. Without it, only a strike force of bomber aircraft would be able to smash any invader crossing the sea badly enough to repel an invasion. Even though it did not yet have such a force, or even a promise of firm plans to deploy one, RAF Far East proceeded to construct a network of airbases in northern Malaya and along its east coast, to enable its non-existent bombers to intercept an invasion fleet far out to sea. This left Malaya Command in a dire predicament. The "period before relief" – the time that the naval base must be held before the fleet could arrive – jumped from 42 days in the 1920s to 180 by autumn 1939. The army was barely strong enough to hold the island and its immediate approaches, but the RAF pointed out that if its new airbases were lost to an enemy they would be used to increase the scale of attack on Singapore itself and insisted that they must all be defended. This analysis was correct, but Malaya Command simply was not strong enough to do so.[4] This mess of contradictions was exposed by the dire change in British military circumstances when France fell in June 1940.

The fall of France forced the British to fight for their very survival at home against a stronger foe. In such circumstances, hard decisions were made that rendered Singapore even more vulnerable than it already was. Prime Minister Churchill rightly decided that risks could be taken overseas and the war still be won, but no risks could be taken with the fight for survival at home. But from that basis, other, more questionable strategic decisions emerged. The chiefs of staff (COS) expressly confirmed RAF Far East Command as the main force in the defence plan for Singapore, even though they could not promise to provide it with the aircraft to play that role until at least the end of 1941. That time lapse forced Malaya Command to stretch itself to cover the airbases in the north and east, complicating its task of making a stand on the peninsula.[5] Worse, the prime minister and the COS then failed to resolve a disagreement over whether or not it was really necessary to make a stand up country in order to defend Singapore. Worse still, Churchill strongly resisted and heavily diluted the COS's efforts to send reinforcements to the Far East. He believed that these forces were more urgently needed elsewhere. He also was convinced, rightly, that salvation lay in inducing the United States to intervene in the war but assumed, wrongly, that with its help any Japanese onslaught could be contained.[6]

A common thread ran through all these arguments, deliberations, and decisions: a pretty widespread underestimation of the Japanese. Most British authorities at home and in the Far East took some convincing to conclude that the Japanese would in fact challenge the Western Powers, then clung to the belief that the Japanese were not strong enough to overrun the Western positions before they could be relieved. Singapore and Malaya received reinforcements, but not enough. When the Japanese finally attacked, the area was defended by a Far East commander-in-chief who had no authority over the RN but whose main mission was to defend its base. The luckless Air Chief Marshal Sir Robert Brooke-Popham had the help not of a fleet but of a squadron of two capital ships, only just arrived, whose superiors in London wanted them to move out of harm's way when war broke out. His air force was too weak to execute the defence plan on which his army was deployed, which left both services spread out and vulnerable. Finally, Brooke-Popham himself was now a lame duck, about to be replaced by Lt.-General Sir Henry Pownall, a younger man with more recent operational experience.[7]

In such circumstances, the defence plans were rapidly compromised and Singapore imperilled. Much credit should go to an efficient and bold invader. But Japanese efforts were assisted by British command blunders that made an already weak position worse. In fact, after four days the defences were in tatters and never recovered. The RN lost HMS *Prince of Wales* and HMS *Repulse* in part because the fleet commander did not call for help from fighter aircraft even after he was discovered and attacked by the Japanese aircraft that sank him. The army planned to pre-empt a Japanese invasion, by moving into Thailand first to seize the areas that they were expected to invade in order to move against Malaya. This plan came unstuck when Brooke-Popham dithered. That dithering weakened the efforts of those same troops to make a stand on the main, prepared defensive line at Jitra. That line was itself placed in at best a mediocre position, because it was the only other way to protect advanced airbases. A bold Japanese assault scattered defenders in superior numbers in two days. This set off a retreat that ended only in Singapore itself, as Malaya Command lost the initiative. As for the RAF, it was so badly outfought, by an enemy that it underrated for no very good reason, that it was forced to all but abandon support of the ground forces after a week, to concentrate on defending Singapore and the now-much-needed reinforcement convoys.[8]

Two command decisions in the second half of December – one in theatre, one in London – shaped the situation that Wavell inherited when he assumed his new command, in practice, on 7 January 1942. The GOC Malaya Command, Lt.-General Arthur E. Percival, made a fateful decision from 18 through 20 December: despite its already difficult position, his army must make a determined defensive stand as far north of Singapore as possible, rather than breaking contact, falling back, regrouping, and concentrating on a shorter front closer to Singapore. Percival had his reasons. His mission was to hold the great naval base – hold it, not just deny it to the enemy. The obvious implication was that the base would be held for the fleet to make use of when it finally arrived. If the enemy closed to within easy air-striking distance or, worse, artillery range of the naval base, it would render the base unusable and the mission would fail. Moreover, it already seemed clear that without strong and timely reinforcements from overseas, especially of fighter aircraft, Malaya Command must in due course be defeated by this enemy, which already controlled the sea and the air and enjoyed tank support. It was essential to keep the Japanese away from the airbases in central Malaya, in order to prevent heavy attacks on the crucial reinforcement convoys closing on Singapore. Percival therefore ordered his vanguard, III Indian Corps, to stand and fight north of Kuala Lumpur – but also to keep itself intact, not to fight to the death.[9]

There might have been a certain strategic logic to Percival's decision, but the way in which he implemented it compromised the very battle that he asked his vanguard to fight. Because it was necessary to stand and fight, but also to cover all points where an enemy in command of the sea might attack on the east coast – Kuantan, Endau, Mersing, and Singapore itself – Percival allowed his army to be brought to battle in detail. He left four of his ten brigades to fight the main battle against the main enemy advance along the west coast, while the other six sat tight. This was too much strength to lose but too little to prevail, not least because III Indian Corps was forced to retreat time and again in order to keep itself intact. As a result, by the end of the first week the corps was badly overstretched, its troops were worn out, and it was still divided. The defence still stood north of Kuala Lumpur, but disaster loomed.[10]

The fateful decision made in London was actually a two-fold non-decision: not to challenge Percival's campaign strategy and not to reconsider the basis of his mission. Churchill raised the first issue just as Percival was making up his mind, asking what sort of defence was being conducted in Malaya and suggesting that Percival be directed to concentrate on defending the immediate approaches to Singapore. The prime minister envisaged a main stand in Johore, with only small rearguards holding up the enemy in the north.[11] This was not the strategy pursued by Percival – and approved by his military superiors. Brooke-Popham endorsed Percival's strategy and, backed by the Far East War Council, recommended it to the COS. There, the new man, General Sir Alan Brooke, who took over as CIGS on 1 December, advised the prime minister to leave campaign strategy to the men on the spot. Brooke was doubtless influenced by the accepted maxim that Singapore could be held only if an enemy was kept well away from the overland approaches through Johore. While this was true enough in principle, it does not explain why no one in London reconsidered whether or not Percival's army was now in any shape or position to fight on, according to conventional wisdom – or even questioned his deployments, although all the other foundations of pre-war defence plans for Singapore were already destroyed. Churchill's approach certainly meant taking risks with the "main battle," but Percival's took risks with the battle at hand. A distracted prime minister, en route for a crucial conference with his newly belligerent ally in Washington, DC, seems to have dropped the matter before Christmas.[12]

Both prime minister and cos compounded this neglect by failing to reconsider Percival's basic task after it became clear that there would be no early reinforcement of the Eastern Fleet. The very basis of British grand strategy for war against Japan was that the fleet would carry the burden of a counteroffensive to repel any Japanese incursion. The naval base at Singapore existed for that express purpose, and the order to hold it ready governed every decision made by Brooke-Popham, Pownall, and Percival. But after the destruction of Force Z, coming on top of recent heavy naval losses in the Mediterranean, it quickly became clear that the Admiralty did not intend to implement the plans on which it had worked for 20 years. As early as 20 December, Vice-Admiral Sir Geoffrey Layton, now C-in-C Eastern Fleet, was authorized to move his headquarters from Singapore if he considered it necessary. On 5 January 1941 he did just that, shifting his staff to Batavia, on Java. This move was more than symbolic. The RN was developing plans to concentrate another fleet east of Suez, but in Colombo, Ceylon, not in Singapore. It saw the Indian Ocean, not Singapore, as the "last ditch" in the war against Japan.[13] This stance left denying the base to the enemy as the only sensible military mission to assign Percival. And Percival knew by January that the RN had no early plans to return in strength to Singapore to relieve it. But nobody told him that grand strategy had changed, and no one altered his mission, so he carried on with the strategy designed to preserve, not just to deny, the base.[14]

No one changed Percival's orders because nobody in the central direction of the war exerted himself to master a fast-moving situation. In the noise and fury of campaigns raging from the central Pacific to north Africa to the central Soviet Union, the collapse of the "Singapore strategy" provoked only a piecemeal response from the prime minister and the cos. Reinforcements were redirected to Singapore, and the orders inherited by Wavell – to hold the "Malay Barrier" – were cut. But even though these orders confirmed that Singapore was no

longer to be a base for an early naval counteroffensive, but merely a
bastion that must be held to deny the area to the enemy, no one
connected that new strategy to how Percival was conducting the
defence of Singapore. Due in no small measure to that oversight,
Percival kept his army divided and vulnerable north of Johore.[15] The
fate of Singapore depended from the start on a race between reinforcements and the Japanese advance. Percival's campaign strategy
reduced the chance of winning that race. It led his army to be defeated
so quickly and so heavily that the available outside help would probably not be enough to turn the tide. The bitter harvest was reaped on
7 January 1942, the very day Wavell took command, when two tired
brigades were caught off-balance on the main road at Slim River by
a Japanese tank-led assault and almost destroyed.[16]

Wavell's first job as he flew in to visit his new command was to
pick up the pieces of what looked like a potential collapse and to find
a plan that would give Malaya Command a chance to make one more
stand far enough north to cover Singapore. No more was really possible by this time. A fair assessment of Wavell's role in the defence of
Singapore requires understanding of the situation that he inherited
on 7 January. Singapore was all but lost before he took charge, and
he had almost nothing to do with this situation. But Singapore was
not yet lost. And Wavell's mission as supreme allied commander of
the area that included Singapore was to do what he could to hold it
for as long as possible – indeed, his orders were to hold it, period.
From the start, Wavell himself regarded retaining Singapore as vital
to plans to hold the "Malay Barrier," let alone to optimistic ideas of
a counteroffensive.[17] Despite his inherited situation, Wavell still had
a job to do, a mandate of leadership, for which he stood accountable.
On the basis of the three questions identified by this study, it must
be said that Wavell did not so stand. Wavell did not always shirk from
tough decisions at the time, but he accepted no public responsibility
for any consequences thereafter. Why?

Wavell's general attitude towards Japanese fighting power can be
summed up in one word: scepticism. Early experience did not challenge this scepticism. Wavell himself knew precious little about the
enemy or the area, having never served east of India and not there
since 1908. The supreme commander was never carried away by some
of the more extreme misjudgments, such as suggesting that the Japanese would not make good pilots because they would not be able to

see well at night, but he did imbibe the generally sanguine appreciation of Japanese capabilities that was all too widespread in London, India, and Singapore in 1941. Obviously the Japanese proved to be more efficient in all elements than expected, but Wavell was not swept along in the other direction either. He saw what the Japanese were doing well but consistently stressed their weaknesses and wondered why they were not being more effectively exploited. The Imperial Japanese Army (IJA) placed too much of a burden on leadership by officers, leaving too little scope for initiative by non-commissioned officers (NCOs) and soldiers. This tendency carried on right up the chain of command. Japanese tactics and strategy tended to be rigid, predictable, and based on dangerously complicated plans. Japanese troops were brave and aggressive, but their leadership had weaknesses. Field units were unlikely to take any initiative even if opportunities arose, working strictly according to plan; the loss of leaders left infantry units ineffective in the attack. Japanese air tactics were also rigid and predictable, just as unlikely to deviate from set plans and patterns.[18]

Given these perceptions, Wavell tended to react to news from the front by insisting on better results and demanding to know why they were not forthcoming. Wavell was aware that many of Percival's Indian army units were tired or raw and that the enemy had the initiative, on land and in the air. He expected the struggle to stem its advance long enough to stiffen the defence as a whole to be a "near-run thing." But he also at first, in mid-January, believed that it could well succeed.[19] And one reason was that he did not rate this enemy as any more efficient than what could be thrown against it, then and in the very near future.

The problem in the air Wavell hoped and believed would be addressed by the introduction of *Hurricane* fighter aircraft to the defence of Singapore. Aircraft sent in crates by ship were hastily assembled, and two squadrons committed to battle, just as the battle for Johore began in mid-January. Wavell was certainly not the only local commander who had high hopes that the new fighters could help turn the tide, but he shared those hopes almost uncritically.[20] The pilots were a mixed bunch, some with combat experience and some without, none with any experience in this theatre or against the Japanese or with time to gain any. Their aircraft were not the latest model, and modifications made to allow them to fly over desert terrain could not be undone and hampered their efficiency.

Nevertheless the supreme commander joined his subordinates in fostering and reporting high hopes – apparently because of an instinctive assumption that modern British aircraft with a smattering of veteran pilots must be able to master the challenge of an Asian air force that so far had proven surprisingly effective, but only against second-line aircraft and units. Surely the rigidity of enemy tactics would level up the playing field. The *Hurricanes* did some damage but were not able to prevail against the enemy, especially the IJN's formidable *Zero*-type fighter, being instead worn down by combat with them. By early February they were all but withdrawn from the battle, leaving Singapore nearly defenceless in the air.[21] Wavell did not cause this problem, but he did act on uncritical assumptions about ways to rectify it. He made decisions based more on preconceptions, seasoned by wishful thinking and lack of choice, than on dispassionate analysis. Unfortunately, his job was to make sure such calculations were not unduly influential.

To the end in Singapore, Wavell misjudged his own forces because he was frustrated at their inability to master an enemy whose general weaknesses he did see. Wavell simply did not absorb the lesson that the IJA taught Malaya Command in the first month of the campaign: what mattered was relative combat power. This Japanese army was more flexible and imaginative a fighter than too many on the Allied side had imagined it would be, whereas the British-led forces proved too rigid, narrow, and predictable in their defensive tactics. The Japanese did a better job of preparing their troops to fight *in Malaya* than the defenders did. His frustration obscured Wavell's appreciation of the performance and potential that he might realistically expect from the forces that he had, constituted and equipped as they were. The most glaring case was that of the 44th and 45th Indian Brigades, two formations hastily rushed to Malaya from India and thrown too early into battle when events left no choice.

As C-in-C India in December 1941, Wavell knew that these formations were not fully trained – not at all trained for jungle conditions or ready for action against a tough enemy. But when called on to send reinforcements to Malaya, he allowed these two brigades, manned mainly by new recruits, to proceed to an active theatre of war. Certainly it was not his fault that changing circumstances meant that the time spent preparing these formations for war in the desert was wasted, but he was expressly warned by the division commander who gave them up that they were simply not ready for battle – period.

Yet he sent them, rather than a more experienced formation, unwilling to deprive India.[22] When fate made Wavell the recipient of his own judgment, he still made too little allowance for how little could be expected of these troops. He operated instead on the premise that a now-reinforced Malaya Command could make a stand and fight its main battle in Johore helped by these new brigades. The results of this overoptimism I explore below. Yet even in the last days of battle, Wavell felt that more could be achieved against this enemy. Relaying an exhortation from the prime minister, Wavell added to it on 10 February in an order of the day that lectured Malaya Command, pointing out that it was much larger than the enemy hurting it so badly, comparing its stand unfavourably with those being made by Soviet and American troops elsewhere, and insisting that with the honour of the empire and the race at stake the army could and must rouse itself and hit back effectively.[23]

His comparisons were unfair, given how different the situations were. In front of Moscow Soviet forces were fighting, with a homogeneous army, for the very survival of their own homeland, on their own territory. In the Philippines, the Americans enjoyed a very strong natural defensive position. Malaya Command had no such advantages. It was a polyglot army fighting to defend a colony that it could not afford to save by destroying it in battle, and one with few natural defences. The tone and wording of Wavell's order also seemed to ignore both the real problems now tearing Malaya Command apart and the fact that many of its superior numbers in uniform were not combat troops. The words may have originated with Churchill, but Wavell shared them by passing on the gist of the message in his own order. This was unwise, being insensitive to the mood on the ground; Wavell surely knew better, having publicly argued that when a general addresses his troops an unfortunate tone may do more harm than good. It convinced too many of his own troops that he did not really understand why they had not put up a better fight and, if anything, sparked a backlash.[24] It is hard to disagree, which suggests that Wavell never really took the measure of Malaya Command either.

This tendency to persist in overestimating what could be done against the enemy ran through Wavell's involvement in the defence of Singapore like a rhythmic chorus – always there, sometimes hard to tell how much it mattered. More dramatic and clear-cut were the specific decisions that Wavell made which seriously influenced the defence one way or another. In order to understand them, we need to grasp two things – Wavell's own job and character, and his evaluations of the senior subordinates over whom he now assumed command. Wavell had no illusions about the nature of the command now thrust on him: "I had been handed not just a baby but quadruplets."[25] Having already seen hard service in the Mediterranean, Wavell was now being asked to take on two concurrent, problematic tasks. He must be the guinea pig for a new system of coalition command – and as such take over, pull together, and salvage separate defensive campaigns in Malaya, the Philippines, and the Dutch East Indies, all already being lost by divided and inadequate forces. He took the job, partly because Churchill and the COS were reluctantly persuaded that in the long run taking up an American suggestion – that this first Allied command should go to a respected Briton – would help cement the vital alliance, but more because a strong sense of duty persuaded him that he had no choice. The job needed to be done, and he was the senior man on the spot – specifically requested by General George C. Marshall, chief of staff of the U.S. army.[26]

But while Wavell certainly had the experience for the post, in other ways he did not suit it. He was sober, steady, diligent, retentive, and all but imperturbable. He had already demonstrated his ability to absorb great pressure and setbacks and struggle on – the very quality that impressed Marshall. But Wavell was also taciturn and far from charismatic – in fact, introverted. He expressed himself much better on paper than in person, did not waste words on pleasantries to improve the atmosphere, and when provoked could speak with an unguarded tongue even at the highest levels.[27] Dealing with politicians was not his strong suit; this proved to be only a minor problem regarding Singapore, but the supreme commander was not beyond making snap judgments about personalities. That did create problems, as did his inability to forge any sort of bond with Malaya Command and its leaders.

Wavell arrived in Singapore on 7 January, the same day as 11th Indian Division's rout at Slim River, half-way down Malaya (see Map 7.1). The division was scattered and close to collapse. Wavell spent the day in Singapore being briefed by Pownall on the situation and on the personalities involved. The Slim River débâcle drew him up country the next day to appraise the situation personally, particularly to see if his field commanders would be able to restore the position.[28] Over the next two days Wavell made several important decisions involving the high command. Certainly the high-pressure atmosphere in which he had to make these decisions is relevant. The coincidence of the defeat at Slim River and Wavell's arrival in Singapore seems almost to be a metaphor for his whole Allied command. One decision was necessary and made unflinchingly. Taking one look at III Indian Corps the day after Slim River, Wavell scrapped Percival's plan to fall back in stages on Johore, fighting all the way, and ordered the army to make a full-scale strategic retreat immediately, abandoning Kuala Lumpur and the central states north of Johore to rearguards and delaying actions.[29] This was now the only sensible course. The two Australian brigades could be brought into action on a narrower front as the peninsula contracted in northern Johore, the enemy's supply line would be stretched at least temporarily, and III Indian Corps would get a chance to regroup. Wavell's other decisions were not so sensible, nor positive in effect.

Wavell had met Percival before but did not know him well. They renewed their acquaintance at a bad time for the latter. GHQ Malaya Command gave the supreme commander an optimistic briefing about its plans for orderly withdrawal. What Wavell saw for himself the next two days convinced him that Percival did not have any grip on the situation or on his army. Wavell was briefed personally by Brigadier I.M. Stewart, recently elevated to temporary command of 12th Indian Brigade, the lead formation scattered by the Japanese tank assault. The exhausted Stewart made a poor impression on Wavell, provoking him to remark that it was one of the most incoherent reports that he had ever heard. At III Indian Corps headquarters, he found the staff struggling to reassemble its scattered formations to block a further Japanese advance. Worse, the corps commander, Lt.-General Sir Lewis Heath, clearly did not share Percival's optimism – it was apparent that he had opposed all along Percival's strategy to fight on in strength north of Johore.[30]

Wavell also received a report from Duff Cooper, hitherto resident minister in Singapore, that raised doubts about whether sufficient action was being taken to bolster the defences of Singapore itself. The report came from Brigadier Ivan Simson, chief engineer, Malaya Command, who had been trying unsuccessfully for over two months to persuade the GOC to make greater efforts to build up fixed defences on the island's almost-wide-open north coast. Wavell and Percival visited the sector on 9 January, and, on seeing for himself the almost-total lack of defences of any kind, even near the causeway, an angry supreme commander demanded an explanation. Percival replied that he felt that it would shake the confidence of both the army and the civil population if they saw defences being built on Singapore itself, perhaps raising doubts about whether the enemy could be held after all. Wavell pointed out "with some asperity" that morale would be damaged much more by enemy troops' pouring across an unde-fended causeway and ordered him to set about building up coast defences forthwith.[31] But the most damaging consequence of these events was that Wavell lost confidence in Percival. This factor pro-duced some decisions that were poorly conceived, or not followed through, or both.

Percival as a rule did not make a good first impression. He was quiet, reserved, thoughtful. His better qualities – a keen analytical mind, relentless work, devotion to duty, and a tendency not to panic – did not necessarily leap out at once.[32] Major-General H. Gordon Bennett, GOC 8th Australian Division and commander of the Australian Impe-rial Forces (AIF) in Malaya, did make a good first impression, at least on Wavell. Bennett was outspoken, charismatic, aggressive, and confi-dent to the point of brashness. He dismissed the current situation as the result of errors made by Heath and of the weakness of his Indian units, complained that his fighting-fit Australian brigades were lan-guishing while the battle was being lost, and insisted that he and his men knew exactly how to stop the Japanese and would do so, given the chance. Bennett talked a good fight and stood out to Wavell as the only senior leader who seemed unaffected by the long retreat, with ideas about how to stop it, fresh troops, and a burning desire to get into the fight. In comparison, Percival seemed to be at a loss; Pownall had already hinted that Percival lacked the ruthlessness needed to pull together an army being heavily beaten.[33] These considerations led Wavell to make his most fateful command decision.

On the evening of 8 January Wavell summoned Percival to his temporary headquarters, kept him cooling his heels for some time, then handed him a new defence plan for the battle to hold Johore and gave the GOC a direct order to implement it forthwith. This plan was the exact opposite of the one developed by GHQ Malaya Command. The staff plan called for III Indian Corps and the AIF to divide the front by a north–south line; III Indian Corps would carry on defend-ing the western sector, and the AIF would hold its prepared positions in the east. Each formation could deploy in depth with clear lines of communication back to Singapore. Instead, Wavell ordered Percival to hand over the main battle in the west to Bennett. The Australian would take charge of the front running from coast to coast from Muar through Segamat to Mersing, concentrating in the northwest. One Australian brigade would move west right away. The other would be relieved and shift west as soon as troops could be spared, once the soon-to-arrive 53rd Brigade was ready to deploy. 9th Indian Division and the just-arrived 45th Indian Brigade completed Bennett's force. The remnants of III Indian Corps would move south to regroup, splitting the front by an east–west rather than by a north–south line – which meant that lines of communication to the main force would now run through the positions of the reserve force. Wavell obviously intended this to be the main stand.[34]

Percival was not given any chance to discuss the plan. While the staff plan seemed risky because it relied on the tired III Indian Corps to carry on bearing the brunt, Wavell's plan assumed Bennett's delivering as he promised. It was on Wavell's part an impulsive move, to say the least. He did not know that Bennett was unlikely to deliver, not only because his own division was riven by internal disputes, caused by his own prickly personality, and by long-standing feuds. The staff of 8th Australian Division was neither large nor experienced enough to handle the load proposed by Wavell. But because Bennett seemed so much more ready to fight than either Percival or Heath, Wavell went with him.[35]

Given his own evaluation and behaviour, Wavell really should at this point have relieved Percival of command. If he had so little confidence in the commander of his most important force that he felt obliged to step in twice in two days to override the plans of the man on the spot and then to give him peremptory orders, one wonders why he felt it safer to rely on Percival to execute his orders properly than to replace him.

Wavell did not even do all in his power to ensure proper carrying out of his orders. Percival made no great effort to accelerate the building of defences on the north coast of Singapore, distracted as he was by the battle at hand. Wavell did discuss the island's defences with the prime minister from the 15th on, in an increasingly grim exchange of telegrams. In the process he pressed the Commander Singapore Fortress with detailed questions on 16 January but did not mention the subject directly to Percival again until the 19th.[36] Percival did develop Wavell's plan for defending Johore, creating Westforce and moving it into place under Bennett to make the main stand. But he made a major change by insisting on leaving the well-trained and acclimatized 22nd Brigade AIF to stand in its positions at Mersing, rather than replacing it with either a Singapore-based brigade or by the 53rd Brigade, nearing Singapore by convoy. The British formation would now move up to the III Indian Corps area, being available to assist Westforce when deployed. This was a departure from Wavell's plan to concentrate the most effective formations for the main battle, and it turned out to be costly.

Bennett made matters worse by deploying his force rashly. The Australian planned to fight an aggressive defence, starting by springing a major ambush on the main road above Gemas, then defending the area above Segamat in depth, counterattacking rather than sitting on fixed positions. For this plan he concentrated both brigades of 9th Indian Division to back up his own 27th Brigade AIF. That left him only the very raw 45th Indian Brigade to hold the entire flank to the west coast, along the Muar River to the coastal town of Muar.[37] Bennett wanted all his muscle for what he thought would be the main battle, so he assigned only one artillery battery to support his weakest formation standing on its own – rather than at least sending one of the battle-tested brigades of 9th Indian Division to guard the flank and grouping the raw formation in the main position. Then he insisted on having the 45th Indian Brigade cover the entire 25-mile front of the Muar River, even though the up-river half of the front led only to a loop road that reached a dead end and could not easily have been used to get behind his main force. Not trusting the Indians to fight aggressively, he insisted on their applying his tactics of active defence based on counterattacks rather than passively holding the river line. To ensure this, he directed the brigade to have both its two forward battalions place two rifle companies – nearly half their strength – north of the river to delay the enemy, the rest digging in on the south bank of the river itself.[38]

These dispositions produced the following situation. Bennett's main force deployed in depth was covered on the flank by one raw and just-arrived brigade that had to stretch itself along too long a line and to divide itself in a way that invited defeat in detail by putting the river between its own halves rather than between itself and the enemy and that received too little support. Obviously Bennett expected the enemy to oblige him by not making any major advance along the west coast.

Wavell returned to Singapore on 13 January, then went up country to Bennett's headquarters at Segamat (see Map 7.2). He and Percival

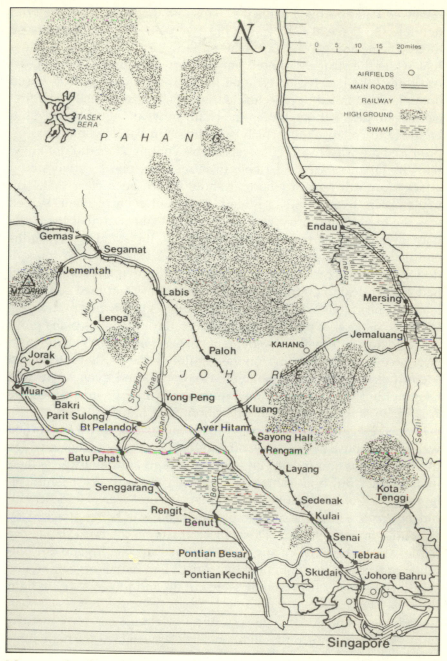

Map 7.2   Southern Malaya.

reviewed and approved Bennett's plans and dispositions. Wavell did not object to Percival's changes in his own plan, or even comment on them. The next day, Wavell gave his superiors in London the warning that while the struggle to hold Singapore was bound to be a "near-run thing," he had reason to hope for success. This view was based on a plan that failed to concentrate the strongest units, as Wavell first envisaged, then left one link in the chain so weak that if hit it would be likely to collapse – in which case the main battle would be compromised anyway. Even if the responsible commanders did not know that the Japanese would be able to launch not one but two strong attacks in northwestern Johore, it should have been clear that Bennett's orders to 45th Indian Brigade were not even prudent. Wavell was the highest authority, with the duty to make sure that the battle plan gave the army the best chance to make the stand on which his entire theatre strategy for ABDA Command was going to hinge – doubly so, in this case, as the basic plan was his own. Certainly Wavell had a great deal to do from 9 through 14 January, not least setting up his own headquarters.[39] But that can only explain, not excuse, his failure to make sure that Percival followed through on his plans properly and to confirm the deployments. Therefore Wavell shares to a large degree responsibility for the results of the battle that ensued according to his outline plan. That battle started even as he was telegraphing London, when the Japanese advance guard tripped the Australian ambush in the late afternoon of 14 January.

Bennett's aggressive defence on the main axis of advance worked well. The ambush at Gemas set off a four-day running battle, in which the Australians and Indians hit the enemy hard and fell back on their own terms.[40] But it all came undone when the west coast flank collapsed. Lack of information was a major factor. Percival and Bennett did not realize that the 45th Indian Brigade was being attacked by the entire Imperial Guards Division until late on the third day of the battle. Meanwhile, the enemy assault carved up the brigade one battalion at a time; the rump, plus two Australian battalions sent in one at a time to bolster the position, were cut off and forced to try to fight their way back. They put up a very tough response, but fewer than 1,000 Indians and Australians, out of an original 6,000-plus, made it through. Percival noted that this confrontation enabled the main force to retreat safely back to the major cross-roads area of Yong Peng, where they could try again to form a defensive line. But the defeat around Muar forced that retreat in the first place, so that they could prevent the enemy from outflanking the main position.[41] And that defeat was hardly surprising, even if the strength of the enemy attack was, given how poorly the raw Indian brigade was deployed.

The defeat was also pivotal in the campaign. It was so rapid and so heavy that Malaya Command was unable to mount another prepared defence on the mainland. The enemy already had a lodgement along the west-coast road, and there were now too few formations to defend all axes of advance that it could use. Wavell was always inclined to consider the worst case before events made it unavoidable. On 16 January he sent the GOC Singapore Fortress a list of direct questions regarding the state of the landward and general defences of Singapore (see above). This was no doubt influenced by the prime minister's inquiries but stemmed mainly from his own inspections. Two days later GHQ Malaya Command produced a map with proposed deployments for the entire army to make a final stand on the island itself.[42]

Wavell then directed Percival to prepare plans for a final retreat and defence, but in strict secrecy – the struggle to hold on the mainland must continue, if at all possible. It was not, as Wavell found for himself when he went again to Singapore on 20 January. The supreme commander did not follow up his direct order to bolster landward defences on the island with any personal inspection. He did order Malaya Command to hold on until at least the end of the month, to cover three more reinforcement convoys due to arrive within the next few days – but he acknowledged that the army would probably soon have to retreat to Singapore.[43] This was all but a death knell for ABDA Command's hastily prepared plans to hold the "Malay Barrier," coming as it did at the same time as the *Hurricanes* failed to regain control of the air.

Wavell based his theatre plans on Singapore's holding out for three months from mid-January. The optimum scenario was that the "main battle" of the campaign, now being fought in Johore, would keep the enemy far enough away so that Singapore could get really powerful reinforcements – strong enough to mount a counteroffensive, not just to bolster the line. The formations involved were actually in the pipeline. Three tough veteran formations were being withdrawn from the Middle East and sent to Wavell: 6th and 7th Australian Divisions and the 7th Armoured Brigade. But their advance guard would not arrive before the end of February at the earliest. Unless the enemy could be kept far enough away, and the air clear enough, they could do nothing to help Singapore. The defeat at Muar and the retreat from the main position made that impossible by making certain a siege of Singapore much sooner even than Wavell feared it might be. Wavell acknowledged as much when he notified Churchill, on 19 January, that a last-ditch defence of the island must now be prepared: "I must warn you however that I doubt whether island can be held for long once Johore is lost."[44]

Now all that he could do was to send in the much weaker reinforcements nearing Singapore and hope that the army could somehow prolong a siege of the island long enough to tie the enemy down. Even this was controversial. The remainder of 18th Division was still at sea, closing Singapore and expected just before the end of the month. Prompted by Wavell's warning, Churchill turned up the pressure for a stiff defence – but he also seriously considered, with the war cabinet and the cos, diverting the remainder of 18th Division to another front that it might be able to bolster more effectively, such as Burma. But the Australians heard of the discussion and warned Churchill in no uncertain terms: "After all the assurances we have been given, the evacuation of Singapore would be regarded here and elsewhere as an inexcusable betrayal."

In the face of such pressure, the central direction of the war backed away from the issue and left decisions to Wavell. Technically this was not incorrect; Wavell's task as supreme commander certainly encompassed deciding where formations being sent him could do the most good.[45] Yet, given the higher political issues involved, leaving the tough call to Wavell alone appears an abdication of leadership. From his point of view there did not seem to be any choice. If the defence of Singapore could be prolonged, this might allow ABDA Command to strengthen itself enough elsewhere to be able to challenge the enemy for control of the air and sea lanes once again. The remainder of 18th Division continued on course, most of it arriving on 29 January. But by 27 January, when Wavell finally authorized Percival to retreat to Singapore, the strategic position of his command had greatly deteriorated in less than two weeks from the beginning of the "main battle" in Malaya – a battle laid out according to the supreme commander's outline plan.[46]

Wavell's role needs to be understood. Bennett and Percival directed the battle itself. The supreme commander could not and did not "micromanage" such a farflung command. But he made the decisions that were his prerogative: to select the man who he felt most likely

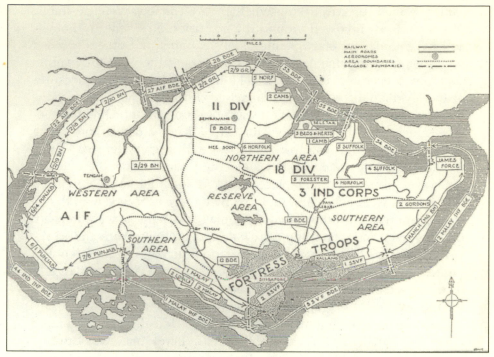

Map 7.3   Final defence plan, Singapore, 8 February 1942.

to mount the best defence and to lay down the outline plan that he believed would give the army the best chance to stand, thereby contributing to his broader strategic plan. Wavell made errors on both counts that accelerated the defeat which drove the army back onto the "naked island" (see Map 7.3). Wavell compromised himself by overruling Percival but leaving him in command, which was highly irregular, and then by not following up his directives properly, which was careless. One cannot say that Wavell did all that he might have to improve ABDA Command's position in his first weeks of command, however tall an order he faced.

Wavell's decision to leave Percival in place was particularly significant because it formed part of a pattern. Wavell's appointment made Duff Cooper's job redundant. Before returning to England, Cooper briefed Wavell at length on the situation. He and others persuaded the supreme commander that the civil government in Singapore was not acting with the speed and efficiency demanded by the emergency. When Cooper relayed the same message in London, the prime minister cabled Wavell directly, asking whether any changes were desirable. The main issue revolved around the governor, Sir Shenton Thomas, and his colonial secretary, Stanley Jones. Cooper and others accused both men of being unable either to understand the need to abandon standard procedures in order to take emergency wartime measures or to galvanize the civil service to act accordingly. These accusations had foundation, and the position was not unimportant. Only the civil government could really drive forward such matters as providing labour for essential war works and bolstering civil defence. These would not decide the issue, but they could help or hurt the defence. Yet Wavell decided not to replace the governor, after being convinced that if Jones was sacked and replaced by a more energetic man things would improve. In other words, Thomas was kept as a figurehead. In this case, and regarding Percival, the motives were the same: Wavell decided that it would provoke too much loss of confidence in higher authority on the part of the troops and the civil population if he dismissed the governor and the GOC – the two men most responsible for the defence of Singapore – for being inadequate.[47]

This line of reasoning must surely be a self-defeating exercise more often than not. That was certainly the case here. Jones was duly let go, and Thomas published a letter to the civil service in the local newspapers on 15 January, insisting that red tape must now be abandoned and fast action was essential. But this was at least a month late, its tone was the palest imitation of Churchill's "action this day" philosophy, and the governor did not follow through to enforce his new orders – all these points being made at the time in critical vein by the Singapore *Straits Times*. No real improvement ensued in civil-service assistance to the war effort, for whatever it was worth.[48] And now the governor was even more discredited, his trusted deputy having been visibly sacked. Wavell thus left in charge a man in whom he had little confidence without even testing the alternative: perhaps sacking the governor might have been seen as the firm resolve of a new team, ready now to fight ruthlessly? So, what gain for Wavell's caution?[49]

Percival's shortfall was more serious. The army retreated into Singapore on the morning of 31 January and from that point on was all but cut off. The rumour mill had persuaded the troops that they were fighting to buy time for the "Fortress" to stiffen its defences – to protect the naval base. When they crossed the causeway, that base was being demolished and evacuated; worse, they were sent to defend sectors on the island's north and west coasts with few if any defensive positions or even fieldworks in place. The GSO1 of III Indian Corps was informed by the staff finalizing the defence plan that there were no finished defences in his sector, nor even any detailed maps of the naval base, which was in the corps area! Yet Percival's plan was to defend the coast itself, to repel any invasion on the water or the beach, rather than leaving only a thin coastal screen and concentrating inland for a counterattack. So now the troops were being asked to defend beaches with few defences, to hold an island that no longer had a usable naval base. Not surprisingly, the effect on morale was very bad indeed, as Bennett and Percival both noted.[50]

Percival stands responsible for the failure to bolster Singapore's defences on the landward side to at least a minimum state while time remained. But Wavell did intervene while there was time to get at least some work done and then failed to follow up effectively. Questions posed did not lead to defences built. On a broader plane, Wavell did not tackle either issue which made Percival balk in the first place. Despite forecasting how discouraged the troops would be to find no defences – suggesting that he felt it necessary to risk discouraging them and civilians by working on defences before the enemy arrived – Wavell did not follow up. Nor did he take up with London the question of the mission assigned to Malaya Command. The other reason why Percival did not devote time and resources to the landward defences of Singapore is that he saw no point. His mission was to hold the naval base so that it could be used, not just to deny it to the enemy. Therefore if it came within artillery range, the mission was over anyway. This view was pedantic. In that case the mission would certainly change instantly to denying the base and the island, as indeed it did.[51] But Wavell did not raise, let alone force, this issue, either to compel Percival to adjust or to require London to reconsider the standing order that he took so literally.

Wavell stands responsible here, because only he was in a position to act in both these directions – it was his duty – and he did not. He did not, despite a full and acrimonious discussion with the prime minister regarding the defences of Singapore, even before the army made its final retreat. Churchill saw the implications very clearly and spelt them out for the COS on 19 January: "Seaward batteries and a naval base do not constitute a fortress, which is a completely encircled strong place. Merely to have seaward batteries and no forts or fixed defences to protect their rear is not to be excused on any ground. By such neglect the whole security of the fortress has been placed at the mercy of ten thousand men breaking across the straits in small boats. I warn you this will be one of the greatest possible scandals that could possibly be exposed."[52] Wavell was not primarily responsible for this situation, but again he did not do everything possible to address it.

Nor can one say that Percival could not be replaced. Pownall half expected to be asked to take his place and was neither tired nor discredited by the fighting up country.[53] Might Pownall not have been more useful as GOC Malaya Command than as chief of staff at ABDA Command? Or perhaps, as has been suggested, as military governor in place of Thomas? After all, Wavell's plans were based on holding Singapore. By early February, Wavell still required Malaya Command to deny Singapore to the enemy for a good two months.[54] Yet it was now very unlikely to be able to do so, and Wavell made decisions that added to rather than relieved its difficulties. ABDA's key bastion was now under siege and in the charge of a general and a governor in whom the supreme commander had little, if any confidence. At the very least, the speed with which Singapore finally fell is a calamity that Wavell cannot completely sidestep.

Wavell did not play a very direct role in the defence of Singapore island itself, which was to be expected. His responsibilities were much greater, and it would have been unwise for him to take over the siege defence, even had it been possible. But his role was not very helpful. Starting with the decisions not to replace those in whom he had no confidence, then moving on to his failure to follow up orders to bolster the landward defences, Wavell did nothing to improve the island's admittedly dire straits. On reviewing the situation and the defence plans, he concluded that the enemy would most likely launch its main invasion to the west of the causeway, across the narrowest stretch of the Johore Straits. He therefore advised Percival to deploy his largest and freshest formation there; that happened to be the 18th Division. But now Wavell rediscovered the maxim of leaving detailed decisions to the man on the spot, did not order Percival to so deploy, and approved his outline plan. Percival was not sure where the enemy would attack, but he leaned to the area east of the causeway, where the ground between the coast and the city was more difficult to defend. He placed the 18th Division there.[55] The Australians deployed right where Wavell expected the Japanese to attack – which they duly did.

The Australian division was now battered and tired, heavily diluted with recently arrived and not fully trained replacements for the losses suffered in Johore. Its commander had already all but given up on the battle, did little to prepare the defence, and started planning his own escape. Its sector had few defences, its southern flank was guarded by another raw and just-arrived Indian brigade.[56] Not surprising, the Australians failed to stop the massive two-division invasion launched by the enemy late in the evening on 8 February, and the Japanese advanced deep into the island before any sort of coherent defence could be pulled together. Worse, Percival failed to assemble his forces for the all-or-nothing counterattack that alone might have repelled the invader, as opposed to prolonging the siege. Instead, he kept the entire 18th Division in place on the north coast for more than two full days, believing that the enemy had large reserves available and was still yet to launch its main assault. There were no large reserves, that assault was already under way, and the Australians were left almost alone to be defeated by it.

Wavell arrived in Singapore for what proved to be his last visit on the morning of 10 February. By that time the defenders were pushed back to an improvised defence line west of the city that already amounted to what Percival sketched out as the final, all-round-perimeter, last-ditch defence of the city area itself, plus some vital high ground and supply dumps to the north. And still there had been no serious counterattack. Bennett's division was in real disarray, and Percival had only just ordered Heath to send a mere battle group of three battalions to help defend the high ground – with the rest of his forces to continue their watch on the north coast. The enemy was now close enough to the city to shell it with field artillery.[57]

There was nothing that Wavell could now have done to salvage the situation, and not much that might have prolonged it. But again his actions fell short. The exhortation to the army that went over so badly (see above) was of course influenced by pressure from London, but also by the sense that the enemy must be very near to overstretching its now-long supply lines and overtiring its infantry. Both these suspicions were not far from the mark. Yet the enemy had its tail up now that victory was in sight, its powerful air force was now pummelling the city and the defenders against virtually no opposition, the island was all but surrounded, and the enemy infantry consisted of very seasoned formations. Malaya Command had a very large number of non-combat and not fully trained troops, no air cover, and poor generalship – the Australians in particular. Wavell did initiate the only obvious step still open – when Percival showed him a plan for a local counterattack to keep the enemy away from the supply dump area, he directed the GOC in no uncertain terms to mount a major counter-attack in three stages, designed to push the Japanese back off the island. Having given this order, he then left the island for the last time. While waiting to depart, he missed a step and fell off the quay onto some rocks and barbed wire, badly injuring his back. It was a fitting illustration of what must for Wavell have been the most frustrating command of his long career.[58]

Percival again did not execute Wavell's orders as directed. Heath was ordered to send another battle group forward, but the attack itself was left up to Bennett's forces plus the small reserves that Percival sent forward to help him in the first two days. All told, these now amounted to no more than a full brigade, so badly depleted and scattered was Bennett's command. Some units moved up to starting positions late on the night of 10 February but were brushed aside by a vigorous two-division assault launched by the enemy, aiming to capture the high ground and open the road to the city itself. The defenders were able to bar the road, but their own aborted attack was pulverized, and they lost the high ground.

Now Percival had no choice but to order a desperate counterattack to regain the hill dominating the vital supply dumps and road to the city. The only formation on hand to mount it was the first battle group sent up by Heath the previous day. It tried but failed, in the only serious attack launched by Malaya Command in the fighting on Singapore island. This was the case even though Percival's fallback strategy was to mount an all-out counterattack if his beach defences failed to repel the enemy. Half of Percival's army remained in place on the northeast and south coasts, watching for another assault that would never come. By the afternoon of 11 February, less than three full days into the battle, the only question left was whether Singapore would collapse in hours or in days – in a defence intended to last at least two months.[59]

Wavell saw what had to be done when he made his last visit but again failed to follow through and make sure that the attempt was made. The tenor of his telegrams now suggests another reason besides pressure of work. With Singapore under direct fire and the army trapped, and a Japanese invasion fleet advancing on Sumatra, he seems to have decided that the island was bound to fall rapidly even if an all-out counterattack was attempted. Even if the enemy was forced to pause to regroup and resupply, it could and no doubt would escalate its air assault and bring up naval forces in close support.

Wavell warned Churchill after his visit that the fall of the island was imminent. Over the next four days he did everything possible to satisfy two conflicting requirements: to keep Malaya Command fighting as long as possible and to persuade Churchill to allow it to capitulate as soon as possible, to spare the city a sacking such as suffered by Nanking in China in 1937. Percival's surrender on 15 February did indeed spare Singapore the horrors of a street-by-street battle.[60] But the real importance of Wavell's involvement with the defence of Singapore itself was indirect. Having overridden Percival already on deployment and plans, why did he not do so again? If a two-month defence of Singapore was so important to ABDA Command's plans to make at least Java, if not Sumatra, really defensible, why was there so little effort to push Percival on the one occasion that it was tried? What did Wavell have to lose by so pushing?

These questions raise the ultimate issue regarding Wavell and the fall of Singapore: so what? What difference did it make what Wavell did, if his chances of saving Singapore were so slim? Does it matter, beyond assigning blame for its own sake, and assessing performance and reputations? It does, for these reasons: the accuracy of the historical record; the repercussions of both the rapid fall of Singapore and the received explanation for that disaster; and the broad question of leadership and responsibility at the highest level of military command, under very adverse circumstances. Despite what by early January 1942 should have been obvious evidence to the contrary, Wavell misread the relative fighting power of his own forces versus the Japanese all through the rest of the campaign. This contributed to decisions that hurt the defence of Singapore more than they helped. Finally, Wavell was quick to find and report the failings of subordinates as causes for the fall of Singapore – but for his own part he noted only the great difficulties of the command forced on him, not any mistakes that he might have made.

Two days after the surrender Wavell told Brooke that the fall of Singapore compromised all his plans, suggesting that ABDA Command as a whole was now in danger. This was of course correct. Unwilling to shoulder any more unsupportable burdens, Wavell pressed for and was granted permission to transfer back to India on 25 February, leaving ABDA Command to the Dutch.[61] By early May, the Japanese overran all the Netherlands East Indies plus Burma, seizing every Western possession between Calcutta and Australia.

This disaster knocked the British truly onto the sidelines in the war against Japan; the surrender of Singapore in particular was a bitterly felt humiliation, as some 125,000 troops in Malaya and Singapore fell into enemy hands with such speed and apparent ease. Pressure for a searching inquiry was instant and remained constant. And Wavell at first agreed with Churchill: there was nothing to be gained and much to lose by launching a post mortem bound to provoke recrimination and controversy in the middle of total war. The investigation could wait until after the war. Wavell went further in the spring of 1942: it was not fair to draw any conclusions with so many of the principals involved now in enemy hands as prisoners of war. Reports and assessments should wait until they could tell their side of the story.[62]

This laudable attitude did not last long. On returning to India as C-in-C, Wavell was directed to oversee the debriefing of many escaped survivors, military and civilian, and to appoint an officer to compile a report on the campaign and the fall of Singapore based on these interviews. The principal author of the report was Major H.P. Thomas, formerly of GHQ Malaya Command, whose last appointment in Singapore was commander of the Mixed Reinforcement Camp. In a covering letter to Brooke dated 1 June 1942, Wavell bowed to propriety: "Finally, I would remind you of what I know you will bear in mind, that the statements available are mainly those of comparatively junior officers with a limited view; and that the great majority of the senior officers whose preparation, planning and conduct of the operations are criticised, have not had the opportunity of explaining their actions." But in the same letter Wavell declared for the record, "I have read, I think, all the principal reports which compose the evidence, and a good many others, and I consider this summary fair and accurate." The report was trenchant in its criticisms: pre-war failures in intelligence, training, and preparations; neglect by the civil government; mistakes in command, strategy, and tactics; inadequate materiel; and, above all, underestimating the enemy. One conspicuous absence was the performance of the highest military authorities; Brooke-Popham's mistakes were implied, and Wavell apparently made none.[63]

The most controversial comments came in two appendices. Wavell explained them as follows: "I have left in Appendix A for your personal information, *since I think it is in the main justified by the evidence*, but I am sure you will agree that anything that would tend to cause recriminations must be avoided and that this Appendix should not have any circulation. I have also allowed Appendix B to remain, since it represents accurately much current opinion." Appendix A was a commentary on a report submitted earlier by Bennett, who made a controversial personal escape from Singapore. Bennett's report was for the most part a self-serving exercise in shuffling blame onto anyone but himself. The comments on it implied in unmistakable terms that the 8th Australian Division collapsed in Singapore without any serious fight because of mass desertions, which undid the defences and accelerated the surrender. Appendix B was a compilation of criticisms of Governor Thomas, so pointed that Wavell felt obliged to vouch for the governor in his letter and to offer to explain in detail for the record why he did not replace him; but he left the appendix in. It also included this sentence: "For the fall of Singapore itself, the Australians are held responsible, while their presence in the town in disproportionately large numbers during the last days, coupled with the escape of large numbers on ships and in boats, has aroused great indignation."[64]

Churchill severely restricted the circulation of this report to prevent controversy with the Australians over its conclusions.[65] But it stood on the record, supplemented later that year by Wavell's official *Despatch on Operations in Southwest Pacific, January 15th–February 25th, 1942*. The *Despatch* appeared only after the war, but it was circulated in the usual official channels while many of the principals remained prisoners of the Japanese. This report toned down its criticisms and made a fair main point: the basic cause of the failure of ABDA Command was the speed and power of the enemy's advance, which gave it no real chance to dig in. But Wavell made this comment regarding the last battle for Singapore: "In Malaya, where the numerical disparity was less, the Japanese troops undoubtedly outmanœuvred ours by their superior mobility, training and preparation. By the time Singapore island was reached these qualities, together with air superiority, had established a moral ascendancy which made the resistance of the Singapore garrison half hearted and disappointing." Wavell admitted no mistakes regarding his part in the defence of Malaya and Singapore. In the list of subordinates mentioned for meritorious service, Pownall was the only officer connected with the campaign, and his inclusion related to his success in setting up an Allied headquarters that in the end did nothing to stop the Japanese.[66]

Wavell never finished his memoirs, dying in 1950 before he could complete them. Privately, he felt bad about his performance in defence of Singapore – at least at the time. On 20 February 1942, barely 100 hours after the fall of Singapore, and with the pain still fresh, he poured out his remorse to his former secretary in a personal letter:

We have lost the battle here [to hold the "Malay Barrier"] by a month or six weeks at least I think – the additional time that we should have gained at least in Malaya and Singapore and the time by which we should have built up in these islands an air force capable of holding and hitting back. I have a hunch the Jap is stretched to the utmost in the air but he is using his forces boldly and well and has been too quick for us … I went four times [five visits] to Singapore and Malaya in a month but never could stop the rot, the front always seemed to be crumbling under my hand. I am still wondering if I might have found the answer somehow. I won't tell you more of the sad story here. You will have seen something of it in the official records and cables and can judge for yourself how my failure came about. I feel I ought to have pulled it off but the dice were rather heavily loaded and the little yellow man threw them with considerable cunning. I hate making excuses. I was given a job and have fallen down on it, whether it was "on" or not others can decide, I feel myself that it might have been but I think it wanted a bigger man than I have ever pretended to be. So that's that. We shall win the war alright in the end.[67]

Wavell also made a confession of sorts in unpublished comments on a draft of Percival's official dispatch. Wavell claimed that he had intended Percival to transfer the 22nd Brigade AIF from its east-coast position to deploy for the coming main battle in northwest Johore even before it could be relieved, accepting risks on the east coast. Percival persuaded him to wait, and the move never took place; looking back, within these restricted Whitehall circles, Wavell commented, "I have always regretted since that I did not insist on the move without replacement." But publicly, he never at any time accepted any responsibility whatsoever for the speed with which Singapore fell or agreed that any of his decisions affecting its defence did so negatively. He left blame for the shoulders of pre-war governments and military advisers, Churchill and the central direction of the war from 1940 on, Thomas and the conduct of the civil government, Brooke-Popham and Percival and the conduct of the campaign itself, and even the Australians and their final collapse.[68]

While all these factors belonged on the list of causes, Wavell was included by his own colleagues over 50 years ago. From the start, the speed and extent of the disaster reverberated at home and within the empire, producing pressure for an inquiry and a scapegoat. Jones was the first, Percival, by default, became the second, backed up by Brooke-Popham. Churchill rejected an investigation as a dangerous distraction in a secret speech to the House of Commons in April 1942, but he published that speech in early 1946. This raised calls in both Australia and Britain for the full inquiry promised earlier by Churchill.

The British government directed the cos to investigate the ramifications of such an inquiry.[69] The brief went down the chain to the Joint Planning Staff (JPS). Its initial conclusions (5 March) were blunt and sensible: any inquiry could not be restricted to any particular aspect or phase of the campaign, such as the final battle for Singapore itself. Because the decisions made in the theatre depended so heavily on grand strategy and British policy as a whole, it would inevitably become a searching assessment of much broader questions: "We consider that the main point which arises from our examination is that it is impossible to discuss our policy in the Far East in isolation. Every theatre was inter-dependent for men and materials which, at the time, were in very short supply." The inquiry should "a) review the progress of the war against Germany and Italy and … decide whether the strategy pursued was correct and whether more forces could have been spared for the Far East, b) review our relations with the Dutch, with the Americans and with the Dominions and India, c) review the whole question of the preparations which were carried out in the years between the two world wars." A review of this nature "could not be carried out without the evidence of the statesmen and military leaders responsible for our policy both before and during the war. This inquiry could not be confined to purely military matters, and would involve a discussion of controversial and delicate political issues."[70] By that the JPS meant mud slinging between the British and the Australians and pointed criticisms of decisions made by authorities at the highest political and military levels.

When the cos pushed one last time for a report on the possibility of holding an inquiry limited strictly to the conduct of the campaign or even to the last battle – one that must focus on the theatre commanders and the Australians – the JPS stood firm (report of 6 May): "It would not be possible to hold an inquiry into the Malayan campaign from the time of the Japanese landing without consideration of wider questions, the discussion of which it has already been agreed would be undesirable. The implications of an inquiry limited to the events on Singapore island would be less serious but we consider that such an inquiry would be most undesirable and likely to stimulate public demand for a wider investigation."[71]

The investigation of this issue lasted from February until June 1946, producing two thorough reports by the JPS (5 March and 6 May) and several discussions by the COS. Throughout, Attlee looked for conclusions to justify the decision that he made at the start – to sidestep any official inquiry, leaving official comment on the matter to be expressed by publication in due course of the *Despatches* of the commanders involved. The reason was understood and stated by the JPS: "Important witnesses would have to be called, the summoning of whom might be very embarrassing. For example, the presence of Mr. Churchill and Lord Wavell would be essential."[72]

That was not possible. Churchill was now leader of the opposition and a world-famous figure, a heroic symbol of British defiance and victory. Wavell was viceroy of India, in the midst of very sensitive political initiatives regarding probable Indian independence. To cross-examine such men in the glare of world publicity, regarding a humiliating defeat, would risk bringing the basis of British policy, and the judgments of the men who made it, under severe criticism. The JPS did not mince words in its report of 5 March. Regarding Wavell: "The Chiefs of Staff had given General Wavell a free hand to divert reinforcements if he considered it desirable. The only result which we can foresee arising out of a public inquiry would be justification or censure of General Wavell's decision to continue the reinforcement of Malaya as long as he did. In view of his present position we consider that any public arguments regarding the correctness of his decisions would be most undesirable." Probing the performance of the civil government in Singapore would "almost certainly disclose, in addition to any military faults, facts to discredit the British Colonial Administration in Malaya and by implication possibly that in other parts of the Colonial Empire."

The report continued that investigation into the state of equipment provided would reveal that the enemy enjoyed a definite advantage. Questions about intelligence collection and appreciation would not only reveal how badly Japanese capabilities were misjudged but also "must include discussion of our methods of gaining information, and this might, as has occurred in the Pearl Harbour [*sic*] inquiry, prove very embarrassing." As for commanders and command decisions: "Particular criticism is likely to be directed at the decision to send the

Prince of Wales and the *Repulse* to the Far East and this question would
certainly involve an undesirable examination of personal relationship
[*sic*] between the Admiralty, the Chiefs of Staff and the Prime Minister." To underline the point, regarding the eight changes in senior
commanders involving Singapore from autumn 1940 to January 1942,
and the organization of the higher command structure itself: "The
discussion of these matters at a public inquiry would bring to light
the reasons for the many changes, and involve discussion of the character and ability of the higher commanders concerned. We consider
such a discussion undesirable. The system of command might also be
discussed, but we see no disadvantage in this."[73]

British authorities refused even to countenance the kind of public
soul searching that the United States undertook with the congressional investigation of Pearl Harbor, because they were afraid that
the answers would reveal just how badly the defence of Singapore,
and preparations for war against Japan, had been handled. An inquiry
into the fall of Singapore would underline the naked fact of Britain's
inability to maintain effective control over the empire, and provide
for its security, since the First World War. This would raise doubts
about the system that elevated the men who made policies and about
the policies that they made – doubts that could impair current efforts
to strengthen British control over the empire and imperial defence.
That might harm the effort to maintain Britain as a first-class power.
So the *Despatches* and official histories were left to tell the story,
and for a generation Percival and Brooke-Popham stood out as the
"guilty men." In due course, pre-war policies and wartime grand
strategy came in for their share of deserved criticism, as over time
historians followed all the trails of causes laid out by the JPS investigation in 1946 – but the damage was done. Wavell escaped almost
entirely. Percival, who played his hand badly but was given a bad
hand to play, carried too much of the burden of blame.[74] That
injustice distorted understanding of the part played in the fall of
Singapore by arrangements for, and decisions of, the highest levels
of command.

It is ironic that the only issue for which the JPS singled out Wavell
was his decision to allow the rest of 18th Division to proceed to
Singapore. This is the least blameworthy of the decisions that he made
which had negative consequences – especially for the men of 18th
Division who suffered the terrible years of captivity under barbaric

Japanese control. Wavell's job was to hold Singapore as the linchpin of the "Malay Barrier." His entire strategy depended on prolonging its defence. From his vantage point, this was a non-decision, and no other commander in his place would have chosen differently. The foul odour partly muffled in public by Wavell's presence was the rank mishandling of imperial, specifically British–Australian, relations, throughout the whole sorry story of the "Singapore strategy."

The British could not face and fight a world war without the unstinting support of the dominions. They could not hope to hold the empire in the Far East without Australian help. They could not even claim to be a world power, during and after the war, without the added strength that the dominions could throw into the imperial pool. But before the war the dominions were not interested in spending money on defence. The "Singapore strategy" became for the Australians a placebo, and for the British, a promissory note. The note was called with the outbreak of war in Europe in 1939. Eliciting Australian help required reaffirmation of the improbable strategy that secured for Australia its "Near North." When the defeat of France in 1940 forced the British to admit that they could no longer hope to send the main fleet to the Far East for the foreseeable future, and made it probable that the rapacious Japanese would move against the weakened Western empires, the Australians exerted themselves to help defend Singapore – but also emphasized how they regarded its defence as quid pro quo for their vigorous contribution to the war against the European Axis. The loss of Singapore produced a bitter public rift between the governments, with Australia claiming to be deceived and beginning its drift into the strategic orbit of the United States.[75] Here, Wavell's failure to take any responsibility, at the time and later, and his willingness to assign blame in haste added to the damage to both imperial relations and the historical record.

The two brigades plus other elements of the 8th Australian Division did indeed haemorrhage from mass desertions in the last days of the final battle, but only after they put up a stiff if short fight against the Japanese onslaught – as the war diaries make categorically clear. The division ceased to function as such, but this was the result far more of failures by its own commanders, and by Malaya Command, than to any other considerations – aside from the enemy. The division did not enjoy any leadership from its higher commanders, who failed utterly to give it the best possible chance, in existing circumstances, to fight effectively.[76] Finally, this problem affected only the speed at which the final battle, let alone the campaign, was lost – not the result. The Japanese had Singapore surrounded and under the gun by the time they invaded an island never meant to withstand a close siege; had they been held longer, they would have rushed in the available air and naval strength and finished the job. Nevertheless, Wavell accepted and lent his authority to reports claiming wrongly that the Australians collapsed without a fight because they were unwilling to fight at all – one can almost hear the ring of the old "bad blood of convicts" accusation[77] – and claimed that this destroyed his plans to defend Singapore and thus hold the "Malay Barrier."

This was misstating the facts of the final battle and distorting what Wavell himself knew was the truth about why Singapore was lost so rapidly. After all, he all but gave up on the island, privately, even before Malaya Command retreated across the causeway for its final stand (see above). And these reports were based almost entirely on interviews with Britons, who remembered all too keenly every episode that they saw or even heard of regarding Australian behaviour in Singapore. Moreover, most of these people were not, as Wavell himself acknowledged, privy to the "big picture" of strategy. Wavell was certainly grappling with an all but insoluble problem; ABDA Command was never really a viable proposition to begin with. But in misrepresenting what happened, and why, he not only clouded the record, which made it harder for readers to draw any useful conclusions about what happened, he also placed a time bomb in British–Australian relations. The British, by insinuation, let the charge of an Australian collapse without a fight in the last battle gain currency as the received explanation for why the siege defence of Singapore was so short and feeble. This strategy helped dilute considerations of previous broader decisions and arrangements that left Singapore so vulnerable in the first place.[78] This was an abdication of responsibility, dishonourable and even pointless.

Churchill stood to answer for underestimating the Japanese and for not pressing matters of theatre strategy, but his key decision was sound and defensible: if from mid-1940 on risks had to be run, the Far East was where they might be run without jeopardizing victory. Instead, to keep the dominions trusting, compliant, and forthcoming, Britain could accept no blame, although perhaps the Australians could. The JPS saw how futile these arguments were bound to be in the long run when it warned the COS not to restrict any inquiry to areas that would focus blame only on Percival and the Australians. It also singled out the question of the morale and performance of the army in the last battle as the most delicate of all: "The allegations concerning the Malayan campaign which are likely to have the most far reaching repercussions are those directed at the morale of the troops ... [T]he recriminations involved by an inquiry must strain relations between the United Kingdom, India and Australia ... The overwhelming fact which would emerge from public inquiry is that there was a breakdown in morale ... The fact that the main attack fell upon the Australians and their failure to prevent the Japanese landing would inevitably lead to further recriminations."[79]

The idea that the Australians broke and ran in Singapore because, when it came right down to it, they were all talk and no action became over time a part of British folklore, while the concept that the British deliberately led the Australians to believe Singapore secure when they knew better became a truism in Australia. When the report that Wavell accepted and signed was finally released for public research in 1992, the Australian reaction was explosive, up to and including an angry statement by the prime minister in Parliament. Wavell could have mitigated this result had he handled the incomplete and lopsided report differently in 1942. He asked instead for a field marshal's baton – and received it, reward no doubt from a prime minister grateful for the soldierly way in which he took on an almost-impossible task with no complaints.[80] By sidestepping blame, Wavell and his superiors, who knew better, made sure that there was no formal inquiry, even after the war, into decisions in matters of great consequence: defence policy, grand strategy, arrangements for higher command, and their impact on the fall of Singapore.

That impact was massive, and critical scrutiny indicates that Wavell must be assigned a minor but definite share in the blame – and some of his actions had more than immediate interest. The British official history, *The Loss of Singapore* (1957), volume 1 in the series *The War against Japan*, was written by S.W. Kirby, an officer who served under Wavell and made no secret of his admiration for him. After its publication, Percival and some others argued that it led to a whitewash of the supreme commander in a publication designed to provide a scapegoat. Sure enough, there was precious little criticism of Wavell within. Even when a frustrated Kirby years later published his own, much more critical work, *Singapore: The Chain of Disaster* (1971), he expanded his criticisms of authorities and decisions in London but still made virtually none of "the Chief."[81] One author was harshly critical of Wavell. Sir John Smyth, VC, in *Percival and the Tragedy of Singapore* (1971), did not blame Wavell for the loss of Singapore but found reason to criticize all his relevant decisions, concluding "Wavell also interfered in the control of operations in Malaya in a way which most commanders would have found quite intolerable."[82] Which way does the pendulum swing?

Wavell handled the defence of Singapore erratically at best. Some decisions he faced unflinchingly: pull III Indian Corps back to Johore; order nearly all RAF squadrons away from the island, when it was invested, to preserve them; and capitulate. Others he shied away from: replace Percival? Replace Thomas? Wavell had reason to know how it felt to lose the confidence of his boss, how that could affect his own efforts, and what it felt like to be arbitrarily ordered by a distant authority to pursue detailed plans – all from his experience in the Middle East, answering to Churchill.[83] Why did he think that his own interventions would not hamper Percival? The maxim "back him or sack him" fits here; even a Wavell biographer does not accept his case for not replacing Thomas, while his principal biographer glosses over the way in which he peremptorily altered plans for defending Johore yet left Percival in charge. The defeat at Muar was a disaster that made an early siege of Singapore unavoidable. Wavell was as responsible for that defeat as Bennett and Percival, and his conscience troubled him at least once on this issue, as expressed in his comments on Percival's dispatch (see above).[84]

Wavell's failure to follow through his orders is inexplicable and was fatal. Why override Percival in Johore but not in Singapore? If landward defences were so crucial, why no serious follow-up? This would have been a prudent exercise of supervision, not "micro-management." If Wavell had to spell out for Percival what steps to take to defend the island, something that Percival should have had in hand, why did he leave him to it? Finally, why no follow-up on the order for one last counterattack? An injured back must have been involved, but it does seem as if the supreme commander was now just going through the motions. In fact that impression persists from start to finish around him, brave words in optimistic telegrams notwithstanding: most sources took Wavell at his word when he called the ability to fight on without ever despairing of defeat a key test of generalship, and claimed to have done so with ABDA Command. That makes his erratic handling of the Singapore problem harder to understand. After all, Wavell himself maintained that an important attribute of success in high command was to be a good judge of character, to know who needed to be pushed and who could be left alone on his own to carry through.[85] Can anyone argue that Wavell lived up to his own standards here?

This failure also brings up what must be the primary point of this study. What could Wavell have done, given what he was and when he arrived? Wavell's job as supreme commander was more than difficult. But he was experienced in facing, as a theatre commander, great odds and major problems from several directions simultaneously, having done so in North Africa and the Middle East in spring 1941. He drew lessons: enemy intentions and capabilities must be correctly appreciated, and one's own strategic priority identified and driven home.[86] Wavell failed miserably to grasp how outmatched his own forces were when war came. He was not alone in this sort of misapprehension, but he was the champion. In due course, praise for the Japanese still did not produce any recognition on his part that his own forces could not do what he wanted at the time. Wavell identified the defence of Singapore as his strategic priority. Yet he did not concentrate consistently on it, or at least make sure that only people whom he trusted were defending it. He could not have saved Singapore – but as theatre commander he did not do all that he could to fight for it. Wasting Pownall's time at ABDA headquarters instead of leaving him in Singapore was a blunder that Wavell never even saw. The thread mishandled helped unravel the whole quilt.

The issue that will always be at the centre of any study of the fall of Singapore is why it was so vulnerable in the first place. Wavell saw part of the answer as early as two days after the surrender: "The trouble goes a long way back: climate, the atmosphere of the country (the whole of Malaya has been asleep for at least 200 years), lack of vigour in our peace-time training, the cumbrousness of our tactics and equipment, and the real difficulty of finding an answer to the very skillful and bold tactics of the Japanese in this jungle fighting."[87]

Yet even though few of these causes implicated him, Wavell avoided responsibility that he should have shouldered. Worse, he dishonourably passed it on to others. To join the chorus of blame shuffling the onus on to the Australians for their misrepresented collapse in the anti-climactic final battle was unworthy, wartime pressure or not. To stand back and allow Percival first to be criticized while unable to defend himself, and later to let him take nearly all the blame for a job that Wavell himself felt Percival was not up to in the first place, were just as bad, if not worse. Wavell helped provide an alibi for British policy and grand strategy, arrangements for higher command, and the hand given Percival to play. That was not leadership in its most demanding sense.[88] Worse, those actions helped distract attention from the crucial question of supreme military command in situations of crisis management.

The folly of the pre-war "Singapore strategy" – the decision to base plans for imperial defence on optimistic expectations very unlikely ever to be realized – was for too long obscured by the smoke and fire surrounding the campaign. The role of the central direction of the war in that campaign was in turn less explored than the performance of local commanders, forced to fight a campaign for which no one was really prepared, except the enemy. Wavell was at the pinnacle of those theatre commanders for the final phase of the campaign. But his handling of the improvised ABDA Command received precious little criticism on any grounds on the assumption that it was all hopeless to begin with.[89] That marginalized any study of this prime example of how a hard-pressed supreme commander identified his most urgent task but failed to do all that he might have to keep on top of it – or at least to make sure that only people whom he trusted to do whatever might still be done were left in charge. Percival "carried the can," even though his inherited strategy was unrealistic and the chain of command to which he answered makeshift and poorly served, from Brooke-Popham through Wavell.

Percival was also blamed for not being ruthless enough to fight for Singapore by all means, fair and foul. How ruthless was it for Wavell to shy away from replacing a general and a governor who did not seem fit for the challenge, for fear of a *possible* grassroots reaction? The summit of theatre command was not helpless, even in this situation, to either accelerate or delay events. Wavell's command decisions accelerated the fall of Singapore and the demise of his own command. In the end, greatness is surely revealed in adversity.

Even Wavell's character, let alone his skill, should have been reconsidered because of this experience. On his last visit to a dying army, Wavell was tempted to stay in Singapore and share the ordeal of surrender and captivity with his troops. Quite rightly he resisted the temptation, which could only have given the enemy the cheap propaganda coup of capturing a full general. Like the soldier that he was, Wavell instead turned back to the daunting duties crowding in on him.[90] But it almost seems as though by that act he resolved from then on to excuse himself, in public, for his role in accelerating disaster. By going along with political expediency in assigning blame, by interfering but not following through, by making mistakes and by the manner in which he did so, tough assignment notwithstanding, Wavell made one final fact clear in his defence of Singapore. Whatever else he was, "the Chief" was not among the great commanders of the Second World War, let alone among the great captains of military history.

NOTES

1 S.W. Kirby, *Singapore: The Chain of Disaster* (hereafter *Chain of Disaster*) (London, 1971), passim.

2 The pre-war "Singapore Strategy" controversy is discussed in N.H. Gibbs, *Grand Strategy. Vol. 1, Rearmament Policy* (London, 1976); W.D. McIntyre, *The Rise and Fall of the Singapore Naval Base* (London, 1979); J. Neidpath, *The Singapore Naval Base and the Defence of Britain's Eastern Empire, 1919–1941* (Oxford, 1981); I. Hamill, *The Strategic Illusion: The Singapore Strategy and the Defence of Australia and New Zealand* (Singapore, 1981); M.H. Murfett, "Reflections on an Enduring Theme: The Singapore Strategy at Sixty," in Brian P. Farrell and Sandy Hunter, eds., *Sixty Years On: The Fall of Singapore Revisited* (Singapore, 2002).

3 Public Record Office (PRO), London, WO172/17, War Diary, GHQ Malaya Command, Sept. 1939; *Operations of Malaya Command from 8th December 1941 to 15th February 1942*, para. 21; Ong C.C., *Operation Matador: Britain's War Plans against the Japanese 1918–1941* (Singapore, 1997), chap. 3.

4 PRO, AIR23/7761, RAF Far East Monthly General Summary of Work, Jan. 1937-July 1939; WO172/2, War Diary, GHQ Far East, June 1940; Ong, *Operation Matador*, 115, n. 86, 117, n. 93; H. Probert, *The Royal Air Force in the War against Japan 1941–1945* (London, 1995), 16–17; C. Kinvig, *Scapegoat: General Percival of Singapore* (London, 1996), 116–17.

5 PRO, CAB80/16, COS(40)592, Far East Appreciation, 15 Aug. 1941; WO172/3, War Diary, GHQ Far East, Appendix, Tactical Appreciation of Defence Situation in Malaya, 16 Oct. 1940; *Operations of Malaya Command*, paras. 24–6; S.W. Kirby, *The War against Japan. Vol.1. The Loss of Singapore* (hereafter *Loss of Singapore*) (London, 1957), 31–6.

6 PRO, CAB120/615, Minister of Defence Secretariat Files, Churchill to COS, 1, 10 Sept., Churchill to Lord Cranborne, 15 Dec. 1940, 5 Jan. 1941; 120/517, 22 Sept. 1940; CAB79/6, COS minutes, 4, 6, 9, 16, 17, 19 Sept. 1940; 79/7, 12, 19 Nov. 1940; 79/8, 13 Jan. 1941; CAB69/2, Defence Committee(Operations) (DC(O))minutes, 9, 29 April 1941;

W.S. Churchill, *The Grand Alliance* (Boston, 1950), 188–92; Ong, *Operation Matador*, chaps. 4, 5; Probert, *Royal Air Force*, 18; Kirby, *Loss of Singapore*, 48–50; Raymond Callahan, "Churchill and Singapore," in Farrell and Hunter, *Sixty Years On*.

7 For pre-war intelligence and appreciations, J.R. Ferris, "Worthy of Some Better Enemy: The British Estimate of the Imperial Japanese Army 1919–1941 and the Fall of Singapore," *Canadian Journal of History* 28 (Aug. 1993), is outstanding. See also P. Elphick, *Far Eastern File* (London, 1997), and R.J. Aldrich, *Intelligence and the War against Japan* (Cambridge, 2000). PRO, CAB79/15, COS minutes, 18 Nov. 1941, JIC(41)439, and CAB79/55, COS minutes, 28 Nov. 1941, indicate how late the authorities in London remained undecided about whether the Japanese would strike north or south. For the establishment of Far East Command under Brooke-Popham, see Kirby, *Chain of Disaster*, 42, 55–7. The decision to deploy Force Z can be traced in PRO, CAB79/13, COS minutes, 25 Aug. 1941, and CAB69/2, DC(O) minutes, 17, 20 Oct. 1941, plus S.W. Roskill, *The War at Sea 1939–1945. Vol. I. The Defensive* (London, 1954), 553–8. The decision to replace Brooke-Popham is discussed in Kirby, *Chain of Disaster*, 119–20, 130.

8 A good general discussion of the disastrous first four days of the campaign is Kirby, *Chain of Disaster*, chap. 14. For the destruction of Force Z, see Roskill, *War at Sea*, 559, 563–4; C. Barnett, *Engage the Enemy More Closely: The Royal Navy in the Second World War* (London, 1991), 406–21; and M. Middlebrook and P. Mahoney, *Battleship: The Loss of the Prince of Wales and the Repulse* (London, 1977). For the mishandling of Operation *Matador*, see PRO, WO172/15, War Diary, GHQ Far East, Dec. 1941, WO172/18, War Diary, GHQ Malaya Command, Dec. 1941, *Operations of Malaya Command*, paras. 128–30, and Ong, *Operation Matador*, chap. 8. The defeat at Jitra is also described in the war diaries. For the defeat of the RAF, see PRO, WO172/18, War Diary, GHQ Malaya Command, Appendix V.1, 10 Dec. 1941, *Operations of Malaya Command*, paras. 42, 125, 127, 132, 152, 158–60, and Probert, *Royal Air Force*, 30–2, 42–5, 48–50. For all the above, the most recent treatment is Brian P. Farrell, *The Defence and Fall of Singapore 1940–1942* (Gloucestershire, 2004), chap. 7.

9 PRO, WO172/18, War Diary, GHQ Malaya Command, 15–20 Dec. 1941; WO172/15, War Diary, GHQ Far East, 15–23 Dec. 1941; *Operations of Malaya Command*, paras. 136, 155, 177–93, 196–205; A.E. Percival, *The War in Malaya* (London, 1949), 152–58; Kinvig, *Scapegoat*, 170.

10 PRO, WO172/18, War Diary, GHQ Malaya Command, Appendices 22–9 Dec. 1941; WO172/20, War Diary, GHQ Malaya Command, Appendices

1–6 Jan. 1942; *Operations of Malaya Command*, paras. 212–13, 257, 260, 262, 268–80; Percival, *War in Malaya*, 192, 198; I. Simson, *Singapore: Too Little, Too Late* (London, 1970), 54–6, 62–3, 67–71; Tsuji Masanobu, *Singapore 1941–1942* (Oxford, 1988) (first published as *Singapore: The Japanese Version*, 1960), 151–2, 157–61; Kinvig, *Scapegoat*, 172–3; S. Falk, *Seventy Days to Singapore* (London, 1975), 148–9, 154–5. The latest narrative study of the campaign, based on thorough archival research, is A. Warren, *Singapore 1942: Britain's Greatest Defeat* (London, 2002).

11 Churchill, *Grand Alliance*, 636–9; Farrell, *Defence and Fall of Singapore*, chap. 9.

12 PRO, CAB69/2, DC(O) minutes, 19 Dec. 1941; CAB79/16, COS minutes, 22–3 Dec. 1941; AIR23/3575, COS to C-in-C Far East, 22 Dec. 1941; *Principal War Telegrams and Memoranda 1940–1943*, vol. 1 (hereafter *PT*, vol. 1) (Lichtenstein, 1976), WO to C-in-C India, 22 Dec. 1941, COS to C-in-C Far East, 22 Dec. 1941; J.R.M. Butler, *Grand Strategy. Vol. III, June 1941–August 1942 Part I* (London, 1964), 413–14.

13 *PT*, vol. 1, C-in-C Eastern Fleet to Admiralty, 13 Dec. 1941, Admiralty to C-in-C Eastern Fleet, 14, 17 Dec. 1941, COS to C-in-C India, C-in-C Far East, 17 Dec. 1941; PRO, CAB80/61, COS(42)7(O), 5 Jan. 1942; ADM199/1472B, Layton Despatch; *Operations of Malaya Command*, para. 229.

14 PRO, WO172/20, War Diary, GHQ Malaya Command, Appendix R.18, 1 Jan. 1942, Appendix F.21, 5 Jan. 1942; *Operations of Malaya Command*, paras. 262, 268–75.

15 PRO, CAB79/55, COS minutes, 11 Dec. 1941; 79/16, COS minutes, JP(41)1050, 12 Dec. 1941, COS minutes, 25 Dec. 1941; CAB79/17, COS minutes, 1 Jan. 1942; CAB69/2, DC(O) minutes, 19, 27 Dec. 1941; CAB80/60, COS(41)277(O), 14 Dec. 1941, COS(41)280(O)(revise), 20 Dec. 1941; LHCMA, Brooke Papers, 3A/V, 20, 24, 25 Dec. 1941 diary entries; LHCMA, Pownall Papers, 20, 30 Dec. 1941, 2, 5 Jan. 1942 diary entries; *PT*, vol. 1, Pownall to Brooke, 27 Dec., C-in-C Far East to WO, 29 Dec. 1941; *Operations of Malaya Command*, paras. 196, 254–6; Probert, *Royal Air Force*, 51–2.

16 PRO, WO172/20, War Diary, GHQ Malaya Command, Appendices W.21, G.22, 6 Jan. 1942, Appendices J.22, L.22, N.22, Q.22, U.22, 7 Jan. 1942; CAB106/195, Extract from Account of Slim River Battle January 1942, Brigadier Selby, 28th Indian Brigade; *Operations of Malaya Command*, paras. 293–4; Percival, *War in Malaya*, 191, 206; I.M. Stewart, *History of the Argyll and Sutherland Highlanders 2nd Battalion* (London, 1947), 75–86; Tsuji, *Singapore 1941–1942*, 171–5, 182; Simson, *Singapore*, 61–6; Kinvig, *Scapegoat*, 175; Kirby, *Chain of Disaster*, 177; Falk, *Seventy Days to*

Singapore, 149–53; J. Moffatt and A. McCormack, *Moon over Malaya: A Tale of Aryglls and Marines* (Gloucestershire, 2002), chap. 3.

17 *PT*, vol. 1, Wavell to Combined Chiefs of Staff (CCS), 15 Jan. 1942; PRO, CAB106/38, *Despatch on Operations in South-West Pacific, January 15th–February 25th 1942* (hereafter *Operations in South-West Pacific*), paras. 5, 13.

18 BL (OIOC), L/Mil/17/20/24, "Japanese Army Memorandum," issued by the General Staff H.M. Naval Base Singapore, reprinted with additions and modifications by the General Staff India, March 1941; PRO, CAB106/38, *Operations in South-West Pacific*, paras. 17, 20, 22, 34; Australian War Memorial (AWM), AWM73/65, Japanese Tactical Methods, report by US Army Observer in Malaya, Feb. 1942; Simson, *Singapore*, 26–7; J. Connell, *Wavell: Supreme Commander 1941–1943* (London, 1969), 36–7; P. Elphick, *Singapore: The Pregnable Fortress: A Study in Deception, Discord and Desertion* (London, 1995), 82–3; Elphick, *Far Eastern File*, 95, 158–9, 166–8; Ferris, "Worthy of Some Better Enemy," 227–51; L. Allen, *Singapore 1941–1942* (London, 1977), chap. 11; Probert, *Royal Air Force*, 27.

19 *PT*, vol. 1, Wavell to COS, 9, 12, 14, 15 Jan. 1942; PRO, CAB106/38, *Operations in South-West Pacific*, paras. 13–14; Connell, *Wavell*, 21; I. Beckett, *Wavell*, in J. Keegan, ed., *Churchill's Generals* (1991), 81–2; J. Smyth, *Percival and the Tragedy of Singapore* (London, 1971), 154–7.

20 Imperial War Museum (IWM), London, Percival Papers, P.21, F.26, Heath comments to Percival on draft report, n/d [written in captivity]; *Operations of Malaya Command*, paras. 196, 254–6, 407; PRO, CAB106/38, *Operations in South-West Pacific*, paras. 8, 13, Appendix A; LHCMA, Pownall Papers, 13 Jan. 1942 diary entry; Probert, *Royal Air Force*, 51–2; Smyth, 145.

21 PRO, CAB106/38, *Operations in South-West Pacific*, para. 21; *Operations of Malaya Command*, paras. 254, 338, 388, 397, 401–3, 405, 408; Percival, *War in Malaya*, 217–18; Tsuji, *Singapore 1941–1942*, 197–8; Probert, *Royal Air Force*, 56–60; Kirby, *Loss of Singapore*, 323–4, 331–2; J.R. Ferris, "Student and Master: The United Kingdom, Japan, Airpower and the Fall of Singapore, 1920–1941," in Farrell and Hunter, *Sixty Years On*.

22 PRO, WO172/15, War Diary, GHQ Far East, Wavell to Brooke-Popham, 16 Dec. 1941; IWM, Percival Papers, File 43, Summary of comments by Lord Wavell on General Percival's despatch, n/d [hereafter Wavell comments]; Smyth, *Percival*, 86–8, 154–7; Kinvig, *Scapegoat*, 176–8, 265 n 3.

23 *PT*, vol. 1, Churchill to Wavell, 10 Feb. 1942; W.S. Churchill, *The Hinge of Fate* (Boston, 1950), 82–7; Connell, *Wavell*, 157–9.

24 Wavell's statement appears in his posthumously published collection *Soldiers and Soldiering* (London, 1953), 31. The field marshal was referring to a commander addressing his troops in person, but the issue is relevant here, as this was the only way in which he could now communicate with the beleaguered Malaya Command rank and file. Connell, *Wavell*, 159, defends Wavell. R. Lewin, *The Chief: Field Marshal Lord Wavell, Commander-in-Chief and Viceroy 1939–1947* (London, 1980), 170, Smyth, *Percival*, 227–33, and Kinvig, *Scapegoat*, 209, do not. The Australian official history, L. Wigmore, *The Japanese Thrust* (Canberra, 1957), 341–2, is savagely critical of both Churchill and Wavell for this hectoring message. Smyth claimed that some commanders were so insulted that they did not pass Wavell's order on to their men. Russell Braddon, an Australian gunner, author of *The Naked Island* (Sydney, 1952), one of the most vitriolic memoirs written by a Malayan campaign veteran, wrote to Percival in 1954: "I have always regarded the late Lord Wavell's final message to the defenders of Singapore as itself utterly outrageous – both to you and the men who served under you. Therein, perhaps, lies the explanation of much of my vitriol." IWM, Percival Papers, File 48, Braddon to Percival, 2 Sept. 1954.

25 Connell, *Wavell*, 71.

26 PRO, CAB80/61 and CAB99/17 document the establishment of ABDA Command; WO172/16, War Diary, GHQ Far East, COS to Wavell, 1 Jan. 1942, spells out the task assigned to Wavell; CAB106/38, *Operations in Southwest Pacific*, paras. 1–4; Connell, *Wavell*, 69–73, and in an appendix, 291–4, the directive given Wavell on 3 January.

27 Connell is the standard biography, written with access to the field marshal's papers. Connell, Lewin, and Beckett all give good portraits of Wavell's character. All agree that his failure to communicate effectively with Churchill, even to understand the need to establish some durable empathy, was the root cause of their failure to work well together. For a personal account, see B. Fergusson, *Wavell: Portrait of a Soldier* (London, 1961). For the most recent assessment, see H.E. Raugh, *Wavell in the Middle East: A Study in Generalship 1939–1941* (London, 1993).

28 LHCMA, Pownall Papers, 5, 8 Jan. 1942 diary entries; PRO, WO172/16, War Diary, GHQ Far East, 1–7 Jan. 1942; Connell, *Wavell*, 78–80.

29 PRO, WO172/16, War Diary, GHQ Far East, Wavell to COS, 8 Jan. 1942; CAB106/38, *Operations in South-West Pacific*, paras. 5–6; *Operations of Malaya Command*, paras. 296–7.

30 PRO, WO172/16, War Diary, GHQ Far East, Wavell to COS, 8 Jan. 1942; WO172/18, War Diary, GHQ Malaya Command, Appendices G.9, O.9,

18 Dec., Appendix W.15, 28 Dec. 1941, Appendix R.16, 29 Dec. 1941,
serial 1651, 29 Dec. 1941; CAB106/38, *Operations in South-West Pacific*,
para. 6; IWM, Heath Papers, LM7, Postwar Correspondence, Heath to
Percival, n/d; *Operations of Malaya Command*, paras. 296–7; Stewart,
History of Argyll and Sutherland Highlanders, preface by Wavell, v;
Simson, *Singapore*, 54–6, 62–3, 67–71; Connell, *Wavell*, 83–5; Kinvig,
Scapegoat, 178; Farrell, *Defence and Fall of Singapore*, chap. 10.

31 PRO, CAB106/38, *Operations in South-West Pacific*, paras. 9, 21; LHCMA,
Pownall Papers, 8 Jan. 1942 diary entry; IWM, Percival Papers, File 43,
Wavell comments; *Operations of Malaya Command*, para. 436; Simson,
Singapore, 68–72, 86–9, 106–7; Churchill, *Hinge of Fate*, 45–6; N. Barber,
Sinister Twilight: The Fall of Singapore (London, 1968), 78–9; Falk, *Seventy
Days to Singapore*, 206–7.

32 Kinvig, *Scapegoat*, passim, is the fairest discussion of Percival's person-
ality and appearance; see especially 111–12, 178, 225–8, and also
"General Percival and the Fall of Singapore," in Farrell and Hunter,
Sixty Years On.

33 PRO, CAB106/38, *Operations in South-West Pacific*, paras. 7–8; LHCMA,
Pownall Papers, 8 Jan. 1942 diary entry; H.G. Bennett, *Why Singapore
Fell* (Sydney, 1944), 16, 47–8, 100; Kinvig, *Scapegoat*, 178–9; Wigmore,
Japanese Thrust, 198–203; A.B. Lodge, *The Fall of General Gordon Bennett*
(North Sydney, 1986), passim, is the best description of Bennett.

34 PRO, CAB106/38, *Operations in South-West Pacific*, paras. 7–8; WO172/16,
War Diary, GHQ Far East, Malaya Command Operations Instruction 32,
8 Jan. 1942, Wavell to COS, 9 Jan. 1942; WO172/20, War Diary, GHQ
Malaya Command, Appendix Q.23, 9 Jan. 1942; IWM, Percival Papers,
File 43, Wavell comments; *Operations of Malaya Command*, paras. 290–1,
299, 346; Percival, *War in Malaysia*, 208–10; Kirby, *Chain of Disaster*, 185;
Kinvig, *Scapegoat*, 178–9; Connell, *Wavell*, 87–8.

35 Kirby, *Chain of Disaster*, 185, at least implies some criticism of Wavell
here. Connell offers none. Lodge details how Bennett poisoned his
relations with many of his Australian superiors and subordinates.

36 *PT*, vol. 1, Churchill to Wavell, 15 Jan., Wavell to Churchill, 16 Jan.
1942; IWM, Percival Papers, File 43, Wavell comments; Churchill, *Hinge
of Fate*, 38–45; Simson, *Singapore*, 106; Connell, *Wavell*, 106–11.

37 PRO, WO172/19, War Diary, GHQ Malaya Command, Operations
Instruction 33, 9 Jan. 1942; IWM, Percival Papers, File 48, Percival to
Kirby, 2 Dec. 1953, comments on official history draft; File 43, Wavell
comments, suggests that the supreme commander wanted Percival to
send up a Singapore-based brigade, bringing 53rd Brigade onto the

island. Whatever Wavell's intention, he allowed Percival to alter the whole plan. *Operations of Malaya Command*, paras. 301–3, 315, 330, 332; Bennett, *Why Singapore Fell*, 47–8; Wigmore, *Japanese Thrust*, 203, 211–12; Lodge, *Fall of General Bonnett*, 109–10; Kinvig, *Scapegoat*, 178–9, 184; Smyth, *Percival*, 155–6.

38 PRO, CAB106/162, Report on Operations of 8th Division AIF in Malaya (Thyer Report); Bennett, *Why Singapore Fell*, 101–4; Wigmore, *Japanese Thrust*, 211–12; Lodge, *Fall of General Bennett*, 109–13; Kirby, *Chain of Disaster*, 198–200.

39 *PT*, vol. 1, Wavell to COS, 9, 12, 14, 15 Jan. 1942; IWM, Percival Papers, File 43, Wavell comments; PRO, CAB106/38, *Operations in South-West Pacific*, paras. 13–14; *Operations of Malaya Command*, paras. 303, 315, 330; Wigmore, *Japanese Thrust*, 203, 211–12; Lodge, *Fall of General Bennett*, 109–10; Kinvig, *Scapegoat*, 178–9, 184; Smyth, *Percival*, 155–6; Connell, *Wavell*, 85–95.

40 The ambush at Gemas is described in AWM52/8/3/30, War Diary, 2/30 AIF; PRO, WO172/20, War Diary, GHQ Malaya Command, Appendix U.26, 15 Jan. 1942; see also Appendices 15–18 Jan. 1942; CAB106/162, Thyer Report; *Operations of Malaya Command*, paras. 347, 368; Bennett, *Why Singapore Fell*, 112–16; Percival, *War in Malaya*, 224; Tsuji, *Singapore 1941–1942*, 192–4; Wigmore, *Japanese Thrust*, 214–18; Falk, *Seventy Days to Singapore*, 167–9.

41 PRO, WO172/20, War Diary, GHQ Malaya Command, Appendices, 16–21 Jan. 1942; CAB106/162, Thyer Report; *Operations of Malaya Command*, paras. 300, 348–70; Percival, *War in Malaya*, 222, 224, 227–33; Bennett, *Why Singapore Fell*, 126–7, 131–2, 144; Wigmore, *Japanese Thrust*, 222–46; Kirby, *Loss of Singapore*, 304; Falk, *Seventy Days to Singapore*, 169–74, 177–9; Kirby, *Chain of Disaster*, 198–205.

42 PRO, AIR23/3575, GHQ Southwest Pacific Command to Commander, Singapore Garrison, 16 Jan. 1942; WO172/20, War Diary, GHQ Malaya Command, 18 Jan. 1942; Connell, *Wavell*, 107–8.

43 *PT*, vol. 1. Wavell to Churchill, 19 Jan. 1942; IWM, Percival Papers, File 43, Wavell comments; Kirby, *Loss of Singapore*, 317; Churchill, *Hinge of Fate*, 47–8. Connell, *Wavell*, 110–12; Kinvig, *Scapegoat*, 187–8.

44 *PT*, vol. 1, Wavell to COS, 9, 12, 14, 15, 19 Jan. 1942; PRO, WO172/16, War Diary, GHQ Far East, COS to Wavell, 31 Dec. 1941; CAB106/38, *Operations in South-West Pacific*, paras. 5, 13, 18, 24.

45 *PT*, vol. 1, Wavell to Churchill, 19, 21 Jan. 1942, Churchill to Wavell, 23 Jan. 1942, vol. 6, COS(W)19, Curtin to Churchill, 28 Jan. 1942, COS(W)20, COS comments on same, 28 Jan. 1942; PRO, CAB106/38,

Operations in South-West Pacific, paras. 18, 21; CAB80/61, Churchill to
Ismay, 21 Jan. 1942; CAB80/33, COS(42)37, 20 Jan. 1942; CAB79/56, COS
minutes, 21 Jan. 1942; CAB69/4, DC(O) minutes, 21 Jan. 1942; CAB65/25,
War Cabinet minutes, 22, 26 Jan. 1942; CAB65/29, confidential annex,
26 Jan. 1942; W.F. Kimball, ed., *Churchill and Roosevelt: The Complete
Correspondence* (Princeton, 1984), vol. 1, telegrams C-159x, 27/1, R-78x,
30 Jan. 1942; Churchill, *Hinge of Fate,* 47–52; Kinvig, *Scapegoat,* 187–8, 194;
Kirby, *Chain of Disaster,* 214–17; Wigmore, *Japanese Thrust,* 285–7. Wavell's
authority to dispose of reinforcements sent to him was spelt out in PRO,
WO172/16, War Diary, GHQ Far East, COS to Wavell, 1 Jan. 1942.

46 PRO, WO172/20, War Diary, GHQ Malaya Command, 27–8 Jan. 1942;
CAB106/38, *Operations in South-West Pacific,* paras. 5, 21, 36; *Operations
of Malaya Command,* paras. 390–2, 407; Connell, *Wavell,* 127–8; Kinvig,
Scapegoat, 188–91.

47 PRO, PREM3/168/3, WP(42)314, Operations in Malaya and Singapore,
8 Sept. 1942: see especially covering letter, Wavell to Brooke, 1 June
1942, and Appendix B; CAB106/38, *Operations in South-West Pacific,*
para. 9; Simson, *Singapore,* 83–9; B. Montgomery, *Shenton of Singapore:
Governor and Prisoner of War* (Singapore, 1984), 106, 117–19; Kirby, *Chain
of Disaster,* 190–6; Connell, *Wavell,* 95–9.

48 Simson, *Singapore,* 78–91, 100–1; Montgomery, *Shenton of Singapore,*
114–24; Kirby, *Chain of Disaster,* 191–6, 229; Percival, *War in Malaya,* 182;
Smyth, *Percival,* 99.

49 Even Connell, *Wavell,* 99, criticized Wavell here, not very subtly.
Lewin's comment, *Chief,* 165, is more pointed: "But the Russians did
not put 'good figureheads' into Stalingrad or Leningrad" – or leave
them there.

50 The final rearguard is discussed in *Operations of Malaya Command,*
paras. 390–2, 396, 460, 462, 465, Falk, *Seventy Days to Singapore,* 190–1,
196–7, Moffatt and McCormick, *Moon over Malaya,* 132–5. For defences,
see *Operations of Malaya Command,* paras. 390, 419, 435–6, 451, 458, 460,
462–5, 594–9, 612; Percival, *War in Malaya,* 254–6, 257, 259; Bennett, *Why
Singapore Fell,* 165; G. Chippington, *Singapore: The Inexcusable Betrayal*
(United Kingdom, 1992), 174–5, 237; D. Russell-Roberts, *Spotlight on
Singapore* (United Kingdom, 1965), 113; Kinvig, *Scapegoat,* 203; Kirby,
Chain of Disaster, 221–2; Lodge, *Fall of General Bennett,* 140–1; Wigmore,
Japanese Thrust, 294–5; R. Holmes and A. Kemp, *The Bitter End*
(Chichester, 1982), 152–3.

51 *Operations of Malaya Command,* paras. 390, 419, 435–6, 451, 594–9, 612;
Percival, *War in Malaya,* 254. Kinvig, *Scapegoat,* 195, is the only other

study to note the effect of his perception of the mission on Percival's decisions on defences for Singapore. On 246, Kinvig suggests that bias in favour of Wavell led Kirby to blame Percival unfairly on this issue in the British official history. See note 81 below.

52 Churchill, *Hinge of Fate*, 38–45.

53 LHCMA, Pownall Papers, 8 Jan. 1942 diary entry.

54 PRO, CAB106/38, *Operations in Southwest Pacific*, para. 24.

55 Ibid.; IWM, Percival Papers, File 43, Wavell comments. *Operations of Malaya Command*, paras. 437, 456, 459–68; Percival, *War in Malaya*, 261, and Smyth, *Percival*, 215, contradict Wavell, claiming that the GOC correctly anticipated where the Japanese would attack. Kirby, *Chain of Disaster*, 220–1, rejects this view, citing the conversation between Wavell and Percival on 20 January and a postwar letter from Percival. That letter is in IWM, Percival Papers, File 48, Percival to Kirby, 2 Dec. 1953, comments on official history draft. PRO, WO172/21, War Diary, GHQ Malaya Command, for February 1942, makes it clear that the largest and freshest division, the bulk of the field artillery, and until the last moment most of the defensive materiel were stationed in Northern Area – where, Percival (when he made up his mind) concluded, the main attack would likely come. Kinvig, "General Percival and the Fall of Singapore," in Farrell and Hunter, *Sixty Years On*, 257–8, agrees.

56 AWM, 52/8/2/22, War Diary, 22nd Brigade AIF, 1–8 Feb. 1942; 52/8/3/18, War Diary, 2/18 AIF, 1–8 Feb. 1942 entries; PRO, CAB106/162, Thyer Report; Wigmore, *Japanese Thrust*, 258; Bennett, *Why Singapore Fell*, 165–71; Elphick, *Singapore*, 288–9; Kirby, *Chain of Disaster*, 223; Lodge, *Fall of General Bennett*, 129–33.

57 For the first three days of the battle of Singapore, see PRO, WO172/21, War Diary, GHQ Malaya Command, serials and appendices 8–10 Feb. 1942; CAB106/162, Thyer Report; AWM, 52/8/2/22, War Diary, 22nd Brigade AIF, 8–10 Feb. 1942, Appendices A and B entries; 52/8/2/27, War Diary, 27th Brigade AIF, 8–10 Feb. 1942; 52/8/3/18, War Diary, 2/18 AIF, 8–10 Feb. 1942 entries; Kirby, *Loss of Singapore*, 387–8.

58 PRO, WO172/21, War Diary, GHQ Malaya Command, Appendix V.58, 10 Feb. 1942; CAB106/38, *Operations in South-West Pacific*, para. 27; Kirby, *Loss of Singapore*, 387–8; Connell, *Wavell*, 155–61; Kinvig, *Scapegoat*, 209.

59 PRO, WO172/21, War Diary, GHQ Malaya Command, Appendices Q.59, X.59, F.60, J.60, O.60, 11 Feb. 1942; IWM, Percival Papers, File 48, Percival to Kirby, 26 Dec. 1954, comments on official history draft, in which Percival claims that Wavell agreed at the time that there was still a threat which obliged III Indian Corps to stand fast on the north coast; AWM,

52/8/2/22, War Diary, 22nd Brigade AIF, Appendices A and B, 11 Feb. 1942 entries; 52/8/2/27, War Diary, 27th Brigade AIF, 11 Feb. 1942; *Operations of Malaya Command*, paras. 520–7, 530–7; Stewart, *History of Argyll and Sutherland Highlanders*, 104–12; Tsuji, *Singapore 1941–1942*, 255–6; Kirby, *Loss of Singapore*, 391–7; Wigmore, *Japanese Thrust*, 346–53.

60 PRO, CAB66/21, War Cabinet situation report, 12 Feb. 1942; CAB79/18, COS minutes, 13 Feb. 1942; CAB106/38, *Operations in South-West Pacific*, paras. 27–9; *PT*, vol. 1, Churchill to Wavell, 10 Feb. 1942, Wavell to CCS, 13 Feb. 1942, Wavell to Churchill, Churchill to Wavell, 14 Feb. 1942, Percival to Wavell, 15 Feb. 1942; *Operations of Malaya Command*, paras. 553, 574–82; Percival, *War in Malaya*, 286, 291–2; Churchill, *Hinge of Fate*, 82–7, 90–2; Kirby, *Loss of Singapore*, 409–10; Wigmore, *Japanese Thrust*, 371–2, 378–80; Connell, *Wavell*, 161–9; Allen, *Singapore 1941–1942*, 175–84.

61 Wavell blamed the rapid fall of Singapore for what he obviously saw as the imminent collapse of his whole theatre and of the Allied defensive strategy against Japan: PRO, CAB106/163, Wavell to Brooke, 17 Feb. 1942.

62 LHCMA, Brooke-Popham Papers, V/5, Signals on Change of Command, Wavell to Brooke-Popham, 10 April 1942. This is confirmed by the field marshal's son: IWM, Percival Papers, File 88, Miscellaneous Letters, Earl Wavell to Percival, no date (early 1950s).

63 PRO, PREM3/168/3, Bridges to Rowan, 17 July 1942, Wavell to Brooke, 1 June 1942, WP(42)314, 8 Sept. 1942. Many of the reports read by Wavell are filed as appendices in WO172/16, War Diary, GHQ Far East, Jan. 1942.

64 PRO, PREM3/168/3, Wavell to Brooke, 1 June, WP(42)314, Appendices, 8 Sept. 1942. Emphasis regarding Appendix A added.

65 PRO, PREM3/168/3, correspondence, Churchill with Attlee and Cabinet Office Secretariat, 17 July–6 Sept. 1942. Churchill's insistence delayed the restricted circulation of this paper from early June to early September 1942.

66 PRO, CAB106/38, *Operations in South-West Pacific*, paras. 34–7.

67 Elphick, *Singapore*, 179–80.

68 IWM, Percival Papers, File 43, Appendix B. A representative list of authors analysing the fall of Singapore and assigning blame includes Allen, Barber, Elphick, Falk, Holmes, Kirby, Ong, Warren, and Wigmore. None assigns Wavell any significant blame, taking a cue from Connell, Kirby, and the basic argument that by the time Wavell arrived nothing that he did could have saved it, so no errors he made were of any consequence.

69 PRO, CAB119/208, Chifley to Attlee, 28 Jan. 1946, extract from COS minutes, 29 Jan. 1946, Attlee to Chifley, 31 Jan. 1946, extract from VCOS minutes, 31 Jan. 1946.

70 PRO, CAB119/208, JP(46)29(Final), Malayan Campaign – Public Inquiry, Annex, Part I, 5 March 1946.

71 PRO, CAB119/208, Extract from COS minutes, 8 March 1946, JP(46)56(S)(T. of R.), 8 March 1946, JP(46)56(Final), Malayan Campaign – Limitations of a Public Inquiry, 6 May 1946.

72 PRO, CAB119/208, Telegrams, minutes, memoranda, Jan.–June 1946; the JPS quote is in JP(46)29(Final), 5 March 1946, para. 4.

73 PRO, CAB119/208, JP(46)29(Final), Annex, 5 March 1946.

74 Compare the treatment accorded to Wavell on the one hand and to Churchill and Percival on the other hand by Allen, Connell, Elphick, Falk, Kirby, Lewin, Widmore, and R. Woolcombe, *The Campaigns of Wavell* (London, 1959). While their decisions were of more consequence, Wavell should not have been excused entirely – especially with regard to Percival. Smyth is not always reliable, having been a friend of Percival's and a subordinate sacked controversially by Wavell during the Burma campaign. Kinvig, *Scapegoat*, chap. 20, gives a more balanced account of the controversy over blame. Percival would have been very exercised indeed to read the documents of spring 1946 contained in CAB119/208. Instead he was cold-shouldered by an establishment that made him carry the entire burden for a collective failure.

75 An over-the-top Australian account of the controversy is D. Day, *The Great Betrayal: Britain, Australia and the Onset of the Pacific War 1939–1942* (London, 1989). A more reliable rendering is D.M. Horner, *High Command: Australia and Allied Strategy 1939–1945* (London, 1982). A full account of British grand strategy is Brian P. Farrell, *The Basis and Making of British Grand Strategy 1940–1943: Was There a Plan?* (New York, 1998). Good summaries of the "Singapore strategy" and the British–Australian controversy are M.H. Murfett, "Living in the Past: A Critical Re-examination of the Singapore Strategy 1918–1941," in *War and Society* 11, no. 1 (May 1993), and "When Trust Is not Enough: Australia and the Singapore Strategy," in C. Bridge and B. Attard, eds., *Between Empire and Nation: Australian External Relations 1901–1939* (Melbourne, 1998).

76 Elphick, *Singapore*, chaps. 13–15, was the first analysis of the Australian collapse on Singapore island. But Elphick did not bother – in this or his subsequent book – to consult Australian records in Australia, especially the formation war diaries. A more complete study is B.P. Farrell, Appendix 3, "Controversies Surrounding the Surrender of Singapore,

February 1942," in M.H. Murfett et al., *Between Two Oceans: A Military History of Singapore* (Singapore, 1999). Warren, *Singapore 1942*, chap. 16, also examined Australian records.

77 Specifically, PRO, PREM3/168/3, WP(42)314, 8 Sept. 1942, covered by Wavell's letter of 1 June 1942, with its controversial appendices.

78 Farrell, *Defense and Fall of Singapore*, Appendix 3, "Controversies"; chap. 9; Warren, *Singapore, 1942*, chaps. 16–17.

79 PRO, CAB119/208, JP(46)29(Final), 5 March 1946.

80 Murfett, "Living in the Past," n. 3. An extreme response to the Wavell report is Roy Connolly and Bob Wilson, *Cruel Britannia: Britannia Waives the Rules 1941–42. Singapore Betrayed, Australia Abandoned* (New South Wales, 1994). The story of Wavell's baton is told by Lewin, 206–8. See also Peter Dennis, "Australia and the 'Singapore Strategy,'" in Farrell and Hunter, *Sixty Years On*.

81 IWM, Percival Papers, File 48, Miscellaneous Papers, Phillips to Percival, 27 Nov. 1954. Kinvig, *Scapegoat*, 246–7, 271 n. 36, quotes Kirby in a letter to Percival dated 16 December 1953! "I have served under Wavell personally and know that his memory is absolutely infallible." The letter is in Percival Papers, File 42. Percival fought with the British official historians for nearly a decade over their drafts and analysis, and much of the acrimony involved Wavell and his comments for the record. Phillips's own view was certainly shared by Percival: "I fear that General Kirby is a very difficult man to tie down. He feels that he has a mission to lay the blame on someone, and is prepared to say that every one was wrong all the time, except possibly General Wavell." Percival's final comments, written in January 1962 regarding drafts of the forthcoming volume in the Grand Strategy series of the official history project, pointedly complained about a chapter ending with some "hasty opinions expressed by Wavell": P.23, F.48.

82 Smyth, *Percival*, 263.

83 J. Connell, *Wavell: Scholar and Soldier* (London, 1964), Book Two; Raugh, *Wavell in the Middle East*, passim; Lewin, *Chief*, chaps. 2–5.

84 Connell, *Wavell: Supreme Commander*, chaps. 3–4, backs away from Wavell's treatment of Percival and his role in the battle plan for the defence of Johore but is more sceptical of his handling of Thomas; Lewin, *Chief*, 165, condemns it bluntly.

85 Wavell, *Soldiers and Soldiering*, 26; Connell, *Wavell: Supreme Commander*, 71–2.

86 Connell, *Wavell: Scholar and Soldier*, Book Two; Rauch, *Wavell in the Middle East*, passim; Farrell, *British Grand Strategy*, Part 2.

87 PRO, CAB106/163, Wavell to Brooke, 17 Feb. 1942; *PT*, vol. 1, Wavell to Brooke, Wavell to Churchill and Brooke, 18 Feb. 1942; Connell, *Wavell: Supreme Commander*, 181–2.

88 In *Soldiers and Soldiering*, 78, Wavell took full responsibility for supporting the diversion of troops to Greece in spring 1941. But on page 92, his comment on ABDA was blunt: "[I]t never had the resources to stem the Japanese attack." This contradicts his immediate reaction, as expressed privately to Joan Bright Astley. Nor did it stop him from making critical remarks about Malaya Command's pre-war preparations, on page 109, and in BL(OIOC), L/Mil/17/5/2223, *A Note on Training for Commanding Officers*, May 1942. Yet he was on record as stating in November 1941, after his visit to Malaya and Singapore, "From the very little I saw and what I heard of the lay-out, I should think the Jap has a very poor chance of successfully attacking Malaya, and I don't think myself, that there is much prospect of his trying." – Connell, *Wavell*, 41. Wavell was not alone in being so wrong, but while the human frailty displayed by forgetting embarrassing mistakes in later years and letting others take the calumny might be all too common, it is not the fibre of supreme command. Wavell's official but unpublished criticisms of the campaign also indicated that he knew full well that the Australian collapse at the end was hardly decisive.

89 An interesting exception is H.P. Willmott, *Empires in the Balance: Japanese and Allied Pacific Strategies to April 1942* (Annapolis, Md, 1982).

90 Connell, *Wavell*, 159; Lewin, *Chief*, 164.

8

Colonials and Coalitions: Canadian–British Command Relations between Normandy and the Scheldt

PAUL D. DICKSON

Canada's wartime experiences were, and are, shaped by coalitions. The country has always fought as part of an empire or in partnership with major powers. The anticipation of that situation has shaped doctrine, training, organization, and equipment policy. Prior to the Second World War, the professional education of officers destined for senior command was predicated on the assumption that they would fight in conjunction with the British forces. The constitutional autonomy recognized by the Statute of Westminster in 1931 did nothing to alter the military's dependence on the British for military expertise or the reality that the forces would still fight in co-operation with the British military – a reality codified in legislation that redefined the relationship between the Dominion and British militaries and provided the framework for cooperation with other nations.

During the Second World War, the legislation created for Canadian senior command a dual accountability: first to the government and then to the chain of command in the British and Allied armies. This provided the framework for the command decisions of Canadian senior officers during the war. That fact, however, has not always informed evaluations of their operational performance. Responsibility and accountability were not always clear-cut and could be contradictory. The conduct of operations immediately following the breakout from Normandy, in early autumn 1944, was an example of this dilemma. By autumn 1944 the Canadian army was not simply a British dependant but was fighting in a multinational coalition operation, operating in a coalition military formation structured in such a way as to render a national army commander dependent on many forces beyond his control. The campaign was hampered by the gradual decline in strength of the combat units of First Canadian Army, supply problems, plus lack of operational support from the coalition forces of which the army was a part. The GOC, General H.D.G. "Harry" Crerar, pressed for greater support and on at least one occasion reduced the scope of operations to take into account the depleted strength of his units. He was harshly criticized for failing to pursue coalition strategy vigorously at a critical juncture of the campaign. Yet he was also attacked for failing to take responsibility for his men by fighting with understrength formations. Where did this national army commander's responsibility lie? To whom was he accountable? Should the military goal have overridden all other considerations?

This study first outlines accountability and responsibility as they evolved during and between the two world wars. It then looks at them specifically in terms of Crerar's relationship with the British chain of command, especially with Field Marshal B.L. Montgomery, in the late summer of 1944, after the Allied breakout from Normandy. It examines in turn the Canadian manpower crisis, an important clash over accountability between the two commanders on 3 September, and the evolving plans vis-à-vis the Scheldt and the Channel ports, complicated by Canadian shortages of personnel and materiel. These few weeks highlighted the paradox that meeting coalition requirements could be at odds with defending national considerations. The conclusion reconsiders Crerar's accountability and responsibility during that brief but crucial period.

Accountability and responsibility are of late subjects of some interest to the Canadian military. Much of the debate surrounding the recent inquiry into the "Somalia Affair" centred on the degree to which the chief of the Defence Staff (CDS) was responsible for the actions of those under his command and to what degree he could be held accountable. The issue was not resolved in the CDS's favour. It was not a new issue, however; it was an important one for the Canadians and British during the two world wars. Indeed, it provides the subtext for any study of command relations between the two. It was the twin questions of accountability and responsibility that shaped the evolution of the Canadians from colonials to nominal partners in the Allied coalition.

The relationship between British and Canadian forces was defined by two related events: the First World War and the Statute of Westminster's Visiting Forces Act. The latter recognized as constitutional law what the Canadian Corps asserted in the former: the right of Canadian forces to choose the nature of their relationship with the United Kingdom, and, as it turned out, with any allied nations. The Visiting Forces (British Commonwealth) Act of 1933 (VFA) was the military corollary to the Statute of Westminster, which in 1931 redefined the constitutional relationship between the dominions and Great Britain. The VFA defined the legal relationship between the Canadian military and that of the other Commonwealth countries. Its main points reflected the complexity of recognizing the autonomy of the Canadian military at the same time as the forces of the Commonwealth countries were tied together by organization, equipment, training, and doctrine, not to mention a shared heritage – a particularly critical component of an army organized around the regimental system. In retrospect it was a remarkable document, in that it allowed for the complete integration of two, or more, independent military forces. While this act recognized that, despite its independence, the Canadian military was very much tied to the British in practice, it also confirmed that there was no desire to lose the real, or perceived, benefits of that relationship.

The act defined two possible relationships into which the Canadian military could enter with its Commonwealth counterparts: "acting in combination" and "serving together." The first prescribed a unified command structure and essentially created, for operational purposes, one force. In many ways, it was simply a continuation of past practice and as such retained the same degree of ambiguity with regard to the relationship between the national government and its army in the field when it served as a component of a larger force. Serving together recognized the evolution of the relationship: in practice it defined a coalition partnership of two independent forces. While the responsibilities of the command structure in both scenarios were relatively clear, the accountability of the Canadian commander was implicit rather than explicit; it did not define the relationship between the civil and the military authority. When under higher British command, the commander was subject to "the powers of command as if he were a member of the home force," but the established precedent was that the senior Canadian officer was answerable to the Canadian government for all operational commitments.[1] It was not immediately clear that this meant all Canadian troops in a given theatre, whether they were under his command or not; nor was it clear how to define accountability when the senior commander made the decisions about military necessity while the subordinate commander had the right of reference to a government if he felt that national considerations were at stake. General Sir Arthur Currie's refusal during the crisis of March 1918 to parcel out his formations, as C-in-C General Sir Douglas Haig required, was the best example of how this authority could be used to break the chain of command. Neither did the VFA clarify whether it was the government or the Canadian senior officer who should make the decision about what constituted a "national consideration" that could outweigh a military one. These details were hammered out in the first years of the Second World War.

Defining the compromise at the core of the VFA was easier than putting it into practice. The ambiguity of the act left to the Canadian senior command a great deal of independence to define its own relationships with the British and the Canadian governments. Both General Andrew McNaughton and General Harry Crerar, the two architects of the wartime relationships, had had their nationalism forged in the battles of the First World War, and both vigorously pursued British recognition of Canada's autonomous position in the Second. They also recognized, and believed in, the value of the British connection. However, the strength of that belief was not static; familiarity did, to a certain degree, breed, if not contempt, then at least suspicion.

McNaughton and Crerar interpreted the VFA as creating a two-fold responsibility for the senior Canadian commander to the Canadian government and to the British commander-in-chief. They considered, however, that they were accountable only to the former.[2] This was not always appreciated by the British – or by the Canadian government, for that matter – who often required gentle reminders that the Canadian forces were independent. The high-strung McNaughton was not so gentle, however, and, while the British got the message, the resulting acrimony worked against him. Although Crerar was also high-strung, he was more adept at masking his feelings while tempering his approach with a sense of diplomacy.[3]

It is somewhat misleading to characterize as national the struggles between the Canadian senior command and the British and between the Canadian senior command and its government. The relationships defined by the VFA were relatively clear on that point: Canadian forces were independent. Rather, the process was one of bringing home to the British the painful reality that they no longer had the convenience of treating the Canadians as British troops and to the Canadians the fact that independence cost money, and sometimes blood. When in 1940 GOC Home Forces Lt.-General Alan Brooke complained in his diary that the Canadians were more difficult to handle than allies, he was reflecting the difficulties inherent in the concurrent transitions from colony to nation and from mother country to equal.[4] It is wrong to see the Canadians and British as simply coalition partners. The relationship was far more complex, particularly early in the war. The fights between McNaughton and Brooke, who from December 1941 on was CIGS, were characteristic of family struggles; Brooke commented on the childlike and touchy nature of the Canadians, who in turn sought autonomy without responsibility. The planning and execution of the Dieppe raid in 1942 constituted a good example of some of the contradictions inherent in this struggle. In its aftermath, there was a definite tightening of the procedures for accountability and responsibility between Ottawa and its senior officers. This was the situation that faced the new army commander, Harry Crerar, as he prepared his forces for the landings in France.[5]

Through to the end of 1943, McNaughton fought most of the political battles, and suffered for it. The animosities generated by his struggles with Brooke played a role, if not the major one, in his removal from command in late 1943. Crerar became army commander in March 1944, and, while most of the British senior command recognized the principle of autonomy, questions of operational responsibility and accountability remained unanswered. Crerar recognized this problem, made aware of it when in April 1944 the Canadian government requested a formal statement from him regarding the feasibility of the upcoming operation, so it could issue formal instructions detailing his responsibilities to the government and the position of First Canadian Army within the British 21st Army Group. While such a statement would follow the precedent set by McNaughton prior to Canadian participation in operations in Sicily,[6] Crerar objected initially, protesting that the government's permission for Canadian involvement in the D-Day invasion was implicit in its placing First Canadian Army "in combination" with 21st Army Group. It appeared that Prime Minister William Lyon Mackenzie King and Minister of National Defence J.L. Ralston feared the worst and were at least preparing a sacrificial lamb in case it occurred. A strongly worded telegram from Ralston, however, moved Crerar to review the plans with Keller and to forward his assessment that he was "satisfied that the tasks allotted ... in the forthcoming invasion of enemy occupied Europe, are feasible operations of war and ... are capable of being carried out with reasonable prospects for success."[7] Crerar did believe this, talking privately of his "supreme confidence that [the] first assault will succeed provided the timing is right."[8]

This exchange showed that, irrespective of the operational chain of command within 21st Army Group, the Canadian commander was ultimately accountable for Canadians when they were committed to operations. Thus, concurrent with the discussions between Crerar, Lt.-General Ken Stuart, the chief of staff at Canadian Military Headquarters (CMHQ) in Britain, and Ralston, Crerar and Stuart determined that formally establishing Crerar's position as Canadian army commander within the British 21st Army Group was necessary to strengthen their hands in the event of problems with the British or other Allied leaders. Crerar wanted to ensure that if he was accountable for Canadians overseas, he could make sure that they were not exposed to unnecessary risks. He seized on the opportunity provided in April by the abrupt refusal by Montgomery, Allied Ground Forces commander, to allow the Canadian prime minister to observe 3rd Canadian Division while it took part in the combined training exercise *Fabius* unless he was ordered to do so by higher authorities, reasoning that "no 'non-professional' people should be about." This was consistent with Montgomery's past approach, but his snub of Mackenzie King raised further questions about his respect for national sensibilities.[9]

Crerar and Stuart staked their ground in late April, presenting their concerns to Ralston's envoy. They argued that the Canadian army commander must not be treated like any other British commander but must be viewed as head of the army of "an Allied nation – as a separate nation [with] independent status."[10] On 1 May, they officially urged Ralston by cable to formally draft instructions to the army commander stating that Ottawa desired both that Canadian formations remain under First Canadian Army except in an emergency and that they all be united under it after hostilities with Germany ceased. Crerar also pressed Stuart successfully to follow the principle that only he, or someone directly responsible to him, could represent Canadian views to Montgomery and U.S. General Dwight Eisenhower, supreme commander of the Allied Expeditionary Force. A spate of cables between the Department of National Defence (DND) in Ottawa and CMHQ ensued, during which the details of the government's instructions to Crerar were hammered out. The most contentious point was the difficulty of ensuring that Canadian commanders were informed of operations without prejudicing operational secrecy, but in time to exercise their right to withdraw Canadians if they felt it necessary. After some debate, and some hesitation by Mackenzie King, cabinet approved the instructions on 24 May 1944. It proved a timely move.[11]

The negotiations – for such they were – surrounding the government's official instructions to its army commander were affected by Montgomery's determined efforts to reduce, for the purpose of operations, the Canadian army commander to the status of a British officer.[12] While the problem, at least as between Crerar and Montgomery, had its roots in Italy and in tensions developing in the run-up to the invasion, the immediate context was Montgomery's determination to assert his control over Canadian troops while minimizing Crerar's operational command responsibilities.[13] Crerar, while seeking government sanction of his position, also wanted to assert the principle that only he could represent to Supreme Headquarters Allied Expeditionary Force (SHAEF) or 21st Army Group the operational interests of First Canadian Army. On this point he was determined.[14]

An inspection of 3rd Canadian Division by Eisenhower, undertaken without Crerar's knowledge, prompted him to use the prime minister's visit to clarify the principle of his operational responsibility. Writing to Stuart, Crerar belaboured the "tendency on the part of SHAEF and HQ 21 Army Group" to ignore Canada's position. Noting what had happened, he urged Stuart to use the prime minister's presence to clarify with the CIGS the "proper procedure in these matters ... on the political level" and explain them to SHAEF. He added ominously: "If the special position of the Commander, First Canadian Army, is not understood at the outset, I can see further and more embarrassing incidents occurring in the future."[15] To ensure that the message was passed to Brooke, Crerar arranged a "private" dinner with the CIGS on 16 May – their first since the end of March.[16]

Stuart, hesitantly, wrote Brooke. He took pains to point out that he and Crerar had great faith in their commanders and had no desire to hinder co-operation between Canadian, British, and American formations; nevertheless, Britain and the United States must acknowledge Crerar's dual responsibilities. Stuart argued: "He commands the First Canadian Army, and he is also the Canadian national representative in respect to all Canadian Formations and Units employed operationally in theatre even though some may not be under his operational command."[17] Brooke readily agreed with the logic of the argument. Montgomery did not.

Montgomery orchestrated an informal luncheon meeting with the Canadian prime minister for 18 May.[18] His approach to Mackenzie King left no doubt as to his position. Montgomery shrewdly blind-sided him, first praising Crerar, then noting that he required more experience and that "there were some things that he had to keep advising him on." He recommended General Guy Simonds as Crerar's replacement and, as remembered by King, moved to his main point: "Montgomery then said there are just two things that I keep before me and before the men at all times. That is to win battles and save lives. From that he went on to say that he hoped that so-called national considerations would not be allowed to override military considerations. In other words, that he should not be obliged to govern his actions because of political necessity where his judgement indicated that there were military reasons which made that inadvis-able. He said more or less directly that Crerar had kept asserting there were national reasons why such and such a thing should be done. He had reference to keeping all the Canadian formations together in the fighting and at all times having Canadians commanded by Canadian officers as against British officers." According to Montgomery, "some of the [Canadian] officers had not had the experience that was needed for commanding, particularly in the initial assault. That it was dan-gerous to have lives of men entrusted to those who had not had the needed experience."[19]

King's answer was ambiguous: "I had from the beginning of the war insisted that no political considerations of any kind should be permitted to override a military consideration. Other things being equal, I felt that so-called national considerations should, of course, be taken into account at all times." Montgomery pressed his advan-tage. He boldly requested that Mackenzie King "back him up" if an emergency necessitated quick separation and amalgamation. King's reply, while not completely affirmative, left no indication that he would back his own army commander against Montgomery.[20]

The prime minister had, momentarily at least, abandoned his army commander. He reiterated his conversation with Montgomery to Crerar and to the Cabinet War Committee on his return to Canada. He expressed some concern that the instructions to the army commander might conflict with his assurances to 21st Army Group's GOC-in-C. Ralston, however, reminded him that "since in our view Canadians fought better together, the concentration of Canadian formations was also a 'military' consideration." After further discussion, King conceded the point and the committee approved the instructions.[21]

Montgomery, emboldened by his meeting with King – "I like [King] immensely and we had a great talk about his Canadians" – seized the initiative. Convinced, correctly, that Stuart was acting as Crerar's voice, Montgomery determined that he had to be firm with the Canadians. He wrote to Stuart on 25 May; while he conceded that Crerar was responsible for the "general welfare and administration of all Canadian troops in the theatre of war" and had "the right to refer any point to his Government," Montgomery "made it quite clear that [he] could not admit that Crerar had any operational responsibility for Canadian troops serving temporarily in another army." Crerar would be treated like any other army commander. "There is no doubt that the national and political feeling is very strong in the Canadian senior ranks. My view is that what people really want is victories," he noted in his diary the next day.[22]

Stuart was prepared to accept Montgomery's position.[23] Crerar, however, was not willing to bow to Montgomery's desire to limit the army commander's operational responsibility: "Quite apart from the specific instructions I have from the Canadian government in such matters, it is obvious that it can only be the senior Canadian Commander in 21 Army Group who *can* accept such responsibility." Crerar restated his desire to co-operate and his admiration for Montgomery's great abilities and qualities as a field commander but observed accurately: "Political relations, international or inter-Imperial, have not been his study, however, and these cannot always be reduced to that 'forceful simplicity' which is his special genius in the matter of military operations." The crux of the matter was this: "Though in practice I expect to be treated, and behave, as any other Army Commander, in principle I … am not. I am the Canadian Army Commander and, as such, am in a different category to the British Army Commander."[24] Exactly.

The issue faded as the invasion loomed. During the Normandy campaign, until First Canadian Army Headquarters became operational, Montgomery was unusually restrained in his approach to the Canadian senior command. When doubts grew about 3rd Canadian Division's commander, Major-General Rod Keller, Montgomery pressed for a resolution but hoped that the Canadians would find one themselves. In his dealings with Guy Simonds, GOC II Canadian Corps, Montgomery was respectful, but not least because Simonds was content to act as a British formation commander and refrained from raising political issues.

Crerar's arrival changed all that. He immediately sought a resolution to the question of command and control. Naturally Montgomery did not want to pursue the issue, and he kept Crerar at arm's length both physically and by opening direct, if infrequently used, channels to Simonds. While the army commander's role in the operations remained limited, the question was marginal. When Crerar asserted himself as army commander, Montgomery reacted. As August 1944 came to a close, the question of Crerar's responsibility for his troops in operations was brought to a head by the manpower crisis that hit all the Allied armies. But the problems faced by Crerar and Montgomery should be understood in the context of other disagreements, over coalition strategy and tactics, that appeared as the Normandy campaign closed and the breakout began. Similarly, the problems between the two men in early September ended a long crisis of confidence in which neither man was blameless. Montgomery's refusal to accept either the fact of Canadian autonomy or what he viewed as its logical extension – Crerar as GOC-in-C First Canadian Army – made him the instigator in their last major blow-up of the war – but Crerar's continual preoccupation with his constitutional position exacerbated the command problems that he encountered. The issue was further inflamed by Montgomery's tendency to treat his army commanders as corps commanders.

The operational dimension of the issue has been well-covered in the essay by Terry Copp and Robert Vogel on Canadian operations in September.[25] From the perspective of the senior command, it was a difficult month: victory appeared tantalizingly close, but the course of changes to command, operations, and strategy followed a predetermined plan rather than reacting to events. Montgomery's position was affected, and he was not happy. Thus Crerar's approach to operations was but one of many things that irritated the newly promoted field marshal that month. He was struggling to secure permission from Eisenhower to undertake his "pencil-like" thrust to the Ruhr, an operation Montgomery was convinced could bring about the collapse of the entire German war effort in the west; not coincidentally it would require his retention as ground forces commander. He had since 15 August been discussing the use of an airborne army to pave the way. On 23 August, Eisenhower rejected Montgomery's plans as neither feasible, given the logistical situation, nor desirable, given the estrangement between Montgomery and the American commanders, with personality problems exacerbated by their doubts about his command abilities. Accordingly, Eisenhower determined to take over direct control of the ground forces while retaining his position as supreme commander, AEF, and to continue with a "broad front" strategy – both as previously intended. Montgomery was left in no doubt as to his position when he was, again as intended, effectively demoted to command of 21st Army Group; neither was his ego salved by his promotion.

Montgomery's operational orders conformed to Eisenhower's strategic concept, but begrudgingly, and with an eye to developing his own plans later. On 26 August, Montgomery ordered First Canadian Army to operate northwards, cross the Seine, and secure LeHavre and Dieppe. All enemy forces "in the coastal belt up to Bruges" were to be destroyed. On the right, Second British Army was to advance rapidly towards Amiens but was instructed to be prepared to support airborne troops who might be dropped in the Pas de Calais to facilitate clearance of the area and to eliminate the threat of the V1 and V2 rockets then raining down on southeastern England.[26] Late on 29 August, Montgomery decided against using airborne troops in the Pas de Calais on the then-correct assumptions that the Channel ports would not be defended and that the German Fifteenth Army would be forced to retreat eastwards by the rapid advance of Second British Army, which had already crossed the Somme, against opposition characterized as "weak," and captured Amiens.

Consequently, Montgomery summoned Crerar to his headquarters, where he received orders to "push" his armoured divisions north along the axis Abbeville–St Omer, to safeguard the British army's increasingly exposed flank and to take over the Abbeville extension of the Somme bridgehead from XXX British Corps. Crerar, however, warned Montgomery that his transport and maintenance needs were such that he could not use more than two divisions north of the Somme. Montgomery was doubtful about this assertion; noting the difficulties arising because the "Canadian army [was] hanging back somewhat," he ordered his chief of staff, Major-General Frederick DeGuingand, to investigate "maintenance matters" with the First Canadian Army staff: "It is essential that the whole of Second Canadian Corps … should be able to operate right up to Bruges and clear the Channel coast, but to do this Crerar says he wants more GT Companies, and if so he must have them."[27]

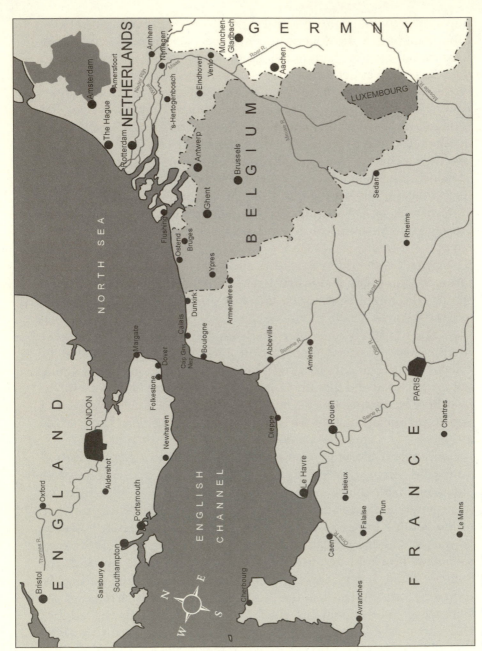

Map 8.1 Northwestern Europe.

Crerar did as ordered. Even though the Canadians and the Poles were meeting stiff resistance from fresh German divisions and incurring heavy casualties while trying to cross the Seine, and despite growing concerns over manpower, on 1 September Crerar ordered his depleted armoured divisions to race for the Somme, having early that morning been assured by his operations staff that there was no significant enemy resistance south of the river. Simonds consequently ordered his corps – exept for 2nd Canadian Division, which was to stay in the Dieppe area and reorganize – to advance on the axis Abbeville–St Omer–Ypres until it reached the line of the Somme; at that point, 4th Canadian Armoured Division – operating at half of its authorized tank establishment and promised a four-day rest – would stop to refit.[28]

These orders were in keeping with Montgomery's wishes; that morning Crerar had, as noted, ascertained what was possible from his early-morning meeting with his senior staff officers, and he met with Dempsey and Montgomery later on 1 September to receive the latest situation report and the orders noted above. After flying back to his headquarters, he issued the necessary orders and met once more with his staff regarding the movement of the tactical headquarters, before retiring because of an attack of dysentery. Neither his operations staff, which reported that 4th Canadian Armoured Division was making good progress and was over half-way from Neufchatel to Abbeville, nor Simonds had perceived any lack of push. Nor was it unreasonable to anticipate a pause for some of the formations to absorb some reinforcements, given the manpower concerns that had been rising fast since early August.

Montgomery, however, was not pleased with the decision to pause 2nd Canadian Division. On 2 September DeGuingand reported that, contrary to Crerar's assertion, "Canadian Army 'Q' say their [transport] sufficient to allow Second Canadian Corps of four divs and Corps tps to operate to Bruges." Later that day, Montgomery wired Crerar: "Second Army now positioned near the Belgian frontier and will go through towards towards Brussels tomorrow. It is very necessary that your armoured divisions should push forward with all speed towards ST. OMER and beyond. Do NOT consider this is the time for any division to halt for maintenance. Push on quickly."[29]

Crerar had very different information. As the Polish Armoured Division arrived at Abbeville it found no British troops, but the initial reports available to the chief engineer suggested that three bridges were captured intact – though by early afternoon Crerar's own flights revealed that this was not the case. 4th Canadian Armoured Division encountered resistance on its front at Airaines, but the Canadians had fulfilled Montgomery's orders; there were concerns about the availability of large-scale air support as the forward troops put more distance between themselves and the airstrips, but it was deemed sufficient for the resistance then being encountered. The minutes of the morning staff meetings also reflected the continued concerns over maintenance.[30]

Crerar's response to Montgomery reflected both this information and his testiness at the barb: "Delighted to learn that Second Army is now positioned near Belgian frontier would advise you that until late this afternoon Second Army troops have not been within 5 Miles of ABBEVILLE and that all bridges R. SOMME Ne PIQUINGY blown with enemy in considerable strength holding north bank. With assistance flank attack 4 British Armd. Bde. from direction PIQUIGNY and Polish Armd. Div. attacking ABBEVILLE across R. SOMME from south Simonds hope secure crossings tonight. Not a case of more Divs. on line R. SOMME but of 2 Canadian Inf. Div. Bns. down to average strength 525 and in my opinion a 48 Hr. halt quite essential in order it can absorb approx. 1000 reinforcements arriving today. You can be assured that there is no lack of push or rational speed Canadian army. ST. OMER and beyond will be reached without any avoidable delay."[31] This reply did not endear him to Montgomery, who was incensed at both what he saw as the Canadians' lack of drive and Crerar's inept handling of the army.

Montgomery's perceptions also created tension between the staffs of First Canadian Army and 21st Army Group. The Canadians were believed to be overly cautious. On 3 September, the result of DeGuingand's investigation into Crerar's claims that the maintenance situation of the Canadian army was holding it back suggested miscommunication within the army headquarters; his report found the Canadians prone to "bellyaching about their inability to maintain their troops forward" but that Crerar's deputy adjutant and quartermaster general, Brigadier A.E. Walford, was "quite happy." More damning was the perception that the Canadian army was hesitant to come to grips with the Germans. Writing to Montgomery on the impending operations against LeHavre, DeGuingand noted that he hoped that "the Canadians do not make too much fuss about Havre [sic], as Bill Williams [21st Army Group's chief intelligence officer] says there is only an indifferent static Bde there besides flak and CD troops. I mention this because David Strangeways, whom I sent forward with a party to get into Rouen at an early stage ... found the Canadian Bde sitting around the City saying that they could not get in owing to opposition. Strangeways then got tired of waiting and drove in with his chaps, finding no-one there!" The 21st Army Group's chief of staff continued to fear that the Canadians were not moving quickly enough, noting a few days later, as he informed Montgomery how necessary it was to secure a port north of Dieppe, that he "hoped Crerar realizes the urgency of the situation" and was taking it up through staff channels.[32]

Were the Canadians overly cautious? Or were the British ignoring the real problems facing the Canadian army? Clearly, Montgomery's dislike of Crerar had an effect on British perceptions. However, the predominant factor influencing Crerar's handling of operations following the Normandy battles was the greatly reduced strength of the units under his command, Canadian and Polish. As well, terrain and logistics hampered the Canadian army, as it turned northwards and began crossing the Seine in the face of stiff German resistance. Understrength units meant increased casualties. Would more lives have been saved had Crerar pushed ahead anyway, possibly helping to finish the war then and there? This is impossible to answer. Crerar, like many others, believed that the war as good as won and thought that allowing Canadian units to refit and absorb reinforcements was not going to affect this result. Nevertheless, he sought to maintain a balance between the coalition's operational needs and the requirements of his own troops. While the links between them were obvious, the correct balance was not.

A euphoria descended on the senior officers and headquarters staff of the British and Canadian armies in late August and early September 1944. The stunning victory in Normandy, and the rapidity of the advance through France and into Belgium, convinced most of the collapse of the German will to resist. The belief that the Germans were nearly finished influenced many in the Allied high command regarding the crossing of the Seine; it influenced Crerar's approach to operations, as well as to the reinforcement crisis in August and September, and his decision to pause to absorb badly needed reinforcements in early September. As early as 24 August, Crerar was guardedly optimistic that the war would soon end. "I believe that the toughest fighting is now over. Indeed, if we were not at war with a government of fanatics, an unconditional surrender would have taken place a week or so ago."[33] However, the biggest factor in his decisions during September was his responsibility to his own troops and to the Canadian government – for the reinforcement crisis.

The manpower issue had long roots. The resulting crisis of the late summer and the autumn of 1944 had been brewing for some time, but, with the heavy fighting, shortfalls reached a critical point.[34] Through July, general-duty infantry casualties of on average 120 per battalion prompted Crerar to draw CMHQ's attention to the increasingly dangerous situation. Listing the shortfalls unit by unit, he went to the heart of the problem: "Am concerned about infantry general duty deficiencies which approximate 1900. Our ability to continue severe fighting or to exploit a break-through would be severely restricted through lack of replacement personnel. I consider this the most serious problem of Cdn Army at the moment and to require most energetic handling."[35]

CMHQ's reply was not reassuring. The situation as it stood forecast up to 15 October was that remustering artillery, service corps, and armoured corps should satisfy approximately 80 per cent of the army's needs. The chief of staff at CMHQ had, before his departure on 25 July, approved a staff recommendation for remustering as infantry up to 25 per cent of the artillery and up to 60 per cent of the service corps; this was based on reports from Brigadier A.W. Beament, officer-in-charge, Canadian section GHQ, 1st Echelon, 21st Army Group, that infantry casualties were dramatically higher vis-à-vis other corps – 78 per cent of infantry, against (British) War Office estimates of 63 per cent – than had been estimated by CMHQ, despite Beament's warnings to that effect to Stuart in December 1943.[36] CMHQ thus suggested that Crerar's accepting personnel who had not completed their training would expedite the arrival of reinforcements in the theatre; otherwise, CMHQ requested affirmation of the present policy to withhold any personnel insufficiently trained to the minimum acceptable standard. Under this policy, it estimated, it could dispatch 3,773 all ranks by 19 August.[37]

On 7 August Crerar consulted with Simonds, who briefed him on the potential shortfall, following operation *Totalize*, of up to 2,500 general-duty infantrymen in 2nd Canadian Division alone. Crerar concluded that CMHQ's numbers were insufficient. Aware that remustering had helped ease reinforcement shortages in Italy, Crerar promoted this as the quickest means to alleviate the problem in northwest Europe.[38] Instructions had already been issued on the 5th to dispatch remustered men to the 13th Infantry Brigade, the designated retraining organization. Crerar cabled his plans to CMHQ on the 8th: "Problem is confined to Infantry General Duty and this cable applies only to that classification. Operations for balance of month likely to involve much heavy fighting. It is quite clear that only solution lies in vigorous remustering and strenuous conversion training. Request careful study of possibility of shortening conversion training by grading on entry and so securing a proportion in four weeks ... In view distinct possibility that operations of next four weeks may prove turning point remustering policy should be based on short view. It is vital that our offensive power be maintained and long term futures must be risked to produce early results."[39]

Two points are notable. First, Crerar emphasized that the problem, and thus the remustering policy, related only to the infantry; remustering of officers, as well as of tradesmen, remained voluntary, except for those in disbanded units, not least because of the morale and political difficulties involved in reassigning higher-paid, skilled tradesmen who had volunteered under specific conditions. Crerar insisted that, regardless of the urgency, all men must be trained to a minimum acceptable standard.[40] Coalition goals could not override professional and national considerations on this issue. Second, however, Crerar was willing to risk the long-term health of the army on the possibility of a decision before the crisis became acute. This was another indication, if any more were needed, that Crerar was, at this point, balancing the state of his army with the needs of the coalition. Unfortunately, his assessment reflected the influence of the optimism – unwarranted, as it turned out – that permeated the Allied high command during the heady days of August.

Reconciling the directive to maintain a minimum standard of proficiency with the need for immediate reinforcements proved difficult. By August, only 1,875 men were remustered, despite Stuart's assurances to Montgomery that steps were being taken to improve the situation. Stuart took pains to control "alarmist" reports to Ottawa regarding the potential problem, hoping that informal measures such as increasing pressure on volunteers to join the general-service infantry would alleviate the situation. Crerar took pains to distance himself from the "gloves-off" effort designed to "persuade NRMA men" to go "GS."[41] Stuart – at this point, a very sick man – while in Ottawa painted a rosy picture of the reinforcement situation, which, while delighting King, was not accurate.

The deputy chief of staff at CMHQ, Brigadier M.H.S. Penhale, crossed over to First Canadian Army Headquarters on 10 August to apprise Crerar and his staff of the limitations of supplying remustered

men in the short period prescribed. Penhale's visit was not recorded
in Crerar's war diary, nor was any record kept of the discussions.
Soon, however, the army staff considered, according to official historian Colonel C.P. Stacey, "the possibility of accepting infantry reinforcements with a lower standard of training." Neither Crerar nor his
staff found this policy desirable and so informed CMHQ; Stuart concurred, but, rather than addressing the problem, suggested that any
men competent enough to complete refresher training "more quickly"
would be sent to alleviate the immediate shortfall. The crisis was not
alleviated, however. The deficiency was such by 16 August that First
Canadian Army Headquarters was encouraging the dispatch as soon
as available of men returned from hospital as well as "otherwise provided" in order to add to "bayonet" strength; the crisis peaked, sta-
tistically, on 31 August, when the shortfall in other ranks was 4,318.[42]

Crerar's position was increasingly difficult. Montgomery and staff
at 21st Army Group were pressing the Canadians to move faster. None
the less Crerar's army was weakening with each passing day. He
pushed for solutions within the army itself. He continued to stress
that the situation must be addressed so that First Canadian Army
could take advantage of the German retreat. On 31 August, Crerar
wrote Stuart that the steps towards remustering should "soon produce
amelioration [of the] existing situation" but emphasized the "urgency
of the existing situation." Following a memorandum by Simonds,
which maintained that discrepancies between casualty figures and
unit establishments were the result of too lenient a view of battle
exhaustion, straggling, and absenteeism – the study itself a measure
of how desperate the reinforcement situation was – Crerar ordered
Walford to pen a harsh memorandum reminding formation commanders that what they were dealing with was desertion. A harsh
reminder sent two days later to the deputy adjutant and quartermaster
general to "get some speed out of the JAG [Judge Advocate-General]
section" suggests that Crerar saw this as an interim solution, as well
as indicating his exasperation with a staff not adapting to mobile warfare as fast as it might have. The result was a precisely worded
reminder to Simonds, directed to the formation commanders, that
absence, cowardice, and desertion should not go unpunished. A final
rejoinder to Stuart in mid-September – that the reinforcement situation
showed no "general improvement over that which obtained a month
ago" and "require[d] [his] personal and urgent attention" – seems to
have been Crerar's last word on the subject before he went off sick.[43]

Was there more that Crerar could have done? At this stage, no.[44] He had only two options besides remustering. First, he could have demanded immediate conscription of NRMA men for overseas service, which would have solved nothing, would have been turned down, and would have been very damaging to the war effort and possibly to army morale. Second, he could also have accepted a shorter training or retraining period – an option that was considered but dismissed. Here was a problem that plagued the higher command, even after the war. Writing in 1956 on manpower and the Canadian army, General E.L.M. Burns observed that it was worth considering whether manpower was wasted in "trying to attain too high a standard of reinforcement training." His conclusion was that the reverse was often true: there were complaints all through the war that reinforcements were untrained despite the 23 to 31 weeks between enlistment and going to the front. They were more likely to be killed or wounded. His solution was to improve liaison between front-line units and base reinforcement units to enhance the actual training rather than shortening the time.[45] This approach again would have had no short-term impact, but in the end it was tried, in November 1944, as Crerar assessed the post-Scheldt state of his army in general and of the officer corps in particular.

It appears then that Crerar was doing everything possible to keep his army fighting. The issue in the late summer and early autumn of 1944 was one of operational capability; in the long term, morale loomed as a key consideration as the reinforcement problem continued and became by November the conscription crisis. While his past responsibility for the creation of this situation is debatable, in the short term Crerar was acting responsibly. The problem was rooted in the acceptance of earlier policies, ranging from policies on proportional wastage rates, through creating too many headquarters and then overstaffing them, to the intensity of the fighting in the Normandy battles.

The problem was not confined to the Canadians. The reinforcement issue loomed as a potential area of conflict in the multinational First Canadian Army, placing Crerar in a delicate situation. On 17 August, the Polish C-in-C, General K. Sosnkowski, requested that Crerar consider the inability of the Polish army in London to make good reinforcements when assigning tasks to the Polish Armoured Division. Crerar responded by reminding him that the British and Canadians were also experiencing manpower problems, concluding with the point that 4th Canadian Armoured Division had a 20 per cent higher casualty rate, suggesting that neither he nor Simonds had been "unmindful of the casualty situation in allotting operational tasks to these two Armoured Divisions."[46] It became more important as the Canadians crossed the Seine.

Crerar's concerns about his army were not shared by Montgomery, who was unhappy with Crerar's handling of operations. He informed Dempsey that, given the possibility that "it must be some time before Canadian army moves up your left flank," he should slow his advance. Fearing the loss of momentum, Montgomery arranged a meeting between his army commanders for 3 September.[47] Again Crerar balked by citing national considerations – in this case, a ceremony scheduled to commemorate the liberation of Dieppe. Anxious to attend the event, Crerar wired Montgomery that unless "operational situation requires my arrival at TAC British Army at 1300 hrs tomorrow would appreciate if meeting could take place say 1700hrs ... Have arranged to be present at a formal religious service and parade elements of 2 CANADIAN DIVISION at DIEPPE commencing about noon tomorrow and from a CANADIAN point of view desirable I should do so. Will however conform with your wishes." Montgomery made his wishes known before day's end on the 2nd: "essential you should attend meeting at Tac Second Army at 1300 hours tomorrow 3 September."[48]

There is some evidence that Crerar, anticipating Montgomery's reply, ignored the message; he was still at his headquarters when it arrived, although he later claimed not to have received anything from Montgomery before flying to meet Simonds in the early morning hours of 3 September. He also claimed to have arranged for any messages from the C-in-C to be forwarded immediately to II Canadian Corps or 2nd Canadian Division.[49] He had made such arrangements: Mann recounted after the war how Crerar, before he left for the Dieppe, had told him that "in no circumstance was he [Crerar] to receive any further communication from Monty until it was too late to cancel his role in the Dieppe ceremonies." Mann recalled that when he had received, on the evening of the 2nd, Montgomery's follow-up message stating that Crerar was "definitely [sic] required," he informed the signals officer that there was an error in decoding and ordered him to send a query, "also in code to delay things, asking for a repeat." First Canadian Army did not reply until 1447 hours on 3 September. In a further attempt to mislead, it read that no reply had yet been received regarding the "deferment [of the] rendezvous" and that Crerar, already in the air, was most anxious to learn if this was acceptable.

When the new message arrived, error-free as expected, Mann had the duty signals officer check the decoding. "As time had now run past any conformity with the Monty order I had it sent on to 2 Div."[50]

Crerar's trips to Dieppe led to a well-known blow-up with Montgomery. The field marshal took Crerar to task and, forgetting himself, chewed him out, stating, "[O]ur ways must part." As Crerar reported later, he pointed out that he "could not accept this attitude and judgement on his part," having "carried out my responsibilities as one of his two army commanders, and as the Cdn Army Comd [sic], in what I considered to be a reasonable and intelligent way, in the light of the situation as I knew it, or appreciated it." He had also emphasized the importance of the ceremony in Dieppe: "I had, as previously explained, a definite responsibility to my Government and country which, at times, might run counter to his own wishes. There was a powerful Canadian reason why I should have been present with 2 Cdn Inf Div at DIEPPE that day. In fact, there were 800 reasons – the Canadian dead buried at DIEPPE cemetery."

Montgomery had continued his hard line until Crerar played the national card: "I replied that I assumed he would at once take this up through higher channels and that I, in turn, would at once report the situation to my government." Faced by Crerar's stance, Montgomery had backed down, but Crerar had persisted, pressing his advantage. They continued to argue, Montgomery wishing to close the matter and Crerar insisting that it be aired. In the end, Crerar satisfied himself with the report to Stuart from which the quotes above were taken.

Crerar's conclusion – "I must state that I received the impression, at the commencement of the interview, that the C-in-C was out to eliminate forcefully from my mind that I had any other responsibilities than to him" – summed up the problems caused by the ambiguity inherent in the new relationship between a dominion force commander and a British superior, when both exercised their prerogatives to the full extent of the existing legislation.[51]

Was this command problem significant from an operational point of view? Not immediately, although events suggest that the most notable repercussion of the clash on 3 September was Crerar's disinclination to question Montgomery's fixation with operation *Market-Garden* and the Ruhr. Montgomery's biographer Nigel Hamilton gives it more weight, characterizing it as a "Fatal Conference" – one "as important for the final course of World War II as Monty's conference with Eisenhower on 23 August, where the Master was forced to accede

to Eisenhower's wishes for the broad front strategy." Observing that
the army commanders, without strong strategic direction from SHAEF
and Eisenhower, "were being compelled to initiate their own strategy," he lays the blame for the direction of the campaign directly at
Crerar's feet: "Crerar's failure, by his absence [on 3 September], to
present the Canadian case for caution in assigning bold missions for
the Allied armies without first ensuring priority to the seizure of the
Channel ports and Antwerp, as well as the capture of the 150,000
Germans reckoned to be retreating along the coast, was to be of profound
significance."[52] Later, he also blames Eisenhower for not "unequivocally" ordering Montgomery to secure the Channel ports and Antwerp.
The nub of his argument, in direct contradiction to all previous char-
acterizations of Montgomery, is that a hapless field marshal, bitter
and confused, was allowed by both his army commanders and his
superior to stumble into the operational quagmire of *MarketGarden*.

Hamilton's point is extreme, and he stretches credulity by suggesting that Montgomery would have been dissuaded by Crerar, but it
does underline the difficulties in fighting as a coalition and the delicate
balance of the command relationships. It also raises the question of
whether Crerar, in direct contradiction to Montgomery's perception,
was forceful enough in pointing out the difficulties of seizing quickly,
with his understrength army, the Channel ports required to support
"a full-blooded Allied advance."[53] Certainly Crerar did not make a
forceful case for the difficulties involved in clearing the ports, but it
is unlikely that he would have done so at the meeting on 3 September
or that it would have had any effect on Montgomery. As of 3 September, intelligence reports from First Canadian Army indicated that "the
enemy did not intend to defend LeHavre, and stiff resistance was not
anticipated"; two days later Crerar's intelligence officer informed the
staff at its morning conference that it was "the probable intention of
the enemy to withdraw to the Siegfried Line or the Rhine before
attempting to establish a def[ensive] line."[54] The main problem facing
Crerar's army was not yet too many tasks, but rather too few men
and resources – in particular, bridging equipment and means to cross
the numerous canals and rivers facing it.

After the war, in a letter to C.P. Stacey suggesting that he was
understating in drafts of the official histories the tactical and administrative difficulties posed by the coastal terrain, Crerar wrote that it
seemed as if the Canadian army always had "ten more rivers to cross
and many, many canals to cross as well."[55] This was a matter of

concern, particularly as First Canadian Army transferred to Second British Army resources such as pontoon and folding-boat equipment, as well as bridging companies, even though it was denuded of supplies and formations following the conference on 3 September, as Montgomery pursued his course. By 7 September, dissatisfied with the pace of the build-up for his own "full-blooded thrust" for the Ruhr, Montgomery rerouted further supplies destined for the Canadian formation; the flow of supplies to Second British Army was increased, and soon *MarketGarden* was ready to go, but at the expense both of ordnance and other stores and, of course, of the general build-up for First Canadian Army. It was no coincidence that on that same day Brigadier Walford observed that "a 10-ton truck was now worth more than a Sherman tank."[56]

There is no record of any further disagreements between Crerar and Montgomery over the speed of Canadian operations. However, this calm seemed a result more of the strained relationship than of any mutual understanding. The situation preoccupied Crerar through at least 4 September, as he spent the better part of that day preparing a memorandum on the incident. It was also on Montgomery's mind, as his venom spilled into his operational reports to Brooke. That same day he observed, "[T]he Canadian Army has had trouble in crossing the Somme as all bridges were blown on their front. They have now got over at Pont Remy and north of Abbeville and are now beginning to move northwards and are now about three miles north of the Somme. The operations of this Army since crossing the Seine have been badly handled and slow."[57] While Montgomery apologized, neither man was overly happy with the command problems.[58] "Monty has been pretty trying on a couple of occasions during the last few days," Crerar wrote Stuart on 5 September. "He is very upset at the loss of operational command over the US Armies, and his nomination to Field Marshal's rank has accentuated, rather than eased, his mental disturbance."[59] By this time he had Montgomery's measure. Stacey wrote in his memoirs, "I remember Crerar saying Monty would always go through a yellow light; but when the light turned red, he stopped." Nevertheless, the strained relationship was a factor in operations through September.[60]

The momentum of the Canadians' campaign through the rest of September was slowly blunted: as their tasks multiplied, the resources allotted shrank. Unit strength continued to decline. Crerar's health also deteriorated. As well, the unwieldy interservice command structure became more important as First Canadian Army came increasingly to depend on the fire-power of Bomber Command, on tactical air support, and ultimately on the guns of the RN. Simultaneously, German resistance stiffened as Hitler reorganized his defences in the west. Field Marshal Gerd Von Rundstedt, dismissed in July, was reappointed Commander-in-Chief West, and the First Parachute Army – a mix of German air force recruits and paratroopers, commanded by Col.-General Kurt Student – was deployed in the Antwerp–Albert Canal sector. Hitler's directive of 4 September designated LeHavre, Boulogne, and Dunkirk, as well as the Scheldt approaches to Antwerp, including Walcheren Island, as "fortresses" to be defended to the last. The German Fifteenth Army, in danger of being cut off by the fall of Antwerp, began on 5 September a strained but organized retreat to a line on the Albert Canal, to the right of Student's parachute army. Over the next two and a half weeks, Fifteenth Army moved close to 90,000 men, 600 guns, and 6,200 vehicles, harassed only by Allied tactical air forces; the newly reorganized and reinvigorated formation implemented Hitler's orders and substantially strengthened the garrisons of the Channel ports, while creating two new fortresses, Scheldt Fortress North and Scheldt Fortress South. By the second week of September, Antwerp was effectively closed to the Allies as the Germans entrenched along the 50-mile approach.[61]

It was at this critical juncture that difficulties with Montgomery threatened to upset the delicate balance that Crerar had struck between Allied objectives and Canadian army realities. The tension between the two commanders may well have shifted the Canadian balance towards favouring the needs of the coalition. Through September, Montgomery stripped the Canadian army of its resources while, with little or no opposition, adding tasks. Simonds's assumption of command in late September did nothing to alter that situation; he proved more accommodating than Crerar and was unwilling to play the national card. Even Crerar seemed more hesitant than usual. As Montgomery defined his priority as Second British Army's drive to the Ruhr, he contemplated no significant role for First Canadian Army.[62] His cable of 3 September directed that 21st Army Group's intention was, first, to "advance eastwards and destroy all enemy forces encountered" and, second, to "occupy the RUHR, and get astride the communications leading from it into Germany and the sea ports." First Canadian Army was to "clear the coastal belt, and ... then remain in the general area Bruges–Calais until the maintenance situation allows of its employment further forward." He issued no other formal directives for 11 days but began to reconsider First Canadian Army objectives as the situation dictated. On 6 September, as it became obvious that Antwerp would not be available as the Germans held the approaches, he asked Crerar for his "opinion on the likelihood of [the] early capture of Boulogne," noting that the "immediate opening of some port north of Dieppe [was] essential for [the] rapid development of [his] plan."[63]

First Canadian Army had already begun to liberate the Channel ports. The forward elements ran up against LeHavre's formidable defences on the 2nd, and it was evident that a set-piece attack, supported by Bomber Command and the RN, was necessary if losses were to be minimized. Consequently, preparations continued until the 10th, after which the fortress was reduced by combined bombardment within three days, with over 11,000 prisoners reported as taken at a cost of 388 casualties. Operation *Astonia* suggested heavy fighting to come. While the garrison commander questioned the efficacy of the bombing, if there was any doubt in the minds of First Canadian Army staff and their commander, the ratio of losses to prisoners of war put them to rest. Crerar accepted that bombers would be a necessary component of his operations to capture the other coastal ports. He later wrote to Air Chief Marshal Arthur Harris, C-in-C Bomber Command, "Yesterday, the C-in-C handed me a large and difficult job to do, in the next week or ten days, which I am now studying. I am already quite convinced, however, that I shall need to call upon you for the maximum support, if it is to be successfully accomplished."[64] Planning for a similar operation to reduce Boulogne had already begun when Montgomery's inquiry of 6 September reached Crerar.[65] Crerar was informed following the morning joint conference that Boulogne would probably require a "treatment similar to LeHavre" – an estimate confirmed over the next few days. The operational method for capturing the ports was thus settled.

Some critics decry the decision to go for the ports or the operations themselves.[66] Were operations against the ports necessary? Or should Crerar have gone directly for the Scheldt? Thanks to Ultra intercepts, Crerar was aware of German preparation to defend the estuary, and so was his staff. As early as 7 September, in sharp contrast to the intelligence report of two days earlier suggesting German withdrawal to the Rhine, the intelligence officer informed the GOC that the Germans would probably "try to form a def[ensive] line along the Albert Canal," offering "stiff resistance with fresh troops."[67] This information, at Crerar's disposal as early as the 5th, prompted his instructions to Simonds to press on with all speed. Once he received Montgomery's request concerning Boulogne, he met twice with Simonds – first to instruct him on the priority for capturing the ports and then to discuss the operations to besiege Boulogne. There is no evidence of Simonds' urging him to bypass the ports, and all agreed on the operational method, which meant that the seige of Boulogne would have to await the fall of LeHavre and the transfer of support resources some 150 miles.[68]

If there were any doubts about taking the Channel ports, they evaporated with successive orders from Montgomery giving priority to obtaining a harbour to support his thrust to the Ruhr. He had calculated that the ports of Dieppe, LeHavre, Boulogne, Calais, and Dunkirk would provide him with enough supplies to get to Berlin; "one good Pas de Calais port" would take him into the Ruhr. The approaches to Antwerp were designated as First Canadian Army's "last priority." Crerar was so informed at a meeting of army commanders on 9 September. This is suggested by his directive to his corps commanders of that day. In the directive, Crerar listed First Canadian Army's tasks as the capture of LeHavre, Boulogne, Dunkirk, and Calais, "preferably in that order," and, "secondary in importance," the "capture or destruction of the enemy remaining North and East of the Ghent–Bruges Canal." Reflecting Montgomery's orders, he did not mention Antwerp. However, a meeting with Eisenhower on 10 September forced Montgomery at least to pay lip service to opening the port.[69] On the 12th, he cabled Crerar stressing the need to move on to Boulogne as soon as LeHavre fell, but he also, for the first time, noted that "the early opening of Antwerp [was] daily becoming of increasing importance" and that the approaches would have to be cleared; there was, however, no urgency in his wire: "grateful for your views as to when you think you can tackle this problem."[70]

Montgomery's inquiry prompted a detailed assessment of the operations and resources required to open the Antwerp approaches. First Canadian Army was already facing problems imposed by the distances between its operations; in addition, supporting services, particularly artillery, engineers, and the air force, were encountering difficulties in maintaining the level of support that the army required. The sieges absorbed the bulk of the army's fire-power. The engineers, taxed to the limit by the river crossings and the paucity of bridging equipment, also had to build or rehabilitate the airfields required by 84 Group. This assignment was in the hands of the new chief engineer, Brigadier Geoffrey Walsh, a permanent force officer who had served as the chief engineer for I Canadian Corps; characterized as cold, he was also efficient.[71] The lack of airfields was important; Crerar's directive of 9 September, reflecting Montgomery's inclination, instructed 84 Group to deal with the Germans in the Ghent area. The first 10 days of September were devoted to constructing airfields in the St Omer area; on the 10th, following requests that certain construction groups be allowed a month to rest and refit, it was decided to abandon all work on these fields and find sites around Lille, further from the ports but closer to the anticipated line of 21st Army Groups' advance. The impact of such delays can only be estimated, but the minutes of the headquarters conference meetings suggest that delays in airfield construction and the priority given the ports severely limited the number of sorties. The crossings on the River Scheldt were, on the 11th, the third and last priority for air operations.[72]

This is one example of how the pace of operations was taxing the resources of the army and the capacity of the still relatively inexperienced headquarters and commander to co-ordinate the allocation of those steadily shrinking resources. The problems were being addressed, and Crerar was active at the policy level, but at the sharp end results were mixed. He pressed for improvements in communication between the armies, corps, and line of communication troops as well as between 21st Army Group HQ and First Canadian Army.[73] He also continued to work on the manpower shortages; he met Stuart on several occasions to discuss this matter and policy questions on the postwar shape and employment of the armed forces.[74] He did not, however, press Montgomery particularly hard for more resources, nor when he did was the issue carried very far.

This was evident on 13 September when Montgomery reassessed the strategic situation. In a letter that he wrote the same day, he implied that he had handed First Canadian Army a task beyond its means in his instructions of the previous day; he now asked Crerar whether he could accelerate operations if some of the objectives were dropped or the priorities were reversed. While he suggested his willingness to "give up" Dunkirk and Calais, his next directive, issued on the 14th, declared that he expected the approaches to Antwerp and the Channel ports, except Dunkirk, cleared with all speed. He thus reversed the policy of operations already in progress and pressed for a greater sense of urgency. While stressing that the "really important thing is speed in setting in motion what we have to do" and that the army would be able to "tackle both ... tasks simultaneously," he now decided that the "setting in motion of operations designed to enable us to use the port of Antwerp was probably the most important." He did not stop at issuing general instructions on how to develop operations. He also suggested Crerar's use of one corps headquarters to control the operations against the Channel ports and the other for the action to open the approaches to Antwerp. He also arranged for heavy bomber support, the use of airborne troops against Walcheren island, and for Crerar's army to take over responsibility for Antwerp in order to develop operations "westward along the neck of the peninsula towards Walcheren."[75]

Here was a formidable range of tasks, beyond the army's capacity to perform speedily – an interpretation reflected in the request that emerged from Crerar's meetings with his operations and planning staff that day. Two alternatives presented conformed with Montgomery's conceptions but recognized that the existing operational situation limited what was possible. At root, the two main issues involved, first, disentangling headquarters and formations from operations already under way and switching them quickly over long distances with limited routes and transportation, and, second, the need for more formations to effectively take over Antwerp and protect Second British Army's flank. The keys were how quickly Calais could be invested and whether Montgomery would free some resources, particularly XII British Corps and 53rd British Division, already responsible for Antwerp; the former would determine whether I British Corps Headquarters could be moved quickly, and the latter, whether it would have to be switched to the right flank, allowing II Canadian Corps to concentrate on the Scheldt. In either case, Crerar estimated that the operations against the Channel ports would take at least 10–14 days and that I British Corps Headquarters could be moved in no less. Finally, while Crerar agreed that the Scheldt operations, which he characterized as "very tough propositions," would require all the support suggested by Montgomery, no detailed study had yet been conducted.[76]

Montgomery was pleased neither with the assessment that such operations were beyond First Canadian Army's capacity nor with the request for further resources. On the 13th, he signalled that both XII British Corps and the 53rd British Division were committed to

MarketGarden; and he ordered – no suggestions this time – Crerar to bring I British Corps Headquarters and 49th Division up to Antwerp as early as possible while grounding 51st (Highland) Division. Yet only ninety minutes later, Montgomery offered a new solution: "Early use of Antwerp so urgent that I am prepared to give up operations against Calais and Dunkirk and be content with Boulogne. If we do this will it enable you to speed up Antwerp business. Discuss this with me tomorrow when you come here for conference."[77]

Crerar placed Montgomery's points before his heads of branches and his advisers who met following the usual morning conference to discuss the implications of operation *Infatuate* – the plan to clear South Beveland and capture Walcheren. The discussions at this conference illustrate another aspect of the coalition that was becoming increasingly important for Crerar: the impact of Allied interservice command organization. Its structure made it difficult to shift the momentum of operations already initiated. First Canadian Army, depending as it did on Bomber Command, the RN, and 21st Army Group arrangements with 2nd Tactical Air Force, was particularly vulnerable to the limitations imposed by these arrangements. With no clear-cut priority assigned, the interdependence of the services became as much of a handicap to assigning priorities as it was a help after they were settled. Once the infantry divisions "peeled off" to engage the garrisons of the Channel ports and the armoured divisions were committed to the Scheldt, switching them became costly in both precious time and transport equipment.

From the army's perspective, the naval and heavy-bomber aspects of the operations had, by the 14th, become interlocked. The naval liaison officer at First Canadian Army Headquarters was asked to consider whether Antwerp could be used if Boulogne and Calais remained in German hands or whether Boulogne could be used if Calais was still in enemy hands. He concluded that Boulogne was not usable without significant loss if the guns of Calais were in German hands; Dunkirk could be masked, but the other ports, from the naval perspective, had to be taken. The decision to employ Bomber Command's resources placed similar constraints on strategic flexibility. Because support by the heavy bombers required nothing short of negotiations, preparations for their use at both Boulogne and Calais were secured at the same time; but the arrangements were not made until the 15th, after a 24-hour delay, because First Canadian Army

Headquarters had to wait for the representative of Bomber Command to arrive. Even then Bomber Command hesitated to commit its full resources until Simonds forcefully made a case that they would ensure a decisive and speedy result. Similarly, the desire of First Canadian Army to bring to bear the full fire-power at its command meant further delays as the Brigadier Royal Artillery arranged, to good effect, for the 14" and 15" guns positioned at Dover to neutralize the German cross-Channel batteries in the Calais–Cape Gris Nez region. The end-result was a masterpiece of all-arms co-operation, but, with the unwieldy Allied command structure, it took time.[78]

The decision to examine the implications of whether to undertake operations against the Channel ports as well as on the Antwerp approaches left open the question of whether to switch corps headquarters as well. If neither Boulogne or Calais was to be attacked, then it was clear to the army staff that instead of implementing the "tentatively planned" move of I British Corps and 49th British Division to take over on the right, both time and fuel could be saved if 2nd Canadian Division and II Canadian Corps took over this responsibility. The same would happen if the specialized equipment destined for Boulogne from LeHavre were stopped. The various advantages and disadvantages of the alternatives were laid before Crerar in time for his meeting with Montgomery later on 14 September.[79]

The meeting did little to clarify the situation but produced two significant changes to First Canadian Army responsibilities: Dunkirk was to be masked, which would free 2nd Canadian Division for operations in the Scheldt, and Antwerp was to engage a greater part of the army's attention: the "whole energies of the Army will be directed towards operations designed to enable full use to be made of the port of Antwerp." Montgomery also directed I British Corps HQ and 49th British Division to move to the right "as soon as possible," grounding 51st (Highland) Division. First Canadian Army operations were thus still subsidiary to Second British Army's and in support of the advance on the "real objective" – the Ruhr.

Crerar's directive to his corps commanders reflected these new instructions, but the new responsibilities left questions. In particular, he was unable to sort out the corps's responsibilities, partly because no one could be certain how strongly the garrisons of the Channel ports would resist, partly because the transport shortages made any unnecessary movement a calculated risk. I British Corps was thus left with two possible roles: if a deliberate siege was necessary to take

Calais, then the corps would undertake it, but if resistance seemed unlikely, then Simonds's corps, already handling the operation, would finish the job before turning its full attention to the approaches to Antwerp. The ambiguity of this directive, which captures the ambiguity implicit in Montgomery's orders to attempt two major operations simultaneously, was not removed until 19 September, when I British Corps was ordered to secure the right flank to free XII British Corps, then supporting the flagging operation *MarketGarden*.[80]

The responsibilities placed on the First Canadian Army and in particular on II Canadian Corps were enormous. First Canadian Army Headquarters directed a front that stretched some 200 miles; its resources were not only limited but decreasing as the headquarters and elements of I British Corps were likely to be grounded; and the operational responsibilities before it were complex interservice operations, using specialized equipment, that required careful planning for transporting those resources over vast distances on two roads. The Canadian staff faced two daunting tasks: the logistical and air-support nightmare represented by maintaining the momentum of operations against the Channel ports and planning as well as initiating operations to free the Scheldt.

The strain of this overload began to show. Crerar and his staff could shape the Channel operations by the speed with which they shifted resources or obtained strategic air and naval support; they thus kept the focus on the ports while slowly developing operations to open up Antwerp. While much of the onus fell on the staff, Crerar maintained his regimen of daily flights to keep the staff alert to major problems. The staff itself performed magnificently; particular credit was also given the transport and service corps, as they moved the equipment used in the capture of LeHavre to Boulogne, some 200 miles, with, as Church Mann described it, "limited transportation," by driving continuously for 24 hours. With *Astonia* complete, *Well hit*, the attack on Boulogne, began on 17 September, later than planned but remarkably early, given the handicaps facing army and corps planners; as it was, 3rd Canadian Division attacked with neither the fire-power nor the troops – two brigades, compared to two divisions – available to I British Corps.[81] Crerar and his headquarters did not, however, force the pace; a certain hesitation in the face of the conflicting tasks emerged, affecting future decisions. Decisions on operations against the ports became so dependent on forces outside the control of First Canadian Army that they took on a life of their own.

Planning for the attacks against the Scheldt estuary reflected the same tendency to react to events, driven by the ponderous decision-making process within the coalition and by the army's lack of a clear-cut objective within its means. Crerar initiated formal planning for operation *Infatuate* on 13 September, following Montgomery's directive; simultaneously the staff grappled with the ongoing planning for taking Boulogne and Calais. There was, however, little urgency in Montgomery's exhortations regarding the Antwerp approaches. Montgomery and his staff remained preoccupied with the Ruhr – de Guingand's main concerns centred on obtaining the use of the Channel ports. First Canadian Army planning and operations staff followed suit.[82] As soon as planning began, however, despite evident concerns over inadequate resources, shifting priorities was not considered. The solution was to rely on the support from other services, but this ensured that operations would develop slowly. Montgomery's rejection of the Canadian request for greater resources only increased the army's dependence on naval and air support. Just how hard it was to produce speedy evaluations when so many parties needed to be involved was underlined on 17 September, when First Canadian Army hosted Admiral Ramsay, Allied Naval Commander Expeditionary Force, plus Brigadier Cutler of the Airborne Army, to discuss plans such as *Infatuate*.

Such steps as were taken to anticipate the operations to clear the approaches and to allocate the limited resources available were upset by both Montgomery and the increasingly stiff German resistance. Crerar signalled his intention to keep a tight rein on his few resources in his directive of 15 September, which forbade any formation movement without express consent of army headquarters, due to the maintenance problem. His attempts to maintain his resources were shattered by the failure of operation *MarketGarden*, which began on 17 September. As Second British Army proved to have insufficient troops and armour to push its offensive the 50 miles towards Arnhem, Crerar's army was stripped to support it. On the 19th, as we saw above, he was forced to commit I British Corps east of Antwerp in order to relieve XII British Corps of responsibilities to allow it to support *MarketGarden*. This proved a major blow for First Canadian Army plans. Crerar's plans to release 3rd Canadian Division to support 2nd Canadian Division's operations west of Antwerp and in the city were scotched, as one of his corps was effectively removed from his operational control, although the army had still to provide precious transport resources for its operations. 3rd Canadian Division was now committed to a deliberate attack on Calais that kept it occupied from 25 September to 1 October.[83]

While Crerar and his senior staff continued to try to squeeze resources out of 21st Army Group, their efforts met with mixed results. At the request of II Canadian Corps, the staff struggled to get two Army Group Royal Artillery formations, one of which was grounded for lack of transport, and, at Crerar's suggestion, to find ways to move stores through the waterways of the Leopold Canal, in preparation for operations against the islands of the estuary. They also sought Dutch troops to relieve their already stretched army troops of guard duties in the liberated areas.[84] The results were meagre. Planning for operations *Infatuate* and *Switchback* – to clear the area south of the Leopold Canal – was based on the assumption that help would be forthcoming in the form of airborne troops, as Montgomery had promised Crerar in mid-September, and as Cutler had reiterated on the 17th, plus the unqualified support of Bomber Command.[85] The assistance of the latter would remain crucial when Simonds replaced Crerar at the end of the month.

Montgomery was eventually forced to support the Canadians as they fought to clear the Scheldt, but he did so because of the circumstances of the campaign rather than because of the efforts of the Canadian commanders.[86] On 27 September Simonds became acting GOC First Canadian Army, remaining as such until the end of the Scheldt operations on 9 November. He proved even more reticent than Crerar when it came to requesting resources, and there is no evidence that he contemplated exercising his rights as the Canadian senior commander. By mid-September, coalition goals predominated. Crerar's health was slipping, but the effects of his earlier struggles were also a factor. Had he exhausted what little goodwill might have existed by fighting for abstract principles? Or was it that the issues during actual operations were not clear-cut? It is difficult to pass judgment on decisions surrounding the manpower issue and the pace of operations. It is impossible to discern whether or not a speedier conclusion to the war would have been, in the long run, less costly than fighting with drastically understrength formations and units.

Crerar appreciated that his tasks were far more formidable than Montgomery and some others allowed. He made some efforts to acquire more resources but in the end fought with what he had. Did he have any alternative? Certainly a more forceful evaluation of the situation was in order, but it is difficult to see how he could have broken off the fighting on his own. Similarly, his choices became increasingly limited as First Canadian Army's dependence on the coalition's interservice assistance increased. Where then did Crerar's responsibility lie?

Constitutionally, Crerar was responsible to the coalition as well as to his government and his own troops. He acknowledged this dual responsibility under which he laboured. While he took pains to balance the two, he generally favoured his national considerations, foremost of which was the welfare of the troops. Crerar believed that it also was in the coalition's interest to maintain the morale of the Canadian troops by keeping them together and providing adequate rest and reinforcement. Montgomery disagreed with this appraisal, and it also could be argued that Crerar was becoming inclined to reconsider, particularly after he was worn down by the tiresome struggles with Montgomery in early September and as he gained more experience in battle. The principled debates of 1943 and the winter of 1944 gave way to the practical realities of fighting and winning the war. However, it would be wrong to see in Crerar's actions a consistent pattern of behaviour and reaction.

The needs of the coalition and the Canadian army were not mutually exclusive, nor was the right course of action apparent, as clear as it may seem in hindsight. Crerar was swayed, at times, by circumstances. In August 1944 he was aware that his troops were reaching the breaking point, but the statistics on battle exhaustion suggest that neither he nor Simonds was sensitive enough to the state of their men.[87] This was a result partly of the tension between the needs of the troops and the demands of the coalition, but it was also the price paid for asserting the autonomy of the Canadian forces. With that autonomy came responsibilities within the coalition. Still, by early September, Crerar was refusing to push the troops any harder than he felt was necessary – a decision criticized as short-sighted and potentially more costly in lives in the long run.

Did these disputes affect operations? They created an atmosphere of mistrust between Montgomery and Crerar. The British C-in-C's doubts about Crerar's military aptitude were confirmed, and fed, by the latter's national sentiments. This mistrust may have hindered Crerar's ability to secure more support from Montgomery during a critical period, although it seems unlikely that Montgomery would have been dissuaded from his goals. Neither did Simonds, who had a much better relationship with Montgomery, pursue more resources, which suggests that too much can be made of the personal issues that surfaced. It seems likely, however, that Montgomery, and his staff, were more than willing to believe that demands for supplies or explanations of the need to slow down to refit were further examples of the Canadian tendency to assert national autonomy when it was convenient. The evidence thus suggests that the British commanders sometimes questioned Crerar's commitment to, and understanding of, coalition goals, at least as defined by Montgomery.

To whom then was Crerar accountable? Montgomery believed that his Canadian commanders were accountable to him, not least because he envisioned the military objectives, defined by him, as precluding all others. Crerar took a broader view of the military effort, recognizing that there could be issues on which Canadian and coalition interests diverged. In practice, national and coalition objectives were rarely contradictory during operations, but Crerar fought to establish the principle that they were not one and the same. His struggle made the divergence, particularly with the British, most evident. Ultimately, Crerar would answer to his own government, his troops, and his national conscience.

NOTES

1 C.P. Stacey, *Arms, Men and Governments: The War Policies of Canada 1939–1945* (Ottawa, 1970), 212.

2 National Archives of Canada (NA), Ottawa, H.D.G. Crerar Papers (CP), Vol. 11, D220, "The Statute of Westminster … 1931"; Stacey, *Arms, Men and Governments*, 211–13; McNaughton was "one of the Canadian representatives who had drafted the Statute of Westminster": J. Swettenham, *McNaughton, Volume 2: 1939–43* (Toronto, 1969), 30–3.

3 Swettenham gives examples of McNaughton's verbosity. See *McNaughton, Volume 2*, 30–1; Stacey also notes McNaughton's confrontational style in *Arms, Men and Governments*, 213–16; Stacey notes that relations were "generally easy, smooth and agreeable" but that the British showed little knowledge of much less appreciation for, the concepts enshrined in the Statute of Westminster or the VFA. See C.P. Stacey, "Canadian Leaders of the Second World War," *Canadian Historical Review* 66 (March 1985). In addition to observing McNaughton's temper, Lester Pearson also noted the difficulties arising from the

failure to reconcile "civil and military authority" through the use of the
VFA. L.B. Pearson, *Mike: The Memoirs of the Right Honourable Lester B. Pearson, Volume 1: 1897–1948* (Toronto, 1972), 168–71.

4 LHCMA, Brooke Papers, 5/4, diary entries, 1940.

5 Dean Oliver provides a good overview of Crerar's generalship and on opinions about it in Lt.-Colonel Bernd Horn and Stephen Harris, eds., *Warrior Chiefs: Perspectives on Senior Canadian Military Leaders* (Toronto, 2001), 91–106.

6 C.P. Stacey, *The Official History of the Canadian Army in the Second World War: Volume III: The Victory Campaign* (hereafter *Victory Campaign*) (Ottawa, 1960), 42–3.

7 Ibid.

8 Deputy Minister National Defence (DMND), Diary, entry, 6 April 1944. Courtesy of J.L. Granatstein.

9 NA, CP, Vol. 3, D49, Crerar to Stuart, 3 May 1944. See, for example, Stacey, "Canadian Leaders of the Second World War."

10 DMND Diary.

11 NA, CP, Vol. 3, D49, Crerar to Stuart, 3 May 1944; RG 2, Records of the Privy Council, Cabinet War Committee Minutes, Vol. 15, 3 and 24 May 1944.

12 Ibid.

13 Imperial War Museum (IWM), London, Montgomery Papers (BLMP), BLM 107/3, "List of recipients of 'notes by C-in-C 21 Army Group'," 20 March 1944; Sir Frederick de Guingand, *Operation Victory* (New York, 1947), 181.

14 NA, CP, Vol. 3, D49, Crerar to Stuart, 3 May 1944.

15 NA, CP, Vol. 8, D176, Crerar to Stuart, 13 May 1944.

16 LHCMA, Brooke Papers, 5/8, diary entry, 16 May 1944.

17 NA, RG 24, Vol. 10,688, 215C1.056(D7), "Cabinet Instructions and Interpretations of same by Montgomery," Stuart to Brooke, 18 May 1944.

18 R.S. Malone, *A Portrait of War, 1939–1943* (Don Mills, Ont., 1983), 237.

19 NA, Mackenzie King Papers and Diaries (MKP), MG 26 J13, diary entry 18 May 1944.

20 Ibid.

21 NA, RG 2 7C, Vol. 15, Minutes of Cabinet War Committee, 24 May 1944.

22 IWM, BLMP, BLM73, diary entries 18 and 26 May 1944.

23 NA, CP, Vol. 3, D67, Stuart to Crerar, 29 May 1944.

24 Ibid., Crerar to Stuart, 30 May 1944.

25 T. Copp and R. Vogel, "No Lack of Rational Speed: First Canadian Army Operations, September 1944," *Journal of Canadian Studies* 16 (fall–winter 1981), 145–55.

26 Public Record Office (PRO), London, WO285/2 Dempsey Papers, M520, General Operational Situation and Directive, 26 Aug. 1944.

27 PRO, WO205/5B, Correspondence Between Chief of Staff and Commander in Chief, Letter to C of S, 1 Sept. 1944; Copp and Vogel, "No Lack of Rational Speed," 147.

28 NA, RG 24 C17, Vol 13,626, GOC8, 1 Sept. 1944; Minutes of Morning Joint Conference (MJC), Main HQ First Canadian Army, 1 Sept. 1944.

29 IWM, BLMP, BLM109/9, M141, Montgomery to Crerar, 2 Sept. 1944.

30 NAC, RG 24 C17, Vol. 13,626, Minutes of MJC, 2 Sept. 1944.

31 Ibid., Crerar to Montgomery, 3 Sept. 1944.

32 PRO, WO205/5B, DeGuingand to Montgomery, 3 and 7 Sept. 1944.

33 NA, CP, Vol. 7, Crerar to Lett, 24 Aug. 1944.

34 NA, CP, Vol. 5, D129, CMHQ to NDHQ, 10 April 1944.

35 Ibid., Crerar to Montague, 4 Aug. 1944; figure from E.L.M. Burns, *Manpower in the Canadian Army 1939–1945* (Toronto, 1956), 92–3.

36 Stacey, *Arms, Men and Governments*, 430–9.

37 NA, CP, Vol. 5, D129, Montague to Crerar, 5 Aug. 1944.

38 Burns, *Manpower in the Canadian Army*, 96–7.

39 NA, CP, Vol. 5, D129, Crerar to Montague, 8 Aug. 1944.

40 Ibid.; G. Hayes, "The Development of the Canadian Officer Corps 1939–1945," unpublished PhD thesis, University of Western Ontario, 1992, 184–8; Burns, *Manpower in the Canadian Army*, 123.

41 Stacey, *Arms, Men and Governments*, 432–4. "NRMA men" referred to troops conscripted and serving in Canada under the provisions of the National Resources Mobilization Act, passed following the fall of France in June 1940. They could be conscripted for service only in Canada; to be sent overseas, they had to volunteer to be designated GS: General Service.

42 Ibid., 438.

43 NA, CP, Vol. 5, D129, Crerar to Stuart, 31 Aug. and 18 Sept. 1944; Vol. 4, D123, Crerar to Simonds, 2 Sept. 1944.

44 NA, CP, Vol. 6, D154, Crerar to Lt.-Colonel W.H. Boswell, 23 Nov. 1944.

45 Burns, *Manpower in the Canadian Army*, 80–1.

46 NA, CP, Vol. 7, D137, Sosnkowski to Crerar, 17 Aug. 1944; Crerar to Sosnkowski, 20 Aug. 1944.

47 PRO, WO285/2, Dempsey Papers, Montgomery to Dempsey, 2 Sept. 1944.

48 IWM, BLMP, BLM109/15, C67, Crerar to Montgomery, 2 Sept. 1944; BLM106/16, Montgomery to Crerar, 2 Sept. 1944.

49 NA, RG 24, Vol. 10,651, D7, Notes re Situation Which Developed Between C-in-C 21 AG and GOC First Canadian Army, 2/3 Sept. 1944, 4 Sept. 1944.

50 Department of National Defence (DND), Department of History (DHist), 86/544, Mann to Foulkes, 2 April 1963 (now at NA); IWM, BLMP, BLM109/19, Mann to 21 AG HQ, 3 Sept. 1944.

51 NA, RG 24, Vol. 10,651, D7, Notes re Situation, 2/3 Sept. 1944, 4 Sept. 1944.

52 N. Hamilton, *Monty: The Field Marshal 1944–1976* (London, 1986), 16, 20.

53 Ibid., 20.

54 NA, RG 24 C17, Vol. 13,626, Minutes of MJC, 3–5 Sept. 1944.

55 NA, CP, Vol. 21, D329, Crerar to Stacey, 10 March 1959.

56 NA, RG 24 C17, Vol. 13,626, Minutes of MJC, 5 Sept. 1944; "Musketeer: The Campaign in North-West Europe III: Some Aspects of Administration," *Royal United Service Institute Journal* 103 (February 1958), 77; Stacey, *Victory Campaign*, 300.

57 NA, CP, Vol. 15, War Diary Sept. 1944; LHCMA, Brooke Papers, 14/30, M156 to Brooke, 4 Sept. 1944.

58 NA, RG 24, Vol. 10,651, Montgomery to Crerar, 7 Sept. 1944.

59 NA, RG 24, Vol. 10,633, D318, Crerar to Stuart, 5 Sept. 1944.

60 C.P. Stacey, *A Date with History* (Ontario, 1984), 236.

61 H.R. Trevor-Roper, *Hitler's War Directives 1939–1945* (London, 1966), 271–2 and Directive 64; J. Ellis, *Brute Force: Allied Strategy and Tactics in the Second World War* (London, 1990), 402–5.

62 Stacey, *Victory Campaign*, 306–9.

63 IWM, BLMP, BLM109/25, Montgomery to Crerar, 6 Sept. 1944.

64 NA, CP, Vol. 6, D155, Crerar to Harris, 15 Sept. 1944.

65 IWM, BLMP, BLM109/28, Crerar to Montgomery, 6 Sept. 1944.

66 For example, see H. Essame and E.M.G. Belfield, *The Northwest Europe Campaign 1944–1945* (Aldershot, 1962), 65, and W.A.B. Douglas and B. Greenhous, *Out of the Shadows* (Toronto, 1977).

67 NA, RG 24 C17, Vol. 13,626, Minutes of JMC, 7–9 Sept. 1944.

68 NA, CP, Vol. 15, War Diary, Sept. 1944.

69 Stacey, *Victory Campaign*, 310.

70 Ibid., 331; IWM, BLMP, BLM109/30, Montgomery to Crerar, 12 Sept. 1944.

71 DND, DHist, 000.9 (D93) Biographies of Canadian Army Officers (now at NA); interview with Finlay Morrison, Crerar's aide-de-camp.

72 NA, RG 24 C17, Vol. 13,626, Minutes of MJC, 7–13 Sept. 1944.

73 Ibid., 10–15 Sept. 1944; Q Mov Policy Letter Number 1, 18 Sept. 1944; Main FCA to Main 84 Gp RAF re Comn Aircraft, 12 Sept. 1944; CP, Vol. 15, War Diary, 7 Sept. 1944.

74 NA, CP, Vol. 15, War Diary, 8 Sept. 1944.

75 IWM, BLMP, BLM109/32, Montgomery to Crerar, 13 Sept. 1944.

76 NA, CP, Vol. 15, War Diary, 10–13 Sept. 1944; Stacey, *Victory Campaign*, 358–9.

77 IWM, BLMP, BLM109/33, Montgomery to Crerar, 13 Sept. 1944.

78 NA, RG 24 C17, Vol. 13,626, Conference Held to Discuss Immediate Problems of *Infatuate*, 14 Sept. 1944; Stacey, *Victory Campaign*, 338.

79 Ibid.

80 Stacey, *Victory Campaign*, 329–36.

81 Copp and Vogel, "No Lack of Rational Speed," 49–50.

82 B.L.M. Montgomery, *The Memoirs of Field Marshal the Viscount Montgomery of Alamein* (London, 1958), 297.

83 T. Copp and R. Vogel, *Maple Leaf Route: Antwerp* (Alma, Ont., 1984), 89–90.

84 NA, RG 24 C17, Vol. 13,626, Minutes of MJC, 15–21 Sept. 1944.

85 Terry Copp's interview with Lt.-Colonel J. Pangman, Planning Staff, First Canadian Army, no date.

86 NA, CP, Vol. 15, D265, War Diary September, Notes for Conference on Operation *Infatuate*, 22 Sept. 1944; DND, DHist, Air 14/911, Notes on Conference – Operation *Infatuate*, 23 Sept. 1944 (now at NA).

87 T. Copp and B. McAndrew, *Battle Exhaustion: Soldiers and Psychiatrists in the Canadian Army 1939–1945* (Montreal, 1990). Some figures there illustrate the problems: in December 1944 it was estimated that 35 per cent of the total casualties in the Italian theatre for the month were battle-exhaustion cases (103); in Normandy, the average for Allied armies was "in excess of one in every four non-fatal casualties" (126).